PSYCHOLOGY

Boris Vukov

Long Beach City College

All images in this textbook are purchased by the author from the following website: www.shutterstock.com.

Editors:

Lisa Goddard-Fitzgerald, MA, English
Sanja Medic, PhD, Neurology
Matthew Lawrence, MA, Philosophy
Katie Heaton-Smith, MA, Psychology
Jeremy Lawrence, BA, English.

Printed in the United States of America. First printing.

For information:

Boris Vukov
Long Beach City College
Social Science Department
LAC Campus
4901 East Carson Street
Long Beach, CA 90808
Email: bvukov@lbcc.edu

Cover art by pathdoc (www.shutterstock.com).

Contents

CHAPTER 1:   1-34

EXPLORING PSYCHOLOGY

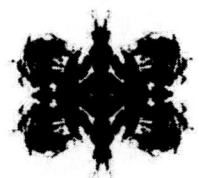

CHAPTER 2:   35-92

PSYCHOLOGY OF PERSONALITY

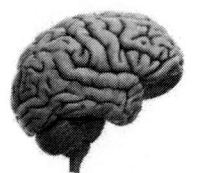

CHAPTER 3:   93-122

BIOLOGICAL PSYCHOLOGY I

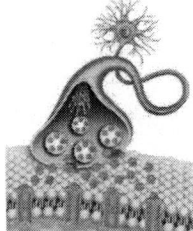

CHAPTER 4:   123-152

BIOLOGICAL PSYCHOLOGY II

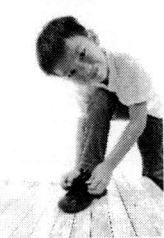

CHAPTER 5:   153-176

LEARNING

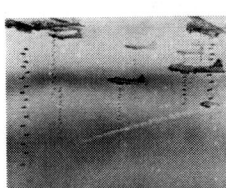

CHAPTER 6:   177-200

MEMORY

Contents

CHAPTER 7:   201-224

COGNITION

CHAPTER 8:   225-252

CONSCIOUSNESS

CHAPTER 9:   253-290

DEVELOPMENTAL PSYCHOLOGY

CHAPTER 10:   291-326

ABNORMAL PSYCHOLOGY

CHAPTER 11:   327-352

SOCIAL PSYCHOLOGY

Exploring Psychology

Chapter One

The field of **psychology** encompasses the scientific study of behavior, mental processes, and physiological reactions (breathing, sweating, brain activity, etc.). Psychology comes from the Greek words **psyche** and **logos**, which, respectively, refer to the mind and studies. Memory, needs, feelings, making decesions, perceiving, imagining, language acquisition, problem solving, and intelligence are all included in the category of mental processes.

The study of behavior includes reflexes, walking, talking, sexual intercourse, and all other types of observable actions. Since it is impossible to directly observe mental states, psychologists must investigate outward, observable behaviors in order to better understand the mental processes behind them. For example, if you observe a person at a store deliberating over which of two similar products to purchase, you may be able to infer their consumerist dilemma by their visible hesitancy, the tilt of their head, the way they pick up one product and then the other. It is the observable behaviors that allow us to understand the workings of their unobservable mental state.

TYPES OF BEHAVIOR

Behaviors can be either **voluntary** (occurring at our will and under our control) or **involuntary** (typically reflexive and not under our conscious control). Analogously, behaviors can be either verbal or non-verbal. A verbal behavior is one that involves the meaningful pronouncement of communicative sounds, such as words or sighs. A non-verbal behavior would involve neither emotive sounds nor words, such as one's posture or eye contact (Brehm, Kassin, & Fine, 2005).

Figure 1. What mental process is indicated by this non-verbal behavior? Fear? Confusion? Happiness?

1

SAME BEHAVIORS IN DIFFERENT CULTURES

There is a great deal of continuity across cultures for some nonverbal behaviors such as emotional expressions. For example, almost universally, cultures recognize a smiling face to convey happiness and a frowning face to convey sadness (Ekman & Rosenberg, 2005). There are, of course, a number of behaviors that do not convey the same messages in different cultures. For example, to signify the word "no" in the United Statesone shakes their head from left to right while in Bulgaria this same head movement means "yes"., A similarly reversed behavior would be forming a circle with your thumb and forefinger. In the United States this could mean "great" or "O.K.," but in Brazil it would be interpreted as an obscene gesture (Axtell, 1993).

When I visited New Zealand for the first time, a behemoth Maori man covered in tattoos approached me. He came so close to me I was convinced he was coming in for a kiss on the lips. Shocked, I froze where I stood, not knowing how to avoid the imminent kiss from this person. But he didn't kiss me; instead, what I later found out is the traditional and accepted Maori form of greeting, he merely rubbed his nose against mine. In times like this—when a mountainous Maori seems to be leaning in for a kiss—that we must be aware of cultural traditions and careful of how we interpret behaviors.

Figure 2. The nose is important for our sense of smell, but it can be useful in expressing a non-verbal behavior as well.

Verbal behaviors can also mean completely different things to people of different cultures. "Da" in Serbian (my native tongue) translates to "yes" in English. But "da" (pronounced "duh") in English typically refers to stupidity.

PHYSIOLOGICAL REACTIONS AND PSYCHOLOGY

Psychologists can also observe and research **physiological reactions**. Physiological reactions are synonymous with bodily functions and include behaviors such as breathing, sweating, and cellular activity, etc. Special equipment is often required to study these processes, though some internal processes are easily observable through an individual's behavior. For example, emotional arousal causes pupil dilation. This specific correlation is demonstrated in Ridley Scott's *Blade Runner*. Detective Rick Deckard, played by Harrison Ford, tests human replicas by asking them questions meant to elicit an emotional responses while observing their pupils for dilation. Studies have shown that pupils automatically dilate when a person experiences an intense emotion (Partala,

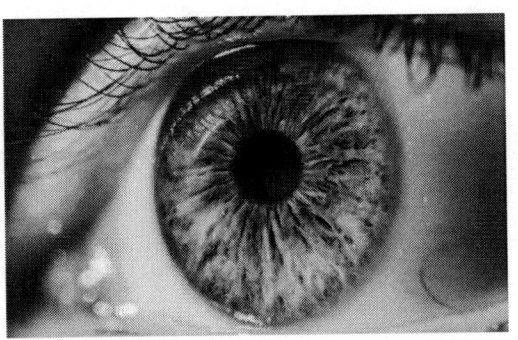

Jokiniemi, & Surakka, 2000; Siegle, Granholm, Ingram, & Matt, 2001). Pupil dilation in response to an emotion, however, is not a trait possessed by the human replicants in *Blade Runner*. This indication gives away the replicant and Deckard "retires" the subject.

Figure 3. Why do you think psychologists spend so much time studying the pupil?

Another example that illustrates how physiological reactions correlate and reveal mental processes is a study regarding the stress levels of men and women when they are forced to imagine their partner cheating on them. The study dealt with two type of disloyalty: (1) a partner developing romantic feelings for another person (for future reference called emotional disloyalty), and (2) a partner becoming physically intimate with another person without an emotional connection (called physical disloyalty). Male and female participants were asked to image their partner acting upon both types of disloyalty. A machine measured the physiological reactions of the participants, capturing sharp increases in heart rate, muscle tension, and sweat production. All of these reactions suggest a stressed mental state. The study found that men exhibited higher levels of stress when imagining the physical disloyalty of their partner, women emotional disloyalty (Buss, Larsen, Westen, & Semmelroth, 1992).

PSYCHOLOGY THROUGH TIME

Figure 4. The history of psychology is as fascinating as its scope is wide.

Psychologist Hermann Ebbinghaus (1850-1909) was correct when he observed that psychology has a long past but only a short history. Ebbinghaus meant that although psychological topics had long been considered and discussed, the official history of psychology did not begin until it became accepted as a social science in 1879. This was the same year that German scientist Wilhelm Wundt (1832-1920) founded the first psychology laboratory. The wonders of the subject matter of psychology, such as the fundamental mechanics of memory, emotions, dreams, and consciousness, have captured the curiosities of humans throughout time. But up until the founding of Wundt's laboratory, much of the study of psychology centered on speculation and opinion. Wundt wanted to create a scientific field, based on evidence and fact, for the study of the mind and its behavior (Thorne & Henley, 2001).

ANCIENT (3500 BC-AD 500) VIEWS ON THE MIND AND BEHAVIOR

There is no shortage of evidence documenting ancient civilizations' reflections on the mind and behavior. The overwhelming majority (if not all) of them, however, are based on opinion rather than scientific research. Most of the opinions that composed the earliest observations on psychology stemmed from ancient philosophy, religions, and physiology; therefore, philosophy, religion, and physiology are often considered the roots of psychology. For example, ancient Egyptians believed that the human soul resided in the heart. After an individual's death, the god Anibus would place the deceased's heart on one end of a scale and the feather of truth on the other. If the heart outweighed the feather, the person was deemed immoral and a ferocious otherworldly beast promptly devoured their mind. But if the heart and the feather were found to be equal in weight, the god Osiris would grant eternal paradise to the deceased individual's mind. It is clear that the ancient Egyptians believed a sense of morality resided in the heart (Brummet et al., 2003). However, contemporary scientific endeavors have pointed out that one's morality resides in the brain. If a person undergoes a heart transplant, their mental processes and sense of morality are not drastically changed. But if a person suffers brain damage, their mental processes and corresponding behaviors often do change. There have been instances where individuals with criminal tendencies suffered brain damage and, afterward, became morally upstanding citizens (Giles, 2004). Conversely, there have been instances of moral paragons becoming unethical individuals post-brain damage (Damasio, 2005).

Figure 5. The god Anubis.

Many ancient philosophers have explored the subject of psychology, but their opinions were not scientifically tested or supported. Aristotle (384-322 BC) concurred with the Egyptian's belief of the brain being unrelated to the soul. He similarly believed that the heart was where the mind and soul resided. The source of this belief was an observation that anger, fear, and other strong emotions produced sensations in the chest (Laver, 1972). Aristotle shared many thoughts on how the world can be perceived through the senses, memory, and dreams. He believed that repetition improved memory, and that dreams during sleep are similar to hallucinations during wakefulness (Sahakian, 1968). Aristotle also believed the mind of a newborn to be a "tabula rasa," a blank slate,

4

and that mental abilities and behaviors are learned through direct experience (Schacter, Gilbert, & Wegner, 2007). Psychologists have since extensively researched this notion.

On the other hand, Plato (427-347 BC) believed that certain dispositions and thoughts—such as concepts of goodness, justice, and beauty—were inherently instilled in a person at birth (Soccio, 2004). Plato believed that experiences serve to uncover ideas that already exist deep within our minds (Thorne & Henley, 2001). The notion of innate functions of the mind has since been scientifically explored. Cicero (106-43 BC), Seneca (4 BC-65 AD), and Marcus Aurelius (121-180 AD) held the belief that all people have the power to control their feelings of anger, fear, and hatred. They believed that being able to conquer these (as well as all other) feelings could lead to the most rewarding accomplishment, serenity and true peace of mind. But, again, Cicero, Seneca, and Aurelius did not conduct scientific studies to verify or disprove their beliefs (Soccio, 2004).

Figure 6. What psychological topics were discussed during the ancient period?

Chinese philosopher Laozi (sixth or fifth century BC) suggested that true happiness could only be reached by withdrawing from society, living in harmony with nature, being consciously aware of one's breathing and proper eating, and remaining involved in sexual practices. Confucious (551-479 BC) believed that happiness was attainable through moral actions. He held that showing genuine empathy towards others, maintaining the desire to grow as a moral agent, and offering help to others to do the same was the path of true happiness. But neither Laozi nor Confucious tested their views with scientific research (Brummet et al., 2003; Soccio, 2004). Today, though, psychologists have the ability to study happiness. One such study involved the prescription of exercises meant to improve the participants' positive emotions. Participants were instructed to first write a letter of gratitude to someone for whom they were grateful but never properly thanks. They were then tasked with reading this letter to the person either in a face-to-face meeting or over the phone. Participants

Figure 7. Does modern research in psychology support Ancient Chinese opinions?

were also instructed to write down, each evening, three good things that happened to them that day and explain why they thought the good things occurred. The study found that engaging in these tasks for only one week helped improve the participants' moods, while the positive effects of noting three good things that happened each day lasted for six months (Seligman, Rashid & Parks, 2006).

Physiology explores how the body functions by studying its chemical and electrical processes, bodily systems, organs, and cells. A portion of contemporary psychology originates, in part, from physiological views. The breadth of physiology encompasses the skeletal, muscle, and nervous systems. It also includes the senses, the lymphatic, immune, respiratory, urinary, digestive, and reproductive systems (Martini et al., 2004; Sherwood, 2004). Inquiries on the relationship between bodily functions and the mind/behavior are apparent as early as the writings of ancient Greek philosopher Hippocrates (fifth century BC). He saw a positive correlation between mental health and proper nutrition and exercise (Magner, 1992). Hippocrates correctly believed the brain to be responsible for sorrow, pain, beauty, and morality (Breedlove, Rosenzweig & Watson, 2007). However, he incorrectly believed that mental abnormalities were caused by a wandering uterus, and therefore only experienced by women. To remedy mental disturbances, Hippocrates would suggest pregnancy. In Hippocrates' time, it was widely believed that gods stealing an individual's mind caused epilepsy; Hippocrates believed that it was an imbalance of black bile, yellow bile, phlegm, and blood in the body. This explanation was closer to the facts of epilepsy that we know today, that epilepsy results from an imbalance of neurotransmitters. Although his views were never tested (and in many aspects false), Hippocrates was right in suggesting a connection between the mind and the physical functions of the body.

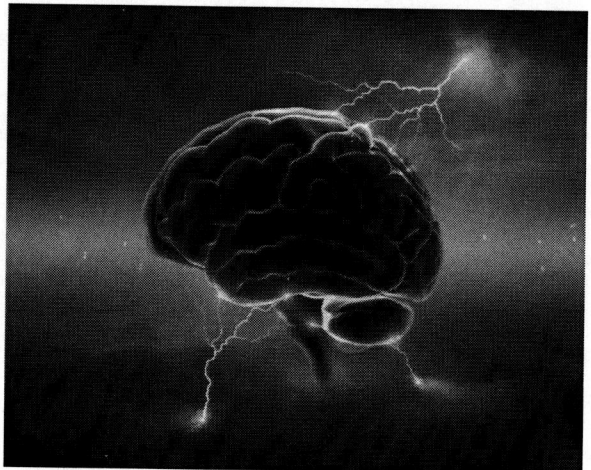

Figure 8. Although the brain heavily influences our mind and behavior, other organs are also important influential factors (as you will see in the biological psychology chapter).

HOW DID THE RENAISSANCE (AD 1300s-1600s) INFLUENCE PSYCHOLOGY?

The medieval era (500-1600s AD) contained two of the most defining yet opposed periods of human history. Beginning with the **Dark Ages** (500-1300s AD), arts and science were suppressed under the ubiquitous rule of the church. For example, church authorities used a religious text, the *Malleus Malleficarum* (The Witch Hammer) to identify, capture, and punish women they believed to be witches. The text portrayed women as sexually insatiable creatures who unending desire made them easy prey for the devil. To the culture of the Dark Ages the only honorable and relevant desire was that of religious fulfillment.

Figure 9. To psychologists, Malleus Malleficarum's position on women is a mere speculation, since it reflects an opinion without supporting research evidence. Later in the chapter you will see how research-based views are achieved.

But once the Dark Ages came to a close, the progressive developments of the period known as the **Renaissance** led to many notable scientific accomplishments and breakthroughs. The Renaissance did away with the infinitely confining nature of the church allowing for freedom of exploration and research. The factors that facilitated this shift are important and worthy of note (Thorne & Henley, 2001). The proliferation and development of cities and metropolitan centers allowed trading companies and technology to expand. This led to an increase of ships and other transportation means of trading, which in turn increased the opportunity for the exchange of ideas.

Another aspect of the Renaissance that promoted freethinking was the invention of the printing press. Prior to the fourteenth century, texts had to be written manually. The rarity of texts meant very few people owned books or even knew how to read. It also slowed the generation of original ideas. The ability to print in mass quantities allowed for the spreading of information through large numbers of common people. Handwritten books were often only written in Latin. But with the invention of printing, texts could be more easily translated into different language, increasing the accessibility of ideas and influencing new theories and academic endeavors to unfold (Thorne & Henley, 2001).

In addition, the founder of Protestantism, Martin Luther (1438-1546 AD), successfully exposed members of the clergy who were, in many respects, behaving in manners contradicting what they preached. Luther attacked the clergy's selling of *indulgences*—written statements absolving individuals of sin. This sudden exposure of the church's corrupt acts caused many people to redirect their focus from religion to the human mind and behavior. Emphasis on the exploration of human behavior, interaction, and functioning rather than God is known as **Humanism** (Thorne & Henley, 2001).

Renaissance astronomers conducted numerous observations and calculations to explore the church's understanding of the universe. It was discovered that sun was the center of the galaxy, not the planet Earth as the church had previously posited. Such a momentous discovery changed the standard way of thinking. This change is called a **paradigm shift**. The discovery of Earth's status as not the center of our galaxy furthered the opportunity for scientific exploration beyond the church's dogma (Thorne & Henley, 2001). All of these factors influenced an environment much more conducive to broader thinking. The human being—its mind, behavior and physiological processes were suddenly opened to new horizons of exploration. The Renaissance was the right time and environment for unconstrained thinking (Leahey, 2004).

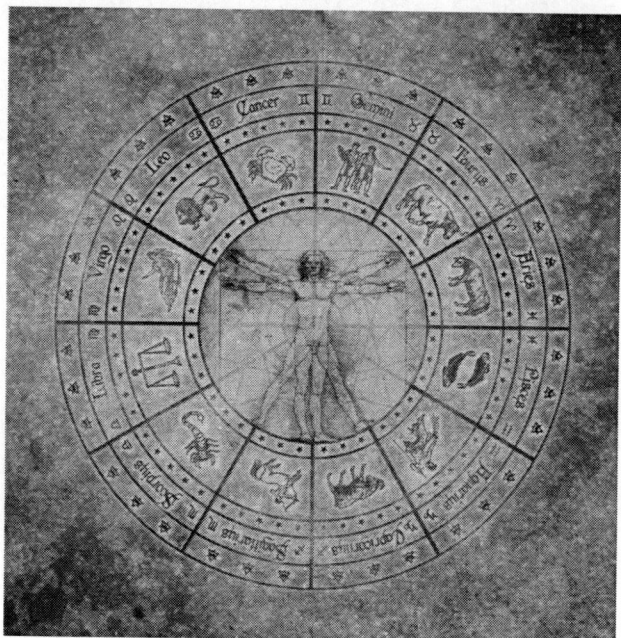

Figure 10. What factors led to the development of Humanism?

Advancements in the fields of physiology and anatomy during this period were also essential for the birth of modern psychology. Leonardo da Vinci (1452-1519) was one of the first researchers to draw bodies he dissected. His detailed anatomical diagrams enabled researchers to better visualize the complex systems of the body (Breedlove et al., 2007). His endeavors into human anatomy also influenced other researchers to focus their energy on humans as well, instead of on God and his relationship with humans.

Through his own dissection ventures, Rene Descartes (1596-1650) noticed the various fibers, organs, and fluids that make up the body, and noted their resemblance to the working aspects of machines. By paralleling the human body to a machine, Descartes proposed the idea that human reflexes involve several steps, each one causing the next. For example, if a person touches fire, the stimulus of heat causes fluid to move through the fibers of one's arm, up to the brain, and back to the arm, ultimately causing the person to quickly withdraw their hand from the heat. Although his views on reflexes in their entirety were proved incorrect, Descartes stimulated researchers to think about human behavior in terms of physiological processes within anatomical structures. His dissections of human cadavers and philosophical reflections on the mind led Descartes to propose the notion that the mind's interaction with the pineal gland in the brain affected behavior. But again, although many aspects of this view were later found to be incorrect, his proposition of the relationship between the brain's physiological process and behavior were unprecedented (Breedlove et al., 2007). Physician William Gilbert (1540-1603) published one of his first papers on electricity in 1600, a topic that would become wildly important for understanding how the brain conducts behavior and conscious experiences (Thorne & Henley, 2001).

MODERN AGE (1600s - PRESENT) VIEWS ON THE MIND AND BEHAVIOR

The Renaissance acted as a springboard for the development of the modern age. The modern epoch is characterized by unconstrained thinking even more abundant than in the medieval period. This is exemplified in **empiricism**, a philosophical school of thought that originated in the seventeenth century arguing that experience and observation is the source of human knowledge. John Locke (1632-1704), David Hume (1711-1776), and George Berkeley (1685-1753) were prominent empiricists. Empiricism significantly influenced psychology. One of the essential pillars of psychology is an understanding that it is imperative for knowledge to come from evidence obtained through formal observation and measurement (Thorne & Henley, 2001).

The modern age has also seen biological discoveries that were vitally important for psychology. Luigi Galvani (1737-1798) and others demonstrated how the nervous system conducts electricity and how changes in the electrical stimulation of the nervous system create changes in mental behaviors and processes. For example, Roberts Bartholow (1831-1904) tricked subjects into "experiencing" visual and auditory stimuli by stimulating their brains with electrical currents (Throne & Henley, 2001). Discoveries pertaining to brain damage also supported the importance of the part the nervous system played in the mind and behavior. Researchers were able to demonstrate how damage to different regions of the brain caused different problems in behaviors and mental processes. Paul Broca (1824-1880) discovered that trouble producing verbal speech could be directly linked to injuries suffered to a specific brain area. And Carl Wernicke (1848-1904) found that if a different area of the brain sustained an injury the subject would still be able to speak but their language would be incomprehensible (Thorne & Henley, 2001).

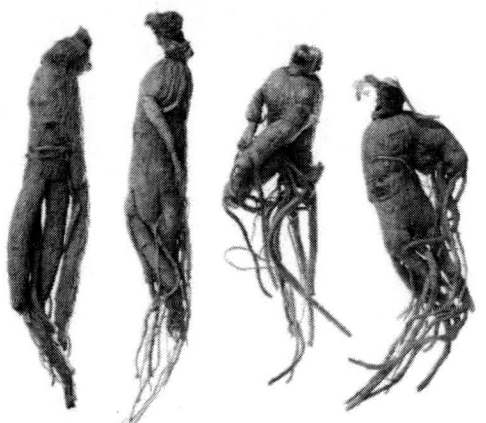

Figure 11. The roots of psychology are religion, philosophy, and biology.

SCIENCE OF THE MIND AND BEHAVIOR

Even though empiricists placed paramount importance on the collection of evidence and this became the basis for advancements in scientific inquiry, we cannot say with complete certainty that the researchers we have talked about so far intended to create a scientific field such as psychology. Instead, Wilhelm Wundt (1832-1920) receives the credit for carving out a recognized field of study dedicated to psychology.

It is widely held that psychology officially became a science in 1879. In his laboratory at the University of Leipzig in Germany, where he was a professor, Wundt launched the field of psychology. It's objective was clear: to scientifically investigate the human mind and behavior. Wundt moved the discussion of psychology from speculation to testable facts. In his lab he performed scientific studies with research participants, instruments, measurements, and data collection. Wundt also created the first psychological journal that he formed with a number of graduate psychology students. Many of Wundt's students later became influential psychologists themselves, including Emil Kraepelin (1856-1926), who contributed extensively to the study of schizophrenia, Charles H. Judd (1873-1946), a pioneer in the field of social psychology, and Lightner Witmer (1867-1956), who founded the world's first psychological clinic (Thorne & Henley, 2001).

Figure 12. It is a common misconception that Freud was the father of psychology when in actuality it was Wundt.

HISTORICAL APPROACHES: VOLUNTARISM

Wundt's goal was to scientifically explore how humans experience the world through conscious vision and hearing. He focused on the structure of consciousness, mainly the experience of intensity (i.e. how bright a stimulus may be perceived) and quality (the color, shape, etc.). In one study, Wundt recorded participants' reaction times to light and compared this data with their reaction time to determining the color of light (Bernstein, Penner, Clarke-Stewart, & Roy, 2008).

Attention span was also a focus of Wundt's; he studied the amounts of stimuli (numbers, letters, words, etc.) that could be clearly held in an individual's consciousness with a single exposure. Wundt's experiments consisted of stimuli flashed on screens for participants to recall. Wundt understood human attention as something that could be consciously directed and selectively used to capture stimuli. He called the view that humans have the ability to choose what we experience **voluntarism** (Thorne & Henley, 2001). Through other studies, Wundt came to the conclusion that the basic aspects of human feelings are pleasure, displeasure, tension, relaxation, and excitement. Wundt pioneered a research technique that relied on participants reporting their subjective experiences called **introspection** (Bernstein et al., 2008). His colleague, Hermann Ebbinghaus, criticized this approach for allowing the human bias into data collection. Ebbinghaus also pointed

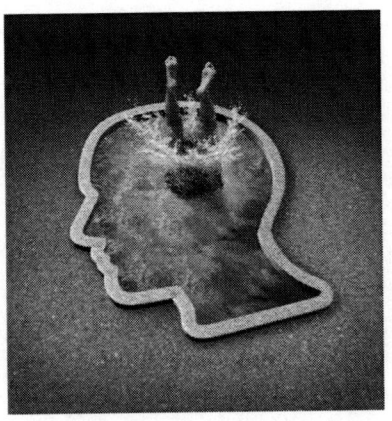

out a major deficit in Wundt's research on human consciousness as it focused almost exclusively on sensation and perception but ignored learning and memory, two similarly important mental processes (Bernstein et al., 2008).

Figure 13. Introspection is like diving into one's own mind (self-exploration).

STRUCTURALISM

One of Wundt's students, Edward Titchener (1867-1927), was influenced to research the *structure* of human consciousness. By using the same method of introspection as his teacher and similar experiments, Titchener explored human sensations (vision, hearing, etc.) and feelings. Similar to Wundt, he studied the intensity, quality, duration, and clarity of these elements. Titchener's primary interest rested on consciousness's basic structural elements; he called this approach **structuralism**. While Wundt saw attention as an act of our will capable of selecting our experience, Titchener understood it merely as a term we ascribe to the clarity of our experience. Another key difference between the approaches of Wundt and Titchener is that Wundt did not see psychology as capable of significantly exploring processes such as language, memory, and thinking. Titchener, however, disagreed. Titchener graduated from Oxford in 1890 (Leahey, 2004) and later founded a psychology laboratory at Cornell University (Thorne & Henley, 2001).

GESTALT

German psychologists Kurt Koffka (1886-1941), Wolfgang Kohler (1887-1967), and Max Wertheimer (1880-1943) believed that Wundt and Titchener were not accurately studying the human mind by breaking its smaller elements and parts. They argued that the whole (**Gestalt** in German) experience is more than the sum of its parts. They pioneered the Gestalt school of thought on the basis that separate elements of experience do not equate to the totality of the experience.

For example, in a now famous experiment, Wertheimer presented to a research subject two lights flashing in rapid succession. In the first stage of the experiment, the time between the flashes was set for one-fifth of a second and subjects reported seeing two distinct flashes. When the time between flashes was reduced to one-twelfth of a second, the research subjects reported seeing only one flash of light. Participants could not discern the individual flashes when they were presented in such exceedingly rapid succession. Their experience involved the flashes becoming combined into a false perception of a single light. This illusion Wertheimer termed the "phi phenomenon" (Schacter et al., 2007). This phenomenon is similar to blinking traffic arrows indicating a lane closure, telling us to change lanes. The signifying arrows seem to be moving when they blink in succession. In reality the light bulbs are not moving; it is simply the pattern of the lights, blinking one after another, that creates this illusion of movement in our mind. Gestalt psychologists would say that our perception of the apparent motion is the result of individual stimuli combining to make a larger experience. The fundamentals of the Gestalt approach are still readily used today in order to understand human perception (Bernstein et al., 2008).

Figure 14. Gestaltists would argue that we see water, but do not see particular hydrogen and oxygen atoms binding to create water. We experience water as a whole, not a mere sum of its parts.

FUNCTIONALISM

American psychologist William James (1842-1910) sided with Gestalt researchers and argued that Wundt and Titchener's approaches to human experience were too simplistic. He thought that studying the mind by examining its parts was like studying a house by looking at its bricks. Instead of studying the elements of the mind, James wanted to know what the greater *function* of the mind was. James's approach to better understand the function of mental processes became known as **functionalism**. According to James, consciousness functions to help individuals better adapt to environments in order to survive and thrive. For example, consciousness can detect a threat of coldness in an environment. The awareness of the oncoming cold prompts a person to find ways to stay warm (clothes, shelter, etc.). In the late 1870s James founded the first psychology lab in the United States at Harvard University. The Harvard lab, however, was used primarily for demonstration, not research purposes.

Figure 15. How would William James perceive the mental processes of an astronaut on the moon?

GENDER AND ETHNIC DIVERSITY IN PSYCHOLOGY

In 1908, Margaret Floy Washburn (1871-1939) became the first woman to obtain a PhD in psychology (Plotnik, 2005). Studying at Cornell University her supervisor was Edward Titchener and she adopted his structuralist psychological approach. Washburn published *The Animal Mind*, an unprecedented work on animal psychology, in 1908. The book delved into her findings on multiple species' perception, learning, and memory. Washburn postulated that animals, like humans, have conscious experience and make conscious choices (Scarborough & Furumoto, 1987). In 1921 she became the president of the American Psychological Association and would go on to teach at several colleges and universities (Thorne & Henley, 2001).

Mary Whiton Calkins (1863-1930) was another notable female psychologist. Her professor at Harvard University, Hugo Munstenberg (1863-1916), recommended Calkins as a PhD candidate. But unlike Cornell, it was not until 1963 that Harvard granted women PhD degrees. At the same time, Calkins was offered a PhD opportunity from Radcliff College. She refused the offer, as she saw it as a chance for Harvard to continue its gender discrimination. This obstacle did not stop Calkins from publishing over 100 essays and four books or from teaching psychology at Wellesley College. The focus of her work and her most notable contributions to the field of psychology were in memory research. She was the first to articulate the primacy vs. recency effect, an observation stating that we are more likely to remember information that we received first (Madigan & O'Hara, 1992). She also published essays on humans' concept of the self and its relationship with others (Wentworth, 1999). By 1903, Calkins was recognized as one of the most prominent American psychologists; in 1905 she became the first female president of the American Psychological Association (Thorne & Henley, 2001).

One of the first prominent Mexican psychologists was George Sanchez (1906-1972). He received his PhD from the University of California, Berkeley and used his research to disprove racial stereotypes. He scientifically debunked the belief that Mexican children were intellectually inferior to Caucasian children. Sanchez determined that reading and intelligence scores are affected when examinations are accurately translated into Spanish and reflect the culture of the test takers. Though his work was originally published in the 1930s, Sanchez's findings are still utilized today in arguments for the adjustment of intelligence tests for fair representation of all cultures. Sanchez's body of work has earned him the title of the Father of Chicano Psychology (Padilla, 1988).

Francis Sumner (1895-1954) was the first African American student to obtain a PhD in psychology in the United States, doing so from Clark University in 1920 (Schacter et al., 2007). His major contributions include the development of an undergraduate psychology program at Howard University, from which more African American psychologists graduated that any other university at the time. Beverly Prossor (1897-1934) earned a PhD in psychology from the University of Cincinnati in 1933 and became the first female African American psychologist. Kenneth Clark (1914-2005) became the first African American president of the American Psychology Association in 1971. Clark's research centered on negative self-image experienced by African American children (Schacter et al., 2007). One his contributions to the field of social psychology was discovering that, statistically, African American preschool children preferred White dolls to Black dolls (Thorne & Henley, 2001). Clark's research identified that psychological harm in African American children was correlated to segregation and its repercussions; his findings greatly influenced the Supreme Court's 1954 ruling on banning segregation in public schools (Schacter et al., 2007).

Figure 16. Since you are now familiar with Clark's research, what sorts of questions come to your mind when you look at this image?

MODERN PERSPECTIVES IN PSYCHOLOGY

Psychology's attempt to understand phenomena from various angles and perspectives make it a broad field. To better understand the different ways psychologists could approach a single phenomenon, we will analyze an example of human behavior through the following perspectives: psychodynamic, cross-cultural, learning, cognitive, biological, humanistic, and evolutionary. It is important to understand that these perspectives are not exclusive and can be amalgamated through eclectic views and approaches.

WHY DID AKIN KILL BATTICALS?

Imagine the following scenario: an honorable knight in training, Akin Fyler, learns of his mother's captivity in the hands of humanoid creatures called Batticals. Arriving at their camp mere seconds before she dies, Akin becomes filled with rage and kills every Battical in the camp, including *innocent* women, children, and babies. Why would he commit such an act if it is a creed of the knights to only kill in self-defense? Different psychological perspectives offer different answers.

PSYCHODYNAMIC PERSPECTIVE

The **psychodynamic perspective** claims that behaviors result from conflicting interactions among three mental structures: the id, the ego, and the superego. The **id** equates to one's impulses, the **ego** to one's reasoning, and the **superego** to one's sense of morality. Sigmund Freud (1856-1939) is credited as the founder of this perspective. But to address the above example—Akin was completely overwhelmed by his aggressive impulse (from the id) to kill and he acted to satisfy his impulse. The surge in his id prevented his ego (the rational aspect) from properly functioning. In a normal instance, the rational ego would have prevented Akin from acting on his first impulses.

14

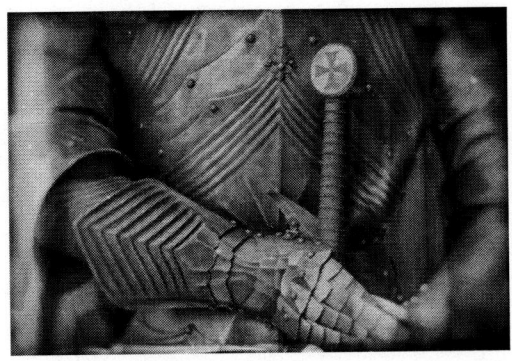

It is not until later, when Akin reflected on the event, that his superego judged his aggressive impulses as morally unacceptable and his ego deemed his violent behavior senseless and against the code of his knighthood. Hatred will still remain in his id, however, towards the Batticals and anxiety will arise from the conflict between his ego, superego, and id (Schultz & Schultz, 2005).

Figure 17. How would the psychoanalythic approach explain Akin's behavior?

FREUD AND PSYCHOANALYSIS

Sigmund Freud emphasized unconscious mental processes as a primary force in shaping human behavior. Freud believed mental disturbances could be remedied by making the patient aware of unconscious conflicts among their impulses, rationality, and moral sense—a therapy he called **psychoanalysis**. Unconscious conflicts, Freud believed, could be "unearthed" and faced in a conscious, mature way, which would pave the way for a cure. Freud proposed other revolutionary ideas as well, such as the development of one's personality through sexual stages and the existence of sexual feelings in children. Freud's original hypotheses remain important in psychology today; they inspire numerous attempts to empirically verify or disprove his idea. Psychoanalysis is still widely practiced and has proved notably successful in helping people control and better understand mental disturbances (Bernstein et al., 2008; Schultz & Schultz, 2005).

JUNG AND THE PSYCHODYNAMIC PERSPECTIVE

Carl Jung (1875-1961) may have posited that Akin killed the innocent Batticals simply because he was acting on a human tendency to be impulsively destructive. This aspect/tendency of the mind Jung called the *shadow*. He simultaneously categorized it as an **archetype**, a primeval

tendency that is inherently passed down from parents to offspring. After he commits his violent act of revenge, Akin confesses to his wife. In his confession he expresses genuine compassion for the Batticals, his Anima archetype (feminine tendencies in a male). According to Jung, archetypes reside in the **collective unconscious**, a mental realm we share with our ancestors of which we are not consciously aware (Crowne, 2007).

Figure 18. The shadow archetype.

15

CROSS-CULTURAL PERSPECTIVE

The **cross-cultural perspective** places an emphasis on the influence of the culture in which an individual is raised (Shweder & Sullivan, 1993). This approach theory would propose that Akin was raised in a culture where he witnessed many instances of violence, where the use of force was a normal problem solving strategy. And in fact, in this example, that is the case; Akin was indeed raised in a kingdoom where violent confrontations were natural occurrences. Additionally, Akin as a child and his mother were both slaves to a heartless owner. The violent act he committed on the Batticals' camp may have been a product of his upbringing. Had he been raised in a more peaceful environment, Akin's actions could have been very different indeed.

LEARNING PERSPECTIVE

The **learning perspective**, influenced extensively by Edward Thorndike (1874-1949) and B.F. Skinner (1904-1990), understands behavior as a product of its *consequences* (results). If an action receives positive consequences (a reward, for example), it is likely that the behavior will be repeated (and thus learned). Alternatively, if an action receives negative consequences, it will most likely not be repeated. This pattern is known as **operant conditioning** (Galef, 1998; Skinner, 1938; Thorndike, 1898). This perspective would suggest that Akin's past aggressive acts being rewarded caused him to massacre the Batticals. Since it was once rewarded, the act is repeated. This, indeed, is the case. Akin was once praised for killing many enemy warlords and was considered a hero. According to the learning perspective, if his past aggressive acts had not been rewarded, it is likely he would not have committed consequent acts.

Figure 19. Akin being rewarded with the knighthood after defending a kingdom.

LEARNING AND BEHAVIORISM

A professor of psychology at Johns Hopkins University, John Watson (1878-1958) believed that psychology should focus on examining observable behaviors in animals and humans. According to Watson, only the observable could be objectively studied and measured. By this account, the mind is a subjective matter and cannot be properly studied. Watson did not deny the existence of human minds, but held that it should not be the focus of scientific investigation; his work centered on how learning affects the development of animal and human behavior. A focus on observable behavior is called **behaviorism**. Behaviorism was the dominant psychological approach from the 1920s to the 1960s, becoming more popular than studies of consciousness. However, the study of consciousness once again became popular in the 1970s and still is today.

LEARNING AND CLASSICAL CONDITIONING

It was first proposed that behavior does not only have to be learned through its consequences by Ivan Pavlov (1849-1936) (Fancher, 1979). Through this learning perspective, known as **classical conditioning**, consider the following: it is possible that as a child Akin witnessed his slave owner shouting at his mother. Angered, little Akin ran off to the desert to be alone. While he was in the desert experiencing this state of anger, he may have noticed the presence of Batticals. If this occurred frequently enough (witnessing the slave owner abusing his mother, running off to the desert, and noticing the Batticals, perhaps on daily basis) little Akin would begin to *associate* the image of Batticals with his anger. Then, later, if he saw a Battical even in a completely new context, he would feel anger. Classical conditioning proposes that Akin killed the Batticals because he associated with them a deep-rooted anger.

COGNITIVE PERSPECTIVE

The **cognitive perspective** suggests that thought processes—such as language, memory, and problem solving—motivate behaviors (Neisser, 1967). For example, Akin did not understand the language of Batticals and perceived their shouts obscenities and threats directed at him. Because of this misunderstanding and the negative connection this formed, he did not feel any empathy towards the Batticals. Instead, he recalled the painful memory of his mother's death in their captivity, which influenced his decision to kill them. The concept that he formed, "the fewer of these creatures, the fewer the problem," justified his violent act.

Figure 20. To kill or not to kill, that is the question.

BIOLOGICAL PERSPECTIVE

The **biological perspective** was pioneered by Donald Hebb (1904-1985), Roger Perry (19 13-1994), and Karl Lashley (1890-1958). Genes, hormones, physiological processes, and anatomical structures are seen as the cause of behaviors and mental processes (Kolb & Whishaw, 2003). The biological perspective would attribute Akin's actions to the biological processes in his body. His violent act may have been caused by his inability to inhibit the surge of activity in his **amygdala** (a brain structure) that resulted in anger. The rational aspect of his frontal lobe was overwhelmed by the amygdala's emotional activity and was therefore rendered ineffective.

But why was Akin unable to inhibit the activity of his amygdala when another knight probably would have been able to if they were put in a similar situation? The biological perspective considers genetics; Akin's overactive amygdala and less active frontal lobe is a result of his genetic makeup. The biological perspective would also postulate that, since Akin was a young man at the time of the violent act, his blood contained more testosterone (a hormone linked to aggression) than an older, calmer peer.

HUMANISTIC PERSPECTIVE

The **humanistic perspective** emphasizes human beings' potential for entire ranges of behaviors and experiences (sadness, joy, generosity, empathy, etc.) and our inherent drive to fulfill our potential (to become self-actualized). Humanists believe that people are progressive by nature,

Figure 21. Akin's remorse.

urging naturally toward *self-actualization* and *growth*. Carl Rogers (1902-1987) and Abraham Maslow (1908-1970) were both strong pioneers in this school of thought. Humanists hold that a person's mind and behavior are influenced by primal needs such as food and shelter, as well as less necessary needs such as friends, social status, and self-realization. It is an ultimate Humanist belief that people are *free* to make *choices* about their own life (Maslow, 1970; Rogers, 1961). The Humanist perspective would say that Akin massacred the Batticals in a moment of weakness, his need for belonging and family temporarily causing a surge in rage and his decision to kill. However, in the future, he may regret what he did, realizing that it was not the morally right thing to do. The time may still come when he will choose the "right" behavior since, like all humans, Akin maintains the potential for both good and bad.

EVOLUTIONARY PERSPECTIVE

Charles Darwin (1809-1882) made major contributions to the **evolutionary perspective** of psychology. The evolutionary perspective states that there are mental processes and behaviors that are directly motivated by survival. Therefore, it is crucial for organisms that want to survive to adapt their behavior accordingly. A process of mental and behavioral change allowing adaptation, and thus survival, is called **evolution**. Behaviors that lead to survival are genetically passed down from parents to offspring (Buss, 1999). If we were to apply this perspective to the case of Akin Fyler, we could argue that his adaptation to a hostile environment gave him the violent disposition that caused him to kill the Batticals. The kingdom into which Akin was born was fraught with violence. Through his training he honed his skills to protect himself and increase his chances of survival. His killing of the Batticals was his adaptation to surviving in a hostile environment.

CAREERS IN PSYCHOLOGY

So far we have summarized the basis of psychology, what it consists of, and how it has developed over time. Its breadth is clear and offers numerous opportunities for careers in the field. An individual with a degree in psychology can be involved in clinical practice, research, teaching, or any combination of careers. Let's take a closer look at the jobs of researchers and practitioners.

Clinical psychologists work with assessing, treating, and preventing psychological disturbances. They may help patients deal with physical pain or emotional pain resulting from traumatic experiences. Clinical psychologists also aid patients in overcoming issues such as panic attacks, schizophrenia, and drug addiction and may specialize in specific populations such as minority groups, LGBTQ communities, or the elderly. Clinical psychologists are often employed by rehabilitation centers, hospitals, and universities (O'Hara, 2005).

Figure 22. What psychological disturbance might this girl be experiencing?

Counseling psychologists (often known as, simply, counselors) interview patients and advise them on major changes occurring in their lives. Counselors generally deal with marriage, family, and career related issues. Counselors may provide vocational/career guidance, marriage mediation, and adjustment advice to college students. They often work at hospitals, universities, and through individual or group sessions (O'Hara, 2005).

Positive psychologists study institutions, character strengths, and emotions that help communities and individuals to thrive. The main goal of a positive psychologist is to share techniques that will generate more positive emotions in the lives of their patients. Positive psychologists' work is concerned with the human capacity for courage, love, compassion, resilience, creativity, moderation, and curiosity. They tend to work in schools, community centers, and workplaces where they aim to promote productivity and opportunity for individuals to grow and improve their selves as well as their societies (Compton, 2005).

Figure 23. What does a positive psychologist research?

Cognitive psychologists' work focuses on research. Specifically, cognitive psychologists investigate the thought processes of perception, problem solving, leaning, creativity, reasoning, memory, and language. Individuals in this line of work spend their time researching the steps of the creative process, memory, the possibilities of artificial intelligence, and computerized models of human thinking (O'Hara, 2005).

Developmental psychologists follow people's psychological development throughout their lives. They may follow subjects all the way from infancy, where they investigate how/when they become self-aware, through old age, exploring how social and biological factors cooperate and collide to create unique individuals. They additionally study speech, the maturation of moral reasoning, and perceptions of death and how it varies by age (American Psychological Association [APA], 2003; O'Hara, 2005).

Educational psychologists research factors that facilitate human learning. Once equipped with this knowledge, educational psychologists develop curriculum and teaching methods meant to improve learning both in and out of school environments (APA, 2003; O'Hara, 2005).

School psychologists work extensively within public and private schools. They may conduct assessments and council students, implement interventions, and consult parents and school staff. School psychologists also work with special needs students, ensuring they are receiving a fair and comprehensive education (APA, 2003; O'Hara, 2005).

Engineering psychologists research methods for streamlining human and machine interactions. They experiment and implement forms of technology that are the most useful, intuitive, and manageable. For example, they may design plane interiors designed to relax individuals who have a fear of flying, or computer screens that are less straining on the eyes. Engineering psychologists are typically hired in industrial settings (APA, 2003; O'Hara, 2005).

Experimental psychologists research various behaviors in human and animal subjects such as motivation, attention, and memory. Experimental psychologists take questions (e.g. "why do many people fear snakes?") and design experiments to help explain the observed phenomenon. They work primarily in academic settings or as private researchers for business, government, and nonprofit organizations (APA, 2003; O'Hara, 2005).

Forensic psychologists integrate the field of psychology with law and criminal justice. They are often tasked with evaluating a defendant's mental ability to stand trial or determining which parent should get custody of a child. They are also often involved in evaluating physical evidence, such as autopsy results of DNA samples. Their expertise in analyzing the accuracy of an eyewitness testimony and other aspects of a court case make them indispensible in the field of criminal justice (APA, 2003; O'Hara, 2005).

Figure 24. Curious about why do some people become serial killers and stalkers? Forensic psychology might just be the right field for you.

Health psychologists study the influence psychological factors have on an individual's development and treatment of illness. One phenomenon they research is what effect one's expectations of recovery have on their actual recovery. Health psychologists design programs to curb substance abuse, teenage pregnancy, poor diet, and other common unhealthy behaviors. This type of psychologist often works in hospitals and through private practices (APA, 2003; O'Hara, 2005; Straub, 2002).

Organizational/Industrial psychologists apply psychological methods and concepts to the workplace and improve the quality of work experience as well as productivity. They may calibrate colors and types of light that can maximize work output and job satisfaction. They are often hired to draw up improvements for businesses' marketing plans. Industrial psychologists are also utilized in selecting optimal employees and training new hires (APA, 2003; O'Hara, 2005).

Neuropsychologists study the relationship between the mind/behavior and the nervous system. They delve into the expessions of love, fear, memory, etc., and the biological processes behind the behaviors. Clinical neuropsychologists are also licensed to assess and treat individuals with psychological abnormalities (APA, 2003; O'Hara, 2005).

Quantitative/measurement psychologists design research methods, analyze collected data, and determine the quality/objectivity of psychological tests (APA, 2003; O'Hara, 2005).

Psychometrists construct, administer, and analyze psychological examinations. Based on the data they collect, psychometrists have the ability to assess a person's skills and predict their performance in future academic or career settings (APA, 2003; O'Hara, 2005).

Social psychologists research how people influence each other. They are interested in how parents or peer groups shape our opinions about people from cultures other than our own. Social psychologists consider what factors influence the length of a romantic relationship, to what extent people obey authority, and what type of leadership proves most effective. They typically work in advertising agencies, government, and businesses (APA, 2003; O'Hara, 2005).

Sports psychologists work exclusively with athletes on all aspects of their performance. They work to develop strategies for helping them concentrate, build confidence, develop imagery skills to attain their goals, minimize frustration, work better as a part of a team, and overall maximize performance (APA, 2003; O'Hara, 2005).

Figure 25. Can you guess what type of a psychologist is depicted here?

THE JOB OUTLOOK

Say you have just finished spending an exorbitant amount of time and energy on obtaining a degree in psychology. The hard work has finally paid off and you have your degree. Now the question is, what can you do with it? The answer depends on the type of degree you have received. A bachelor's degree could possibly get you hired as an assistant at mental health or correctional centers. You could also begin working as a research assistant in a lab. Teaching psychology at high schools would also be an option, as long as you meet state certification requirements. Many graduates with a bachelor's degree in psychology obtain jobs in public affairs, administrative support, and health or biological science. The job field is as wide as the field of psychology itself, encompassing counselors, probation officers, personal analysts, and authors (APA, 2003; O'Hara, 2005).

A master's degree would allow for job opportunities in counseling, clinical, or academic psychology as well as the options of working in the field of quantitative psychology or as a psychometrist. Individuals with master's degrees in psychology often work in data collection and analyst positions for governments, private companies, and universities. With a master's degree one could also teach at most high schools and community colleges (APA, 2003; O'Hara, 2005).

The largest range of high-paying careers is available to those who have earned a doctorate degree. While doctoral graduates often find employment in research or teaching positions at colleges and

22

universities, most have jobs in counseling, clinical, and school psychology (APA, 2003; O'Hara, 2005).

Statistically, 25 percent of individuals with degrees in psychology work in colleges, universities, and professional schools, performing researching and publishing their findings; 40 percent run private practices, and consult businesses and other organizations; 18 percent work in hospitals, counseling centers, and clinics administering therapies for mentally disturbed patients; 7 percent are employed in other miscellaneous fields, conducting research for private institutions, the military, or working with lawmakers to shape public and educational policy; 6 percent are directly employed by businesses and government sectors, assessing the workplace and finding ways to improve productivity and employee satisfaction; and 4 percent work in schools as counselors or specifically in establishments for the developmentally disabled (APA, 2006).

Hopefully you now have a broader understanding of the career opportunities for psychologists and, as you continue reading this book, consider psychology as a viable and profoundly rewarding field of research and work. You may even begin to consider a career in psychology for yourself.

PSYCHOLOGY IS A SCIENTIFIC FIELD

The field of psychology has four main goals: to *describe*, *explain*, *change*, and *predict* mental processes and behaviors. Describing something means to identify its features. For example, when a patient has hallucinations, a psychologist is curious about the characteristics of those hallucinations. Does a patient see things that are unreal? Do they hear voices? If so, what kinds of voices? What are they saying? The goal of explaining refers to psychology's attempt to provide reasons for why mental processes/behaviors occur. What is causing these hallucinations? Is it substance abuse? Genetics? Is it a combination of genetic vulnerability to hallucinations and an influence of a stressful environment? What kind of a stressful environment? Is it perhaps a car accident injuring a certain region of the brain? In terms of change, psychologists will try to reduce or eliminate hallucinations so that the patient can experience a better quality of life. Lastly, prediction refers to the anticipation of when, where, why, and how intensely hallucinations will come back. This hallucination example is just one we can look at to begin to understand the four goals that govern the field of psychology. The goals can be seen as pillars of psychology, and the greater filed of psychology as a type of temple. All the pillars support the

Figure 26. Space telescopes above Earth remind us of sciences, such as astronomy and exploring the cosmos. Psychology uses an identical method for its discoveries; the inner universe that it explores is as vast as the cosmos.

23

structure; but the central pillar, in the middle of the temple, is the scientific method.

Psychology is a scientific field, since it utilizes the **scientific method**. What does the scientific method consist of? It begins with something Sir Isaac Newton once said. He stated that the only reason he could see farther than others is because he stood on the shoulders of giants. Well, not real giants, but instead people who made some significant contribution to the body of knowledge. In other words, Newton was aware of the accomplishments of previous researchers, and by relying on those accomplishments he was able to develop original, groundbreaking ideas. The next step was attempting to verify these new ideas. What I am describing here are the stages of the scientific process: being immersed in a particular field of interest, studying what others have discovered (this is also called a *literature review*), and then, after becoming familiar with others' discoveries, coming up with one's own, original *predictions* of how phenomena are related. A prediction of this sort is called a *hypothesis* or an *educated guess*. It is "educated" since it emerges from an already accumulated body of knowledge. It is a guess since it takes a researcher a step into the unknown, into the realm of the possible and the likely, yet unexplored. But it must be added that every hypothesis must also be a *testable* guess. This means that once it is stated, the goal is to *verify* (or test) the validity of the hypothesis. Let's now turn our attention to the topic of how a research study is designed.

DESIGNING A RESEARCH STUDY

Designing (creating) a research study begins with a *topic* of interest. Let's say that we are interested in violence, specifically whether exposure to TV violence causes viewers to be violent. Our hypothesis is going to be: *exposure to TV aggression increases aggression in people* (a hypothesis is always a statement, not a question). To test this hypothesis, one of the first things we need to do is come up with a *definition* of aggression so that aggression can be observed and measured. We are looking for a *behavioral definition* of aggression, in other words we need to find out what behavior(s) reflect aggression. "Aggression" on its own is a vague notion that will need to be refined if we want to measure it precisely. What type of aggression are we talking about? We need to be very precise within a scientific field so that proper measurements can be taken. Slapping, kicking, hitting, punching, saying bad words to another person, all these behaviors are reflections of aggression. So, we have arrived at a *behavioral* definition of violence. A behavioral definition is also called an *operational definition* since we use behaviors to operate on the environment.

What is the next step in designing a study? How do we *measure* the behaviors reflecting aggression? Let's say we want to see how aggressive children

Figure 27. Why is it important to have an operational definition of violence in psychology?

24

operate in a particular area. We ask for permission to observe children when they play in a schoolyard, and after the permission is granted we simply observe their behavior and record instances of aggression (in the form of the already-defined behaviors). We may observe five slaps, 12 kicks, and 13 bad words a day from the group of children. We can also say that the behavior we are interested in measuring (aggression) is a *variable*, something that can *change* or *vary* (tomorrow there can be more or less kicks, for example).

The behavior variable can depend on certain factors such as exposure of children to TV featuring aggressive content, since children learn through observation and imitation, something that your literature review has convinced you of. Thus, the behavior that we want to measure (aggression) depends on a condition (TV exposure). Such behavior, one relying on the input of a condition, we call a *dependent* variable. TV exposure is a variable too (there can be more or less exposure). It is called an *independent variable* since the behavior of interest (aggression) depends on it, and not the other way around. Now, suppose that our research team hears of a community that does not have any TV sets now, but will in 6 months. This is a perfect opportunity to see whether the amount of aggression (the dependent variable) changes as a result of children's exposure to violent TV (the independent variable). Thus, we will measure aggression in children before and after TV exposure to compare whether the amount of aggression changes.

After TV becomes available in the community, we continue the practice from before; we observe groups of children. The process of recording the behavior of our interest is called *data collection*. Any research study relies heavily on data gathering, since the *data* are recorded behaviors that we observed. Without data, whatever we say is merely an opinion and speculation, and therefore cannot be taken seriously in science. Proven claims must be supported by data. Since we observe the children without participating in their behaviors, this study is considered *non-participant observation* (a study where researchers participate in the study is called *participant observation*).

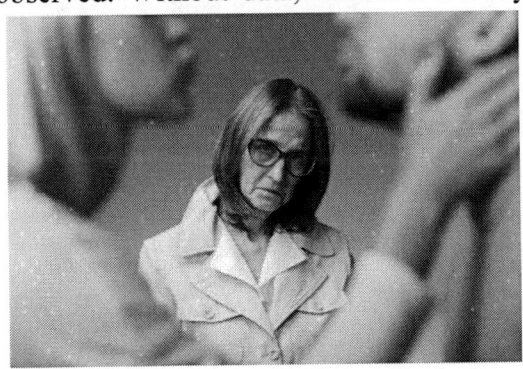

Figure 28. A non-participant observer's role is to simply monitor and record the behaviors of others (not to intervene).

We again measure the behaviors that we have outlined as indicating aggression, and we discover a tremendous jump in aggression displayed by children! We conclude that, since only one aspect of the community has changed (the introduction of TV), that exposure to TV channels caused an increase in aggression. Overcome with excitement, we write a paper about our findings, to share (or *disseminate*) our knowledge with others. We submit that paper to a journal where experienced researchers review our paper, and approve it for publication. A few weeks later, however, criticism from some readers arrives. Critics claim that at the same time TV channels were introduced, a major highway was built connecting the community with the rest of the region, and that our results are inconclusive due to this unaccounted for factor. Initially we are in denial. We soon realize that we need to face reality, and that what we thought was a *causation* was merely a *correlation*. Let's look at what these terms, correlation and causation, mean.

DESIGNING A RESEARCH STUDY: CAUSATION AND CORRELATION

The goal of utmost importance in science is to detect *causation*, a process where one variable makes another variable happen. In the above example, we thought that exposure to violent TV produced an increase in aggression. But, the increase of aggression could be brought on by other factors, like the introduction of a major highway (traffic, irritability, road rage, accidents and associated anger). So we cannot say with complete certainty that the increase in aggression is due to violent TV programs. It is equally likely that it is due to the newly built highway, or maybe a combination of both. This means exposure to

Figure 29. The Holy Grail of psychology is to identify cause-effect relationships.

violent TV is merely associated (correlated) with the increase in violence. The construction of the major highway is similarly associated, but it is radically important to remember: *correlation is not causation.* Correlation is when a variable (exposure to violent TV) happens and another variable (increase in aggression) follows. But in this case we are not sure whether the exposure to violent TV produces the increase in aggression or if it is some third variable producing this increase. But at the same time we cannot be certain that the highway is causing the increase in aggression either.

A *direction* of the correlation is a useful concept. When correlation is *positive*, it means that as one variable changes in one direction, another variable changes in the same direction. For example, there is a myth that younger people are happier. However, it is likely that an advanced age offers more experience and stronger insight into future outcomes and opportunities, which could lead to a better mood. But, it is not accurate to say that age causes better mood. Cities with more churches have more instances of crime, which makes this a positive correlation too, but this does not mean that more churches somehow causes crime. Cities with more churches are simply larger and have greater populations, heightening the likelihood of crime. This points to the already established fact that correlation is not causation. *Negative* correlation means that when one variable changes in one direction, another variable changes in the opposite direction. When variables are not correlated (for example, shoe size does not have any relationship with a score on an intelligence test), that's neither negative nor positive correlation; instead, there is a non-existent or zero correlation. Also, an important consideration is the *strength* of a correlation. A higher intelligence score is only

26

moderately correlated with higher income, for example, meaning that there is room for other factors to influence higher income (such as hard work, motivation, and persistence) (Huffman & Dowdell, 2015).

DESIGNING A RESEARCH STUDY: CONTROLLING VARIABLES

Returning to our study regarding aggression and TV: an additional independent variable (the highway) snuck into our study without our awareness of it. An overlooked variable that may have an influence on the behavior of interest is called a *confounding variable*. How do researchers *control* such variables that can obscure accurate measurements? One way is to create a type of a study called an *experiment*. The study on the community without TVs was not an experiment. In an experiment researchers control the variables; they can *manipulate* them to see how they influence the dependent variable. With this ability to control the situation, we could resume the study, this time with a lower chance of a confounding variable. Then, if we saw fit, we could decide to introduce a confounding variable (the highway) to see how aggression changes (if at all) as a result. Initially, we were unable to manipulate the highway condition, rendering the study not an experiment. Manipulation of independent variables within an experiment can reveal whether they cause changes in the dependent variable (Huffman & Dowdell, 2015).

DESIGNING A RESEARCH STUDY: AN EXPERIMENT

Picture a different study, an experiment structured like this: we want to see how *marijuana* (an independent variable) and *cocaine* (another independent variable) influence rats to *keep track of time* (the dependent variable). Our hypothesis is that these drugs will have absolutely no effect on rats' time tracking ability. We create one group that will be injected with marijuana, and another group that will be injected with cocaine. We create identical circumstances for both groups of rats (so that results cannot be attributed to differences in circumstances). They are kept in the same cages, at the same temperature, in the same room. It is also important to ensure that all subjects are of the same genus of rat, the same age, etc. The only difference between the groups is the type of drug given to them. We call the rats the *experimental groups*, since they are the groups where

our *intervention* occurs. But, we also need to involve a third group of rats that will be injected with a substance that does not have any impact on them (water, for example). This third group is called the *control group*. A control group is important since we need to establish the everyday, normal, baseline behavior of the rats when they are not given any drug. We use the control group as a *reference point* so that we can *compare* the altered groups with the control group.

Figure 30. "Oh no, I am next," says the rat anticipating a painful injection.

27

Before any injections of water or drugs, the rats are trained to press a button exactly 12 seconds after they receive food. This training takes time, since if they press the bar after 10 seconds or 13 seconds they will not receive a food reward, but they will eventually perform the task accurately, since they are motivated by food. The data collection (observing rats' behaviors under the influence of drugs and water) process starts, and we observe that rats given cocaine regularly press the button after eight seconds instead of 12; rats on marijuana after 15 seconds, and rats given water 12 seconds. Then we *interpret* these findings to mean that marijuana slows down the perception of time, cocaine speeds it up and water has no effect. Thus, our hypothesis is not *supported* (or it is *rejected*) since the collected data does not match our hypothesis.

Why did water have to be injected to form a control group? Couldn't we just have a control condition without an injection? A control group without an injection would not be the best option, since we need to see whether the act of injecting a substance (whether drugs or water) influences rats' behavior. Imagine that the rats in the control group press the button after 16 seconds on average. Since water does not influence rats' body in any significant way, it can be concluded that there was something about the process of the *injection* of water that influenced their impairment in time tracking. Perhaps an inexperienced technician hurt these rats by administering the injection to a sensitive area on the body. Thus, injecting water is important to establish *consistency* in substance administration across all conditions so that the difference in results can be attributed only to the difference in the substances, not to the process of injecting those substances.

DESIGNING A RESEARCH STUDY: SUBJECT VARIABLES

Famous psychiatrist Sigmund Freud was criticized for drawing conclusions about humanity based only on samples of white, young women from Vienna, Austria. It is safe to say that his research sample was not *representative* of the entire population of humans. How can a researcher attain a sample of participants that is representative of the entire population? *Random selection* is a procedure that ensures that each member of the population of interest has an *equal chance* of being included in the sample. A study can be *advertised* in such a way that everyone has an equal chance to see it, like posting it on youtube which is accessible to an overwhelming majority of people. When individuals submit their names for a study, a computer program can randomly select a number of participants. However, many psychological studies are conducted at colleges and universities, and research participants are relatively educated students. This demographic may not seem to be highly representative of the entire population, unless students are the population of interest for a study. Thus, we

Figure 31. Many research studies use students for participants. Does this represent an entire population (non-students, for example)?

need to be aware that the results of those studies *may* not be applicable to non-students, but instead reflect approximations.

Random selection is a method to reach the representative segment of a population of interest (say, women in America, or, more specifically, women pianists in Zimbabwe, Africa, etc.). But once the sample has been secured researchers then need to make a selection of who will be in the experimental group and who will be in the control group. This is done through *random assignment.* This is a process through which participants are, again, randomly assigned to one group or another. This balances *subject variables* (sex, socioeconomic status, intelligence score, etc.) across any number of groups, since we do not want the dependent variable to change as a result of subject variables (Alexander, 2014).

DESIGNING A RESEARCH STUDY: DEALING WITH BIAS

Bias refers to an expectation of a person or situation, and behavior in accordance with that expectation. One such bias is called the *placebo effect* (also known as the belief effect). The placebo effect is when the dependent variable changes because of the participant's belief that their behavior will change. It has been observed, for example, that depressed patients who are made to believe a pill containing only sugar is in fact an anti-depressant start to really feel less depressed. Thus, it is sometimes important to eliminate the placebo effect by not letting patients know whether they received treatment or not. This is called a *single-blind study*; patients do not know who received a medicine and who received sugar pills. An even more effective way of reducing a placebo effect is a *double-blind study* where neither the patient nor the researcher knows who received the medication or the placebo (still, somebody, like a secretary, must know who got what).

Why would a study benefit from a double-blind situation? This is because researchers are only human, and therefore subject to human bias (so called the *experimenter bias*) as well. If a researcher knew who received treatment and who did not, it is very likely that they would, whether intentionally or not, evaluate patients who received medications as having fewer symptoms than is the case. They would impose their bias. This may be seen especially in situations where drug companies fund research studies. Positive evaluation of a drug's effectiveness works well for a company

Figure 32. Placebo is a pill that does not have any significant effect on the human body and mind. It can be empty or containing some ineffective substance like water.

selling the drug, and for the researchers who will continue to be paid for this research. Or, a researcher may simply expect, by relying on logic, to see less symptoms in someone they know is on a medication. To prevent all these possible biases, a double-blind study removes (or minimizes) expectations from the equation (Myers & Hensen, 2006).

When we discussed the study of aggression and TV viewing, we mentioned the *non-participant observation* strategy. A study can be designed to include researchers as participants. This would be *a participant observation* strategy. These observational techniques have the advantage of capturing the behavior of interest in its natural, spontaneous state. However, a disadvantage is that a researcher in a non-participant study may influence the behavior of participants to change and become unnatural, once participants realize that someone is observing them. Thus, concealing the researcher is important, so that participants do not perceive the observing eye. In a *participant observation*, the disadvantage remains that a researcher may influence changes in the behavior. A participant observer, however, may be stimulated to act and distort the results of a study. For example, an observer who is trained in psychology knows that when more people are present at a social scene, this increases the likelihood of a person requiring help not receiving the aid they need. Thus, the researcher may run to help a subject regardless if there is only one other person or 20. But that is a very different behavior from most people.

Figure 33. Would you be able to act naturally if you knew that you were being observed?

There is also a *survey* strategy, a set of questions that participants are asked to answer, so that a researcher can better understand their attitudes, symptoms, or dispositions. A survey can be administered in an interview (face to face, on the phone, or over the internet). However, participants can still conceal the truth. Usually, monetarily rewarding a person to participate controls the tendency to lie on the survey. An advantage is that these surveys can be a means of gathering large amounts of data in a short period of time. (Graziano & Raulin, 2010).

A *case study* is another research technique in which a researcher focuses exclusively on an individual, examining their mental processes and behaviors of interest. Later we will examine the cases of Phineas Gage (a person who became overly emotional after a part of his brain was damaged) and Henry Mollaison, a person who underwent brain surgery to remove the part of his brain responsible for creating memories, rendering him incapable of memorizing new information. Case studies are reflections of what happened to a single individual. In other words, these cases are not representative of the population. But case studies, on the other hand, are known for containing an incredible amount of details about that individual.

The previously mentioned techniques are *non-experimental*. However, the hypothetical study of rats on drugs was an example of an experimental instance. We saw that an experiment can manipulate variables, identify cause and effect relationships, and provide a high level of control of the confounding variables. Surveys, case studies, and observational techniques are considered to be *descriptive studies*, since they are not used to manipulate variables. However, these techniques can be used in experiments. For example, immediately after participants are given a drug, they are asked to take a survey of their experience, while the control group takes the same survey but did not receive the drug. A case study can include experiments conducted on a participant where that same person's behavior is measured before some intervention and again after the intervention. A person's behavior being measured once, again later for a second time, and then compared, is called *within-subject design.* Research studies that measure correlations (direction and strength) between variables are *correlational studies*. The aforementioned study on TV exposure and aggression was an example of a mixture of non-experimental and correlational study.

REFERENCES

American Psychological Association. (2003). *Careers for the twenty-first century.* Washington, DC: Author.

American Psychological Association. (2006). *2003 Doctorate employment survey.* Washington, DC: APA Research Office.

Alexander, P., Flint, W. R., Flome, R., Hakala, C., Hayashi, C., Jones, J., July, W., Nguyen, B., Patry, M., Shobe, E., Sweetman, A., Thomas, B., Vukov, B., Wark, V., & Yakel, A.D. (2014). *Psychology: exploring our universe within* (4th edition). Boston, MA: Pearson Custom Publishing.

Axtell, R.E. (1993). *Do's and taboos around the world* (3rd ed.). New York: John Wiley.

Bernstein, D.A., Penner, L.A., Clarke-Stewart, A. & Roy, E. J. (2008). *Psychology* (8th ed.). Boston: Houghton Mifflin.

Breedlove, M.S., Rosenzweig, M. R., & Watson, N. V. (2007). *Biological psychology: An introduction to behavioral, cognitive and clinical neuroscience* (5th ed.). Sunderland, MA: Sinauer Associates.

Brehm, S., Kassin, S., & Fein, S. (2005). *Social Psychology* (6th ed.). Boston: Houghton Mifflin.

Brummet, P., Edgar, R., Hackett, N., Jewsbury, G., Taylor, A., Bailkey, N., et al. (2003). *Civilization past and present* (10th ed.). Boston: Allyn & Bacon.

Buss, D. M. (1999*). Evolutionary psychology: The new science of the mind.* Boston: Allyn & Bacon.

Buss, D. M., Larsen, R. J., Westen, D., & Semmelroth, J. (1992). Sex differences in jealousy: Evolution, physiology, and psychology. *Psychological Science, 3*(4), 251-255.

Compton, W. (2005). *Introduction to positive psychology.* Belmont, CA: Thomson Wadsworth.

Damasio, A. R. (2005). *Descartes' error: Emotion, reason, and the human brain* (paperback ed.). New York: Penguin Books.

Ekman, P., & Rosenberg, E. L. (Eds.). (2005). *What the face reveals: Basic and applied studies of spontaneous expression using the facial action coding system (FACS).* New York: Oxford University Press.

Galef, B. (1998). Edward Torndike: Revolutionary psychologist, ambiguous biologist. *American Psychologist, 53,* 1128-1134.

Giles, J. (2004). Neuroscience: Change of mind [Electronic version]. *Nature, 430,* 14.

Graziano, A. M., & Raulin, M. L. (2010). *Research methods: A process of inquiry* (7th ed.). Boston, MA: Pearson

Huffman, K., Dowdell, K. (2015). *Psychology in Action* (11th ed). Hoboken, NJ: John Wiley & Sons.

Kolb, B., & Whishaw, I. Q. (2009). *Fundamentals of human neuropsychology* (6th ed.). New York: Worth Publishers.

Laver, A. B. (1972). Precursors of psychology in ancient Egypt. *Journal of the History for the Behavioral Sciences, 8,* 181-195.

Leahey, H. (2004). *A history of psychology: Main currents in psychological thought* (6th ed.). Upper Saddle River, NJ: Pearson Education.

Madigan, S., & O'Hara, R. (1992). Short-term memory at the turn of the century: Mary Whiton Calkins's memory research. *American Psychologist, 47,* 170-174.

Magner, L.N. (1992). *A history of medicine.* New York: Marcel Dekker.

Martini, H. F., Ober, W. C., Garrison, C. W., Welch, K., Hutchings, R. T., & Ireland, K. (2004). *Fundamentals of anatomy & physiology* (6th ed.). Upper Saddle River, NJ: Prentice Hall.

Maslow, A. H. (1970). *Motivation and personality* (2nd ed.). New York: Harper & Row.

Myers, A., & Hansen, C. (2006). *Experimental psychology* (6th ed.) Belmont, CA: Thompson Wadsworth.

Neisser, U. (1967). *Cognitive psychology.* New York: Appleton-Century-Crofts.

O'Hara, S. (2005). *What can you do with a major in psychology? Real people, real jobs, real rewards.* Hoboken, NJ: John Wiley & Sons.

Partala, T., Jokiniemi, M., & Surakka, V. (2000, November). *Pupillary responses to emotionally provocative stimuli.* Poster session presented at the Eye Tracking Research & Application Symposium, Palm Beach, FL.

Rogers, C. R. (1961). *On becoming a person.* Boston: Houghton Mifflin.

Scarborough, E., & Furumoto, L. (1987). *Untold lives: The first generation of American women psychologists.* New York: Columbia University Press.

Sahakian, W. S. (Ed.). (1968). *History of psychology: A source book in systematic psychology.* Itasca, IL: F. E. Peacock Publishers.

Schacter, D. L., Gilbert, D. T., & Wegner, D. M. (2007). *Psychology.* New York: Worth Publishers.

Schultz, D., & Schultz, S. (2005). *Theories of personality* (8th ed.). Belmont, CA: Thomson Wadsworth.

Seligman, M. E. P., Rashid, T., & Parks, A. C. (2006). Positive psychotherapy. *American Psychologist, 61*(8), 774-788.

Sherwood, L. (2004). *Human physiology: From cells to systems.* Belmont, CA: Brooks/Cole-Thomson Learning.

Shweder, R. A., & Sullivan, M.A. (1993). Cultural psychology: Who needs it? *Annual Review of Psychology, 44,* 497-523.

Siegle, G., Granholm, E., Ingram, R., & Matt, G. (2001). Pupillary and reaction time measures of sustained processing of negative information in depression. *Biological Psychiatry, 49,* 624-636.

Skinner, B. F. (1938). *The behavior of organisms: An experimental analysis.* New York: Appleton-Century-Crofts.

Soccio, D. (2004). *Archetypes of wisdom. An introduction to philosophy* (5th ed.). Belmont, CA: Wadsworth/Thomson Learning.

Straub, R. (2002). *Health psychology.* New York: Worth Publishers.

Thorndike, E. L. (1898). Animal intelligence: An experimental study of the associative processes in animals. *Psychological Review Monograph Supplements, 2* (Whole No.8).

Thorne, B., & Henley, T. (2001). *Connections in the history and systems of psychology* (2nd ed.). Boston: Houghton Mifflin.

Wentworth, P. A. (1999). The moral of her story: Exploring the philosophical and religious commitments in Mary Whiton Calkins's self-psychology. *History of Psychology, 2,* 119-131.

Psychology of Personality

Chapter Two

DEFINING PERSONALITY

Personality is defined as a relatively consistent way of interacting with the world. Let's break down this definition into its elements that need to be explored a bit more. We *interact* with the world through our mental processes, behaviors and physiological processes. By the *world* we mean the external world (other people, animals, objects, situations, etc.) and the internal world (our own mental processes; for example, you react in a certain way when you have a toothache—going immediately to a dentist, or perhaps procrastinating). Personality is a *consistent* way of interacting, since personality, by definition, refers to something stable or enduring, as opposed to mental

processes, behaviors and physiological reactions that change from moment to moment, day to day. Personality is a *relatively* consistent way of interacting, since our personality can change; therefore, personality is not something set in stone, but it is something alterable. The following pages will discuss various theories about how personalities develop and what their structures are.

Figure 1. In Greek, persona means mask. Actors wore masks that portrayed certain personalities.

THEORIES OF PERSONALITY: PSYCHODYNAMIC

Within the framework of the psychodynamic theory, the mind is a very dynamic (activity laden) environment, where various mental processes constantly interact, influencing one another and the behavior. Let's have a closer look at this theory.

The founder of the psychodynamic theory is psychiatrist Sigmund Freud (1856-1939). He was a physician, a psychiatrist whose patients often complained of the following symptoms: blindness or an inability to see well in both or one eye, deafness or an inability to hear well in both or one ear, stuttering, stomach aches, headaches, diarrhea, arm and/or leg paralysis, numbness in the face or other parts of the boy. Freud used the term *"talking cure"* to refer to the approach he used to treat his patients' psychological problems. Freud noticed that once the patients were able to face their problems, and once he was able to bring their psychological issues to their awareness, that they could acknowledge and accept their problems without being emotionally overwhelmed by them; the aforementioned symptoms (stuttering, headaches, etc.) of many patients were either gone completely, or they were substantially reduced. Freud also gave a more technical name to his "talking cure,"—that name was **psychoanalysis**. Psychoanalysis consisted of three major steps: 1) access the subconscious level of the mind where the psychological problems resided, 2) identify precisely those problems and 3) bring these issues to one's awareness.

In order to understand psychoanalysis better, let's start by explaining what kinds of problems, or **conflicts** we are talking about here. What kind of conflicts? *Internal* conflicts that happen within the mental processes of our minds. Mental processes, in other words, can contradict one another, according to Freud. To understand the idea of conflicts better, we need to understand the basic mental processes of anyone's personality. Those mental aspects are: id, ego and superego. They can become conflicted on a daily basis, even many times during the day (Schultz & Schultz, 2005).

Figure 2. According to Freud, inner conflicts are the driving forces within our personalities.

ID

Id (translated from Latin, meaning "it") refers to mental processes such as *impulses* (or urges), for example an impulse to eat, to quench thirst, to have sex, to sleep, to light up a cigarette or to aggress against someone. These impulses are pre-rational, meaning they initially appear in our consciousness without our rational evaluation of them. For example, you are at your wedding, and you are about to cut the cake with your future spouse; suddenly, you get a strong urge to urinate. First you become aware of that urge, and only after you become aware of it, does your rational thinking kick in and you say to yourself, "it would be a good idea to go to the bathroom instead of making a mess in my clothes. If I urinate here, I will embarrass myself in front of everyone else." That's your rational thinking talking. Urges (impulses) occur during the phase before rational thinking even starts; those urges are pre-rational, and some of them are also **irrational,** like the urge to slap your irritating boss, who can easily fire you. In Freud's view, urges, instincts, drives and impulses are the same thing with different names.

The id is governed by a **pleasure principle**, meaning that the id strives toward immediate satisfaction (**gratification**) of its urges. The id wants the satisfaction here and now, like a baby or a very young child. For example, a few days ago, my four-year-old daughter did not accept any of my arguments against us having a dog, and she cried a river of tears demanding that her dog appear immediately in the car while we were driving on a highway. She literally said, I want it right now, daddy, right now! She refused to hear any of my rational concerns, like she is only four, and the dog's walking, feeding and other responsibilities would most likely fall on myself and her mother, which we don't have time for. She said, through tears, that she is an adult and that she will take

care of all that. The id is just like my daughter; it craves immediate satisfaction without anticipating the consequences of that satisfaction, without thinking whether the immediate satisfaction can realistically or appropriately happen. So, think of the id as that baby or a very young child that still lives inside of us. Luckily, there is the ego, a mental process that can block (or inhibit) our id. Let's turn to ego then (Schultz & Schultz, 2005).

Figure 3. Don't let your id ruin your wedding.

EGO

Ego (translated from Latin, meaning "I" or "myself") refers to our rational thinking. The ego can pay attention to more than one factor while the id's attention is only narrowed to the immediate satisfaction if its impulses. The ego can weigh the consequences of the id's impulsiveness. If the ego thinks that the consequences of immediate satisfaction of the id's urges is not going to be realistic, then the ego makes a decision to stop the id's aspirations. If the ego believes that the consequences are going to be favorable (like when you feel an urge [id] to drink water to quench

thirst), then the ego agrees with the id's aspirations. So, the ego is all about making informed decisions, problem solving through reasoning, paying attention, analyzing, planning, and weighing the consequences of our actions. The id is pre-rational and often irrational, and the ego is rational. The ego is governed by the reality principle, meaning the ego considers realistic demands, limitations and possibilities (Schultz & Schultz, 2005).

Figure 4. August Rodin's sculpture titled "The Thinking Man" resembles Freud's concept of the Ego.

Superego (translated from Latin, meaning "beyond I") is a mental process that manifests as our system of moral values, our sense of morality. Picture the superego as an angel who sits on your shoulder and judges your deeds, thoughts and feelings, and then decides whether they are morally acceptable or not. When we feel guilty, it means that the angel on our shoulder (superego) is

disappointed with how we have behaved, thought or felt. The superego has very high moral standards, and it wants us to be moral, law-abiding citizens, who follow the moral law perfectly all the time. Of course, different people may have a different set of moral values, but the point is that once we deviate from our system of values, we feel guilty (anxious) about letting our principles down (Schultz & Schultz, 2005).

Figure 5. The superego could be resembled by an angelic entity, a being of high moral values.

INNER CONFLICT

Id, ego and superego often get into conflicts. For example, a few months ago there was a heartbreaking situation in another country where a 15-year-old girl was kidnapped, tortured and killed by the kidnapper. A part of me (id) wanted the death penalty for the kidnapper, and not only that, but my id wanted brutal, eye-for-an-eye death. Then, my superego rebelled and said to me that if I participate in the petition for the death penalty, that I am also the killer just like the kidnapper; that I am cruel, just like the kidnapper. The superego insisted that the kidnapper probably had some brain damage or some horrible upbringing (or both) that shaped his personality not leaving him a lot of choice to avoid his own uncontrollable impulses. The superego also added that the kidnapper could be reformed into someone who realizes his mistake; that people, including myself, should show mercy and willingness to help the kidnapper regain his lost soul. My id then said to my superego to go to hell, and my superego lectured my id that it was not ethical to say that and to be mean to others since their feelings are getting hurt. Then my ego, the rational part, finally showed up and said that it is not smart for me to be so conflicted, so tortured; my stress is not good for my mental health, and that stress can lead to physical bodily problems like ulcers, and that the argument between the id and superego should come to an end. So, the ego was contradicting both the id and superego. I was in a situation of being totally torn apart, a part of me (id) still wanted the death penalty, and another part of me (superego) was still firmly against it, and yet the third part (ego) was still against this antagonism that the id and superego were in. That was a classic case of an **internal conflict**. I am sure that if you look into your own personal experiences, you have encountered similar situations. Freud maintained that an internal conflict leads into **anxiety**. By anxiety he meant a feeling of discomfort that can manifest as frustration, being under stress, anger, fear, guilt and shame. He added that there are certain ways our minds help us out with these conflicts and the resulting anxiety; those ways are called **defense mechanisms** (Schultz & Schultz, 2005).

Figure 6. Sigmund Freud.

DEFENSE MECHANISMS

A **defense mechanism** is an automatic process, like a reflex—something that we do not choose to express; instead, it happens below our awareness and intention. Defense mechanisms protect us against conflicts and resulting anxiety. So for example, consider the following scenario: Your id wants you to slap your irritating boss, and your ego tells you not to do it, since you will lose your job (remember, the ego is not concerned with morality; the ego just rationally weighs the consequences of our actions/behaviors and recommends the behavior that maximizes our benefits and minimizes our losses). Since you are conflicted now about your boss, when you get home,

Figure 7. Displacement.

you express your boiling aggression (coming from anger towards your boss; from your id) to someone (or something) who will not make you lose your job if you hurt that person—so, you start to argue with your significant other (sound familiar?), or you kick your dog. Or you punch the wall.

That defense mechanism is called *displacement*. Through this defense mechanism a person is allowing the id's impulse (anger) to be freely expressed, but the id's anger is displaced onto someone or something else other than the primary target (boss). In this way, the ego is silenced since it does not have a reason to tell you "you will lose your job" any longer.

Another example would be a defense mechanism called *repression*. Consider the following example: a religiously devoted family goes to church every Sunday to worship. One day, mother and father leave their seven-year-old daughter with the priest to keep an eye on her, while the parents are doing some other important things. However, the priest sexually molests the child. The child's id wants to kill the priest, yet her superego rebels against that and says that it is important to forgive, and that killing people is immoral. The ego also rebels against the id and emphasizes that killing is not acceptable since she will end up in some correctional institution and not be able to see parents, friends or have a normal life (see, ego is rational, not moralizing). The child is conflicted and, therefore, very anxious. Repression then becomes activated. Repression is *forgetting*, meaning she cannot remember anything about the molestation; she cannot remember that it even happened, so she is no longer aware of the conversation among the id, ego and superego. In the chapter on memory, you will see that in some cases, people really do suppress their memories, and only later on, after the event is over (sometimes years later) they uncover those previously suppressed memories. But, it is much more common that people cannot forget a traumatic experience.

Yet, another defense mechanism that Freud often discussed is *denial*, and it works like this: You are on a date, one thing leads into another, and you find yourself in a situation where you would like to have sex with your date. Your id, oh that lil' devil, demands that you have sex without any protection, so that the experience is the best possible. However, your ego rebels against the id's foolish impulse and requires your immediate action to use protection (condom, for example) in order to prevent sexually transmitted diseases and/or pregnancy. You are conflicted and anxious. Then, denial steps in totally supporting the id's wish, stating that there should be no protection since condoms break all the time, and that there really is no research that shows that wearing a condom is important. Thus, your id's impulse is expressed, and your ego is silenced. Another example would be when a loved one is killed in war, for example. The id says "I want to live happily ever after with my loved one who is coming back any minute," and the ego says "I am terribly sorry to inform you but the loved one is dead." Denial, of course, is going to contradict the reason (such as, someone is misinforming us, the loved one is very much alive, wounded but did survive), and the id will continue to live, for a while, in its unrealistic bubble. You are probably getting the idea that defense mechanisms do not really fix anything; they do not really make peace among the

Figure 8. Denial is not a river in Egypt (do not deny your denial).

40

id, ego and superego. You are right! These mechanisms are not helpful in the long run at all; they just skillfully create an illusion in our minds that everything is under control and that we are not conflicted at all. Defense mechanisms are like some magicians who work with smoke and mirrors, creating their illusions for gullible people. Magic tricks work by directing people's attention away from where the trick is happening; the same goes for defense mechanisms—they shift our attention away from the conflict. However, in reality, we are still conflicted. We just don't easily see the conflict any longer (due to the work of the defense mechanisms) since it is swept under the rug, yet still in the room (the mind) (Shultz & Schultz, 2005).

SO, HOW DOES THE PSYCHOANALYSIS WORK?

Defense mechanisms, as we already saw earlier, do not resolve conflicts; they (mechanisms) just remove the conflicts from our awareness and place them on the "back burner"—into the subconscious layer of our minds. That layer of the mind (Freud called it the **unconscious**) is inaccessible to us; it is an environment where the conflicts are not perceived. They contain a certain "negative energy" since they are made from friction between opposing mental forces (the id vs the ego vs the superego). With the passage of time (and that time varies from a person to person), these conflicts start to manifest themselves affecting our bodies. The conflicts become symptoms, such

as headaches, paralysis, stuttering, etc. Thus, Freud used psychoanalysis to access the conflicts (that we can also conceptualize as mental processes) in the subconscious environment. So, how did he access the conflicts when they reside in the layer that is located away from our awareness?

Figure 9. Our consciousness is like the part of iceberg that protrudes above water; below the waterline is the unconscious.

DESCENDING INTO THE UNCONSCIOUS

To access the conflicts in the subconscious environment, psychoanalysis employs three approaches: **free association, slips of the tongue** and **dream analysis**. Free association refers to saying aloud anything that comes to one's mind. Any phrase, sentence or word that a patient *hesitates* to say aloud, however, is an important breakthrough since that's the area of the patient's anxiety (feeling stressed, uncomfortable), that's the area of conflict. So, if the patient starts the word "father" without willing (or being able) to pronounce it completely and moves to another word instead, Freud insists on going back, encouraging the patient to free associate about his or her father. The next word or a phrase related to the father that the patient resists to pronounce, means that Freud is getting closer to the conflict that has something to do with the father of the patient. Many times Freud discovered that a patient wanted to kill his or her father, which was unacceptable from the superego and/or the ego point of view. According to Freud, free association is a useful approach since these vocalizations happen so fast that they can be faster than the defense mechanisms. This is to say that under free association the defense mechanisms don't have time to push the conflicts into the subconscious environment, and the conflicts pop into the patient's awareness. Resistance or hesitation to pronounce a word (or a phrase or a sentence) means that the defense mechanisms are working and trying to suppress the conflict below the consciousness (into the subconscious layer).

Another approach that Freud used was *slips of the tongue*. Those are certain *errors* in speech that to Freud were not merely innocent mistakes but very useful windows into our conflicted minds. To better understand this idea, consider the following slip of the tongue by one of my students. He was standing in a line to buy ice-cream. A great looking woman with huge breasts was standing in front of him. She sneezed and he said to her, "breast you, I mean bless you." Freud would say that this slip of the tongue is indicative of a conflict happening within the man: his id has sexual impulses towards the woman, and his ego and/or superego disapprove of those impulses. A defense mechanism buries the conflict into the subconscious space. We don't pay too much attention to every single word we say, since talking is an automatic process for us, so sometimes conflicts take advantage of that lack of defense and the conflicts come to the surface, to express themselves when our defense mechanisms are not "watchful" enough.

Freud placed the heaviest emphasis on the importance of *dream analysis*, saying that dreams are a royal road to the unconscious mind. He maintained that dreams contain images that are actually *symbols*. These symbols stand for something else or represent something else. That "something else" is conflict. So, knowing exactly how to interpret dream symbols (going beyond their face value) allows a psychoanalyst to identify the conflict. For example, these hieroglyphs (Egyptian symbols) most definitely do not say "there is some bird next to an inverted cross, above the cross is a pac-man and there is a flying saucer above."

Figure 10. Dream symbolism is based on representation, not on the appearance.

An Egyptologist would probably tell us an elaborate story represented by these hieroglyphs, but the story would have nothing to do with the things I said about pac-man, bird, etc. I didn't engage in any *interpretation*; I merely looked at the images and spelled them out, but that's wrong since those are symbols, and they stand for something else (Schultz & Schultz, 2005).

Let's have a look at a dream by Alexander the Great (356 - 323 BC) and examine how Freud would interpret it. During his conquest of the city of Tyros, Alexander dreamed about Satyros (a mythological creature) dancing on Alexander's shield. Whenever Alexander tried to catch the creature with his hand, Satyros elusively escaped. Finally, Alexander caught it. And woke up. Freud would tell Alexander that the dream-scene of Satyros dancing on a shield is a symbol: The word "tyros" means the city of Tyros. The word "sa" means "yours." Freud would say that

Alexander is very conflicted about the city of Tyros: his id wishes to conquer the city immediately. On the other hand, the ego thinks that Tyros is very difficult to conquer, that Alexander needs more time, and to be more persistent to secure a victory. Alexander had a dream interpreter who offered an interpretation similar to Freud's. Alexander listened to his reasoning (ego); he was persistent and patient, and he eventually conquered the city.

Figure 11. For Freud, dreams were a direct road to the unconscious.

HOW AND WHY DO PEOPLE DIFFER?

Personalities of people differ in the number of different defense mechanisms they use and how often they use them. Remember, we do not consciously decide to use specific defense mechanisms. These mechanisms occur automatically; they are triggered by some subconscious layer of the mind.

PSYCHOSEXUAL STAGES OF DEVELOPMENT

Freud's view of the development of one's mind (which includes personality) is heavily influenced by his or her sexual development that goes through certain stages. It is important to note that the term "sexual experience" for Freud did not mean "erotic experience" only, but "sexual experience" meant, to him, any pleasurable experience, even eating chocolate. Thus, **psychosexual development** means the development of the psyche (the mind) influenced by pleasurable experience.

Each stage of development presents a certain obstacle to an individual, and in case the obstacle is not overcame, the individual remains stuck (**fixated**) on that particular stage of development. This fixation influences certain undesirable personality characteristics to develop. Being stuck on a stage means not to be able to progress successfully through the next stage, so a person would be

43

developmentally held back. Let's have a look at those psychosexual stages of development, according to Freud (Schultz & Schultz, 2005).

THE ORAL STAGE OF DEVELOPMENT

Freud perceived this stage to last from birth to when the child is 2 years old (24 months). During this period, a child received pleasure via the *mouth*. Very often a child (during this period) puts everything in its mouth, such as marbles, rocks, toys, spoons, rugs, ants, and without adult supervision, the child would put very dangerous things in its mouth too, naively seeking the stimulation (pleasure) of this activity. Freud perceived the mouth as the "pleasure zone", an area of the body that provides pleasure (satisfaction) when stimulated by objects (Schultz & Schultz, 2005).

If parents allow too much stimulation (overindulgence) of their child's mouth (meaning to put almost everything in the mouth for as long as the child wants), Freud argued that the child can become fixated on this oral stage. This fixation can lead to an *oral personality* characterized by the following: being passive (since parents were the ones who provided satisfaction of the child's impulses), naïve (too trusting of others, due to having parents who almost always provided satisfaction), overly optimistic (since the child could always get satisfaction), restless (often seeking pleasure through the mouth, like eating and smoking), dependent on others (since others [parents] were the providers of pleasure) and

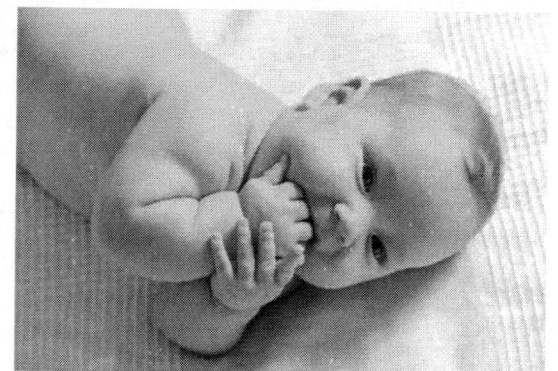

Figure 12. An infant in the oral stage.

impatient (pleasure was almost immediately provided by parents. In cases where the parents *excessively* limit the child's desire to put things in the mouth, the child can become *fixated* on the urge to please/pleasure its mouth. This type of frustrated child may also develop *oral personality*, characterized by the following tendencies: social withdrawal, aggression, mistrust toward others, and pessimism about the world. When facing frustration later in life (beyond the oral stage), the child with oral fixation (due to overindulgence of the mouth or under-gratification of the mouth) would likely show these behaviors that use the mouth to a large extent: talking often, arguing often, smoking, drinking (alcohol), overeating. A major conflict that the child experiences during this phase is conflict between its id (I want to put everything I like in my mouth) and the reality principle ("you can't," the parents say), but this reality principle is not internalized yet into the mind of the child; it manifests as external parental limitations that they impose on the child. The child will later develop its ego and superego from the views of their parents (Schultz & Schultz, 2005).

44

THE ANAL STAGE OF DEVELOPMENT

After the oral stage, there is the *anal stage*. It lasts from approximately 2 years old to 3 years old. During this time, children become increasingly able to control their anal muscles, so they learn how to go to the bathroom and how to delay going to the bathroom. The anal area is the zone of pleasure for this age range. Children are toilet trained during this period, and they often go to the bathroom when parents tell them not to (at the beach with hundreds of tourists around), and they don't go to the bathroom when parents tell them to. These behaviors (going to the bathroom when the child wants to, and not going to the bathroom when the child decides) appear to be a rebellion against the parents. So, the pleasure is multidimensional (stimulation of the anal area provides pleasure, plus rebelling against parents is satisfying as well).

Figure 13. How does rebellious behavior manifest during the anal stage of development?

If children become stuck on the behavior of not wanting to go to the bathroom, they may develop an *anal-retentive* personality, which includes the following traits: being extremely neat, stingy, hoarding things, cognitively inflexible (rigid), overly conscientious and stubborn. If they become stuck on the opposite behavior of going to the bathroom when they should not, then the children may develop *anal-expulsive* personality, which involves cruelty, defiance, messiness, recklessness, high levels of disorganization. The major conflict at this stage is again a clash between the child's id (I want to have and do what I want here and now), and the reality principle imposed on the children by their parents. Later, this reality principle will be internalized into the child's mind in the form of the ego. The superego will be internalized too from the parents' system of moral values (Schultz and Schultz, 2005).

THE PHALLIC STAGE

This stage lasts from 3 years old to 6 years old. During this stage, children receive a considerable amount of pleasure from stimulation of their genitals (penis = phallus; that's why this stage is called *phallic*). Children begin to masturbate, like adults, during this stage. During this stage children develop an *Oedipus complex*--a certain behavioral pattern characterized by a conflict (to be mentioned later) that can be dangerous if one does not overcome it. Let's explain this complex: In Greek mythology, King Oedipus killed his father and married (and had children with) his mother. Well, he did all that without knowing that those people were his parents, but this story inspired Freud to name the previously mentioned pattern "the Oedipal complex." During the phallic stage, boys lust (you read that correctly) for their mothers (like Oedipus did), and want to kill their fathers (like Oedipus did) since boys perceive their fathers as competition. Boys develop anxiety since they are afraid of their fathers' retaliation. Since boys are afraid that fathers will cut off their penises, removing a significant source of pleasure, boys develop *castration anxiety*. Castration is the removal of testicles, so castration anxiety is not the best term but close enough.

The boy's id sexually wants his mother, but his ego instructs him to abandon those ideas since his penis will be cut off. So, the boy is conflicted. Repression (defense mechanism) makes the boy forget the entire complex, pushing the conflict into the boy's subconscious layer. The boy starts to identify with the father, mimicking father's behaviors (shaving together, for example), and accepting his father's views of the world (including his father's superego). In this way, *vicariously*

through his father, the boy can possess his mother. Freud believed that the boy resolves his Oedipal complex (and conflict) through repression of the complex and identification with his father.

If a boy remains fixated on the Oedipal complex (without being able to resolve it), he develops a *phallic* personality, which can follow him though life, and this personality type is characterized by the following aspects (any combination of the patterns listed below is possible):

Figure 14. Why is identification an important behavior in the Oedipal complex?

- Being promiscuous (can't commit to one person since he fears castration)
  - This fear goes back to when he feared castration for being attracted to his mother (in other words, he is still stuck on that castration fear)
- If the boy doesn't develop promiscuity, he may develop asexuality (not being interested in sex since he still fears castration for developing sexual interests)
- Narcissism since he fears castration, and narcissism convinces the boy of his invincibility.
- Extreme courage to overcome the castration anxiety, holding him back, ruining his confidence.
  - Through courageousness, the boy tries to assert his masculinity
- Homosexuality since he is attracted to his mother, not to other women
- The boy has not identified with his father figure, and for that reason, he possesses feminine characteristics (Schultz and Schultz, 2005).

Figure 15. How would Freud interpret this image?

Girls lust for their fathers and want to murder their mothers. Freud also called this situation the Oedipus complex, but some of his followers termed it, perhaps more appropriately, the *Electra complex* since in Greek mythology Electra arranged the murder of her mother. Electra was the daughter of Agamemnon, a king who conquered the famous city of Troy. When he came back home from Troy, his wife (Electra's mother) killed him for sacrificing one of his daughters to gods so that they would favor him in the conquest of Troy. Electra was furious when she learned that her mother killed her father, so Electra arranged a murder of her mother. Now you see why Freud's followers named this complex the Electra complex. Also, during the phallic phase, girls develop *penis envy*—they would very much like to have a penis as their father has. In the Electra complex situation, what the girl thinks will never work since the mother is stronger and the girl will be punished for her wish to kill her mother and to sexually have her father. Also, the girl does not want to lose her mother's love. So, how can a girl resolve the Electra complex? Through repression of the complex and identification with the mother. But, if she remains stuck in the complex, she may develop the following *phallic personality* characteristics:

- Homosexuality
    - A girl dislikes men since her father disappointed her taking her mother instead. Thus, the girl can't trust men and turns towards other girls.

- Overly dependent since she feels inferior, due to penis envy.
    - Even if a woman resolves the Electra complex, Freud believed she still has some remaining penis envy. Freud believed that ongoing penis envy is the reason why some women feel less confident than men.
    - Being seductive since she has penis envy. For this reason she feels inferior to men and wants to conquer them with her looks and charm (Schultz and Schultz, 2005).

Figure 16. What would Freud say causes female homosexuality?

This stage lasts from 6 years old until puberty (12-14 years old). During this period, the child is preoccupied with school work, hobbies, sports and developing friendships, primarily with the members of the same sex. So, sexual instincts are *sublimated* (expression of the id's impulse in a socially acceptable way) in the aforementioned areas (Schultz and Schultz, 2005). In other words, nothing juicy or controversial occurs during this stage. Disappointed?

This stage lasts from puberty through adulthood. Pleasure is obtained from the stimulation of genitals. But, genitals also lead to another kind of satisfaction—having children. During this stage, an important milestone is forming: romantic relationships. Also, additional progress happens in this stage—one starts to work. Sublimation plays a very important role in expressing the id's urges through one's work/occupation. Painters, for example, will express their sexual urges by painting erotic scenes in their paintings. Butchers will express their aggressive impulses via cutting meat. This stage allows individuals to develop a genital personality—being able to love a member of the opposite sex and work productively and creatively (Schultz & Schultz, 2005).

Figure 17. How would Freud explain a surgeon's motivation to perform their work?

FREUD'S IDEAS: TRUE OR FALSE?

Freud used a certain method of collecting data (records of people's experiences), and that method was a **case study.** He simply recalled (from his memory) the session after the session was over, emphasizing that taking notes during the session would only distract the therapist. It is possible that Freud did not perfectly remember important points of the session. Maybe he did, but we can't be sure. Further, Freud's notes were checked by researchers, and they did not notice Freud's patients stating that they were seduced by their fathers; however, Freud often did say that the patients were seduced by their fathers. This indicates that Freud added aspects that he thought would make sense but that those aspects did not really happen (Kihlstrom, 1994). Next, most of Freud's patients were young, unmarried, well educated, upper class women who lived in Vienna (Austria). Freud's patients encompass a very narrow research sample that cannot be effectively used to apply the results to all of humankind.

One of the most important principles in science is replicability of results. This means that we can be more accepting of a result if a different person in a different research environment repeated (replicated) the result of some other researcher. But, most of Freud's patients were not examined by other therapists. Perhaps those other therapists would obtain a totally different result and evaluation. In addition, Freud argued that the most important phase of personality development is from birth to the age of 5. Personality development is only slightly influenced (if at all) after this crucial period. However, research indicates that our development is a life-long process.

Figure 18. Freud argued that the most crucial time of development is until the age of five.

The subconscious layer of the mind (the unconscious) has been supported by many studies. It turns out that there are mental processes below our awareness that can influence our other mental processes and behaviors. Let's discuss an interesting study: research participants were divided into two groups, group A and group B. They were all exposed to beverages that they could purchase. Before they were allowed to purchase anything, though, there were pictures of happy faces shown to group A, and pictures of angry faces presented to group B. The interesting part is that the images of faces were presented for such a short amount of time that those images were **subliminal** (below awareness), meaning that research participants were not conscious of those images. The result of the study was that people presented with the happy faces drank more, and people presented with the angry faces drank less. It seems that the content in their subconscious mind influenced their willingness to drink (Winkielman, Berridge & Willbarger, 2005).

Research does support Freud's view that psychological problems during daily life are expressed in our dreams. World War II veterans have war-related nightmares decades after those events (Schredl and Piel, 2006). Palestinian children exposed to life-threatening situations during the day, dream about those situations at night (Valli, Revonsuo, Palkas, and Punamaki, 2006). However, research does not find conclusive evidence that psychological problems during the day are *symbolically* represented in dreams.

Watson and Getz (1990) discovered that children ages 3 to 6 are more hostile towards the parent of the same sex and more affectionate towards the parent of the opposite sex. This finding provides some support for the Oedipus complex idea. Also, in some people, oral personality tendencies are observed, and in some people anal personality tendencies; however, research has not found oral and anal fixation to be responsible for the emergence of these tendencies (Westen, 1998). The phallic personality type has not been supported by research evidence, especially not the concept of penis envy in women (Schultz & Schultz, 2013).

Figure 19. Make an educated guess as to why a woman may like to wear high heels, according to Freud.

In terms of testing the idea of a slip of the tongue, Motley (1987) had three groups of men in his study. They were presented with identical pairs of words that flashed on the screen. The task was to say those words aloud. Men from group A were connected to a machine, and they were told that the machine would shock them with electricity during the study (although the idea was fictional—no shocks would be given). Men from group B were accompanied by an experimenter who was a sexy woman, and those in group C neither experienced the sexy experimenter nor the story about the electric shocks. When the pair of words on the screen was *brood nests*, men from group B who were the most sexually anxious (as measured by a questionnaire) said *nude breasts* aloud. When the pair of words on the screen was *sham dock*, the men from group A, who were the most anxious about the "impending" electric shocks, said *damn shock*. Group C made no slips. So, this study supports the notion that there are errors in speech that may very well reflect one's anxiety.

Displacement has been scientifically supported (Bushman, Bonacci, Pedersen, Vasquez & Miller, 2005). Repression has been confirmed as well (Myers & Derakshan, 2004). Denial too. (Tallandini & Caudek, 2010). Cramer (2007) found support for projection and identification. However, evidence is missing for the idea that these mental processes relocate the conflicts to the subconscious region of the mind (Schultz & Schultz, 2005).

NEO-PSYCHOANALYTHIC APPROACH

There are certain people in the field of psychology who were greatly influenced by Freud's views and generally embraced many Psychoanalytic ideas, but these individuals disagreed with certain aspects of Freud's perspective and added their own, unique contributions to the Psychoanalytic approach. Let's have a look at these individuals and their contributions.

CARL JUNG (875-1961)

Jung was a psychiatrist. There was a time when Freud considered Jung to be like his son, and Freud wanted Jung to lead the psychoanalytic movement after his death. However, Jung disagreed with Freud on some important issues, and took his own path…

Jung believed that Freud overemphasized instincts (urges or impulses), such as aggression instinct and sexual instinct and neglected the role of other driving mental processes, such as creativity and spirituality. Further, Jung divided the *unconscious* into two compartments: the **personal unconscious** and the **collective unconscious**. The personal unconscious refers to subconscious (not aware of them) mental processes that we acquire through our *personal* experiences gained throughout our lives. Jung's idea of the personal unconscious is equivalent to Freud's idea of the unconscious. Those subconscious mental processes can influence other mental processes and our behaviors.

Among these subconscious mental processes residing in the *personal* unconscious are **complexes**. A complex is a mental process that is a certain concept (power or justice, for example), but this concept is also linked with our personal memories, wishes, dreams, plans, thoughts and feelings associated with that concept. For example, imagine a scenario where a woman is enthusiastically trying to become a judge (within the legal system). She wants to understand where this strong wish comes from and finds a psychoanalytic therapist, hoping that the therapist will be able to help her understand herself better. Later on, during a successful psychoanalysis, she becomes aware of her

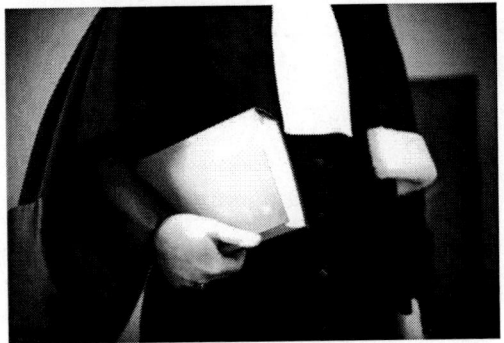

previously subconscious mental processes that she repressed: she loved her father very much. He was murdered by a criminal who broke into their home when she was 14. She swore that day that she would bring criminals to justice. On the same day, she made a decision to study law, to become a judge. That was her plan, and she would stick to it, no matter what. Oedipus and Electra complexes would be additional examples of complexes that derive from our personal family lives with our parents.

Figure 20. What complex may motivate a person to become a judge?

The unconscious has the *collective unconscious* aspect as well. Here reside Freudian urges that are common to all humans throughout history and even prehistory. But, Jung identified other human urges as well, such as creativity and spirituality (to form a connection with a divinity or more divinities). Within this collective unconscious sphere also resides human tendencies to respond to various situations and stimuli. For example, we have a tendency to develop Oedipus and Electra complexes, like all humans do. So, these tendencies are human mental and behavioral patterns. Another example of these human patterns is this: we have a tendency to respond to a snake with fear. But, it is not that we are born with a fear of snakes; it is just that we have a tendency *to fear*, and we need to learn that *a snake* can trigger fear. A baby does not fear snakes, but it learns to fear them later on as a consequence of exposure to human experience (reading about them, watching documentaries, perhaps the child's neighbor was bitten by a snake, etc.) Jung called these tendencies archetypes, so let's turn to them next (Schultz & Schultz, 2005).

JUNG'S ARCHETYPES

Archetypes are tendencies to respond to the world. For example, one archetype (of many) Jung called a **hero archetype**, which meant that people have a tendency to sometimes act like a hero. But, people also have a tendency to perceive someone else as a hero. These archetypes are also presented in books and movies, and people can visualize them well—those visual representations of archetypes are **archetypal images**. Batman, Spiderman, Superwoman are all archetypal images of heroes. An archetype called the **shadow** refers to our tendency to be spontaneous, vital, emotional, but also evil (destructive) too. The **persona** archetype is our tendency to "wear a mask" in the public (to play a role), in other words to be someone else publicly than what we are privately.

Figure 21. What archetypal image is depicted in this picture?

The **animus** archetype refers to our masculine tendencies (boldness, dominance, to name a few)--males *and* females have this archetype. The **anima** archetype refers to our feminine tendencies (nurturance, empathy, and the like)—men *and* women have anima. The **self**-archetype, is the most important archetype, and it is our tendency to seek the unity or integration of all archetypes into a balanced or harmonious whole. **Individuation** is the term Jung used for this integrative process. Individuation is accomplished through a conscious realization that we do possess archetypes and

by an acceptance and acknowledgement of all of our archetypes, without denying any. The archetypal image representing self-archetype is a **mandala** (a circle). Individuation should also be understood as a process of becoming a fully developed individual. Jung believed that the archetypes are passed genetically from parents to their offspring. Thus, archetypes have been passed to us from our ancestors who lived long ago (Schultz & Schultz, 2005).

Figure 22. A mandala.

JUNG'S PERSONALITY TYPES

Jung proposed that people can be divided into two groups: those who are **extraverted** and those who are **introverted**. Extraverted people feel very comfortable being around other people, while introverted people are most comfortable when they are by themselves. Let's examine extraversion and introversion in more detail. Extraversion refers to following: being outgoing possessing good social skills, being actively involved in events involving other people, being involved in a lot of different activities and enjoying that lifestyle, being active and making things happen, having an attitude that the world is one's home, being able to understand a problem better when talking out loud about it and hearing what others have to say on the subject, preferring to work in a group of people, having a lot of friends and knowing many people. Introversion is associated with the following characteristics: focusing on ideas, pictures, memories, and reactions that are inside of one's mind (the inner world); preferring to do things alone or with one or two people the person is comfortable with; reflecting on issues for a longer amount of time.

Figure 23. Extraverted hermit crabs.

Jung further proposed that there are four additional tendencies that people display: thinking, feeling, sensing and intuiting. *Thinking* refers to focusing on the discovery of the basic principles that can be applied to everyday reality, preferring to analyze pros and cons when making choices, using consistency and logical in making decisions, preferring to be impersonal so that one cannot be influenced by other people's attitudes or wishes, enjoying scientific fields where logic is important, believing that telling the truth is more important than being tactful, tending to be too task-oriented, and being indifferent or uncaring toward other people's feelings.

Feeling refers to making decisions by weighing what people care about; being concerned with values and what is best for people involved; focusing on establishing and maintaining harmony among people; being caring, warm, and tactful; communicating with others; expressing concern for others; being compassionate. Overall, feeling is a belief that being tactful is more important then telling the truth, being idealistic and indirect. *Sensing*, on the other hand, refers to paying attention to what one can see, hear, touch, taste, and smell; focusing on the actual, present, current, and real; noticing facts and details; focusing on the practical use of things. Sensing is a belief that experience speaks louder than words and trusting experience more than words and symbols.

Intuiting refers to learning by thinking a problem through, rather than by hands-on experience; being interested in new things and what might be possible; thinking more about the future than the past; working with symbols or abstract theories; remembering events more as an impression of what it was like than as actual facts or details of what happened; solving problems by leaping between different ideas and possibilities; preferring to see the big picture, rather than the details and fact; thinking about new possibilities without trying to make them a reality; and coming up with solutions by relying on gut feelings (or hunches).

Figure 24. Based on cinematic representations of wizards, what Jungian type categorizes most of them?

Jung further proposed that there are four types of extraverted individuals and four types of introverted individuals: extraverted thinking, extraverted feeling, extraverted sensing, extraverted intuiting, introverted thinking, introverted feeling, introverted sensing and introverted intuiting. When you read this information about Jungian personality types, you probably recognized certain tendencies in yourself from most, if not all, of these types, right? It is important to notice that Jung argued that every one of us is to some extent extraverted and to some extent introverted, but only one of these personality aspects is *dominant* in each one of us. Also, every one possesses the abovementioned mental processes of feeling, thinking, sensing and intuiting, but *only one* process dominates within an individual (Schultz, 2013; Myers & Briggs Foundation, 2017). For example, I had two or three intuitive experiences in my life, but there are people who have this type of experience on a daily basis. They are the intuiting types, not me

JUNG'S VIEWS: TRUE OR FALSE?

Just like Freud, Jung was criticized for his subjective method of data-gathering. For example, he relied on his memory about the patients whom he saw, and memory is often known to be an erroneous tool. Just like in Freud's case, the interviews conducted with Jung's patients were not recorded in a way that someone else could verify the accuracy of Jung's observations. Also, just like Freud, Jung too used a narrow sample of the population that cannot help us make generalizations about the mind of all people. For example, Jung often based his views of the human mind in general by relying on his own dreams and wakeful mental processes. Further, Jung's writings were extremely difficult to understand since his thoughts did not always follow one other logically (Noll, 1994). Even Jung himself confirmed that point by stating, "I can formulate my thoughts only as they break out of me. It is like a geyser. Those who come after me will have to put them in order" (Jaffe, 1971, p.8). So, it is possible that some aspects of Jung's writings were more like inkblots for which readers provided their own interpretation of Jung's ideas, and were not likely things that Jung intended to say.

In terms of the assessment of Jung's personality types, the personality differences clearly emerge between extraverted individuals and those who are introverted. That concept is widely accepted in psychology (Schultz & Schultz, 2005). In terms of the assessment of 8 psychological types that Jung proposed, studies seem to confirm the existence of those types. Although, those studies utilized an MBTI test (to be discussed later in this chapter), and the fundamental problem is that an MBTI is criticized for reliability and validity, which casts some doubt on the accuracy of this research. Also, as you will see later in the chapter, there may be more personality types than what Jung originally proposed (Schultz & Schultz, 2005).

Archetypes are very difficult to study scientifically since Jung proposed that they are passed genetically from parents to offspring. According to Jung, they are not created by upbringing or any other environmental aspects (church, school, peer group, etc.). So, the question is then, how do we look for archetypes? What technology and methods do we use to reveal them? And where are they? In genes, or in the proteins that genes make? What particular genes (since there are so many of them)? Are archetypes in the brain or elsewhere in the body, or both?

Figure 25. What archetype would be the most difficult to study?

Alfred Adler, a psychiatrist, believed that a major motivating force in life is an **inferiority feeling,** which can be seen even in childhood but also later on in life. Infants perceive their dependence on others as their inferiority. Infants will attempt to **compensate** for that inferiority, where compensation means to try to overcome their inferiority. So for example, infants will notice that adults walk but they cannot. Therefore, the infants are frustrated and try hard to walk, first by sitting, then by reaching, then by crawling and then finally by walking. So, the inferiority feeling is a driving force that allows development to happen. There is also an **inferiority complex**, which

is more a perception of one's own inability to overcome his/her inferiority feelings. A person with an inferiority complex has a very negative opinion of him/herself, lacks confidence, is depressed, anxious and cannot function in a healthy way.

Figure 26. When was the last time you felt inferior? Was it a complex or simply a passing feeling? If it was a complex, perhaps reading this book will help you overcome it!

There are several sources of the inferiority complex:

- Organic source
  - Some biological defect like defective organs or body parts
- Spoiling or pampering
  - When these individuals are no longer the center of attention, they are crushed and cannot function well in a social situation due to a lack of skills. They also have serious difficulties solving problems and making decisions on their own since that was done for them. They believe in their own personal deficiency when facing obstacles.

- Neglect
  - These individuals were not provided with care and love since parents were neglectful or even hostile towards them. These individuals can develop feelings of worthlessness. They view others with distrust and harbor a lot of anger towards the world.

A person with an inferiority complex may develop an exaggerated sense of self- worth, of one's abilities and accomplishments. This exaggeration is called the **superiority complex**. A person manifesting this complex is boastful and looks down upon others. So, a superiority complex is not beneficial for self and others; however, striving for superiority (perfection) in terms of improving oneself is progressive and recommended. Aspiring to reach this perfection is a motivating force that moves our development forward. Some mental processes that Adler saw as very helpful in the quest for superiority are planning, hoping, expecting success, and actively working on realizing our goals.

Adler did not place emphasis on the subconscious process shaping the development of our personality; he emphasized our *conscious* striving towards perfection, and he believed that this striving is an innate tendency that we genetically inherit from our parents. **Fictional finalism** was a motivating force emphasized by Adler, and it refers to an ultimate goal (finalism) that we choose to impose on ourselves as well as a need to move towards it. **Fictional** means that the goal is not yet reached and persists in our imagination only, until it is reached. While Freud believed that we strive to reduce tension (created by the conflicts), Adler believed that tension is constantly created and needed so that we can move forward towards goal-realization. So, Adler believed in the expansion of tension. For example, a painter who wants to become famous for inventing a new painting style is not going to benefit from relaxing all the time, but he or she needs to put a lot of work and research of other painters into the creation of a new style that nobody has seen before.

Figure 27. Hitler thought he was entitled to rule the world and exterminate people. What complex does this indicate?

Another important concept that Adler proposed is **the creative power of self.** This refers to our ability to choose and significantly influence the direction of our life and personality, even though genetics and the environmental forces, for example upbringing, have a tendency to shape us. Adler also proposed the notion of **early recollections** (memories until we are 5 years old) as being very indicative of some of our personality tendencies manifesting now. Specifically, he argued that if asked to recall some of our earliest memories, we will recall certain situations and/or behaviors and/or mental processes (real or imagined) that characterize us *now*. For example, Adler, was a fearful man who overcame his fear. He recalled one of his earliest memories about walking through a graveyard to get to school. He recalled being terrified of the graveyard. But, he also recalled that one day he ran back and forth through the graveyard several times, which made him used to it. So, during that event, he displayed the inferiority feeling and a compensation (exposure to the graveyard to get used to it). However, when Adler asked around about the graveyard, it turned out that nobody could confirm that there was ever a graveyard next to his school! So, the story was a fiction of his mind! Nevertheless, the story revealed certain personality tendencies of Adler—being fearful yet tackling that fear (like running through the graveyard) in order to overcome fear.

Adler, just like Freud and Jung, saw value in dream analysis. He saw dreams as visual stories depicting our current problems and what we plan to do about those problems. So, in his dream analysis approach, Adler focused on the here and now (current problems), as well as the future (what to do about our current problems). One of Adler's dreams illustrates this position well: before he went to the USA to present his views on personality, he felt fearful about the reception of his ideas. A night or so before his trip on a boat, he dreamed that his boat sank and that he had to swim hard for his life. Eventually, he reached land. So, Adler would say that his current problem (fear) was manifested in the dream (shipwreck) and that he planned to win the audience (reaching the land) not by charm only but by hard work of presenting the evidence and logic in an organized and clear way (swimming is hard work). Adler, obviously, believed in dream symbolism, but he did not see dreams as wish fulfillments and hiding conflicts (Schultz & Schultz, 2005).

Figure 28. How does Adlerian dream analysis differs from Freudian?

ADLER: THE IMPORTANCE OF BIRTH ORDER

A very famous aspect of Adler's view of personality was an idea that birth order plays a prominent role in shaping our personalities. According to Adler the **first-born** child will develop the following tendencies in life:

- Nostalgia for the good old times of the past, and anxiety, due to not so good times now
  - This tendency can be traced to the time before "dethronement" of the first-born child, an event that happens when the second-born child arrives. Before the "dethronement," the attention was focused on the first-born, which made the child feel good, and after the second-born arrived, the attention shifted towards the second-born child
- Pessimism about future
- Focus on obtaining power (since it was lost when the second-born arrived)
- Insecurity (due to not being the focus of attention after the arrival of the second-born)
- High level of intellectual maturity since he/she exercises problem-solving and decision-making in the process of caring for the younger child(ren)
- Good organization skills and focus on details (since they have to help in the process of raising the younger child(ren))
- Inclined to discipline others (due to participation in upbringing of the younger child(ren))
- Hostility towards others (due to their anger and frustration for losing their "throne")

The second-born children have a tendency to exhibit the following behaviors:

- Indifferent to power since they did not experience having it
- Optimistic about the future since they were not dethroned
- Ambitious and competitive, due to competing with the first-born
- Potential to underachieve in case the first-born cannot be outperformed by the second-born

The youngest child has a need to surpass older siblings, so s/he develops fast. These children are:

- High achievers
- Helpless and dependent on others if excessively pampered

Figure 29. What type of an event removes a first-born child from the throne, and how does that affect the child?

The only child has the following tendencies:

- Always expects to be the focus of attention
- Learned neither to share nor to compete
- Very disappointed if his/her abilities do not bring sufficient praise and recognition

It should be noted that these birth-order effects are not **deterministic**, meaning they do not set the mentioned tendencies in stone; rather, these birth-order effects only influence the personality development. These effects can be overpowered and blocked by the creative power of self (Schultz & Schultz, 2005).

ADLER'S VIEW: TRUE OR FALSE?

A major criticism of Adler's work is an approach that was based on his own memories of the sessions he conducted. He did not verify the accuracy of the recollections of the individuals he saw. On the other hand, a study seems to confirm Adler's view of dreams. In this study research participants were given a task to perform a difficult puzzle, which was impossible to solve and created frustration in the participants. Then, the participators fell asleep. Some were awoken during their dreams (indicated through rapid eye movements), and the other group was allowed to dream. In the morning, those who were allowed to dream reported significantly more frustrating dreams of the puzzle they could not solve (Grieser, Greenberg and Harrison, 1972). More studies are needed, though, to confirm Adler's notion. Further, studies have shown that adults who have inferiority feelings are persistent in trying to achieve their goals (Strano and Petrocelli, 2005).

The concept of early recollections has been confirmed in various studies. Davidow and Bruhn (1990) showed that adolescent delinquents recalled early memories of breaking rules and not being able to form social relationships. In some other studies, for example, when physicists, mathematicians and psychologists were asked about their early memories, they recalled themes of curiosity, independent thought and doubt (skepticism) about the information from their authority figures (Clark, 2005; Kasler & Nevo, 2005). Also, most research studies support Adler's view that the first-born children would display a high intellectual performance. Those studies show that first-born children score higher than other children on intelligence tests (Herrera, Zajonc, Weczorkowka & Chichomski, 2003; Kristensen & Bjerkedal, 2007; Zajonc, Markus & Markus, 1979). However, there are some studies that do not show this pattern (Holmgren, Molander & Nilsson, 2006).

Many research studies suggest that the first-borns strive for power. Those studies looked at the achievement scores of the first-borns as a reflection of their power. So, for example, the first-borns completed more years of formal education, worked in more prestigious fields (Herrera, Zajonc, Weczorkowka & Chichomski, 2003; Kristensen & Bjerkedal, 2007; Zajonc, Markus & Markus, 1979), scored higher on tests assessing managerial or CEO functioning (Holmgren, Molander & Nilsson, 2006). Some studies show that first-borns are more anxious than younger children (Schacther, 1963, 1964), but other studies show the opposite pattern (Gates, Lineberger, Crockett & Hubbard, 1988), so the results are mixed on this subject. A study showed that second-borns are 10 times more competitive than older children when they play baseball (Sulloway & Zweigenhaft, 2010).

In terms of the youngest-child research, it has been shown that most people who suffer from alcoholism are the youngest children in the family and that they have been pampered when they were young (Laird & Shelton, 2006). Surprisingly, many studies have shown an *opposite* pattern from what Alder predicted about the only child. These studies show that only children have a higher level of achievement and intelligence than individuals who have older siblings. Similarly, only children also have the same social and emotional skills as people who have siblings (Falbo & Polit, 1986), and only children have greater initiative, aspiration, productivity and self-esteem than children with siblings (Mellor, 1990).

Figure 30. Who would be expected to win in a competitive game, a first-born, middle, or youngest child?

NEO-PSYCHOANALYTHIC VIEW: KAREN HORNEY (1885-1952)

Karen Horney was a psychiatrist who used psychoanalysis to treat her patients. She introduced many innovations to the original Freudian psychoanalysis. Some innovations dealt with the method of how she evaluated what was wrong with patients. For example, one innovation was not to require patients to lie down on the couch as Freud demanded, but to give them freedom to behave in a way that made them feel comfortable (to sit, to walk, etc.) while in her office. Horney also saw Freud as being cold, rigid and detached from his patients, so she believed in a friendly attitude towards her patients. Some innovations were conceptual, as you will see in the following paragraphs (Cherry & Cherry, 1973).

Horney argued that the most important phase in one's personality development is childhood, specifically the child's relationship to his/her parents. During childhood, children develop the **safety need** for security and the absence of fear. The lack of a sense of security and the presence of fear can negatively shape children's personality development. Parents are the key factor influencing this need. The safety need will not be satisfied if parents display the following behaviors: preference for a sibling, inconsistency, promises that are not kept, humiliation, ridicule,

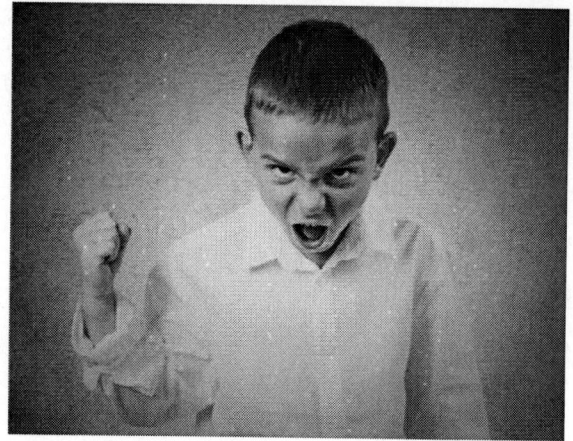 intimidation, and ingenuous displays of affection. Due to these behaviors, children can develop a condition called **basic anxiety,** manifesting as helplessness, loneliness, fear, guilt and hostility. Children suffering from basic anxiety perceives the world as a place of betrayal, neglect, cheating and attacking.

Figure 31. Basic anxiety.

A child suffering from basic anxiety may use the following strategies to protect him/herself from that basic anxiety:

- Securing affection and approval
    - through bribing and/or threatening others
- Submissiveness
    - manifesting as compliance with what others want so that they can be pleased
- Striving for success and power
    - so that one can feel untouchable and superior
- Withdrawing from others
    - so that the person is not hurt by others

The problem is that the abovementioned strategies exist to defend against pain, not to help one reach happiness. These strategies can become a part of one's personality and a basis for the emergence of **neurotic needs**—their satisfaction reduces one's **neurosis** (anxiety). Neurotic needs manifest themselves as an *intense* striving for the following:

- Affection from others
- Approval from others

- A dominant partner
- Power over others
- Exploitation of others
- Prestige

- Admiration by others
- Achievement
- Self-sufficiency
- Perfection

A person suffering from a **neurotic personality** has *all* of these neurotic needs. Some neurotic needs are more intense than others. Horney suggested that these needs exist as *mild tendencies* in healthy individuals. However, these tendencies manifest consistently and intensely in those with a neurotic personality. Horney proposed that a person who has a neurotic personality strives to become perfect, which is totally unrealistic since perfection does not exist. These individuals experience the **tyranny of the should** —they constantly require themselves to be perfect in various spheres of life (I should be a perfect mother, I should be a perfect employee, etc.) and they always feel anxious for not being able to reach the unattainable perfection of self. Also, Horney proposed that someone with a neurotic personality displays **neurotic competitiveness**—an intense urge to strive towards a victory at all costs. The person is anxious while striving, but the anxiety increases if the victory is not attained. By "victory" Horney meant not only a victory in sports, but excelling in various spheres of life (Schultz & Schultz, 2005).

Figure 32. Will many victories satisfy neurotically competitive people?

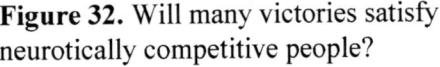

HORNEY'S VIEW: TRUE OR FALSE?

Horney is criticized for not having a substantial record of sessions, as well as for relying on her memory for what patients said. Memory is a very unreliable mental process, as you will see in a later chapter. A research study suggests that female and male children (late childhood) who seem to have neurotic needs, such as power over others, exploitation of others, prestige, admiration by others and achievement, displayed these needs as adults too. This idea supports the notion of the stability of these needs. Further, male children who displayed neurotic needs, such as self-sufficiency and perfection also displayed these needs as adults too; however, female children with these needs during late childhood did *not* display the needs as adults. Male children who were assessed to have neurotic needs, like affection from others, approval from others and a dominant partner no longer displayed those needs when they were adults. Female children with these neurotic needs during late childhood *did* display the same needs as adults (Caspi, Bem & Edler,

1989). So, some aspects of Horney's views seem to be supported while other aspects seem not to be.

In a study research participants were asked to recall things they did during the week and to indicate whether they did these things because they should do them or because they really wanted to do them. Also, they were asked to fill out a questionnaire about their satisfaction with life. It turns out that individuals who believed that they were doing things because they *should*, were less satisfied with their lives than individuals who did things because they *wanted* to (Berg, Janoff-Bulman & Cotter, 2001). This study seems to confirm Horney's notion that there is more dissatisfaction in individuals who impose on themselves what they should do. In terms of neurotic competitiveness, another study showed that people who were anxious and exhibited lower self-esteem, had high scores on a test designed to measure competitiveness (Ryckman, Thornton & Gold, 2009). This is something that Horney predicted.

NEO-PSYCHOANALYTHIC VIEW: ERIK ERIKSON (1902-1994)

Another major representative of Neo-psychoanalythic thought is Erik Erikson, whose theory is extensively discussed in the chapter on developmental psychology. However, we will review a few general and fundamental ideas regarding Erikson's view. Erik Erikson was trained by Anna Freud (Freud's daughter) to become a psychoanalyst with a focus on child development. Although Erikson utilized many aspects of psychoanalysis, he introduced numerous innovations in psychology of personality. According to Erikson, the most important aspect of development, the one that moves us forward, is a sense of trusting others, which can result from proper parenting. A sense of trust is the foundation for the development of our sense of predictability (the world is an ordered place), a sense of reliance on others (not being alone), a sense of having hope (a belief that a goal can be reached) and a sense of self-importance (self-respect). When children experience these mental processes, they can develop independence to explore the world.

Figure 33. Stages of development play a prominent role in Erikson's theory of personality.

Erikson believed that there are certain stages of development that unfold throughout our entire life span. Obviously, he placed an emphasis on the importance of development through life, not on a specific time frame in childhood or midlife. Each one of these stages contains a certain **crisis**, or a problem that a person needs to overcome to move to the next stage of development. In order to move to the next stage, a person needs to adapt to a challenge/crisis of the previous stage. Once the person moves to the next stage, s/he develops a **strength** (a virtue). Each movement to the next stage produces a different strength (Schultz & Schultz, 2005). For more details about these eight stages, find that section in the chapter on developmental psychology.

HUMANISTIC VIEW: ABRAHAM MASLOW (1908-1970)

According to the humanistic view, the following factors are absolutely critical in shaping our personality: aspiration (striving), having a goal, goal attainment, change (transformation), free-will, making choices, self-actualization. **Self-actualization** is a process of manifesting (or realizing) one's potential. For example, one wishes to become an astronaut and works toward that goal and eventually becomes an astronaut. The humanistic view is not concerned with the subconscious processes shaping our personality. The influence of genetics on the development of the personality is also not a considerable concern for the humanistic view. The humanistic perspective focuses on the idea that humans can thrive, grow and attain their goals by making the right choices exercising their free will (Alexander, 2013).

Abraham Maslow (1908 – 1970) is one of the most famous humanistic thinkers in the field of psychology of personality. He conceptualized self-actualization as a driving force in one's life. Let's explain this. Most people have a certain dream, goal or talent worthy of pursuing and concentrating on. These people, in the process of this pursuit, try to actualize (manifest or realize) that part of their self. For example, consider someone who likes to write a lot and who has a dream of becoming a well-respected novelist. That person will write and at some point finish that writing to his or her liking. Perhaps that person will be totally fulfilled with that writing, and the person will consider him or herself to be a writer. If that's the case, the person is self-actualized. But, let's say a person is not totally fulfilled with the idea of being the only one who is perceiving him or herself as a writer; instead, he or she wants to become

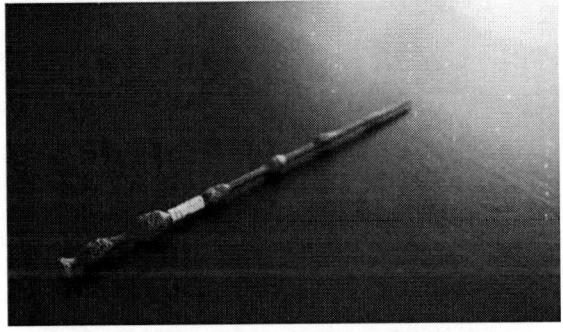

Figure 34. The author of the Harry Potter series, J.K. Rowling, was first rejected by many publishers. Only later, due to her persistence to reach self-actualization, did she become an extraordinary success.

perceived by others as a well-known writer so that others can benefit from these writings. So, that person will send the manuscript to agents so that the text can get published. If the person does not succeed in publishing the work (if the potential is not realized), he or she may not feel self-actualized. So, it really depends on that person's subjective *perception* of what the end of the journey is. We determine, in other words, with our own interpretation of reality (perception), when our potential is realized (actualized) (Maslow 1968, 1970b). Of course, we can't satisfy our need to write while we are starving or gasping for air or needing sleep. Therefore, there is a certain hierarchy of needs that must be taken into consideration. This is to say that we first need to satisfy some more **basic needs** (biological of physiological) before we move to more complex needs, such as the need for self- actualization. Basic needs are the strongest needs and they are a need to:

- Breath
- Eat
- Quench thirst

- Sleep
- Urinate
- Defecate

The next level of needs are **safety needs,** such as the need for security. This need can, for example, be seen in children who form an emotional bond (attachment) with those who provide shelter, protection from danger and satisfaction of basic needs. Another type of a safety need is the need for structure and routine. This need can be seen in humans striving for a predictable order in life. The next set of needs are **belongingness and love needs**. Most humans need to belong to some group, like a group of friends, a club at a college, a sports team, a church or a political party. Being in a romantic relationship with another person is another example of belonging to a group (a group of two people is called a **dyad**). The need to belong to a group is also oftentimes mixed with love. For example, friends are a group, and they love each other (friendly love). A parent and a daughter are a family group, in which parental love involved. A romantic couple expresses a romantic love towards one another, and so on.

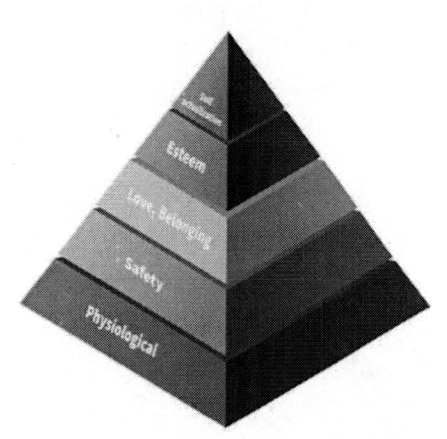

Figure 35. Maslow's hierarchy of needs.

The next set of needs are **esteem needs,** which manifests as a need for *self-respect*, in other words, a need for having an appreciation and a high opinion of oneself. Esteem needs also manifest as our need *to be respected by others*. The highest level of personality development results from our perception that we have a certain potential that we want to realize, like the writer example above. The term "potential" here refers to a dream and/or a goal and/or a talent that one has. As we strive to actualize that potential, a new set of needs arises (called **meta-needs**), such as needs for:

- Perfection
- Beauty
- Uniqueness
- Goodness
- Justice
- Meaningfulness

- Truth
- Peace in the world
- Simplicity
- Completion (to finalize projects)
- Independence
- Freedom

- Feeling alive
- Viewing the world, people and situations from different perspectives
- Unity with the universe
- Comprehension of how the world and the universe work

People working on self-actualization manifests the following tendencies:

- Being unbiased
  - display objective perception of the world
- Accepting htheir weaknesses and strengths, and those of other people and society
- Being open and natural (spontaneous, genuine, no pretense)
- Tolerating others (not prejudice towards people)
- Having deep lasting friendships with a few people
  - But not being unconventional necessarily
- Having a clear sense of a mission
- Not striving for support of others
  - Strive for privacy
- Having mystical experiences
  - Communicating with God, spirits, angels
    - But mystical experience can happen when not working on self-actualization
- Having empathy (compassion) for humans and animals
- Attracting followers
- Creating
  - Having original (unique) and socially-useful ideas
  - Displaying flexible thinking
  - Willing to experiment (and make mistakes)
- Resisting social pressures to influence their work
- Exhibiting humility

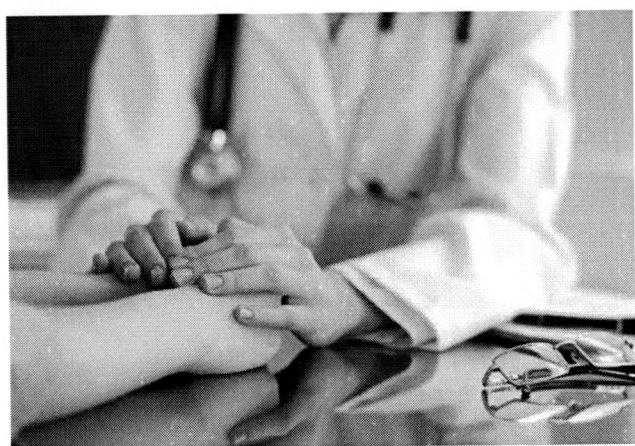

Figure 36. What behavior does a doctor display when indicating the presence of a patient's self-actualization needs?

Inability to become self-actualized can lead to frustration and depression. Maslow proposed that very few people (around 1%) work on their self-actualization. So, why such a small number of people? Maslow's answers are as follows:

- These needs are the weakest; thus, people are not that motivated (driven) by them.

- If parents are overprotective and not permitting their children to explore new ideas nor practice new skills, this is exactly the opposite from parental encouragement that needs to be present for one's work on self-actualization (later in life). Many parents have this negative parenting style.
- For working on self-actualization, a person should have other needs fulfilled to some extent, and many people are not that fortunate since many are not loved: they may be hungry, homeless, sleepless, sick, in pain and broke.
- Then, there is a **Jonah Complex,** referring to our doubts in our own abilities. There was a man, Jonah, from the Bible, and he was called by God to be a prophet, but Jonah was afraid of it. Only later he accepted this significant mission. Working on self-actualization is difficult, and this self-doubt (Jonah complex) that we will not succeed and become actualized, separates us from a successful work on self-actualization.
- Many people want to reach big goals fast and with the least amount of effort. Self-actualization, however, is a difficult process that takes a lot of sacrifice, self-discipline and hard work.

Maslow maintained that only one type of a need dominates a person and that higher needs are weaker, and the lowest needs are the strongest. Higher needs appear later in life, while lower needs manifest frequently in infancy. Satisfaction of higher needs leads to growth, contentment and happiness. A need does not have to be fully satisfied (but it has to be satisfied to the extent that a person can focus on other needs) before the person moves on to the next need in the hierarchy. Maslow believed that the abovementioned needs are genetically inherited from our parents. The ways we attempt to satisfy these needs make us different from one another. Needs are innate, and behaviors that we employ to satisfy needs are learned (Maslow, 1970b, 1971; Schultz & Schultz, 2005).

Figure 37. Is an actress or a homeless person more likely to work on self-actualization needs?

MASLOW'S VIEW: TRUE OR FALSE?

Maslow has been criticized that his definitions of important concepts are vague and inconsistent. He used a small sample of people to make generalizations about all of humankind. When Maslow analyzed famous personalities to come up with the self-actualization notions, he selected the personalities whom he admired and did not analyze other famous people whom he did not admire, so he was selective, which again cannot be something positive when trying to make generalizations about the entire human race. Maslow also often relied on projective tests to generate his view of personality, and we know that those tests are controversial and do not impress the scientific community as a reliable and valid way of assessing personality. So, obviously Maslow lacked the rigor of the scientific method.

However, there is some support for his view of personality. For example, a study found the existence of the 5 types of needs that Maslow outlined, and the same study discovered that people were more concerned with lower needs than the higher needs (Graham & Balloun, 1973). Another study did show the existence of safety, belonging and esteem needs. However, it showed that safety needs were not as strong as these other needs (Williams & Page, 1989). In another study, participants who satisfied their needs more (from basic to self-actualization), experienced less anxiety, which goes along with Maslow's view (Lester, 1990). In other studies people who have satisfied their need for self-esteem (meaning they have a higher score on self-esteem) also tend to experience the following:

- More competence and productivity, function better in various situations, receive more job offers, are rated more favorably by recruiters (Ellis & Taylor, 1983).
- Less anxiety, depression, smoking, and school-dropout rates, as well as fewer difficulties at work, fewer financial problems, as well as fewer criminal convictions. Overall, these individuals exhibit more control of their negative emotions (Brown, 2010).
- Fewer physical health problems (Routledge et al., 2010; Stinson et al., 2008).
- All of the above goes along with Maslow's view.

In terms of self-actualization needs (which is also called **self-determination** in current literature), those needs have been demonstrated in studies (Deci & Ryan 2009; Ryan & Deci, 2000). Also, the individuals who have satisfied these needs to a higher extent, show higher scores in everyday functioning and feeling of satisfaction with life in comparison to people who have lower scores on self-actualization (Podlog & Eklund, 2010).

HUMANISTIC VIEW: CARL ROGERS (1902-1994)

Carl Rogers, a psychologist, is another significant contributor to the humanistic view. He believed in the existence of **a positive regard,** which is our need for acceptance, approval and love from others. Caretakers are the ones who first start to satisfy (or not) this need in children. This need is a basis for developing of a **positive self-regard**, which is our need for acceptance, approval and love that we receive from *ourselves*. If our caretakers did not satisfy the positive regard need, then it is likely that we would not be able to satisfy our need for positive self-regard.

A positive regard and positive self-regard contribute to our (positive) mental health. According to Rogers, one's mental health should be understood as **congruence** (synchrony or consistency) between **self-concept** (our *perception* of who we are) and our **experiential world** (our mental processes and behaviors displayed in everyday situations). For example, if a person sees herself as a helpful person, yet also manifests opposite behaviors, this is **incongruence** (between what the person thinks of herself and the actual experience of hatred manifesting through her behaviors). To protect herself against anxiety, due to the realization of this incongruence, she will find excuses for her behaviors and deny that they even happened. Our mental health, however, refers to our *realistic* self-concept, the one that matches our experiential world. This accuracy results from an **unconditional** (no matter what) positive regard in childhood that is received from parents. This means that children have to know that they are loved, accepted and acknowledged, no matter how many mistakes they make. The unconditional regard that we receive as children creates our feeling of self-worth. Mental health *also* refers to a congruence existing between our self-concept and our **ideal-self** (who we would *like* to be). In other words, our ideal-self should be realistic, reachable and we should be aware that our ideal-self is a *goal*, rather than something already established and reached. When one believes that he or she has reached the ideal-self, yet actually hasn't, that person is running the risk of living an unrealistic, illusory life, and once he or she realizes this illusion, anxiety and/or depression may develop. The goal is to reduce the discrepancy between the self-concept and the ideal-self.

Figure 38. What is unconditional regard and how does it impact children?

Rogers created a **person-centered therapy,** which assists people in reaching their congruency. This therapy attempts to help by modifying either self-concept so that it is in tune with the experiential world or by modifying an ideal self-concept to be more reachable (more in tune with the self-concept) or both. Within the scope of Roger's person-centered therapy, the clients can direct their own personality growth. This means that therapists do not instruct clients what to do with their lives; instead, the clients make decisions, while the therapist just helps clients see the different options they have. The therapist's main role is to provide an unconditional positive regard, with no judgment, to clients and to help them perceive the incongruity in their lives. Clients are also encouraged to examine (to face) the roots of their problems, as opposed to avoiding their feelings and thoughts about their self and the world.

Rogers disagreed with attempts to reach one's subconscious mental processes, believing that "reaching" those contents hidden away from the client's awareness may very well be the therapist's subjective interpretation of what is going on, not what the client is actually experiencing. For

Rogers, we are constantly involved in the process of development of our self, and the process never stops. Being fully functioning is a *direction,* a "path" that does not seem to end (Schultz & Schultz, 2005).

Figure 39. In client-centered therapy, a person makes a choice while the therapist helps them see the options.

ROGERS'S VIEW: TRUE OR FALSE

Rogers tape recorded and video recorded the sessions with his clients (who gave him permissions to do so), to help those researchers who wanted to explore aspects of his view. So, Rogers's work is considered to be a very significant contribution and innovation from a scientific standpoint. Next, a study found that there is a significant reduction in the discrepancy between one's self-concept and one's ideal self after person-centered therapy ended (Butler & Haigh, 1954). Various studies have shown that more dis-alignment between one's self-concept and ideal-self, that person shows more anxiety, self-doubt, depression, social incompetence and lower self-esteem (Moretti & Higgins, 1990; Straumann, Vookles, Berenstein, Chaiken & Higgins, 1991; Nolan, 2008). Further, in a study evaluating the amount of unconditional positive regard in families, it was found that children raised in a family with low levels of unconditional positive regard displayed poor coping skills during their childhood, fluctuations in their self-esteem and resentment towards their parents. Those negative behaviors were not observed in the families, in which parents used more unconditional positive regard (Assor, Roth & Deci, 2004). In another study, adolescents who received more unconditional positive regard from their parents, were more open to receiving social support from others, as opposed to children with less unconditional positive support from parents. Also, the adolescents with parents displaying more unconditional positive regard also involved in more behaviors that were in synchrony with their talents and interests (Harter, Marlod, Whitesell & Cobbs, 1996). The aforementioned findings support Rogers's views.

The behavioral approach argues that we *learn* behaviors, and our personalities are a set of observable behaviors. Genetics provides us with some basic reflexes (basic behaviors) when we are born, which influence our tendencies and vulnerabilities to illnesses, but our behavioral repertoire is largely influenced by *learning* as we live our lives. The role of genetics cannot be denied; it provides us with an *ability* to learn, since genetics creates cellular networks within our nervous system that provide us with a biological mechanism allowing us to learn. Mental processes cannot be denied either, and the behaviorists acknowledge them, but they argue that in order to measure mental processes, we have to measure *behaviors* that are observable manifestations of mental processes. Albert Bandura adopted a behaviorist perspective but with an emphasis on a social context (others). From that social context we learn behaviors through observing what others do and imitating their actions. But a person is not just a passive recipient of the messages from the social environment; instead, the person actively influences the social environment too. After the individual influences the social environment, this environment responds to that individual. This mutual influence between the environment and the individual, Bandura called **reciprocal determinism**. So, this mutually inclusive process goes on indefinitely shaping the person's *perceptions* of the social environment and himself or herself. A person's *behaviors* are influenced by that person's *cognitive processes* (problem solving, making decisions, weighing the consequences of our actions, planning, etc.), and these cognitively shaped behaviors further influence the *environment*—this view is called **triadic reciprocity**. For example, the boy in the picture notices his older sister reading a book; he takes one too. And, since a girl her age is interested in reading, she initiates a conversation with him—something that he was hoping for since he misses talking to his sister who seems to have time only for her friends lately.

Figure 40. Triadic reciprocity.

An especially important concept in Bandura's view of personality is **self-efficacy,** which is a feeling of one's *competence* in dealing with life's problems and demands. Having a low feeling of self-efficacy makes one feel helpless, with a sense that every attempt is an exercise in futility. If one has a strong feeling of self-efficacy, then that individual is persistent and determined, and often times that person does prevail. The question is what makes some people develop a low feeling of self-efficacy and other people have a robust feeling of self-efficacy? *Prior achievements* increase our feeling of self-efficacy, and *prior failures* to accomplish tasks decrease it. Many people set themselves up for failure by trying to attain hard-to-reach goals very quickly, so having more realistic goals that are easier to achieve over a longer period of time can increase one's self efficacy.

Vicarious experience is another factor that can increase self-efficacy, according to Bandura. This experience refers to observing others (models) who complete a task successfully, so that the observer can be motivated and assured that the achievement can be realized. Observing models who fail to accomplish a task, however, can usually influence people to doubt their own achievement too, and it can decrease self-efficacy.

Figure 41. Successful athletes motivate us to try to succeed in anything we do.

Verbal persuasion is another factor that influences self-efficacy. This influence refers to an attempt to convince someone of his or her competence or at least a potential to be competent. This persuasion should be based on reality, though, to be effective. In other words, the persuasion should not encourage people to do the impossible. If verbal persuasion takes a negative form so that people are told that they cannot do something (when they realistically can), it can seriously reduce the self-efficacy feeling. A feeling of **composure** influences self-efficacy too; the more composed (less tension, less agitation, less fear) we feel, the more self-efficient we feel. Composure is especially important in stressful situations. So, how do we become more composed individuals? Bandura recommended proper diet, stress reduction techniques (meditation, for example) and exercising (Schultz & Schultz, 2005).

BANDURA'S VIEW: TRUE OR FALSE?

Science attempts to measure various aspects of nature, and Bandura has been praised for his attempt to measure or *quantify* (assign numerical values) behaviors and mental processes. For example, he would ask how angry one feels on a scale from 0 to 5. Further, Bandura is well-known for using experimental and control groups as well as for defining his dependent variables (behaviors of interest) and independent variables (imposed conditions or environments that influence those behaviors) in behavioral/observable terms. His use of statistics is praised as well.

A study of teenagers and their parents has shown that when parents report more self-efficacy about their parenting (meaning they believe that they excel as parents), their children also show stronger efficacy than the children whose parents have a lower self-efficacy regarding their parenting skills. Children with higher self-efficacy experienced less anxiety, displayed a better academic performance, had more open and honest communication with their parent, than children of parents who reported less self-efficacy (Steca, Bassi, Caprara & Fave, 2011). Another study showed that substance abuse is lower and self-efficacy is higher in teenage boys whose parents have higher self-efficacy feelings too (about dealing with life problems) (Nebitt, 2009). Obviously, feelings of self-efficacy in parents play a prominent role in the upbringing of children, but it is not exactly clear what particular channel (prior achievements and/or vicarious experience and/or verbal persuasion and/or competence) shapes self-efficacy in children. A study also showed that people stronger in self-efficacy had higher scores on job satisfaction surveys, as well as commitment to their workplaces and job performance than those individuals who had lower self-efficacy scores (Salas & Cannon-Bowers, 2001). The higher the feeling of self efficacy in adolescents, the more resistant they are to peer pressure to smoke (Schwarzer & Fuchs, 1995). The lower the self-efficacy, the greater the amount of alcohol use in adults (Taylor, 2000). Various studies show that people who display higher self-efficacy scores deal better with stress than those who have lower scores (Cozazarelli, 1993; Hagedoorn & Molleman, 2006). Thus, studies seem to support the view that self-efficacy is beneficial for the development of our personalities. Bandura is, however, criticized for not equally recognizing the importance of internal mental processes (especially emotions and motivation) as he acknowledged the importance of the observable behaviors (Schultz & Schultz, 2005).

TRAIT VIEW

The trait view conceptualizes personality as a set of characteristics (or traits or **factors**). A **characteristic** is a *typical* way a person responds to the stimuli that he or she is exposed to. This definition was offered by psychologist Gordon Allport (1897-1967). Similarly, psychologist Raymond Catell (1905-1998) viewed personality as a system of traits, which allows us *to predict* how a person will behave in a situation. Allport believed that genetics (heredity) shapes our personality in terms of intelligence, temperament (emotional reactions) and physical appearance, but he emphasized that the foundation the genetics provides can be shaped/modified by environmental influences, so he believed in an interaction between heredity and the environment. Catell, was more precise about the specific contributions of heredity versus environment to our personality. Through his research data, he showed that genetics influences our intelligence (80 percent of intelligence is due to genetics, and 20 percent of it to environmental shaping). Genetics also influences (80 percent) how timid or bold we are. Further, genetics primarily influences how serious or happy-go-lucky we are, how tough minded or tender-minded we are. On the other hand, how submissive or dominant, and how relaxed or tense we are is shaped predominantly by our environment.

Figure 42. According to Catell's research, what factor primarily influences our relaxed state of mind?

One third of our personality is shaped predominantly by genetics, and two thirds by environmental molding. Both Allport and Cattel recognized that our personalities are influenced by **situations** to which we are exposed. For example, if an extraverted individual found himself or herself in prison (or a prisoner of war), s/he may display introverted behaviors (withdrawn). So, depending on the situation, the dominant trait before the situation may become less dominant, and vice versa—the weaker trait before the situation may assume the dominant role in the new situation.

Hans Eysenck (1916-1997) was a psychologist who also advocated for the trait view. In his opinion, our personality entails three dimensions: Extraversion versus Introversion, Neuroticism versus Emotional Stability and Psychoticism versus Impulse Control. These dimensions are characterized by certain traits outlined below:

The Extraversion versus Introversion dimension is characterized by the following traits:

- Sociability
- Liveliness
- Activity
- Assertiveness
- Sensation Seeking
- Being adventurous

A person scoring high on the abovementioned traits would score high on the extraversion aspect. A person scoring low would be assessed as being dominated by the introversion aspect.

The Neuroticism versus Emotional Stability dimension is characterized by the following traits:
- Anxiety
- Depression
- Guilty feelings
- Low self esteem
- Tension
- Irrationality
- Shyness
- Moodiness

A person scoring high on the above traits would score high on the neuroticism dimension. A person scoring low would be assessed as being dominated by the emotional stability aspect.

The Psychoticism versus Impulse Control dimension is characterized by the following traits:

- Aggressiveness
- Coldness (not affectionate)
- Egocentricity
- Being impersonal
- Impulsiveness
- Being antisocial
- Creativity
- Tough-mindedness

A person scoring high on the abovementioned traits would score high on the psychoticism aspect. A person scoring low would be assessed as being dominated by the impulse control aspect.

Eysenck's research indicates that genetics has a predominant role in shaping all three dimensions (and their traits). An exploration of the influence of heredity on behavior is called **behavioral genetics**. Eysenck also believed that the environmental aspects, as well as different situations, can influence personality, but that their effects are not as nearly as significant as the role of heredity (Eysenck, 1990a). Eysenck's research often consisted of a comparison between identical twins (very much genetically alike) versus fraternal twins (less genetically alike than identical twins). He observed that when identical twins are reared in different environments, their personalities are still very much alike. His research also showed that adopted children are much more like their biological parents than the adoptive parents, even when children did not have contact with their biological parents. This research indicates that there is a considerable genetic influence on personality (Schultz and Schultz, 2005).

Robert McCrae (1949 -) and Paul Costa (1942 -) believed that Eysenck noticed *too few* dimensions (only three) and proposed a Five-Factor Model, which consists of the following *five* dimensions: **O**penness to Ideas versus Disinterest in them, **C**onscientiousness versus Irresponsibility, **E**xtraversion versus Introversion, **A**greeableness versus Antagonism, and **N**euroticism versus Emotional Stability (OCEAN is the abbreviation). McCrae and Costa define personality as a mental structure of five dimensions and their traits. Their personality test, NEO Personality Inventory, contains items reflecting these 5 factors (traits). More information regarding this test will be discussed later in this chapter. Research has indicated that agreeableness is influenced primarily by environmental aspects, and the remaining four dimensions are influenced predominantly by genetics (Bergeman et al., 1993; Pedersen, Plomin, McClearn & Friberg, 1988).

Research done in 55 countries indicates that women score higher than men on the following dimensions: extraversion, agreeableness, conscientiousness and neuroticism (Schmitt, Realo, Voracek & Allik, 2008). Most psychologists accept the Five Factor Model as the most valuable trait view (Schultz & Schultz, 2005). Later in the text you will learn more about the NEO PI test, in the context of personality assessment, a section which we examine next.

Figure 43. What does this image suggest about the extraversion/introversion dimension of the individual in the jar?

HOW TO FIGURE OUT SOMEONE'S PERSONALITY?

Imagine this: you are on a date with someone you like, and you begin to like that person so much that you are frightened by the thought of a disappointment. What if this amazing person is just telling you what you want to hear? But, what if the person is for real? So, what do you do? Should you stay or stand up and go? Wouldn't it be great to have some personality test so that you could very quickly, on the spot, figure out that person's personality? So, is the person you like someone who is just wasting your time, or should you tie the knot with that person? I will have to disappoint you and tell you that a quick and easy way to figure out (assess or evaluate) one's personality does not exist. However, there are ways that can give you a pretty good idea of one's personality, but it takes some time to assess personality. We will mention them next.

Figure 44. How can we finally figure out a person's personality?

PERSONALITY ASSESSMENT: INTERVIEWS

An **interview** is a process of asking questions so that the person interviewed can respond to those questions. The interview can be **structured** or **unstructured.** A structured interview contains questions that are set in form and order of presentation; in this type of an interview, it is important to ask all questions in the way they are written. Why such inflexibility? The answer is that some situations seem to require that inflexibility. For example, when a psychologist interviews a person who suffers from a mental illness (such as being a psychopath), it is important to cover all questions so that all important aspects of the illness can be understood and that client can be optimally helped. Also, it is important to read the questions precisely as they are written so that the person who conducts the interview does not confuse the interviewee with ambiguities of his/her imprecise verbal expression. Going along with the previously specified wording of questions ensures that the interviewer sticks to the plan (as opposed to losing focus). Paraphrasing questions is recommended only when necessary (when the interviewee asks for help). However, in an unstructured interview some questions can arise spontaneously on the behalf of the interviewer, and the written questions can be paraphrased by the interviewer. An unstructured set of questions allows for a more relaxed atmosphere (for some people it is very important to get relaxed before sharing some intimate details about themselves) since when one conducts a structured interview, the situation is more artificial, uptight and less pleasant.

The problem with any type of interview is that the person being interviewed can be dishonest, and sometimes it is not possible to detect the dishonesty through a mere interview. Indeed, it is sometimes impossible to detect dishonesty in any way (the polygraph machine cannot reliably detect lies either). People do not necessarily have to lie; they can simply be unaware of their true mental processes and behaviors, and sometimes they can even have false memories (memories for events that never happened, for example "remembering" to save people who needed help when that never happened in reality). In addition, the interviewer, not the interviewee, can sometimes be a "weak link." This means that the interviewer contaminates the perception of the interviewee by bringing his/her own expectations and perceptions of the person being interviewed. For example, when interviewing a serial killer, one may perceive more aggression (in that person) than there really is. Alternatively, one may observe the serial killer trying very hard to control his/her aggression (Schultz & Schultz, 2005).

PERSONALITY ASSESSMENT: BEHAVIORAL EVALUATION

Personality assessment relies exclusively on an *observation* of one's behavior, verbal and/or nonverbal. In this respect, a psychologist would monitor (observe) speech patterns (changes in tone, for example) that would indicate aggression, sadness, joy, fear, lack of confidence, difficulties focusing on one topic, high levels of self-absorption (talking about self a lot, even when not asked, etc.). In a family therapy setting, for example, the "bossy" individual within the family can be identified by observing how that person talks to other family members; likewise, the overly submissive person can be detected too in the way that person talks and responds to others. Of course, only one assessment is not enough; a behavioral assessment should be done on several occasions over time to have a **reliable** (consistent from one observation to another) personality evaluation. Aside from verbal behavior, nonverbal behavior can be evaluated as well. A trained professional would rely in this case on eye contact, gesturing, facial grimacing, and posture. In this case, too, a frequent observation would provide a more accurate evaluation (Schultz & Schultz, 2005).

Figure 45. A nonverbal behavior.

PERSONALITY ASSESSMENT: PERSONALITY INVENTORIES

Personality inventories (self-report inventories or self-report tests) consist of multiple choice and/or true false items that a person (taking the inventory) has to consider and decide about which item applies to him or her. These items reflect people's thoughts, feelings, values and needs. These inventories are questionnaires. They are **objective**, meaning there is no room for interpretation and no room for an unstructured format on behalf of the one who is administering these tests. These inventories have written items, and the person taking the test can fill out an inventory either online or as a paper and pencil test. The results are scored according to certain scoring rules via a computer (to avoid any subjectivity). These tests have a high degree of **validity** (they measure what they are supposed to measure; they are intended to measure personality and that is what they do) (Nevid et al., 2008).

The MMPI (Minnesota Multiphasic Personality Inventory) is the most widely used psychological test throughout the world! (Butcher, 2010). The MMPI has a high validity (Garb, Glorio & Gove, 1998) contains items about one's defensiveness, depression, **anxiety** (fear, guilt, frustration), **paranoia** (a **delusion** or a false belief about intentions of others to harm and/or spy on the person who is being paranoid), **hallucinations** (an unreal sensory experience like hearing voices when they don't really exist), **gender role** (one's expectation of how genders differ behaviorally and mentally), a potential for addiction, shyness, self-doubt, responsibility, an inability to disclose, family dysfunction, **narcissism** (excessive self-absorption or having a big "ego"), **mania** (euphoria or being extremely happy, irritability, inability to concentrate), **psychopathic** tendencies (to manipulate others, to lie, to not feel fear, inability to

Figure 46. Paranoid delusion.

control one's urges [to harm others, for example]), alienation from self, alienation from others, experiencing symptoms of an illness when there is no detectable cause of that illness (so called **hypochondriasis**), and some other items. So, for example, an *item* (evaluating a presence of paranoia) goes something like this: People often conspire against me so that they can kill me. This item is not identically written like this in the MMPI, but it is along those lines (this is merely an example). Although the MMPI was designed (initially in 1943, and there were subsequent editions later on) to evaluate personality of individuals who suffer from a mental illness, this test can also be used on healthy people. Since the abnormalities mentioned above (narcissism, psychopathic tendencies, hallucinations, etc.) are not present in a healthy individual, the test can measure an absence of those abnormalities. The MMPI can be used on adults, and there is also a version for adolescents. The adult version has approximately 567 items, and the adolescent version has around 478—these are obviously, very long tests, which is also their main disadvantage since people get bored and tired during the process of taking this test. Clinical psychologists (who work with mentally ill patients) use the MMPI to diagnose mental conditions, but the MMP is frequently used by employers to evaluate the personality of future employees and if those employees are susceptible towards some mental illnesses (Schultz & Schultz, 2005).

PERSONALITY ASSESSMENT: NEO PI PERSONALITY INVENTORY

The NEO PI test was constructed in 1978 by Robert McCrae and Paul Costa and has gone through several revisions aimed towards improving it. This test has a high validity (Allik et al., 2010). The NEO PI is used primarily for evaluating the personality of a healthy individual. The test measures the following aspects (technically called "factors") of personality: Neuroticism, Extraversion, Openness (to experience), Conscientiousness and Agreeableness. The NEO PI is administered to help people decide their profession. The test is also utilized by employers to evaluate the personality of future employees. The test can be also used in other settings.

If someone has high scores on Neuroticism, that person displays the following tendencies (traits):

- Easily upset (angered easily)
- Anxious (fearful)
- Self-pitying
- Shy, fearing rejection

- Worried
- Depressed (feels discouraged and pessimistic)

- Impulsive (cannot restrain urges or impulses)
- Vulnerable

If someone, however, has low scores on Neuroticism, that person shows the following tendencies:

- Even tempered
- Able to control impulses
- Emotionally stable (as opposed to mood swings)
- Comfortable with themselves
- Calm
- Invulnerable

Figure 47. Calmness indicates a low presence of Neuroticism.

If someone has high scores on Extraversion, that person displays the following tendencies:

- Full of energy (likes to be busy)
- Cheerful (prone to feeling happy)
- Seeking excitement (looking for thrills)
- Assertive (likes to take charge)
- Oriented towards others
- Warm or affectionate (approaches people easily and makes friends easily)
- Sociable (likes to be within a group of people)

If someone, however, has low scores on Extraversion, that person shows the following tendencies:

- Passive
- Seeking a quiet environment
- Quiet and withdrawn (likes to be alone)
- Oriented toward self

If someone has high scores on Openness (to experience), that person displays the following tendencies:

- Dislikes routine
- Challenges convention
- Curious
- Intellectual (likes to think and solve problems through thinking)
- Imaginative (prone to fantasy/daydreaming in order to create a more interesting world)
- Creative
- Artistic (appreciating art and beauty in art)
- Appreciative of aesthetics (beauty of nature, objects, people)
- Adventurous (trying new activities)

Figure 48. Based on this photograph, how would you classify this person on the OCEAN traits mentioned thus far?

If someone, however, has low scores on Openness (to experience), that person shows the following tendencies:

- Down to earth
- Practical
- Conventional
- Appreciative of routines
- Not interested in the intellectual sphere

If someone has high scores on Agreeableness, that person displays the following tendencies:

- Trusting (believes that others are governed by good intentions)
- Straightforward (avoids lies and deception)

- Altruistic (feels that helping others is rewarding)
- Compassionate (kind)
- Modest (no boastfulness)
- Cooperative (values compromising)

If someone, however, has low scores on Agreeableness, that person shows the following tendencies:

- Mistrusting of others
- Hostile
- In opposition to others (does not like to cooperate)

If someone has high scores on Conscientiousness, that person displays the following tendencies:

- Competent or self-efficient (able to accomplish tasks)
- Organized
- Reliable
- Aspires towards excellence
- Cautious (makes decisions without rushing/ decides in an informed way)
- Self-disciplined (imposes rules and limitations on him or herself in order to accomplish tasks; for example, a person allows him or herself only a certain amount of sweets per day in order to stay slim).

If someone, however, has low scores on Conscientiousness, that person shows the following tendencies:

- Incompetent
- Disorganized
- Unreliable
- Irresponsible
- Sloppy
- Makes premature decisions

(Barondes, 2011).

Figure 49. Would a person who leaves a sink looking like this be considered conscientious?

PERSONALITY ASSESSMENT: THE MYERS-BRIGGS TYPE INDICATOR (MBTI)

The MBTI was created in the 1920s by Katherine Cook Briggs (1875–1968) and Isabel Briggs Myers (1897-1980) (Katherine was Isabel's mother). This self-report inventory (or test) is often used by employers to evaluate the personality of their future employees. The test was based on

Jung's view of 8 personality types, but this test adds some additional aspects to Jung's view, and actually assesses 16 personality types. Just like Jung, the MBTI assesses these personality aspects: extraversion, introversion, thinking, feeling, sensing and intuiting. However, the MBTI also adds aspects, such as *judging* and *perceiving*. "Judging" in the MBTI refers to a preference to focus on living a settled life with the least amount of ambiguities as possible, making clear decisions about the situations we deal with in the world that surrounds us, planning ahead and getting work done before having fun. "Perceiving" refers to a preference to take in information and not make a final decision so that more information can be obtained. Perceiving also refers to a flexible and spontaneous way of life, and a preference to understand and adapt to the world rather than organize it. Perceiving does not mean having accurate perceptions of reality, and judging does not mean being judgmental. For example, one of the 16 types (see below) is: INTJ, which stands for introverted, intuitive (N stands for intuiting), thinking and judging type. That cluster of tendencies indicates the dominant pattern of personality aspects in a person. (Myers & Briggs Foundation, 2017).

All 16 types (you do not need to memorize them, this is just for your information) are below:

- ENTP
- ENFP
- ESTP
- ESFP
- ENTJ
- ENFJ

- ESTJ
- ESFJ
- INTP
- INFP
- ISTP
- ISFP

- INTJ
- INFJ
- ISTJ
- ISFJ

Many researches criticized the MBTI for not being a valid measure of personality types (meaning that it cannot accurately evaluate people's personalities) and for lacking reliability (when people take the test in a few months, they may fit into a different personality type then) (McCrae & Costa, 1989; Stricker & Ross, 1964; Pittenger, 1993; Gardner & Martinko, 1996; Boyle, 1995). However, other researchers claim that the MBTI is a valid and reliable test (Bruce & Borello, 1986; Capraro & Capraro, 2002). At best, it can be said that there are mixed results (researchers have a divided opinion) about the validity and reliability of the MBTI.

PERSONALITY ASSESSMENT: PROJECTIVE TESTS

Projective tests are based on the following assumption: if a person is given an *ambiguous stimulus* and asked to interpret that stimulus, the person will project (impose) his or her own personality on the stimulus. The person who scores the test can, in this way, evaluate the personality of the individual interpreting the stimulus. The most famous projective tests are the Rorschach Inkblot

Test and the Thematic Apperception Test (TAT). Let's discuss these tests and dispel some myths about them.

The Rorschach Inkblot Test got its name from its creator, Hermann Rorschach (1884-1922), who developed it in 1921. The test consists of ten cards with an inkblot on each one of them, and a person is asked to tell what he or she sees on the picture. The responses are recorded by a test administrator, and then the responses are interpreted by that person. The Rorschach test is a **subjective** test (not objective), due to the fact that the administering person has to offer his or her *opinion* about the personality of the test taker. The story behind the development of the test is

interesting. Even as a child, Hermann loved to play a game called Klecksography with his friends. The game consisted of interpreting the inkblot shapes. He was so interested that his nickname was "Inkblot." When he grew up, he became a psychiatrist, and to pass time he played the Klecksography game with his patients. He noticed that psychiatric patients (suffering from a mental illness) responded differently to the same inkblots than individuals who did not have a mental illness. These results motivated Rorschach to create the test aimed at evaluating the personality of people. He created 10 cards with an inkblot on each of those cards. Why 10? Why not 11 or 15? The answer is much more

Figure 50. An inkblot, used in Rorschach's projective test.

simple than you may think: Rorschach did not have *money* to buy more than 10 cards! He published his writing about the test, but the test was not accepted by critics, and the publication failed miserably, selling very few copies. Several months after this publication, Hermann died (Schultz & Schultz, 2005).

Ironically, after his death many psychologists and psychiatrists began using the Rorschach test, and it is still used today. But, we need to emphasize that mental health professionals (psychologists and psychiatrists) are divided on the usefulness of the Rorschach test. Some mental health professionals believe that the test lacks validity, in a sense that it does not assess personality but a temporary mental process that a person is experiencing. (Garb, Wood, Lilienfeld & Nezworski, 2005). For example, if a person sees on this inkblot the rising of the Devil on the lake (notice his reflection in the "water") about to start killing people, it does not mean that that particular perception reflects a murderous personality or preoccupation with sin; instead, the person may be influenced by some horror movie viewed last night, and the scenes from that movie stimulate the person to think along those lines. So, the test may evaluate only temporary mental processes, as opposed to an enduring personality.

Some psychologists also perceive the test as lacking *reliability*, meaning that if two different people administer the test, they obtain different results (Garb et al., 1999; Hunsley, Lee & Wood, 2003). However, some other psychologists perceive the test as valid and reliable (Viglione & Taylor, 2003; Weiner, Spielberger & Abeles, 2001). So, the jury is still out on this one, and it is a situation of so-called "mixed views," or a controversy, in other words. I am definitely not going to recommend to you to specialize in the Rorschach test before there is more consensus regarding the validity and reliability of this controversial test. But you can play Klecksography as much as you want! Yet, here is some advice: if you really get hooked on the game, please don't give your child some strange name--like Inkblot.

PERSONALITY ASSESSMENT: THEMATIC APPERCEPTION TEST (TAT)

In the Thematic Apperception Test (or TAT) a person is presented with 31 images that depict some ambiguous situations. The person is asked to provide a story, specifically what led to the current situation, what the thoughts and feelings of people in the situation are, and what might be a likely outcome of the current situation. So, the person is asked to make sense of the situation by integrating it with an already established understanding of the world. The term "apperception" refers to making sense of an idea by assimilating (integrating) it to the body of ideas one already possesses. The TAT situations are much more structured than Rorschach inkblots, since the TAT situations depict a snapshot from someone's life, including clearly visible people, objects and animals. But, the situation is still vague; it can be interpreted in many ways. Have a look at figure 51. You will see how vague and open to interpretation the picture is. The image is not the original one from TAT, but that's the idea.

Figure 51. A typical TAT situation can be interpreted in many different ways.

Henry Murray and Christina Morgan developed this test in 1935. The problem until recently was that mental health professionals did not use a scoring system that was universal (the same for all of those who administered the test), and different professionals interpreted the results in different ways using their own scoring systems (which makes the test highly unreliable). Recently, there were attempts to create a scoring system that could be used in the same way by those who utilize this test, and it seems that the test now has more validity and reliability-- but they are still not nearly as high as the MMPI and NEO PI tests (McClelland, 1999; Westen, 1991; Woike & McAdams, 2001).

REFERENCES

Archer, S. L. (1982). The lower age boundaries of identity development. *Child Development*, 53, 1551-1556.

Alexander, P., & Yakel, D. (2014). *Psychology Exploring Our Universe Within* (4th ed.). Boston, MA: Pearson Education.

Allik, J., & McCrae, R. R. (2004). Towards a geography of personality traits. Patterns of profiles across *36* cultures. *Journal of Cross-Cultural Psychology, 35,* 13-28.

Assor, A., Roth, G., & Deci, E. (2004). The emotional costs of parents' conditional regard: A self-determination theory analysis. *Journal of Personality*, 72, 47-87.

Barondes, S. H. (2011). Making Sense of People: Decoding the Mysteries of Personality. Upper Saddle River, NJ: FT Press.

Berg, M. B., Janoff-Bulman, P., & Cotter, J. (2001). Perceiving value in obligations and goals: Wanting to do what should be done. *Personality and Social Psychology Bulletin*, 27, 982-995.

Bergeman, C. S., Chipeur, H. M., Plomin, R., Pedersen, N. L., McClearn, G. E., Nesselroade, J. R., et al. (1993). Genetic and environmental effects on openness to experience, agreeableness, and conscientiousness: An adoption-twin study. *Journal of Personality, 61,* 159-179.

Boyle, G J (1995). "Myers-Briggs Type Indicator (MBTI): Some psychometric limitations". *Australian Psychologist* 30: 71–74.

Brown, J. (2010). High self-esteem buffers negative feedback: Once more with feeling. *Cognition and Emotion, 24*(8), 1389-1404.

Bushman, B., Bonacci, A., Pedersen, W., Vasquez, E., & Miller, N. (2005). Chewing on it can chew you up: Effects of rumination on triggered displaced aggression. *Journal of Personality and Social Psychology*, 88, 969-983.

Butcher, J. (2010). Personality assessment from the nineteenth to the early twenty-first century: Past achievement & contemporary challenges. Annual Review of Clinical Psychology, 6, 1-20.

Butler, J. M., & Haigh, G. V. (1954). Changes in the relationship between self-concepts and ideal concepts consequent upon client-centered counseling. In C. R. Rogers & R. F. Dymond (Eds.), *Psychotherapy and Personality Change.* Chicago: University of Chicago Press.

Capraro, Robert M.; Mary Margaret Capraro (2002). "Myers-Briggs Type Indicator Score Reliability Across: Studies a Meta-Analytic Reliability Generalization Study". *Educational and Psychological Measurement* (SAGE Publications) 62 (4): 590–602.

Caspi, A., Bem, D.J., & Elder, G. H. (1989). Continuities and consequences of interactional styles across the life course. *Journal of Personality*, 57, 375-406.

Cherry, R., & Cherry, L. (1973). The Horney heresy. The New York Times Magazine, p. 12ff.

Clark, A. (2005). An early recollection of Albert Einstein: Perspective on its meaning and his life. *Journal of Individual Psychology*, 61, 126-136.

Conway, M., & Holmes, A. (2004). Psychosocial stages and the accessibility of autobiographical memories across the life cycle. *Journal of Personality*, 72, 461-480.

Cozzarelli, C. (1993). Personality and self-efficacy as redictors of coping with abortion. *Journal of Personality and Social Psychology*, 65, 1224-1236.

Cramer, P. (2007). Longitudinal study of defense mechanism: Late childhood to late adolescence. *Journal of Personality*, 75, 1-24.

Davidow, S., & Bruhn, A. R. (1990). Earliest memories and the dynamics of delinquency: A replication of study. *Journal of Personality Assessment, 54,* 601-616.

Deci, E., & Ryan, R. (2009). Self-determination theory: A consideration of human motivational universals. In P. Corr & G. Matthews (Eds.), *The Cambridge handbook of personality psychology* (pp. 441-446). New York: Cambridge University Press.

Ellis, R., A., & Taylor, M. S. (1983). Role of self-esteem within the job search process. *Journal of Applied Psychology*, 68, 632-640.

Eysenck, H. J. (1990). Genetic and environment contributions to individual differences: The three major dimensions of personality. *Journal of Personality, 58,* 245-261.

Falbo, T., & Polit, D. F. (1986). Quantitative review of the only child literature: Research evidence and theory development. *Psychological Bulletin*, 100, 176-189.

Garb, H. N. (1999). Call for a moratorium on the use of the Rorschach inkblot test in clinical and forensic settings. *Assessment, 6,* 313-317.

Garb, H. N., Florio, C. M., & Grove, W. M. (1998). The validity of the Rorschach and the Minnesota Multiphasic Personality Inventory. Results from meta-analyses. *Psychology Science, 9,* 402-404.

Garb, H. N., Wood, J. M., Lilinfeld, S. O., & Nezworski, M. T. (2005). Roots of the Rorschach controversy. *Clinical Psychology Review, 25,* 97-118.

Gardner, W. L., & Martinko, M. J. (1996). "Using the Myers-Briggs Type Indicator to study managers: A literature review and research agenda". *Journal of Management* 22: 45–83.

Gates, L., Lineberger, M. R., Crockett, J., & Hubbard, J. (1988). Birth order and its relationship to depression, anxiety, and self-concept test scores in children. *Journal of Genetic Psychology, 149,* 29-34.

Graham, W., & Balloun, J. (1973). An empirical test of Maslow's need hierarchy theory. *Journal of Humanistic Psychology*, 13, 97-108.

Grieser, C., Greenberg, R., & Harrison, R.H. (1972). The adaptive function of sleep and dreaming on recall. *Journal of Abnormal Psychology*, 80, 280-286.

Hagedoorn, M., & Molleman, E. (2006). Facial disfigurement in patients with head band neck cancer: The role of social self-efficacy. *Health Psychology, 25,* 643-647.

Harter, S., Marold, D.B., Whitesell, N.R., & Cobbs G. (1996). A model of the effects of perceived parent and peer support on adolescent false-self behavior. *Child Development, 67,* 360-374.

Herrera, N., Zajonc, R., Wieczorkowska, G., & Cichomski, B. (2003). Beliefs about birth rank and their reflection in reality. *Journal of Personality and Social Psychology*, 85, 142-150.

Holmgren, S., Molander, B., & Nilsson, K. (2006). Intelligence and executive functioning in adult age: Effects of sibship size and birth order. *European Journal of Cognitive Psychology*, 18, 138-158.

Hunsley, J., Lee, C. M., & Wood, J. M. (2003). Controversial and questionable assessment techniques. In S. O. Lilienfeld, S. J. Lynn, & J. M. Lohr (Eds.), *Science and pseudoscience in clinical psychology* (pp. 39-76). New York. Guilford Press.

Jaffe, A. (1971). *The myth of meaning: Jung and the expansion of consciousness*. New York: Putnam.

Kasler, J., & Nevo, O. (2005). Early recollections as predictors of study area choice. *Journal of Individual Psychology, 61,* 217-232.

Kihlstrom, J. F. (1994). Psychodynamics and social cognition. *Journal of Personality*, 62, 681-696.

Kristensen, P., & Bjerkedal, T. (2007). Explaining the relation between birth order and intelligence. *Science*, 3161, 1717.

Laird, T., & Shelton, A. (2006). From an Adlerian perspective: Birth order, dependency, and binge drinking on a historically Black university campus. *Journal of Individual Psychology*, 62, 18-35.

Lester, D. (1990). Maslow's hierarchy of needs and personality. Personality and Individual Differences, 11, 1187-1188.

Maslow, A. H. (1968). *Toward a psychology of being* (2nd ed.). New York: Van Nostrand Reinhold.

Maslow, A. H. (1970). Motivation and personality (2nd ed.). New York: Harper & Row.

Maslow, A.H. (1971). *The farther reaches of human nature*. New York: Viking Press.

McCrae, R R; Costa, P T (1989). "Reinterpreting the Myers-Briggs Type Indicator From the Perspective of the Five-Factor Model of Personality". Journal of Personality 57 (1): 17–40.

Mellor, S. (1990). How do only children differ from other children? *Journal of Genetic Psychology*, 151, 221-230.

Moretti, M. M., & Higgins, E. T. (1990). Relating self-discrepancy to self-esteem: The contribution of discrepancy beyond actual-self ratings. *Journal of Experimental Social Psychology*, 26, 108-123.

Motley, M. T. (1987, February). What I meant to ssay. *Psychology Today*, pp. 24-28.

The Myers & Briggs Foundation (2017). *Psychological Type and Relationships*. Retrieved from: http://www.myersbriggs.org/type-use-for-everyday-life/psychological-type-and-relationships/

The Myers & Briggs Foundation (2017). *Psychological Type and Relationships*. Retrieved from: http://www.myersbriggs.org/my-mbti-personality-type/mbti-basics/sensing-or-intuition.htm

Myers, L., & Derakshan, N. (2004). DO childhood memories colour social judgements of today? The case of repressors. *European Journal of Personality, 18*, 321-330.

Nebbitt, V. (2009). Self-efficacy in African American adolescent males living in urban public housing. *Journal of Black Psychology*, 35(3), 295-316.

Nevid, J. S., Rathus, S. A., & Greene, B. (2008). *Abnormal psychology in a changing world.* (7th ed.). Upper Saddle River, NJ: Pearson/Prentice Hall.

Noaln, G. (2008). Teacher communication of unconditional positive regard (love) to students in secondary school environments. *Dissertation Abstracts International Section A: Humanities and Social Sciences, 4978.*

Noll, R. (1994). The Jung cult: *Origins of a charismatic movement*. Princeton, NJ: Princeton University Press.

Pedersen, N. L., Plomin, R., McClearn, G. E., & Friberg, L. (1988). Neurotocism, extraversion, and related traits in adult twins reared apart and reared together. *Journal of Personality and Social Psychology, 55,* 950-957.

Pittenger, David J. (1993). "Measuring the MBTI...And Coming Up Short." (PDF). *Journal of Career Planning and Employment 54* (1): 48–52.

Podlog, L., & Eklund, R. (2010). Returning to copetition after a serious injury: The role of self-determination. *Journal of Sports Sciences*, 28 (8), 819-831.

Routledge, C., Ostafin, B., Juhl, J., Sedikides, C., Cathey, C., & Jiangqun, L. (2010). Adjusting to death: The effects of mortality salience and self-esteem on psychological well-being, growth motivation, and maladaptive behavior. *Journal of Personality and Social Psychology*, 99(6), 897-916.

Ryckman, R., THornoton, B., & Gold, J. (2009). Assessing competition avoidance as a basic personality dimension. *Journal of Psychology: Interdisciplinary and Applied*, 143(2), 175-192.

Salas, E., & Cannon-Bowers, J.A. (2001). The science of training: A decade of progress. *Annual Review of Psychology*, 52, 471-499.

Schachter, S. (1963). Birth order, eminence, and higher education. *American Sociological Review*, 28, 757-767.

Schachter, S. (1964). Birth order and sociometric choice. *Journal of Abnormal and Social Psychology*, 68, 453-456

Schmitt, D., Realo, A., Voracek, M., & Allik, J. (2008). Why can't a man be more like a woman sex differences in Big Five personality traits across 55 cultures. *Journal of Personality and Social Psychology, 44*(2), 496-506.

Schredl, M., & Piel, E. (2006). War-related dream themes in Germany from 1956 to 2000. *Political Psychology, 27*, 299-307.

Schultz, D. P. (1990). *Intimate friends, dangerous rivals: The turbulent relationship between Freud and Jung.* Los Angeles, CA: Jeremy Tarcher.

Schultz, Duane P., & Schultz, Sydney Ellen. (2013). Theories of Personality. Belmont, CA. Wadsworth.

Schwarzer, R., & Fuchs, R. (1995). Changing risk behaviors and adopting health behaviors: The role of self-efficacy beliefs. In A. Bandura (Ed.), *Self-efficacy in changing societies* (pp.259-315. Cambridge, England: Cambridge University Press.

Steca, P., Bassi, M., Caprara, V., & Fave, A. (2011). Parents' self-efficacy beliefs and their children's psychosocial adaptation during adolescence. *Journal of Youth and Adolescence, 40*, 320-331.

Strano, D., & Petrocelli, J. (2005). A preliminary examination of the role of inferiority feelings in the academic achievement of college students. *Journal of Individual Psychology, 61*, 80-89.

Straumann, T. J., Vooklesm, J., Berenstein, V., Chaiken, S., & Higgins, E. T. (1991). Self-discrepancies and vulnerability to body dissatisfaction and disordered eating. *Journal of Personality and Social Psychology, 61*, 946-956.

Stricker, L J; Ross, J (1964). "An Assessment of Some Structural Properties of the Jungian Personality Typology". *Journal of Abnormal and Social Psychology* 68: 62–71.

Sulloway, F. J. & Zweigenhaft, R. (2010). Birth order risk taking in athletics: A meta-analysis and study of major league baseball. *Personality and Social Psychology Review, 14*(4), 402-416.

Tallandini, M., & Caudek, C. (2010). Defense mechanism development in typical children. *Psychotherapy Research. 20*(5), 535-545.

Taylor, M. (2000). The influence of self-efficacy on alcohol use among American Indians. *Cultural Diversity and Ethnic Minority Psychology, 6*, 152-167.

Taylor, S. E., Kemeny, M. E., Aspinwall, L. G., Schneider, S.C. Rodriguez, R., & Herbert, M. (1992). Optimism, coping, psychological distress, and high risk sexual behavior among men at risk for acquired immunodeficiency syndrome (AIDS). *Journal of Personality and Social Psychology, 63*, 460-473.

Thompson, B., & Borrello, G. M. (1986). "Construct Validity of the Myers-Briggs Type Indicator". *Educational and Psychological Measurement* (SAGE Publications) 46 (3): 745–752.

Valli, K., Revonsuo, A., Palkas, O., & Punamaki, R. (2006). The effect of trauma on dream content: A field study of Palestinian children. *Dreaming, 16*, 63-87.

Viglione, D. J., & Taylor, N. (2003). Empirical support for interrater reliability of Rorschach comprehensive system coding. *Journal of Clinical Psychology, 59*, 111-121.

Watson, M. W., & Getz, K. (1990). The relationship between Oedipal behaviors and children's family role concepts. *Merrill-Palmer Quarterly, 36*, 487-505.

Weiner, I. B., Spielberger, C. D., & Abeles, N. (2002). Scientific psychology and the Rorschach inkblot method. *The Clinical Psychologist, 55*, 7-12.

Williams, D. E., & Page, M. M. (1989). A multidimensional measure of Maslow's hierarchy of needs. *Journal of Research in Personality, 23*, 192-213.

Winkielman, P., Berridge, K., & Wilbarger, J. (2005). Unconscious affective reactions to masked happy versus angry faces influence consumption behavior and judgments of value. *Personality and Social Psychology Bulletin, 31*, 121-135.

Zajonc, R. B., Markus, H., & Markus, G. B. (1979). The birth order puzzle. *Journal of Personality and Social Psychology, 37,* 1325-1341.

Biological Psychology I

Chapter Three

WHAT IS BIOLOGICAL PSYCHOLOGY?

Biological Psychology is the scientific exploration of how different biological systems influence mental processes and behaviors. **Biological systems** are nervous, cardiovascular, urinary, digestive, respiratory, endocrine, lymphatic, immune, muscular, skeletal, reproductive and integumentary (skin, hair, nails and sweat glands). Don't worry if you are not familiar with these systems since one of the goals of this chapter is to explore their elements and functions. An additional goal is to examine how the nervous system influences these other systems. The cells within the nervous system create our mental processes, but the cardiovascular system (the blood vessels, blood and heart) brings nutrients (food) to those cells. Without the proper blood supply, the cells of the nervous system die or become dysfunctional. As a result of these nervous system cells' disintegration or deficiencies, our mental processes and behaviors become impaired (malfunction) too. So, saying that the nervous system is the only one responsible for the mental processes and behaviors is simply not true. Even though the nervous system has an extremely significant role in creating mental processes and behaviors (as you will soon see), *all* biological systems influence the mind and behavior too. It is also important to mention that all biological systems influence one another, so think of our organism as the unity of all biological systems.

BIOLOGICAL SYSTEMS CONNECTED

Let's illustrate a connection between two biological systems, specifically the immune system and the nervous system. But, first we need to examine a few important concepts related to the immune system. **Immunity** is our body's ability to resist harmful influences, such as physical trauma (bumps, cuts, scrapes, etc.); chemical and thermal burns; extreme cold; ultraviolet radiation; viruses; bacteria; fungi and parasites; and cancer cells (abnormal cells within the body). The immune system refers to the interaction among several biological systems to provide immunity. The biological systems involved in the immune system are usually the lymphatic, cardiovascular, integumentary, respiratory, digestive and nervous systems. The immune system resists harmful influences through barriers (skin and mucous membranes), cells and the chemicals these cells release, as well as organs and the chemicals they release (Marieb & Hoehn, 2013).

The following example is based on a true story. Sammy was a teenager when he began to suffer from certain *compulsions* (actions/behaviors that a person feels forced to do). Some of these compulsions were such that he had to perform them in order to eliminate, or at least reduce his *obsessive* (recurring and intrusive) fears and worries; for example, he would not sleep in his bed since he was frightened of the stripes on his blanket, so he would sleep in a chair. When compulsions exist with a purpose to get rid of obsessions (about fears and worries), then we can view them as symptoms of an obsessive compulsive disorder (OCD) (Lombroso & Schahill, 2008). So, Sammy slept in a chair in order to eliminate or reduce his fear of the blanket (Kanal uporabnika malotuINmalotam, 2011).

But, in addition to OCD symptoms, Sammy suffered another kind of compulsion—*tics*. Tics are compulsions that are not purposeful like OCD compulsions; instead, tics are purposeless; this is to say that tics are compulsions (like sudden running, using profane language, shaking hands, shaking head, etc.) that happen for no apparent reason (something that the patient will confirm to you verbally, stating that he/she does not know why a particular compulsion happens). Tics are usually a part of a condition called Tourette's syndrome (Murphy et al., 2010). So, Sammy was a sufferer of OCD and Tourette's symptoms (Kanal uporabnika malotuINmalotam, 2011). But, you may wonder whether two conditions can coexist within a person, and the answer is, yes. When two or more conditions coexist within an individual, we refer to it as *comorbidity*. Sammy was given medications called SSRIs, which are typically given to OCD sufferers. When SSRI medications reach the brain (through the bloodstream after being digested), they influence the accumulation (or an increase) of a certain chemical in the brain called serotonin (Pinel, 2014). 6-8 weeks after serotonin presence increases in the brain, OCD symptoms reduce in some patients (Breedlowe, Rosenzweig, & Watson, 2007).

Sammy was also given medications called neuroleptics to combat Tourette's syndrome. After being ingested, these medications reach the brain through the bloodstream and reduce the levels of a chemical called dopamine that seems to be present in Tourette's sufferers in higher than normal amounts in structures, such as the caudate nucleus (a nucleus is a cluster of cells) and the

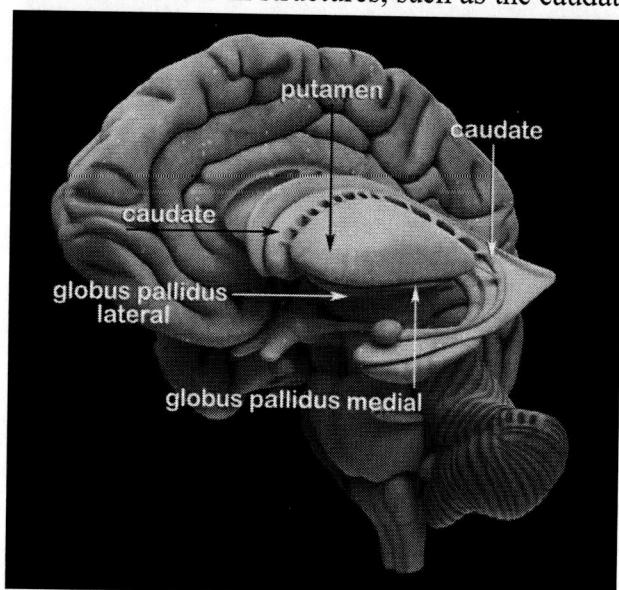

Figure 1. The basal nuclei.

putamen nucleus, which are both located in a larger structure called the **basal nuclei**. It seems that too much dopamine in these structures influences tics/compulsions in Tourette's (Gilbert et al., 2006). The basal nuclei are composed of some additional structures, such as the lateral globus pallidus nucleus and the medial globus pallidus nucleus (Martini et al., 2012).

The effect of neuroleptics on Tourette's is less compulsive behaviors. However, neither SSRIs nor neuroleptics worked for Sammy. The reason was the following: the real culprit for Sammy's disorder was something more fundamental than OCD symptoms and Tourette's symptoms—he was infected with a bacterium called streptococcus (also called strep). He was asymptomatic (without symptoms of the strep infection, like sore throat), so nobody even suspected a strep infection. Once bacteria enter (infect) our body, the immune system becomes activated and starts to fight them by producing chemicals called antibodies. However, in some people, like Sammy, the immune system makes a mistake and starts to attack its own body, for some unknown (or idiopathic) reason. In Sammy's case, that's exactly what happened, and his immune system attacked his nervous system's tissue (the brain) damaging it. When the immune system contains this error and attacks its own body, the resulting condition (in this case the combination of OCD and Tourette's) is called an **auto-immune condition** (Kanal uporabnika malotuINmalotam, 2011).

Sammy's brain damage influenced the emergence of OCD and Tourette's symptoms. These symptoms characterize a condition called PANDAS or Pediatric Autoimmune Neuropsychiatric Disorder Associated with Streptococcus (Lombroso & Scahill, 2008). The physicians detected antibodies for strep inside of Sammy's blood and realized that Sammy had a strep infection. Then, they prescribed medications (antibiotics) against strep. Killing the bacteria with the antibiotics meant that Sammy's immune system didn't have a reason to be activated any longer, and Sammy's symptoms slowly began to retract. But why didn't SSRIs and neuroleptics work when they are the standard treatment for OCD and Tourette's conditions? They didn't work because they just treated the symptoms, not the cause (strep bacteria), which was constantly creating new symptoms. Even if SSRIs and neuroleptics were helpful in reducing some symptoms, new symptoms were continuously being created since the cause (such as the strep infection) was not removed from Sammy's body (Kanal uporabnika malotuINmalotam, 2011).

The story about Sammy is an illustration of a destructive link between the immune system and the nervous system, but the immune system (specifically the lymphatic aspect of it) and the nervous system

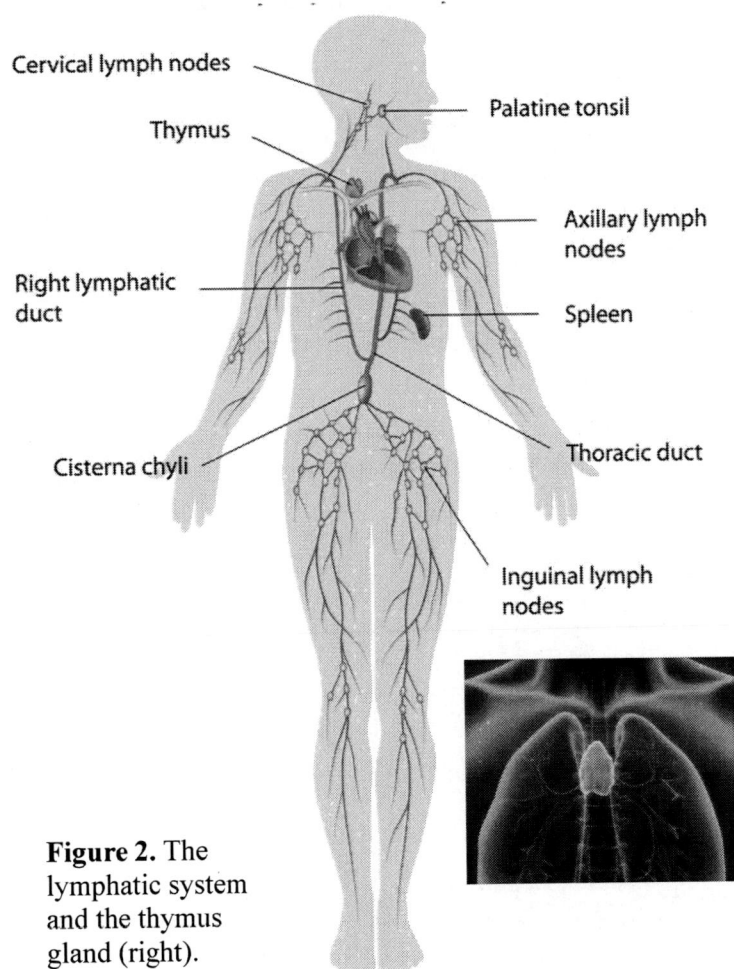

Figure 2. The lymphatic system and the thymus gland (right).

95

are known to have a mutually positive influence too. For instance, the lymphatic system's vessels carry leaked fluids from tissues that surround the nervous system structures so that these fluids don't accumulate and obstruct the nervous system's functioning (Martini et al., 2012). Also, the thymus gland of the lymphatic system produces hormones, as well as chemicals (cytokines), that establish normal levels of some hormones produced by a brain structure called the **hypothalamus** (Marieb & Hoehn, 2013). Likewise, some hormones of the thymus gland stimulate the secretion of hormones from the pituitary gland, located in the brain.

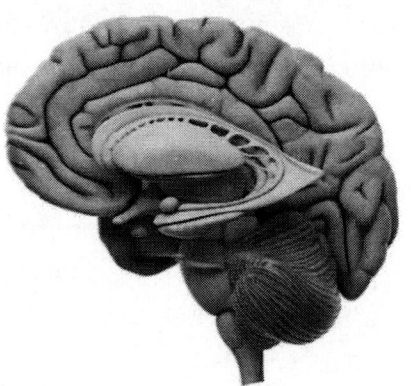
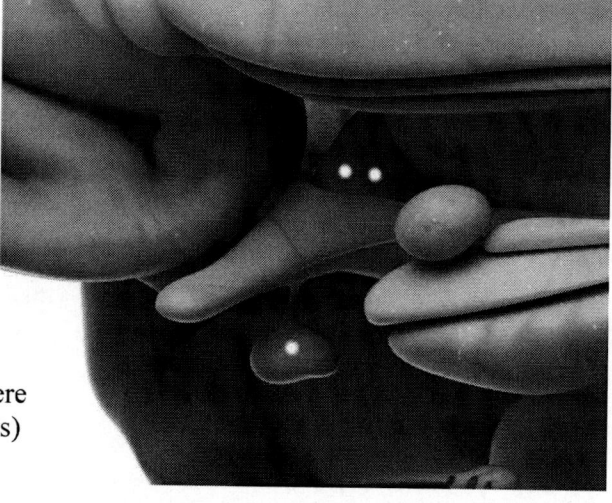

Figure 3. Above: the brain with a hemisphere removed. Right: the hypothalamus (two dots) and the pituitary gland (one dot).

Removal of the thymus gland lowers the levels of endorphins (feel-good chemicals) produced by the brain, and proper functioning of the thymus gland is associated with normal levels of endorphin production by the brain (Marieb & Hoehn, 2013). The nervous system can influence the immune system too. For example, the experience of psychological stress (which is produced by the cells of the nervous system) can lead to a decrease in the immune function. Cells of the brain and the spinal cord produce cytokines that facilitate the immune response. Nerves (fibers that leave the brain and the spinal cord) connect with cells of the lymph nodes, spleen and skin.

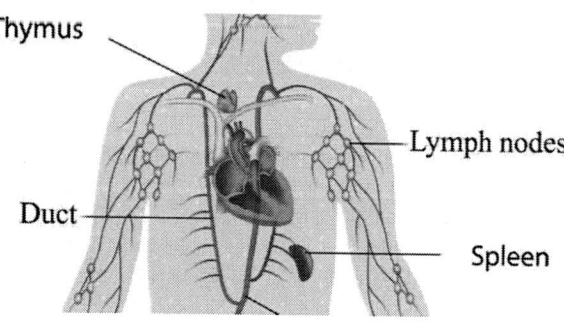

Figure 4. The lymph nodes, spleen and thymus gland.

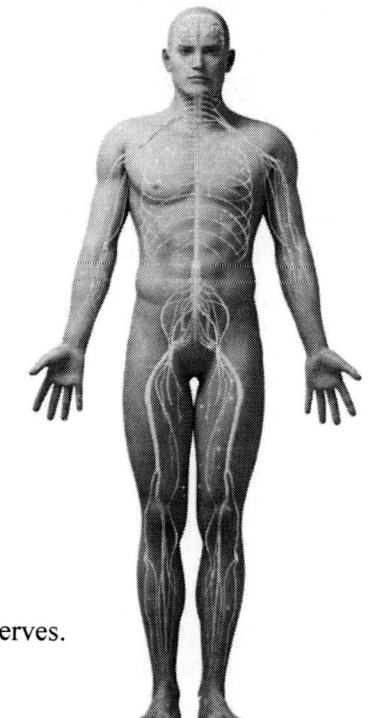

Figure 5. Nerves.

These nerves release chemicals (such as neurotransmitters) onto the aforementioned cells, enhancing their immune functions (Marieb & Hoehn, 2013; Martini et al., 2012).

THE NERVOUS SYSTEM

The nervous system is an information receiving, processing and sending network composed of the brain, the spinal cord and **nerves**. Nerves are fibers originating from the brain and the spinal cord, connecting the brain and the spinal cord to various tissues and organs. The spinal cord is located inside the spine—a structure composed predominantly of bony elements (**vertebrae**).

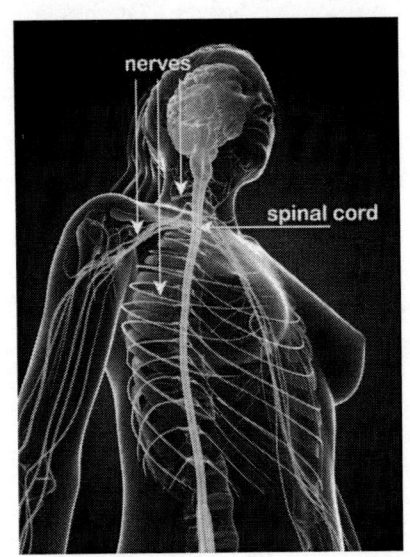

Figure 6. Nerves originate in the spinal cord and the brain.

This very complex network (the brain, the spinal cord and nerves) allows us to *receive* information from the outside world, and to receive the information about our body (when we have some pain, an itch, an accelerated heart-beat, etc.) Also, this network allows us to *influence* (act upon) the outside world (like drive a car or talk to friends) and to influence our "inner world" too (such as our brains sending information to our hearts to beat). So, the nervous system has two major functions: **sensory** (to receive information) and **motor** (to stimulate the activity of the parts of our body, such as organs, limbs, etc.). The nervous system is divided into the **central nervous system (CNS)** and the **peripheral nervous system (PNS)** (Carlson, 2013).

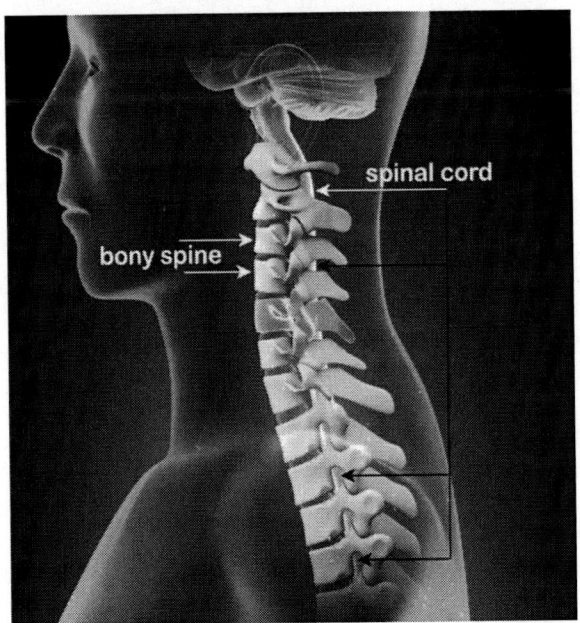

Figure 7. The bony spine is composed of vertebrae and the spinal cord.

The **central nervous system** is composed of the **brain** and the **spinal cord.** The central nervous system is called "central" because the brain and the spinal cord, which are connected, are located along the central vertical axis of the body. This central axis divides the body in two halves. The brain is also an organ capable of making decisions, so the brain obviously has a central role in our lives since we need to make decisions many times during any given day. The vast majority of those important decisions are transmitted along the spinal cord (we will see how soon) through nerves (fibers that arise from the spinal cord) to the other parts of the body (heart, fingers, legs, tissues, etc.). Thus, the spinal cord has a central role in our lives too (Pinel, 2014).

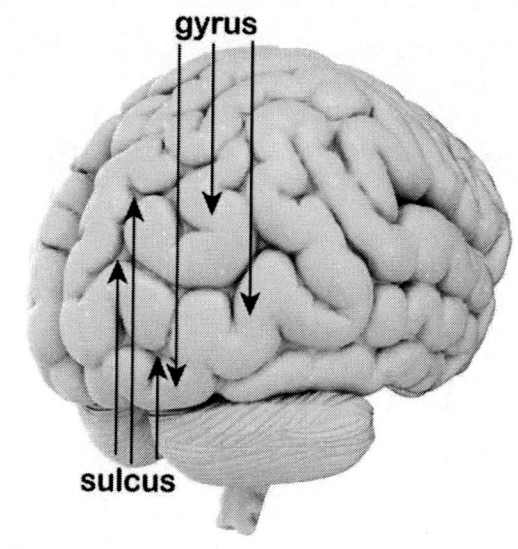

Figure 8. The brain's surface is composed of gyri (bumps) and sulci (valleys).

CORTICAL AND SUBCORTICAL STRUCTURES

The brain is composed of the **cortex** (the surface of the brain) and **subcortical** (below cortex) structures. We previously saw some of the subcortical structures in chapter one, such as the basal nuclei, the limbic system, pons, and medulla. Another important subcortical structure is the **brain stem**--a collection of several distinct smaller structures, such as the **midbrain,** which includes superior colliculus and inferior colliculus (these colliculi are collectively called *tectum,* meaning "roof") and the cerebral peduncle (called *tegmentum,* meaning "floor"). The brain stem also consists of pons and medulla oblongata (Marieb & Hoehn, 2013; Martini et al., 2012).

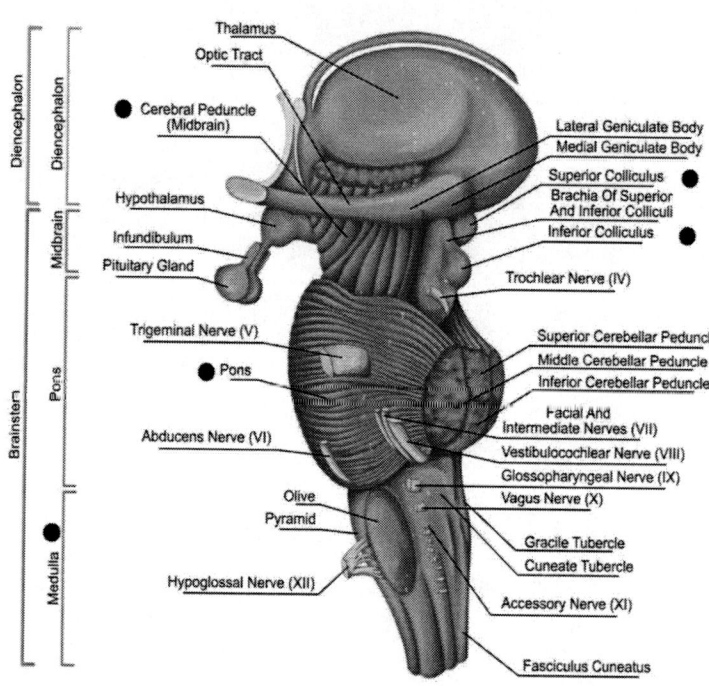

Figure 9. A diagram of the brain stem.

Localization of function, an important and frequent term in biopsychology, refers to certain *areas* of the brain that are responsible for certain functions. By **functions** we mean mental processes, behaviors (actions) and physiological (bodily) processes (breathing, heart-beat, rapid eye movements during sleep, etc.) We will go into the details of localization much more in later chapters; for now, let's briefly mention some basic aspects of the brain's regions that influence our functioning. For example, the brain-stem influences breathing, heart-rate, rapid eye movements, and blood pressure to name a few. The thalamus is known for collecting sensory information (from the skin, eyes, ears) and sending the information towards the cortical structures for more processing. The hippocampus (of the limbic system) is important for transferring information from the short term memory (temporary memory) into the long term memory storage (a more permanent type of memory). The parietal lobe collects sensory information (pain, temperature, touch) and processes it, giving us a conscious experience of that sensation (like hot air blown over your face when you use a hair-dryer). The temporal lobe processes memory and learning (Pinel, 2014; Kalat, 2013). The frontal lobe influences us to control our impulses, including those within social situations (we don't slap our boss even though we might have an impulse/urge to do so; that is the frontal lobe kicking in!) The frontal lobe is also involved when we need to make a decision, solve a problem or speak. But, keep in mind that the information in the previous two paragraphs is a simplification since the already-mentioned structures perform *other* functions as well, which we will see throughout this book (University of Bristol, 2010).

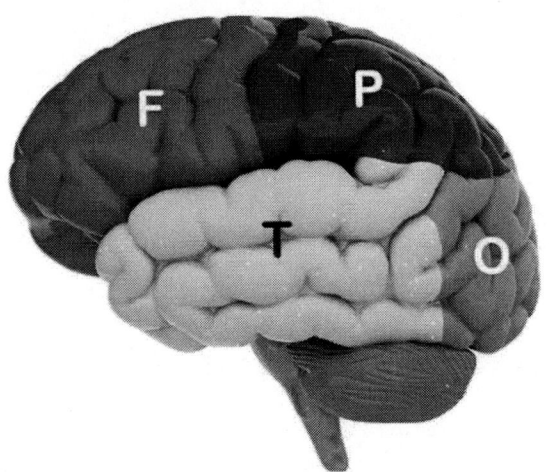

Figure 10. F: frontal lobe, P: parietal lobe, T: temporal lobe and O: occipital lobe.

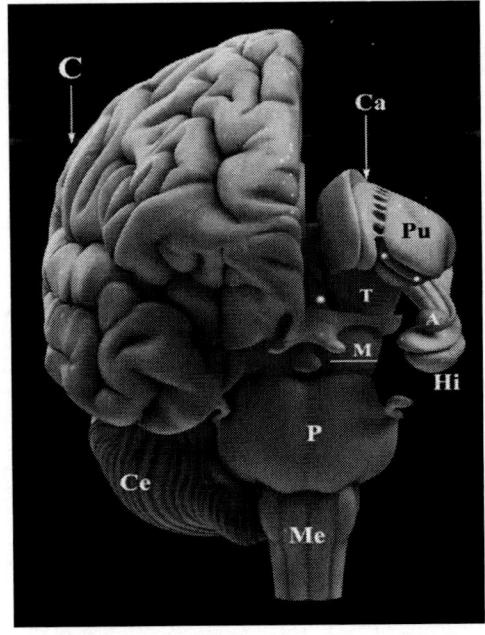

Figure 11. C: cortex, Ca: caudate, Pu: putamen, two dots: pallidus, A: amygdala, Hi: hippocampus, T: thalamus, white dot: hypothalamus, M: midbrain, P: pons, Me: medulla, Ce: cerebellum.

The brain is an organ that creates our mental processes and our conscious experience of those mental processes. Not having the brain means no experience of love, hate, joy, dreams, needs, seeing, hearing, tasting, and so on. The brain can sense the outside world (people around us, for example) and our inner world (a tooth-ache, for example). The brain can do this sensing through *nerves*. The nerves that arise from the brain are called the **cranial** nerves and the vast majority of them arises from the brainstem. There are 12 pairs of these nerves meaning that one nerve arises from each hemisphere, and they are marked in Roman numerals (I, II, III, etc.)

Some cranial nerves have a **sensory** function (to *receive* information). So, a sensory function of a cranial nerve (trigeminal, for example) is to bring the information to the brain about what is happening to the person's face. Is it cold? Is it hot? Is it being touched? Is it being kissed? Does it hurt? Another sensory cranial nerve

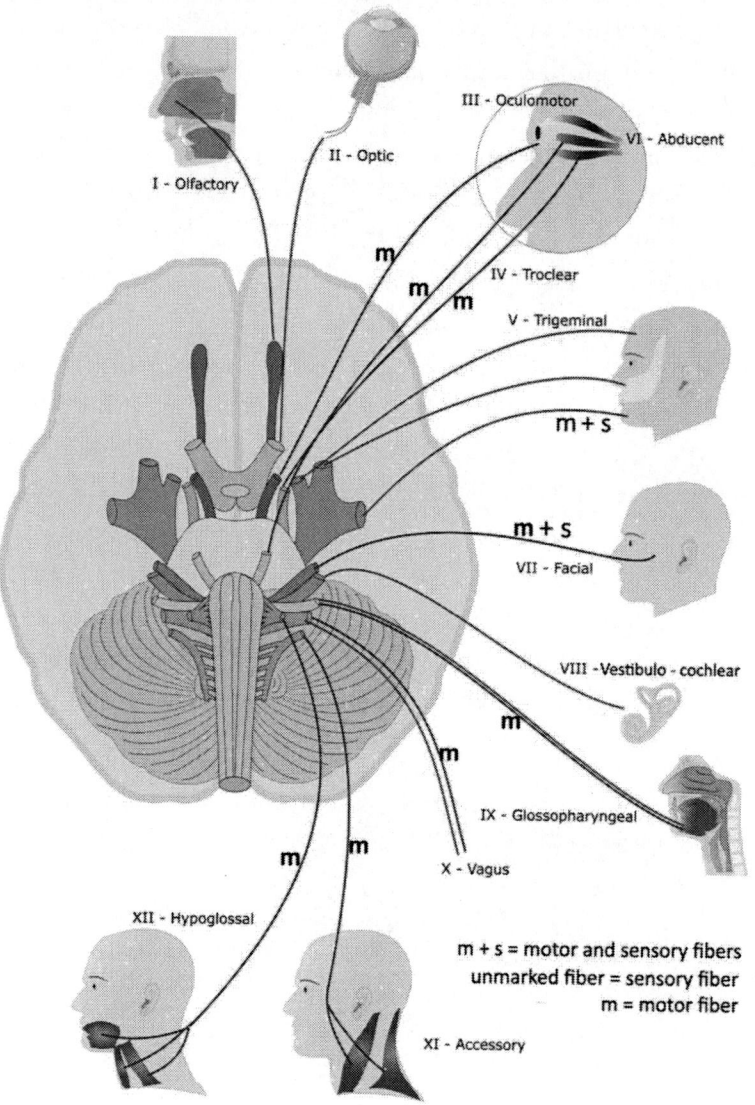

Figure 12. The motor (m) and sensory (unmarked) cranial nerves.

(optic nerve, for example) brings the brain the information about the visual stimuli pertaining to the outside world. Are there any paintings on the walls? What is the color of the wall? How many people are in the room? So, through sensory function of cranial nerves, the brain receives the information about the world (outside and inner). There are *two* of each of the cranial nerves, and many of them branch out. The functions of the sensory cranial nerves are:

Olfactory nerves (I) – receive olfactory (or smell) **stimuli** (information) from the nose.

Optic nerves (II) – receive visual stimuli from the eyes.

100

Trigeminal nerves (V) – receive stimuli from the nasal cavity, skin of the forehead, upper eyelid, eyebrow, nose, lower eyelid, upper lip, upper gums, upper teeth, cheek, upper palate, pharynx, lower gums, lower teeth, lower lips, tongue and lower palate (tissue underneath the tongue).

Facial nerves (VII) – receive taste stimuli from the **anterior** (front) two-thirds of the tongue

Vestibulo-cochlear nerves (VIII) – also known as acoustic nerves or auditory-vestibular nerves

• receive sound information from the inside of the ear

• receive information from the inside of the ear about balance (standing upright in space)

• receive information from the inside of the ear about the orientation and movement of the head.

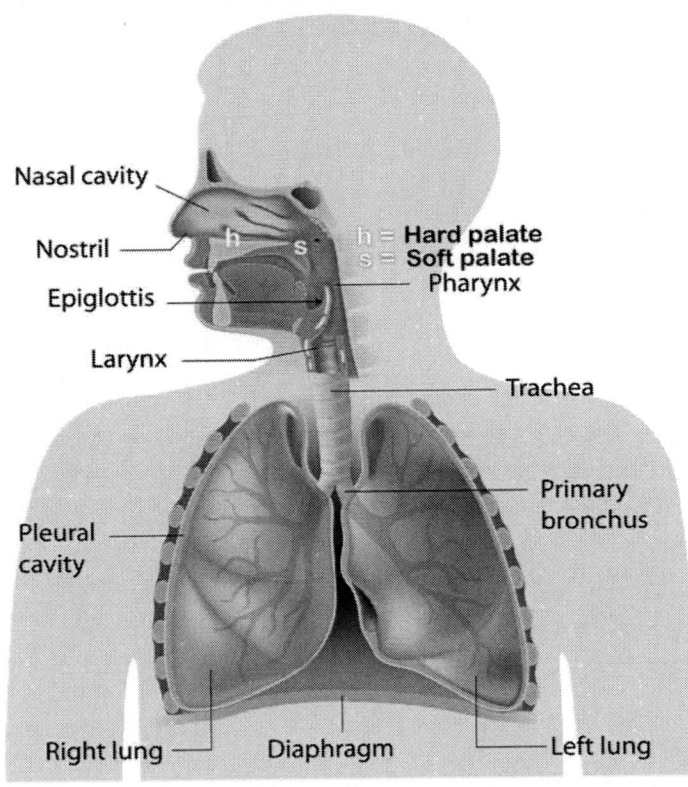

Figure 13. The nasal cavity, pharynx and larynx.

Glossopharyngeal Nerves (IX) -

• receive taste stimuli from the **posterior** (towards the back) third of the tongue

• receive information from major blood vessels of the neck about blood pressure and dissolved gas concentrations

• receive touch, temperature and pain information from the pharynx and soft palate

Vagus nerves (X) -

• receive touch, temperature and pain information from the external ear, the lower part of the pharynx, the larynx (influences breathing and sound production) and esophagus

- receive information about the functioning of the digestive system (the information comes from the pharynx , esophagus, liver, gallbladder, spleen, large and small intestines)

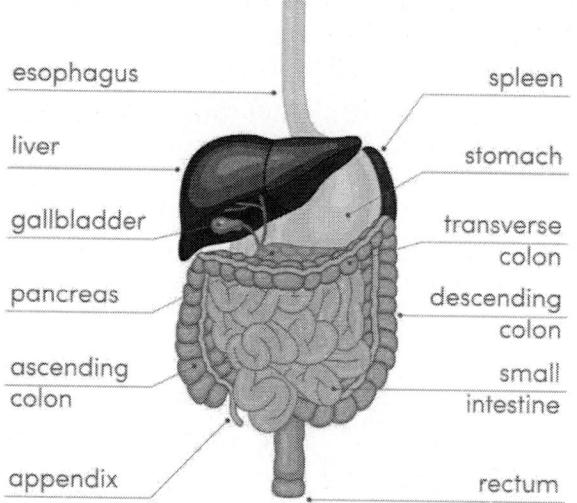

Figure 14. Digestive system structures.

- receive information about the functioning of the lungs, heart, bronchi and trachea and diaphragm (a structure influencing breathing)

- receive information about the functioning of the larynx.

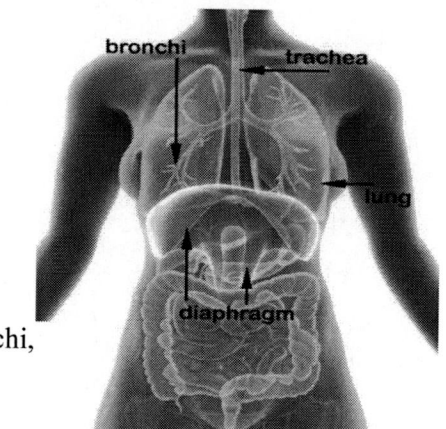

Figure 15. The lungs, bronchi, trachea and diaphragm.

Cranial nerves are classified as the peripheral nervous system, even though they come from the central nervous system (Martini et al., 2012; Marieb & Hoehn, 2013).

THE BRAIN AND SENSATION: SPINAL SENSORY NERVES

Our brain senses the world through the cranial nerves—a fact that we have already established. But, the brain senses the world through **spinal nerves** too. These nerves originate in the *spinal cord* and connect to various parts of the body. So, when we sense someone's touch on our skin, for example, the nerves from our skin carry the information about that touch to the spinal cord (from where the spinal nerves originate), and from there to the brain so that the brain can create our conscious sensation of touch. The spinal nerves that perform a sensory function are called **spinal sensory nerves** (Martini et al., 2012). All spinal nerves branch out at some point after they leave the spinal cord.

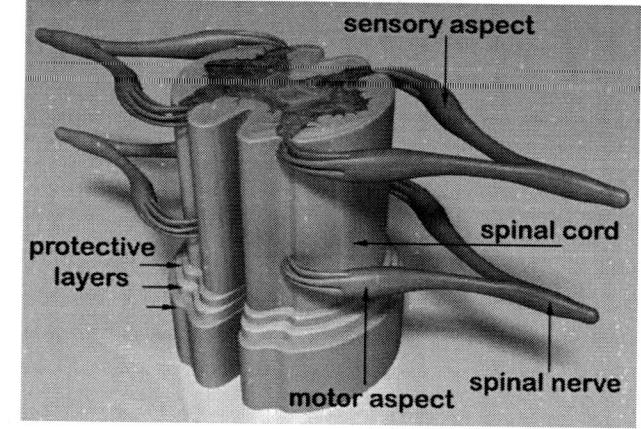

Figure 16. The sensory and motor aspects of spinal nerves.

Previously, we discussed how the brain performs sensation through sensory cranial nerves and sensory spinal nerves; however, the brain *initiates behaviors* (our actions) through different types of cranial nerves called **motor** cranial nerves. A motor function of a cranial nerve is to *activate* parts of the body involved in our behaviors. So, for example, a cranial motor nerve helps us move our eyes. Another motor cranial nerve helps us move our head, and so on (see the list below for more details). Focus now on motor cranial nerves only. The vast majority of the motor cranial nerves originate from the brainstem too (just like sensory cranial nerves). Below is a list of motor cranial nerves and their functions (you are only responsible for the functions; no need to memorize names since you will forget them the day after testing):

Oculomotor nerves (III) – synchronize movement of the right and left eye (this synchronization avoids double vision); facilitate pupillary enlargement and the accommodation reflex (focusing on near or distant objects); influence an eye to look up, down and diagonally, influence the upper eyelid to go up

Trochlear nerves (IV) – move eyes down and to the side and synchronize movement of the right and left eye

Trigeminal nerves (V) – move jaw for chewing (mastication)

Abducens nerves (VI) – move eyes to the side and synchronize movement of the right and left eye

Facial nerves (VII)

- move muscles of facial expression

- stimulate the secretion of tears (they flow down onto the eye surface) from the lacrimal gland

- stimulate secretions from glands in the nasal cavity

- stimulate salivation from salivary glands in the mouth

Glossopharyngeal Nerves (IX)

- control muscles that stimulate swallowing

- control salivation of the salivary gland of the cheek (parotid gland)

Vagus nerves (X)

- control muscles, stimulating swallowing

- control muscles stimulating the function of lungs, heart and digestive system

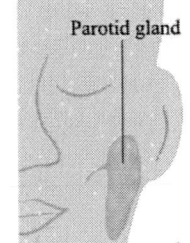

Figure 17. The location of the salivary gland.

- stimulate voluntary swallowing by controlling muscles of the soft palate and muscles of the pharynx

- stimulate movement of the muscles of the larynx/vocal cords (for sound production)

Spinal Accessory nerves (XI)

- stimulate movement of the muscles of the neck (so it can turn)

- stimulate movement of the muscles of the upper back (so that the upper back can move)

- stimulate voluntary swallowing by controlling muscles of the soft palate and muscles of the pharynx

- stimulate movement of the muscles of the larynx/vocal cords (for sound production)

Hypoglossal nerves (XII) – stimulate voluntary movements of the tongue.

You probably noticed from the text above, that *some* cranial nerves that have sensory function *also* have motor function. These cranial nerves are called **mixed nerves** since they have both sensory *and* motor function. Those cranial nerves are Trigeminal, Facial, Vagus and Glossopharyngeal, but you don't need to know their names for testing purposes (Martini et al., 2012).

THE BRAIN AND BEHAVIORS: SPINAL MOTOR NERVES

The brain influences the **initiation** (triggering or starting) of our behaviors (running, for example), by working in unison with the spinal cord. For example, when you decide to run, that decision (the information) travels from your brain, through the spinal cord. From there, the information continues to travel through the cord's *spinal* motor nerves, and these nerves branch out and **innervate** (supply or connect to) your leg muscles, activating the muscles, which move your legs. Spinal nerves are (like cranial nerves) classified as the peripheral nervous system (even though they originate from the central nervous system) (Martini et al., 2012). We mentioned that certain "information" travels through the nervous system. What kind of information are we talking about? It is definitely not miniature letters carried by cute little elves running fast and sweating through our nervous system. The "information" is a complex *message* composed of *electricity* and *chemistry*, but more about that later in chapter four when we examine the functioning of a single cell of the nervous system.

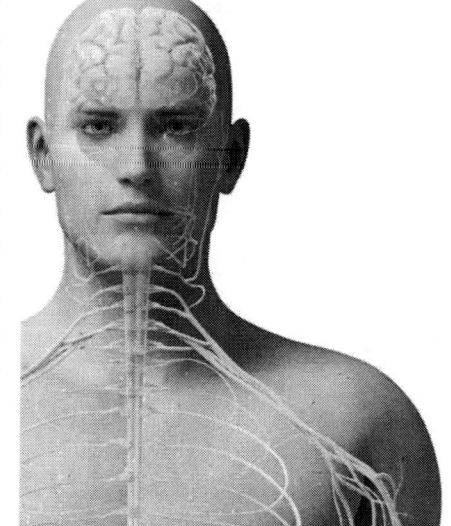

Figure 18. Spinal motor nerves innervating arm muscles.

The brain also influences *physiological* (or bodily) *processes*, such as breathing, heart rate, rapid-eye movements (indicating dreaming during sleep), and others. An important characteristic of these physiological processes is that they happen **involuntarily**, without our will to initiate them. The involuntary information (to control breathing, for example) is created in the brain (below our awareness), then that message travels to the spinal cord, to its spinal motor nerves, and through those nerves to the organs that perform breathing. However, there are physiological processes that we can influence; for instance, we can stop breathing for some time. We can also expose ourselves to erotic stimuli, which will likely produce an erection or vaginal lubrication. If we concentrate on a task very hard, our brain activity will increase in the prefrontal cortex (mainly in that region) and will reflect that heightened concentration.

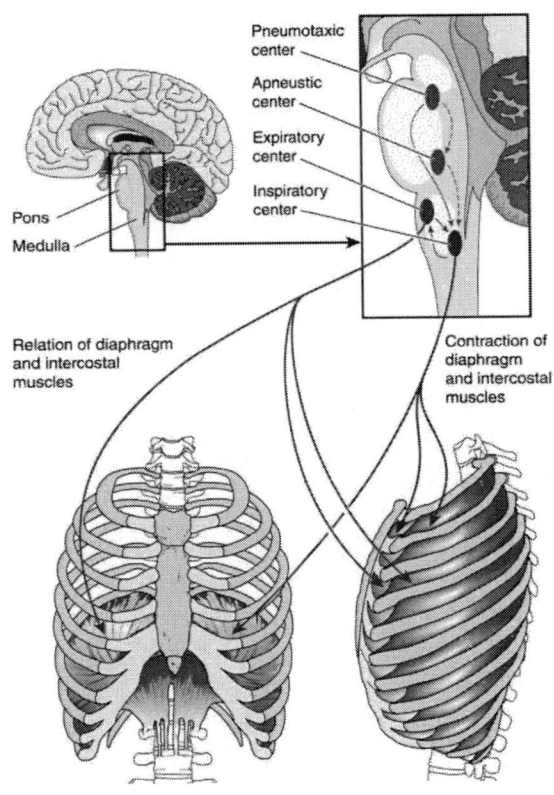

Figure 19. The brainstem innervations of the diaphragm and the intercostal muscles.

The brainstem regions of pons and medulla control breathing. These regions (through a network of neurons) connect with and activate certain spinal nerves. These nerves innervate and activate the muscles of the diaphragm and the muscles between the ribs. Contraction of the diaphragm muscles increases the volume of the thoracic cavity (where the lungs are), and the movements of the rib muscles allow the expansion (inhaling) and contraction (exhaling) of the ribs (Martini et al., 2012; Marieb & Hoehn, 2013).

THE BRAIN AND THE PHYSIOLOGICAL PROCESSES: HEART ACTIVITY

There is a certain region in the *brain stem* that influences heartbeat, specifically to slow it down (when we are relaxed, for example). The brainstem region sends a motor *cranial* nerve (Vagus nerve) to the heart to make it beat slower. The spinal cord also sends its motor *spinal* nerves to the heart to make it beat faster when we are under stress, for example. (Sherwood, 2004).

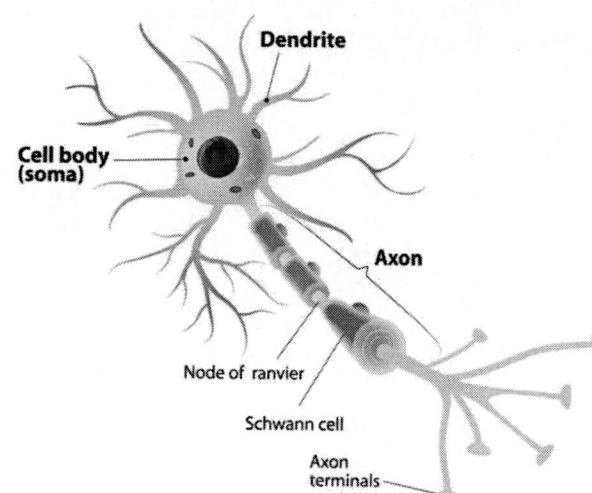

Figure 20. A Neuron and its parts.

A **neuron** is a cell, and it is a basic unit of the nervous system. Focus on the *cell body* and then on the *axon*. Those two terms will be mentioned very soon, so you should be able to visualize them. The **white matter** is a portion of the spinal cord comprised mostly of axons, and the **gray matter** is the butterfly shaped portion containing predominantly cell bodies.

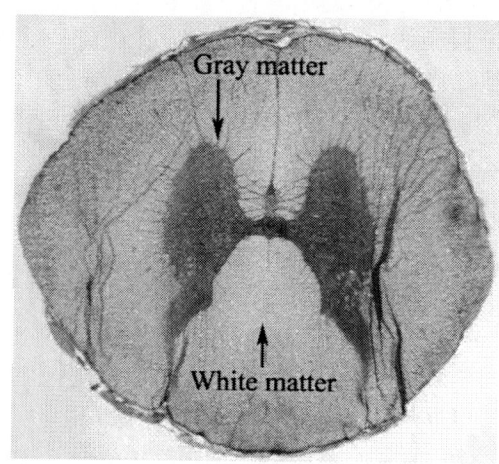

Figure 21. A cross-section of the spinal cord.

Spinal nerves are located on both sides of the spinal cord. These nerves are *mixed*, meaning they are sensory and motor. The motor function is realized through the **ventral** (facing the stomach) **root** of the spinal nerve, and the sensory function through the **dorsal** (facing the back) **root** of the spinal nerve. Hence, the ventral root is closer to the stomach than to the back, and the dorsal root is closer to the back than to the stomach (Breedlowe, 2007).

Dorsal root – is composed of a bundle of many *axons* dedicated to performing sensory function. When these axons leave the spinal cord, they spread to innervate organs and tissues

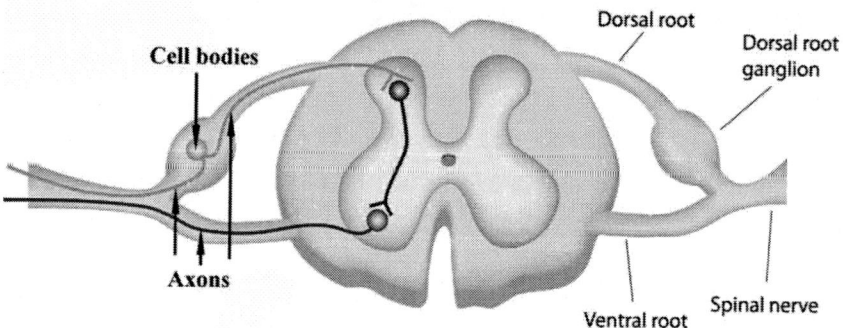

Figure 22. The ventral and dorsal roots and their basic structure.

(like the skin on the arm) *receiving* the information from those organs and tissues (somebody touches you on the leg, for example, and you sense that touch through the dorsal root). The information (that someone touched you on the leg) then travels (through spinal nerves) back to the spinal cord. From there, the spinal cord sends that information (through the network of neurons) to the brain, where the brain processes the collected information and gives us the experience of sensation. Without the brain's involvement, however, that information never becomes our conscious experience, such as "somebody touched me." (Marieb & Hoehn, 2013; Martini et al., 2012).

Dorsal root ganglion – is a *bulge* in the dorsal root. The *ganglion* (bulge) contains *cell bodies* that give rise to axons. These axons make up the spinal nerve (see figure 23) composed of axons, some *myelinated* (contain a fatty substance called myelin) and some unmyelinated (do not contain any myelin). The difference between the myelinated and the unmyelinated axons will be discussed in chapter four. Cell bodies (in the dorsal root ganglion) send their axons to the gray matter in the spinal cord, communicating there with *sensory* cell bodies (see figure 24). From there, the information travels (via connecting neurons) to the brain. The ganglion's sensory cell bodies also communicate with the spinal cord's *motor* cell bodies that send their motor axons (via the ventral root) to *organs* stimulating these organs' activities. The motor cell bodies also send their axons (via the ventral root) to stimulate *muscles* that are involved in movements of our body. As mentioned earlier, from the dorsal root ganglion, sensory axons are directed *towards* the spinal cord. However, from the dorsal root ganglion, sensory axons are *also* directed to go in the opposite direction of the spinal cord to innervate organs and tissues so that these axons can *receive* the sensory information.

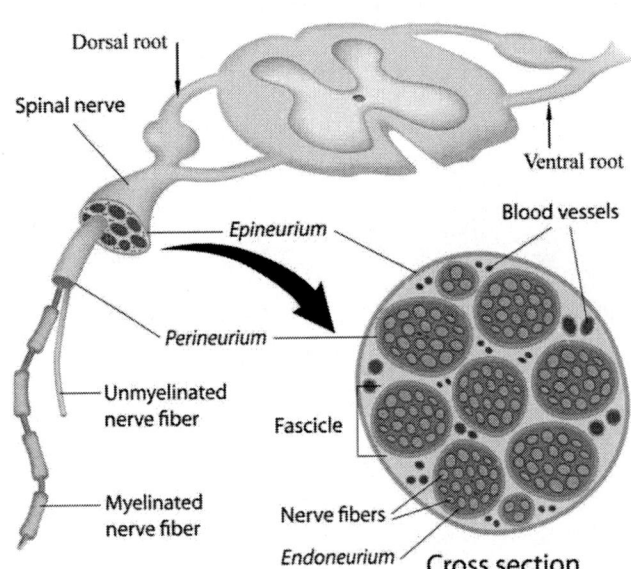

Figure 23. The anatomy of the spinal nerve.

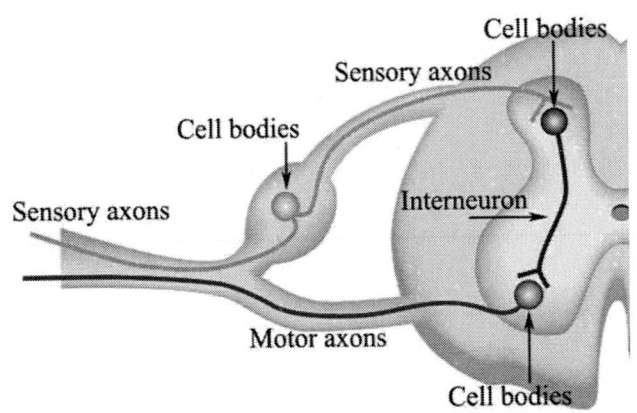

Figure 24. Sensory and motor components of the spinal nerves.

Ventral root – is a collection of axons bundled together, but that bundle specializes in *motor* function. Those axons go from the spinal cord to other tissues and organs in the body stimulating their activity. The dorsal and ventral aspects of the spinal nerve work together. When, say, a bug bites you on your thigh, that sensory information travels through axons to the cell bodies of the dorsal root, then the information is passed to the cells in the spinal cord, and from there the message is transmitted through the ventral root to the muscles to move the leg, to shake off the bug (Marieb & Hoehn, 2013; Martini et al., 2012).

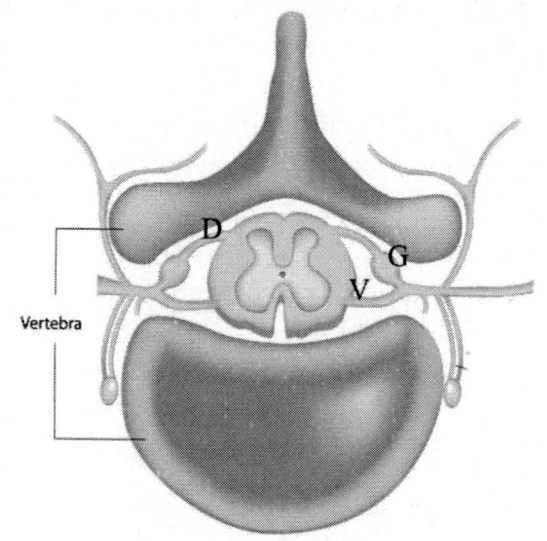

Figure 25. D: dorsal root, V: ventral root, and G: dorsal root ganglion.

NERVES OF THE PERIPHERAL NERVOUS SYSTEM

The peripheral nervous system is composed of **nerves**. These fibers originate from the central nervous system: from the brain stem (cranial nerves), and from the spinal cord (spinal nerves). Even though nerves originate from the central nervous system, they spread towards the periphery of the body (away from the center), and that's why the nerves comprise the peripheral nervous system. A nerve is a structure that contains bundles of axons. Each bundle contains many axons (thousands!). There are blood vessels near these bundles of axons. The blood is the source of nutrients for the axons since the blood contains various nutrients for the axons and other parts of the cell (Martini et al., 2012; Marieb & Hoehn, 2013). In the peripheral nervous system, bundles of axons are called a nerve; however, in the central nervous system, bundles of axons are called a **tract**. A cluster of *cell bodies* in the central nervous system is called a **nucleus** (remember the caudate and putamen nuclei). However, a cluster of cell bodies in the *peripheral* nervous system is called a **ganglion** (remember the dorsal root ganglion from this chapter) (Pinel, 2014).

THE DIVISION OF THE PERIPHERAL NERVOUS SYSTEM

The peripheral nervous system is composed of the following:

- o motor aspect
  - composed of the somatic system and the autonomic system

- o sensory aspect
  - composed of the somatic system and the autonomic system.

The motor aspect of the peripheral system contains the **somatic system**. This system *mainly* allows our **voluntary** behavior, meaning we can make a conscious decision to produce that behavior at will. This behavior is directed towards our environment. Our behaviors consist of the movement of our body parts. We move parts of our body (arms, legs, neck, trunk, fingers, eyes, etc.) with the help of our *muscles*. Specifically, when those muscles contract, that *contraction* produces movement. When the muscles *relax*, however, that stops the movement and behavior. Muscles that allow the *voluntary* movement of various parts of our body are attached to the bones of our skeleton. These muscles are called *skeletal*. Thus, the somatic system within the peripheral motor part is also called the *skeletal system*. The skeletal muscles attach to the skeleton via *tendons* (a type of tough tissue). Tendons attach the muscle to the bone (Martini et al., 2012).

Recall high-octane scenes from your favorite action movie. You probably remember a lot of voluntary movement in the video: moving arms, hands, legs, facial features (grimacing), and other forms of movement. All that movement is based on certain changes affecting the muscles that supply the skeleton of arms, legs, face and other parts of the body. That change is a **contraction** (shortening) of a muscle. That contraction is the key to understanding how muscles and movements work. Muscles have two states of existence, *contraction* and *relaxation*. Some muscles, when they contract, pull the tendon; the tendon pulls the bone and the **flexion** (bending) of the body part is performed. When other muscles contract, they pull the tendon, the tendon pulls the bone and the **extension** (stretching out) of the body part is performed (Martini et al., 2012).

When a voluntary movement happens, then **antagonistic** (opposing) muscles are at work at the same time. While one muscle contracts creating flexion, at the same time, the other muscle relaxes. That principle of voluntary movement through *muscular antagonism* exists throughout our bodies. In addition to flexion and extension of a body part, the muscles (through their contraction) also perform *rotation* of a body part by relying on the same mechanism that we mentioned earlier: muscles contract and pull tendons, the tendons pull the bones, and the rotation of the body part happens (Martini et al., 2012).

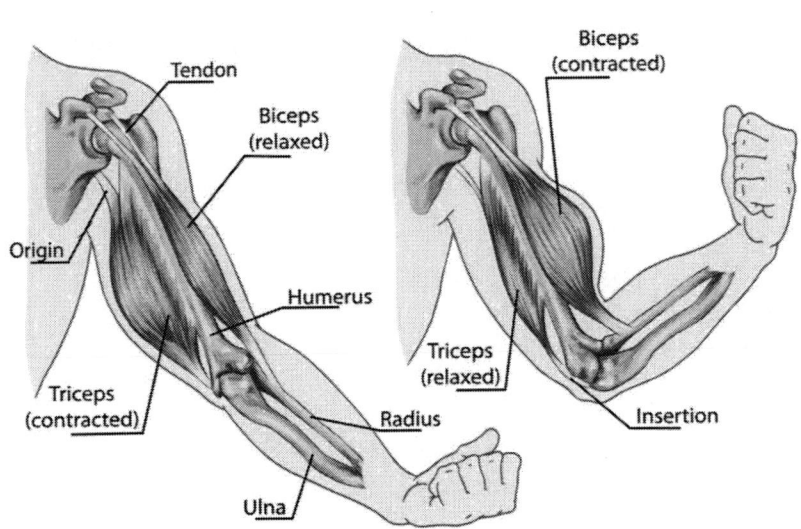

Figure 26. When the triceps contract, the biceps relax. This causes the arm to extend. Alternately, when the biceps contract, the triceps relax. This causes the arm to flex.

But how does the muscular contraction even happen? What is causing it? The answer is nerves are causing the muscular contraction. The somatic system innervates (through nerves) skeletal muscles. Motor nerves of the somatic system stimulate the skeletal muscles to contract, and by doing so, we can engage in voluntary behavior. When motor nerves of the somatic peripheral nervous system are not stimulating skeletal muscles, then muscles relax and our movement stops.

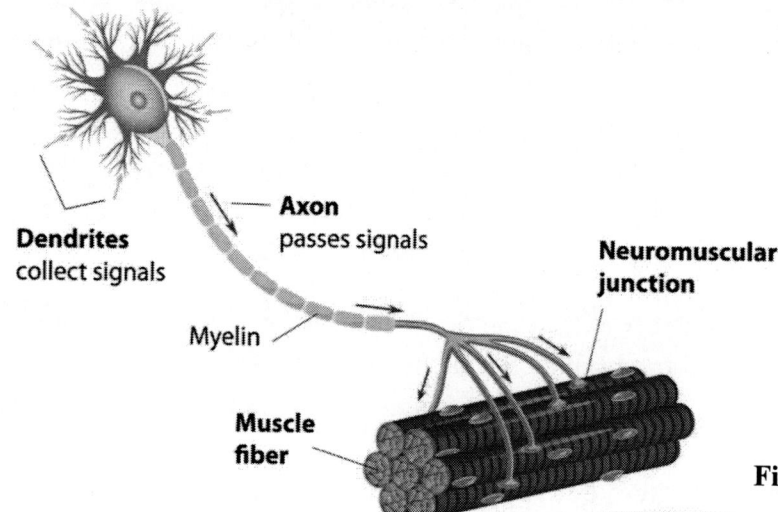

The connection between the nerves and the muscles is called a **neuro-muscular junction**. There is a large number of neuro-muscular junctions between the cranial nerves and the skeletal muscles and between the spinal nerves and the skeletal muscles (Martini et al., 2012).

Figure 27. A neuromuscular junction.

THE PERIPHERAL SYSTEM'S MOTOR ASPECT: SOMATIC SYSTEM AND REFLEXES

So far, we have said that the somatic system controls our voluntary behavior. But, there is an exception—this system also controls **reflexes,** which are **involuntary** behaviors (that happen automatically). These reflexes are produced by skeletal muscles innervated by somatic peripheral nerves.

A **reflex arc** is a mechanism that involves a *presentation* of a stimulus, a *reception* (through a *sensory* nerve) of that stimulus, and a *transmission* of that stimulus via a sensory nerve to the spinal cord. From the spinal cord, the received message about the stimulus is passed onto the *motor* nerve originating in the spinal cord. These motor nerves innervate various body parts allowing those body parts to *move* in response to the stimulus. For example, when something (a *stimulus* like a mallet) taps one's knee area, that person's leg-extension *response* happens almost immediately, due to that knee-tap stimulus. Think of reflexes as **stimulus-response** relationships. In between sensory and motor

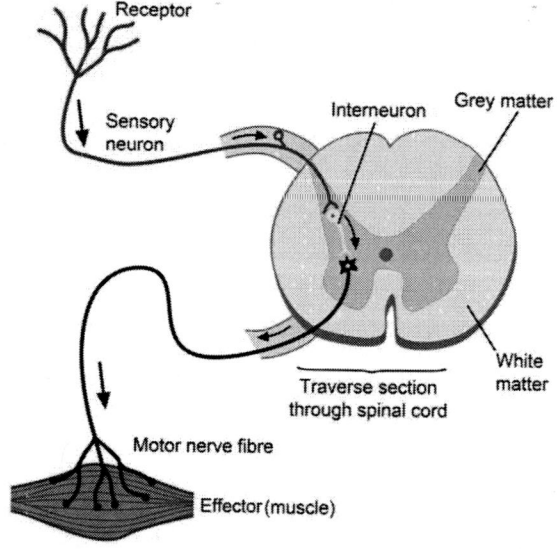

Figure 28. Reflex arc.

110

neurons are usually interneurons (association neurons) connecting them. The reflex arc is a story of a communication between the *somatic sensory part* (of the peripheral system) and the *somatic motor part* (of the same system) (Martini et al., 2012).

THE PERIPHERAL SYSTEM: SENSORY ASPECT AND ITS SOMATIC SYSTEM

Our sensations (pain, for example) from muscles, tendons and joints (all involved in voluntary behaviors), begin as the information *received* by sensory nerves connected to those body parts. These nerves are a part of the somatic sensory system. The information is passed through those nerves to the spinal cord, and from there to the brain. In the brain, the information is transformed into our awareness of sensations (for example, pain) in our muscles, tendons and joints. Skin, the largest sensory organ, is innervated by the somatic spinal nerves. The somatic nerves also innervate *sensory* organs such as eyes, tongue, ears and nasal cavities. These innervations are accomplished through cranial nerves. (Kalat, 2013).

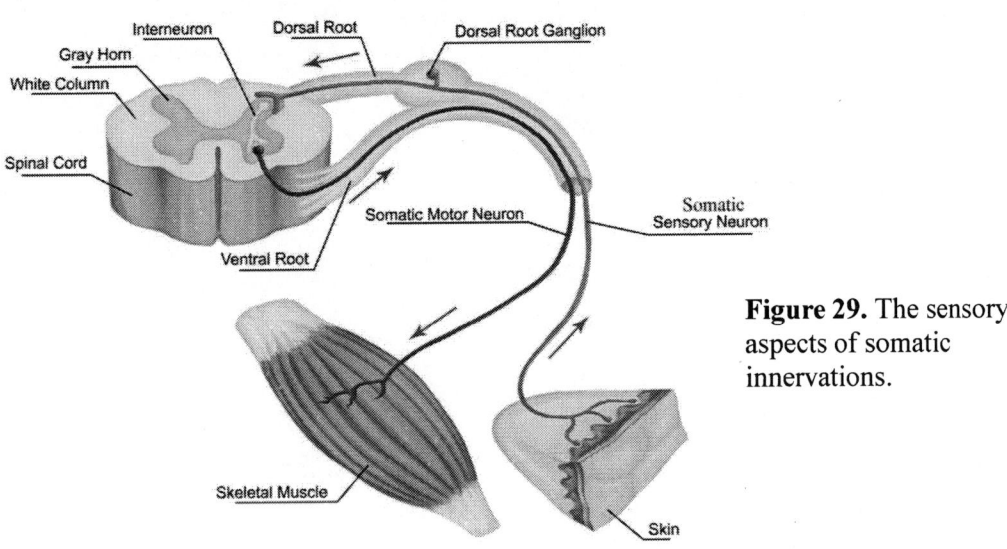

Figure 29. The sensory aspects of somatic innervations.

THE PERIPHERAL SYSTEM: MOTOR ASPECT AND ITS AUTONOMIC SYSTEM

The motor aspect of the peripheral system contains the *autonomic* system. The autonomic system is also called the "visceral system" since its nerves innervate many of our **internal** (or visceral) organs, such as the larynx, trachea, lungs, heart, liver, pancreas, spleen, stomach, small and large intestines, glands (sweat, salivary, adrenal), kidneys, urinary bladder, blood vessels, portions of the eye (that control pupil enlargement, pupil constriction, and accommodation of the lens), gallbladder, rectum, uterus, fallopian tubes, ovaries, prostate gland, seminal gland and genitals (involved in orgasm, erection and vaginal lubrication) (Martini et al., 2012; Marieb & Hoehn, 2013).

Most of the above-mentioned visceral organs contain **smooth** muscles. Unique to the heart is the **cardiac** muscle. Glands (like ovaries, testicles, prostate, seminal vesicles) contain **glandular epithelium** (a sheet of cells). The autonomic nerves innervate smooth and cardiac muscles (via neuro-muscular junctions) and the glandular epithelium (via neuro-glandural junctions). The autonomic system also innervates skin stimulating the sweating response. The autonomic system uses its *motor* nerves to stimulate the functioning of the already-mentioned organs. So, the motor function of the autonomic system is to *stimulate* the functioning of the organs, but also to reduce or even block these organs'

activity. The visceral parts of our body function on an **involuntary** basis, meaning even if we don't think of those body parts, they still operate beyond our awareness (Martini et al., 2012; Marieb and Hoehn, 2013).

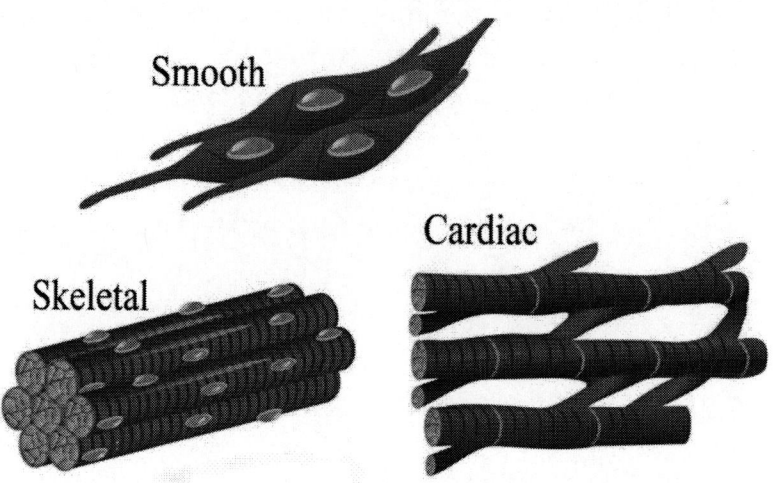

Figure 30. Three types of muscles.

The autonomic system has two motor sub-systems: the sympathetic system and the parasympathetic system. The sympathetic system helps the body respond to stressful or exciting situations. Dealing with stressful situations is realized through *running away* from it or by *confronting* it (called **fight or flight** response). Both situations (stressful and exciting) are termed *arousing* in psychology. The sympathetic system innervates various body parts stimulating their activity. By doing so, it performs the following functions:

- widening (or dilating) pupils so that we get more light and have better vision

- increasing heart rate (the heart pumps faster) and increasing heart contraction. These increases bring more oxygen and glucose (a carbohydrate) to the cells of the body parts so that they can work optimally

- widening (vasodialation) of blood vessels in the heart and of the blood vessels in the skeletal muscles throughout the body. This vasodilation increases the blood flow to those parts of the body so that they can respond quickly to the demands of the situation

- narrowing (vasoconstriction) of blood vessels in parts of the body that are not critical for an arousing situation (such as the digestive organs and kidneys). This vasoconstriction

112

reduces the blood flow to those parts of the body. This reduction results in decreased activity of those parts of the body

- decreasing digestion by constricting the muscles that control the movement of food forward

- increasing respiration (or breathing) by dilating the respiratory airways so that air that moves in and out encounters less resistance. In this way, the optimal amount of oxygen (from the air) moves to the body parts that are significant for the arousing situation

- inhibiting (preventing) the emptying of the bladder. This is accomplished by constricting a muscle (internal urethral sphincter) that controls the urine flow through the urethra (a cylinder that leaves the bladder, taking the urine out through the process of urination). When the muscle is constricted, the urine flow (through the urethra) cannot happen. The external urethral sphincter, however, is controlled voluntarily by the somatic spinal nerves, which means that one can decide not to urinate and delay the urination in that voluntary way

- inhibiting defecation by constricting the anal muscles

- stimulating liver processes to create glucose and fat, both of which are fuels for cells. After being created, glucose and fat are deposited into the bloodstream, reaching cells involved in responding to the arousing situation, such as the muscle cells involved in movement and brain cells

- inhibiting the pancreas to secrete the hormone insulin. Since insulin removes glucose from blood, this inhibition of insulin allows glucose to stay in the blood

- stimulating a small amount of salivation from the salivary glands in the mouth. The amount is significantly smaller than the optimal amount during a non-arousing event; hence, some researchers perceive this stimulation as a sign of a reduction in salivation. Salivation helps digestion, a process not crucial for an arousing situation

- stimulating sweating (which refers to secretions from sweat glands) to cool down the body. Muscles work harder in arousing situations, so the body generates more heat. Sweating is triggered to counteract the overheating of the body. Overheating influences malfunctioning of the mechanisms regulating temperature. This further leads into an improper functioning of proteins, phospholipids and lipoproteins. The result is a collapse of the cardiovascular system, muscular system and other organs. Convulsions, coma, and in rare cases, even death can result

- increasing the blood pressure, via vasoconstriction, in some blood vessels. This process forces blood to organs that are significant for responding to an arousing situation, and it provides the sufficient flow of blood in case of blood loss (due to injuries, for example)

113

- stimulating the adrenal glands (there is one on top of each kidney) to release epinephrine and norepinephrine hormones. The role of epinephrine is to enhance the mentioned effects of the sympathetic system. Norepinephrine also enhances the sympathetic effect, but this hormone does not cover such a wide range of functions as epinephrine does. For example, norepinephrine is not involved in the dilation of respiratory airways

- stimulating ejaculation from penis and vaginal contractions (Martini et al., 2012; Marieb & Hoehn, 2013).

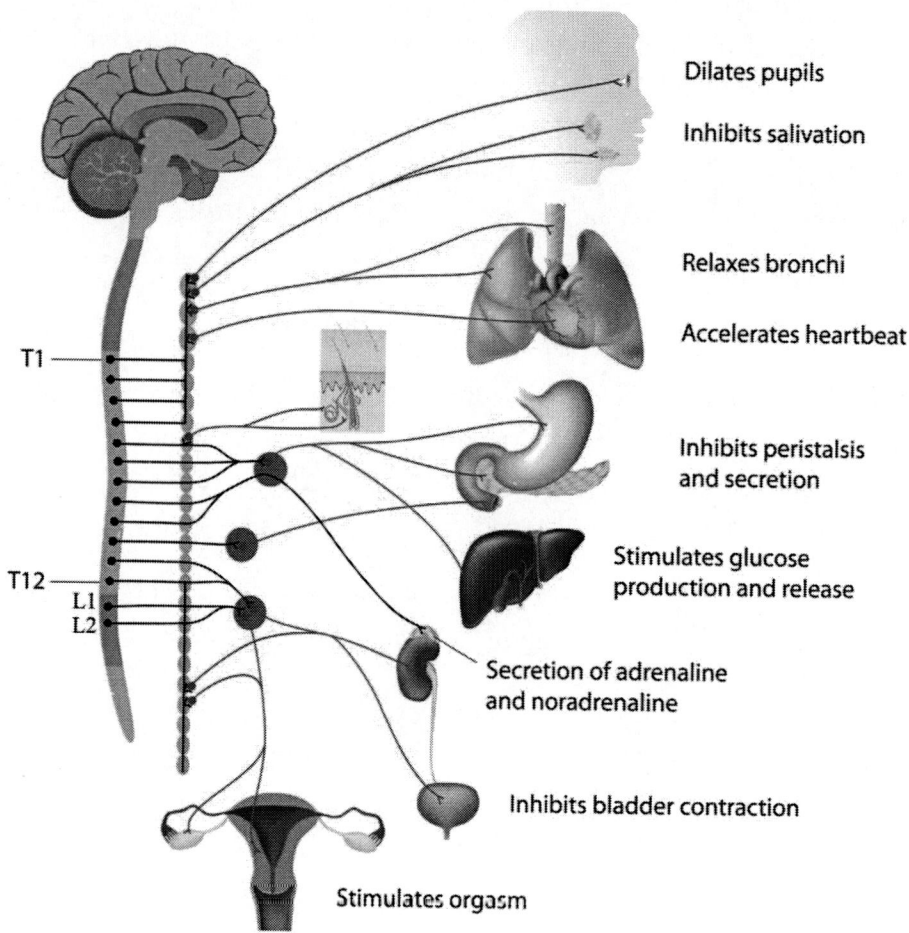

Figure 31. The Sympathetic system's innervations of various organs. Next to the spinal cord is a sympathetic chain—a long, vertical structure connecting sympathetic ganglia.

While the sympathetic system *energizes* the body to respond to an arousing situation, the parasympathetic system calms the body down when the arousing situation has passed. Also, the parasympathetic system is involved in the process of energy conservation so that the energy can be used in the future when the sympathetic system needs it to respond to an arousing situation. To accomplish the relaxing effect on the body's organs, the parasympathetic system facilitates the following:

- stimulates the narrowing (constriction) of the pupils, which reduces the amount of light that comes to eyes. In this way we get sufficient amounts of light for normal vision required for non-arousing situations. This pupillary constriction also influences focusing on close objects

- influences bulging of the lens, a process required for focusing on close objects

- stimulates lacrimal glands (located on top of our eyes) to produce tears important for lubrication and cleansing of eyes. Tears are also associated with emotional reactions.

- decreases heart rate (the heart pumps slower) in serene situations when there is no need for an increased action of the heart

- decreases the force of the heart contraction. The decrease in heart rate and the decrease in the force of heart contraction bring sufficient amounts of oxygen and glucose to the cells of the body parts that are facing a non-arousing situation.

- does not innervate skeletal muscles or tissues of the body wall.

- increases digestion of the digestive system. This process is done by nerves that stimulate the contractions of the muscles in the walls of the digestive tract. These contractions influence the movement of food through the digestive tract. Also, nerves stimulate glands of the digestive system to release hormones and enzymes (proteins) important for digestion. In non-arousing situations digestion is an important process (in arousing situations, however, digestion is not a priority)

- stimulates the pancreas to secrete insulin, a hormone that influences the removal of glucose from blood. In non-arousing situations, cells do not need the same amount of glucose as in arousing situations

- constricts the respiratory airways, which decreases respiration (breathing), so that there is sufficient airflow to accompany the mental state of relaxation

- stimulates bladder emptying by contracting the muscles in the wall of the bladder

- increases salivation from salivary glands in the mouth. Saliva contributes to the digestion process since it allows us to sense taste. Without sufficient amounts of saliva, food doesn't taste good or is tasteless! Food particles must be moistened by saliva so that they can be tasted by the tongue. Also, saliva contains proteins (enzymes) that break down carbohydrates (in food) in the mouth. In addition, saliva facilitates swallowing by moistening particles of food and providing a slippery environment; saliva also facilitates chewing

- influences mucous glands under the tongue to produce mucus important for coating food, which reduces friction and helps digestion

- increases vaginal lubrication, and stimulates penile and vaginal erection via vasodilation. No innervation of other blood vessels (Martini et al., 2012; Marieb and Hoehn, 2013).

THE PARASYMPATHETIC SYSTEM AND ITS ANATOMY

The parasympathetic system does have ganglia too, but it does *not* have a chain connecting its ganglia vertically as was the case with the sympathetic system. The ganglia of the parasympathetic system are located within the organs the system innervates (even though on the images ganglia are usually depicted outside organs). There are two locations from which the parasympathetic nerves originate: the *brain stem* (cranial nerves III, VII, IX and X) and the *sacral section* of the spinal cord. From these locations the nerves terminate in the ganglia, where these nerves communicate with the ganglias' cell bodies that send axons to innervate the tissues and organs. The oculomotor nerves (III) influence the smooth muscles of the eyes to initiate pupillary constriction and bulging of the lens. The facial nerves (VII) influence the tissue of the lacrimal glands to produce tears. Facial nerves also influence the secretions of the mucous and salivary glands.

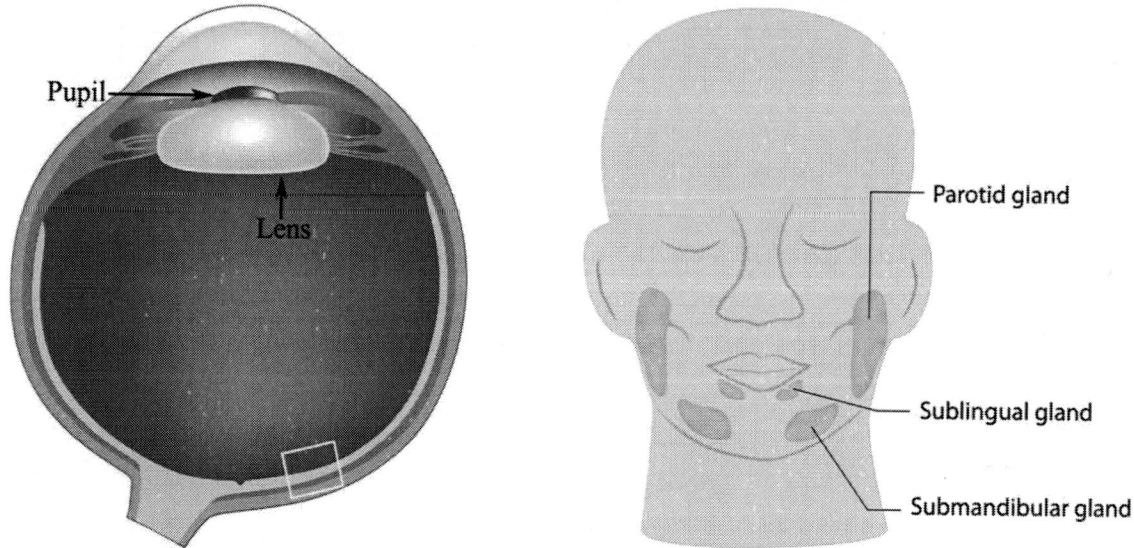

Figure 32. While the eye pupil is an opening, the lens is a structure.

Figure 33. Salivary glands.

116

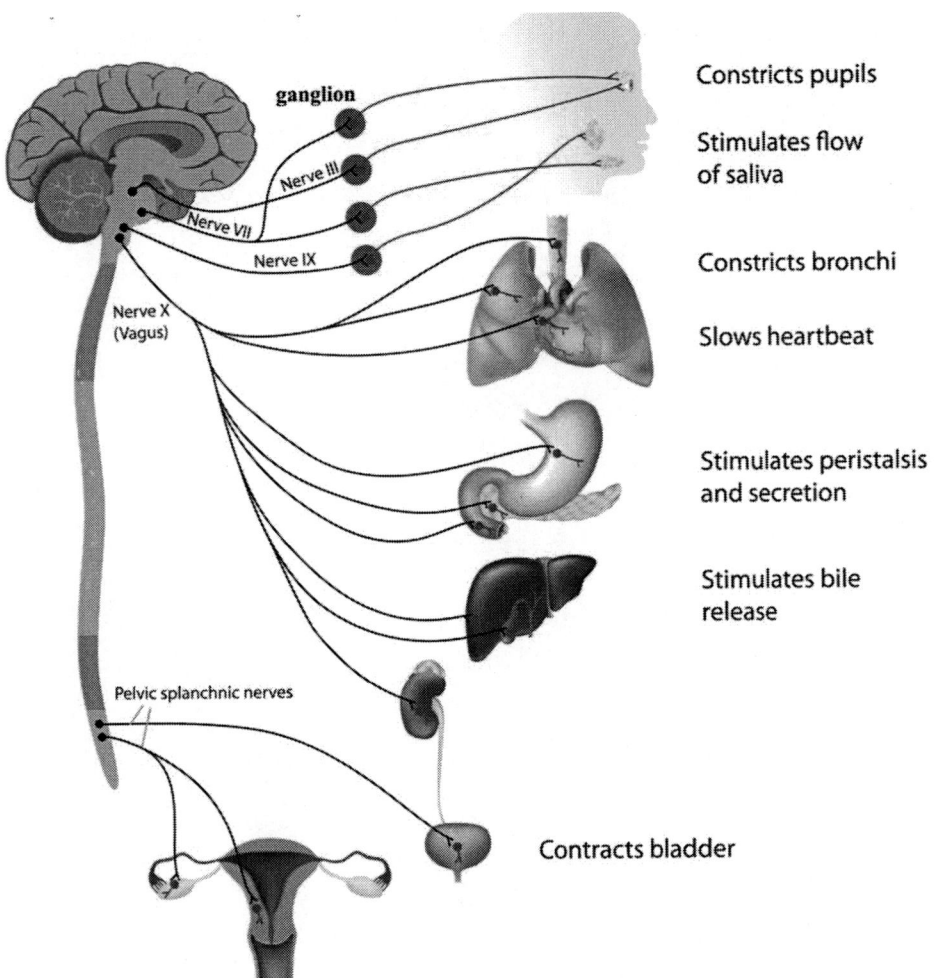

Figure 34. The parasympathetic system. Notice the absence of the chain of connected ganglia.

Glossopharyngeal nerves (IX) influence the parotid salivary glands, and vagus nerves (X) influence the activity of the organs such as heart, lungs, liver, gallbladder, stomach, pancreas, large and small intestine and rectum. The sacral spinal nerves connect with the ganglia, and their nerves stimulate the parasympathetic function of the urinary bladder and genitals (Martini et al., 2012; Marieb and Hoehn, 2013).

SYMPATHETIC AND PARASYMPATHETIC SYSTEMS ACT TOGETHER

Almost all organs that are innervated by the sympathetic system are also innervated by the parasympathetic system. These two systems should be perceived as harmoniously working together at any given moment to maintain the balance of our organism. The systems should not be seen as if they fight each other. Sweat glands, adrenal glands, muscles constricting blood vessels, and muscles that erect hairs of the skin have only sympathetic innervations (Martini et al., 2012; Marieb and Hoehn, 2013).

As you already learned, the peripheral system is composed of the sensory and motor aspects. The sensory aspect is composed of the somatic and autonomic systems. Through the *sensory* autonomic system, the brain receives the information about the functioning of the body parts that are innervated by the autonomic system's sensory spinal nerves and sensory cranial nerves. Once the sensory information about organs is collected by these nerves, the information is transmitted (via spinal and cranial nerves) to the brain, which analyzes that information and, on the basis of that analysis, makes decisions that influence the activity of the body parts (via motor spinal and cranial nerves) (Martini et al., 2012; Marieb and Hoehn, 2013).

For example, some people suffer from a condition in which their respiratory (breathing) system is not working properly. This disorder leads to an abnormal *decrease of oxygen* in the blood. The results are the following abnormalities: heart problems (irregular heartbeat and abnormally high blood pressure), headaches, fatigue, anxiety, and nightmares.

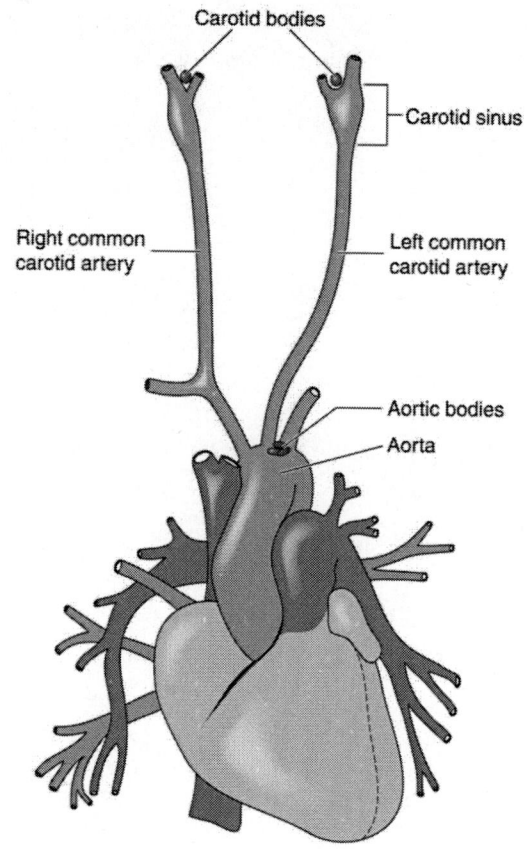

Figure 35. Chemoreceptors are located in aortic and carotid bodies.

How is a drop in oxygen detected? Through a mechanism that involves the sensory autonomic system. Specifically, the abnormal oxygen level in the blood is detected by the *chemoreceptors,* which are *sensory neurons* of the sensory autonomic system. Chemoreceptors are located in the *carotid bodies* within the carotid arteries. Carotid arteries are in the neck. Also, the receptors are in the *aortic bodies* within the aortic arch. The aortic arch is a part of the heart (Martini et al., 2012).

After detecting a drop in oxygen, the chemoreceptors send their messages (via cranial nerves IX and X) to the nuclei of medulla to influence the increase of oxygen delivery to the body through *peripheral vasoconstriction* (narrowing of the blood vessels), so that the flow of blood is increased (elevated blood pressure) in the body. In this way, more oxygen (in the blood) is being delivered to the body (including the brain). Also, the chemoreceptors stimulate (via cranial nerves) the medulla to influence an *increase in heart-rate* so that more blood (containing oxygen) circulates throughout the body providing nutrition for its parts (including the brain). These oxygen-increasing effects also occur when the chemoreceptors detect a *decrease in hydrogen ion* (an atom) *concentration* (called "pH level") and/or an *increase in carbon dioxide level* (CO_2) in blood. The information about the detected oxygen changes is passed from the chemoreceptors via cranial nerves to the medulla. The medulla contains its own chemoreceptors too. These sensory neurons detect, in the nearby cerebro-spinal fluid (CSF), the levels of carbon dioxide (CO_2) and the levels of hydrogen ion concentration ("pH level"). An increase in CSF's CO_2 levels and/or a decrease in CSF's pH level trigger a response in the medulla that increases the presence of oxygen in the body (Martini et al., 2012). Let's examine this response.

On the basis of the information (from the aortic and carotid chemoreceptors) regarding a drop in blood oxygen levels, a drop in blood hydrogen concentration, an increase in blood CO_2 level, and the medulla's own information regarding the CSF's increased level of CO_2 and/or a decrease in pH, the medulla sends messages through motor nerves to the lungs' and diaphragm's muscles. These motor messages stimulate the movement of the lungs and the diaphragm. The movement of these structures leads to an increased rate of lung inhalation, which brings more oxygen to the body. The movement of the aforementioned structures also leads to an increase in lung-volume during inhalation, which provides more oxygen to the body (Martini et al., 2012).

Going back to the story of experiencing a drop in oxygen, the brain is sometimes not powerful enough and can't fix the problem of oxygen deficiency, even though the already-mentioned mechanisms try to correct the problem. Once, however, the patient's breathing has improved, through a prescribed air-blower (a device that brings more oxygen to the respiratory system), there is, then, a sufficient level of oxygen in the blood, and the symptoms go away (Howard, 2006).

PERIPHERAL SYSTEM: DORSAL AND VENTRAL ASPECTS OF THE SPINAL NERVES

Now that you are familiar with the somatic and autonomic systems, let's also add this concept: each *ventral* aspect of a spinal nerve contains *motor autonomic* (visceral) axons and *motor somatic* axons. Each dorsal aspect of a spinal nerve, however, contains *sensory autonomic* (visceral) axons and *sensory somatic* axons (Sherwood, 2004; Martini et al., 2012).

PERIPHERAL SYSTEM: ITS DIVISION DEPENDS ON ONE'S PERSPECTIVE

Also, this is a good time to mention that the division of the peripheral system depends on one's perspective. For example, in this book (and some other books), the peripheral system is divided into sensory and motor aspects. Sensory is divided into somatic and autonomic, and the motor into somatic and autonomic. However, in other books, the peripheral system is divided into the somatic system and the autonomic system. Then, the somatic system is divided into its sensory and motor aspects. The autonomic system, too, is divided into its sensory and motor aspects (sympathetic and parasympathetic) (Pinel, 2014).

These differences in dividing the nervous system should be seen as an exercise in viewing the same thing (the peripheral system) from a different perspective. I am telling you this since when I was introduced to these differences, I was confused at first and thought that some books must be wrong. But then I realized that both divisions are just different perspectives, and that both are accurate.

REFERENCES

Breedlowe, M. S., Rosenzweig, M. R., & Watson, N. V. (2007). *Biological Psychology: An introduction to behavioral, cognitive and clinical neuroscience* (5th ed.). Sunderland, MA: Sinauer Associates, INC.

Carlson, N. R. (2013). *Physiology of Behavior* (9th ed.). Boston, MA: Allyn and Bacon.

Kalat, J. W. (2013). *Biological Psychology* (11th ed.). Belmont, CA: Wadsworth, Cengage Learning.

Kanal uporabnika malotuINmalotam. (2011, September 12). *Skrivnostna diagnoza - PANDAS in avtoimunski progesteronski dermatitis 1/3.* [Video file]. Retrieved from http://www.youtube.com/watch?v=H1MmASiMyeI.

Kanal uporabnika malotuINmalotam. (2011, September 12). *Skrivnostna diagnoza - PANDAS in avtoimunski progesteronski dermatitis 2/3.* [Video file]. Retrieved from http://www.youtube.com/watch?v=UvMLCRdJ-6o.

Lombroso, J. P., & Scahill, L. (2007). Tourette syndrome and obsessive-compulsive disorder. *Brain Development,* 30(4):231-237.

Marieb, E., & Hoehn, K. (2013). *Human anatomy and physiology* (9th ed.). Glenview, IL: Pearson Education.

Martini H. F., Nath, L. J., Bartholomew, F. E., & Ober, C. W. (2012). *Fundamentals of anatomy and physiology.* (9th ed.). San Francisco, CA: Pearson Benjamin Cummings.

Lohbauer, P. [Paul Lohbauer]. (2010, Nov 10). *Trigeminal neuralgia: Important things to know if you have facial pain-UF neurosurgery* [Video file]. Retrieved from https://www.youtube.com/watch?v=ypckUpTtXPs

Pinel, P. J. (2014). *Biopsychology* (9th ed.). Boston, MA: Pearson Education.

Sherwood, L. (2004). *Human physiology: From cells to systems* (5th ed.). Belmont, CA: Thompson Learning.

University of Bristol. (2010, Mar 03). *How the human brain works*. [Video file]. Retrieved from
  https://www.youtube.com/watch?v=9UukcdU258A.

Biological Psychology II

Chapter Four

You are probably asking yourself what the above heading has to do with biopsychology. When a person can't see the forest from the trees, it means that he or she is so focused on the particular (like individual trees), that the perception of a whole (the forest) escapes that person. Likewise, it is crucial to understand why we are going to explore the cell of the nervous system, which is something so particular, so seemingly insignificant, even microscopic. We must explore the cells since without cells, mental processes, behaviors and physiological processes, cannot exist. So, don't forget that we explore cells to see (understand) the entire "forest"-- the whole of the mental processes, behaviors and physiological processes.

A NEURON

A **neuron** (a cell within the nervous system) creates its own electricity. This electrical current (composed of moving atoms called **ions**) flows through the neuron reaching its end point. There, the electrical current influences the release of chemicals called **neurotransmitters**. These neurotransmitters bind to the nearby neuron, stimulating it to generate an electrical impulse. The electro-chemical activity travels via connecting neurons to the brain, where the brain *translates* this electro-chemical activity into our own subjective experience of a mental process (a memory or a wish, for example). Neurotransmitters also influence the functioning of our various organs and external behaviors (walking, for example) by binding to

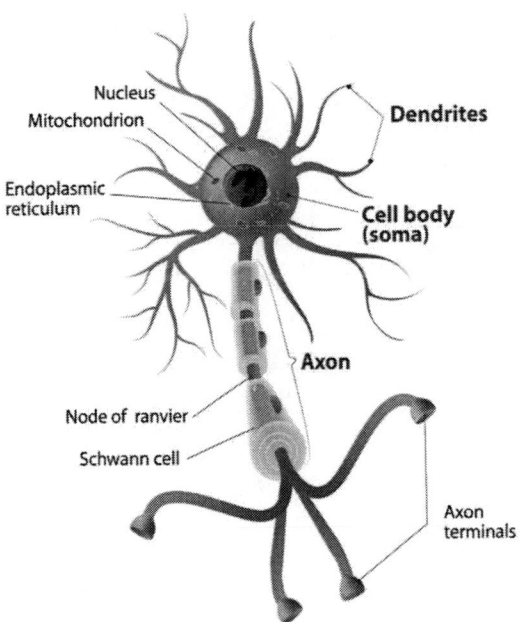

Figure 1. Neurons are the basic unit of the nervous system.

the muscles in the walls of the organs, to the muscles of our limbs and to the tissues of the glands. However, when the binding of the neurotransmitters is altered (blocked, increased or decreased), the mental processes, physiological processes and behaviors are affected, sometimes profoundly (as you will see throughout this book). Therefore, neuronal activity, such as the production and release of neurotransmitters, as well as the reception of the neurotransmitters, has a very significant influence on the mental, behavioral and physiological processes (Pinel, 2014; Kalat, 2013).

There are two types of cells within the nervous system—neurons and glial cells; we will first talk about neurons. A neuron is a *microscopic* structure. There are about 100-150 billion neurons in the brain (Breedlove, 2007), and about 1 billion neurons in the spinal cord (Kalat, 2013). For now, visualize the dendrites, cell body, axon and axon terminal since we will be talking about these components often. **Cytoplasm** refers to the neuron's content, which can be divided into the **cytosol** (a liquid) and **intracellular** (inside cell) structures (so called **organelles**) that perform certain cellular functions. The cytosol contains nutrients (sugars and amino acids), ions (atoms), proteins and waste products. A neuron is surrounded by a watery substance—**extracellular fluid**. The cytoplasm of an axon is called an **axoplasm** (Martini et al., 2012).

This communication among neurons depends a lot on **dendrites**, located on the cell body. Dendrites (from the Greek word "tree") are neuronal extensions specializing in receiving chemicals (or **neurotransmitters**) that are released from other neurons. Many neurons, thousands, can communicate with the dendrites of one neuron. Dendrites contain **receptors** (structures made of proteins) that receive the already-discussed chemicals from other neurons. Dendrites have outgrowths that are called **dendritic spines**, and these spines contain receptors too. The more dendritic spines a neuron has, the larger the area is for receiving chemicals from other neurons, so the dendritic spines enhance the communication among neurons (Martini et al., 2012). Axons communicate (or **synapse**) with the dendrites; thus, this type of communication is called **axon-dendritic**.

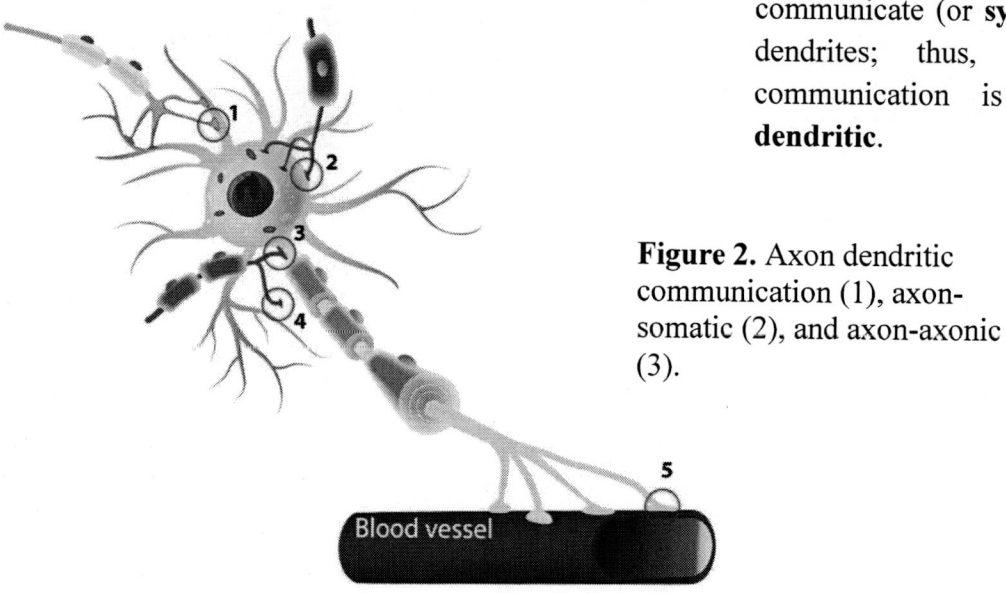

Figure 2. Axon dendritic communication (1), axon-somatic (2), and axon-axonic (3).

Neurotransmitters are released from one neuron onto the dendrites (onto their receptors, specifically) of another. Neurotransmitters are stored in **vesicles** (sacs) and released from the vesicles (located within the ending of a neuron) when the neuron to neuron communication occurs. Neurotransmitters cross the gap (**synaptic cleft** or a **synapse**) between neurons and move from presynaptic neuron (located before the synapse) to the postsynaptic neuron located after the synapse (Marieb & Hoehn, 2013).

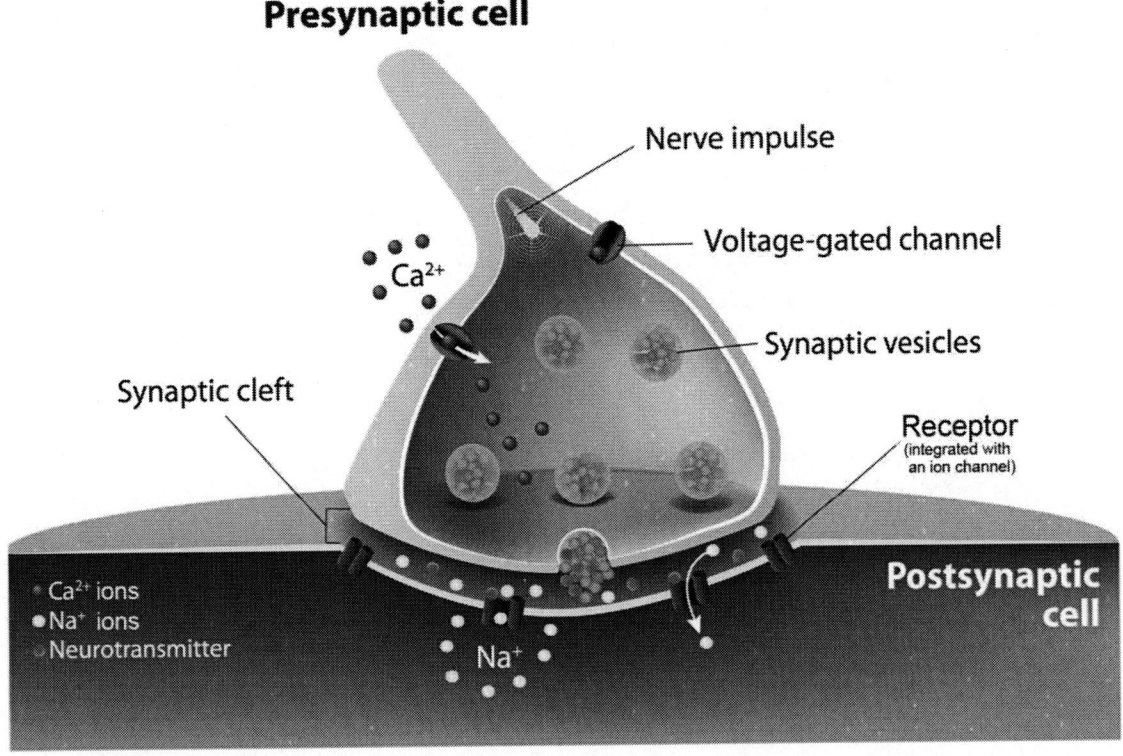

Figure 3. Vesicles of the presynaptic cell releasing neurotransmitters onto the receptors of the postsynaptic cell.

AXON

An axon is an elongated structure composed of the **axoplasm** (axon's cytoplasm) containing filaments, microtubules, vesicles, lysosomes, peroxisomes, mitochondria and enzymes. Axons usually do not contain the endoplasmic reticulum and Golgi apparatus. The axoplasm is surrounded by **axolemma**, which is the same neuronal membrane we have already discussed, but it is called axolemma in this case since it covers the axon. The axon conducts the electrical impulse towards the axon terminal, where the electrical impulse stimulates the release of the neurotransmitters. The axon also serves as a location where the neurotransmitters from other neurons can attach (specifically to the receptors on that axon), and by doing so they stimulate the creation of electricity in that axon. Some neurotransmitters from other neurons attach to the axon and can prevent the production of electricity in that axon. By doing so, these neurotransmitters make the axon inactive, rendering it unable to produce either electrical current or release its neurotransmitters (Martini, et al., 2012; Marieb & Hoehn, 2013).

An axon can be **myelinated** or **unmyelinated** (dendrites, however, are always unmyelinated!) Myelin is a substance composed of mostly fat and protein, and it is created by **Schwann** cells that reside in the Peripheral Nervous System (PNS). In the Central Nervous System (CNS), however, the myelin is created by cells called **oligodendrocytes**. A myelinated axon conducts the electrical current faster than the unmyelinated. Another role of the myelin is to provide a barrier (insulation) for the axon so that the electrical current from that particular axon doesn't leak. This leakage of the current (flow of ions) prevents the normal function of that particular neuron. Also, the insulation prevents the "spilling over" of the electrical current (ions) into another axon of another neuron since this spilling would cause disturbance in the conduction of electricity in that other neuron. The myelin sheath is not continuous; instead, it comes in segments—each segment is one Schwan cell or segment of an oligodendrocyte. Spaces between Schwann cells are called **Nodes of Ranvier**. These nodes are located on an axon where myelin does *not* exist (Martini, et al., 2012; Marieb & Hoehn, 2013).

A Schwann cell wraps around the axon, and by doing so, it creates the myelin. In the PNS, the myelin is a set of many Schwann cells lined up along the axon. The unmyelinated axons also have Schwann cells surrounding them, but the coiling (wrapping around the axon) is not present. The rotation around the axon, however, is crucial for the genesis of the myelin. Within the CNS, the myelin sheath is not created by Schwann cells; instead, myelin is created by oligodendrocytes in the CNS. In the CNS, a single oligodendrocyte cell creates the entire myelin sheath (all myelin segments) and not only for an axon of one neuron, but also for axons of different neurons. Nodes of Ranvier also exist in the breaks of the myelin sheath of the CNS. In axons that are not myelinated, oligodendrocytes do not cover a larger area of an axon, so that makes the axon unmyelinated too even though other parts of that same axon may still be covered by oligodendrocyte glial cells. Olygodendrocytes also provide structural support

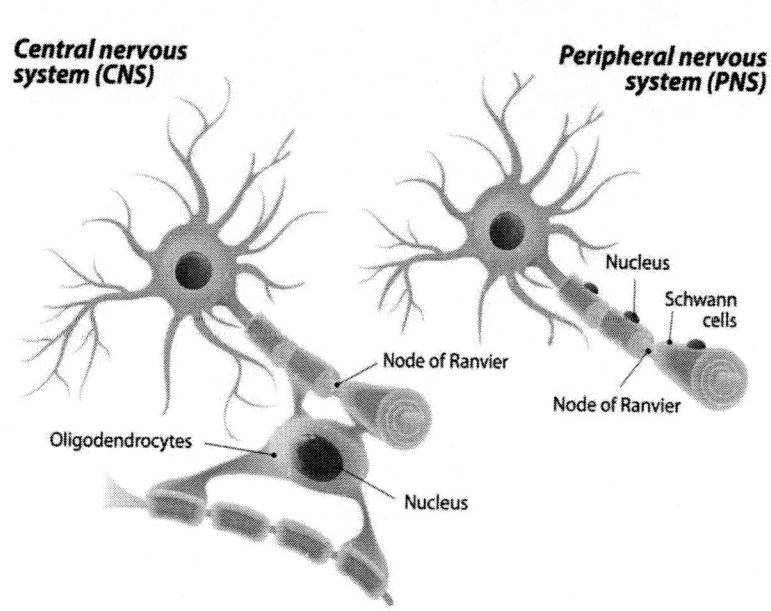

Figure 4. Schwann cells and oligodendrocytes during myelin production.

since they hold axons in place through the process of myelination (Martini, et al., 2012; Marieb & Hoehn, 2013).

Axons can grow an additional axon or more than one additional axon. An axon that arises from the main axon is called **axon collateral**. It usually arises at a 90 degree angle, from the Nodes of Ranvier (in myelinated axons), and the function of the collateral is to allow a neuron to have more communication (synapsing) with other cells (than when a neuron has only a single axon). After the myelin sheath ends, there is a point where the smaller branches start to arise. Those smaller branches are called **telodendria (axonal branches, terminal branches** or **terminal arborization,**— depending on what textbooks and journal articles you read). An axon can have thousands of telodendria (Martini, et al., 2012; Marieb & Hoehn, 2013).

Some neurotransmitters (many of them are made of an amino acids or a chainf of amino acids) are synthesized in the cell body, specifically on the ribosomes of the rough endoplasmic reticulum (RER). After their synthesis, the neurotransmitters are transported (via transport vesicles or round sacs) from the adjacent smooth endoplasmic reticulum (SER) into the nearby Golgi apparatus (GA) that refines them and packages them into secretory vesicles. These secretory vesicles, via *microtubules* (located throughout a neuron), eventually reach the farthest point of an axon which is called an **axon terminal**. This terminal is also called the **end button** or **synaptic knob, synaptic end-bulb** or **synaptic terminal**—depending on what textbooks and journal articles you read. Some neurotransmitters are synthesized in the *cell body*, but it is also true that in some neurons their neurotransmitters are synthesized in the *axon terminals*. These terminals contain ribosomes, ER and GA—important components for neurotransmitter synthesis. In *some* neurons, however, the axon terminal does not contain the endoplasmic reticulum (RER and SER); thus, that particular portion of those axons is not engaged in transmitte synthesis. Also, in *some* neurons that same part of the axon does not contain the GA either, so the packaging of these transmitters into vesicles does not

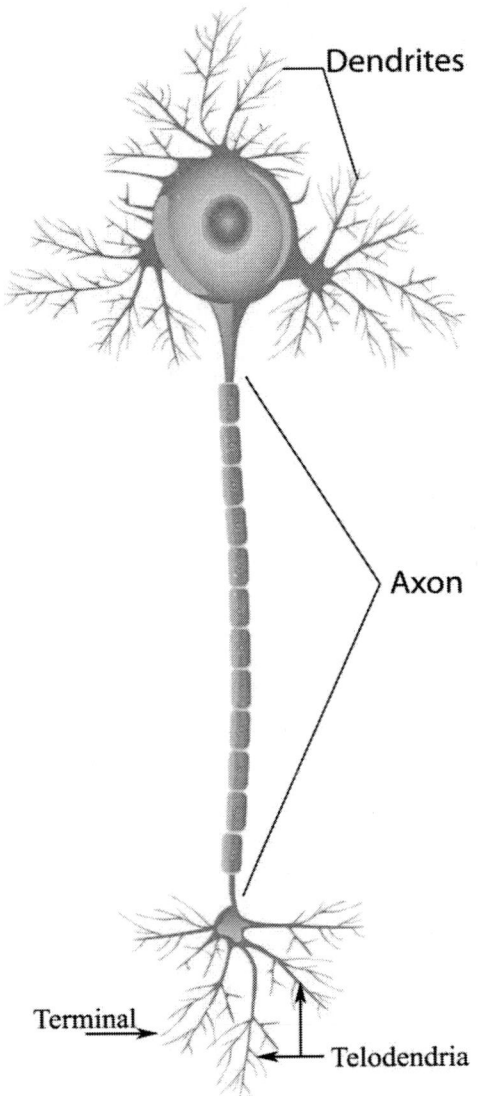

Figure 5. The axon terminal and telodendria. RER, ER, GA, ribosomes and microtubules are organelles (little organs) within neurons.

happen in that part of the axon. To compensate for the absence of the ER and GA, however, the neuron has microtubules, which allow transport of important substances from the cell body's ER and GA to the axon terminal. Microtubules are hollow cylindars made of proteins. It is easy to make a mistake and visualize vesicles moving through them; instead, the microtubular transport happens along the *surface* of these hollow structures (Marieb & Hoehn, 2013).

After neurotransmitters are released into the synapse, they attach to the receptors of a synapsing neuron. Shortly after, they *detach* from receptors, and synaptic enzymes break them down. Then, a mechanism in the axon terminal absorbs these neurotransmitter remnants back into the terminal. There, in the end buttons, the re-assembly of the neurotransmitters occurs. As you already know, the neurotransmitter creation happens on the ribosomes of RER (Martini at al., 2012; Marieb & Hoehn, 2013).

TYPES OF NEURONS (A ZOO OF DIVERSITY)

So far we have considered only one shape of a neuron; however, neurons come in different shapes and sizes. Especially interesting are **anaxonic** neurons since they are without an axon. These neurons don't need to have an axon since they are squeezed between two neurons. Anaxonic neurons transmit messages over very short distances (Martini, Nath & Bartholomew, 2013; Marieb & Hoehn, 2013).

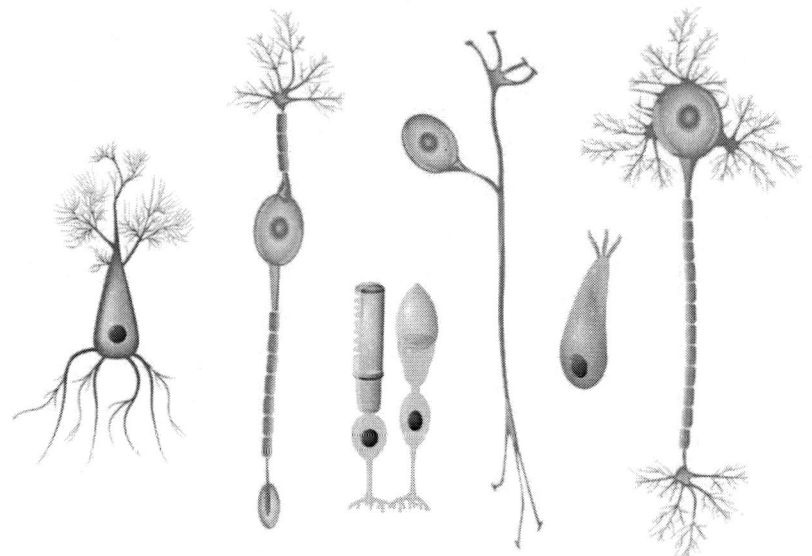

Figure 6. Neurons can come in different shapes.

MOTOR AND SENSORY SYNAPSES (CONNECTIONS)

There are different types of synapses that neurons can establish, such as a neuron activating or blocking another neuron, a neuron activating or blocking a muscle or a neuron activating or inhibiting a gland. A neuron can affect a skeletal muscle (in our limbs, for example), a smooth

128

muscle (in the walls of organs), the heart muscle and the tissue of a gland. These are all **motor** synapses, and neurons that are performing the activation or inhibition are motor neurons. Sensory neurons, on the other hand, *receive* the information from neurons, muscles, glandular tissue and sensory receptor cells. Receptor cells are still neurons, but some look very differently from neurons you have seen thus far. They are embedded in the sensory organs such as the tongue, skin, eyes, ears and nose. Sensory information eventually ends up in the spinal cord and is further transmitted (from one cell to another) to the brain so that we get an experience of that sensory information. In chapters eight and nine we examine these sensory receptors more closely. **The pre-synaptic neuron** is located *before* the synapse, and the **post-synaptic neuron** is located *after* the synapse. Is a pre-synaptic neuron a sensory or motor neuron if it receives sensory information and transmits that information to another neuron? Some books will still call that neuron a sensory neuron since it receives and passes on the sensory information. Other books, however, will label it a sensory neuron as long as it receives the sensory information, but it would be termed a motor neuron at the point of activating or inhibiting the next neuron (Martini et al., 2012; Marieb and Hoehn, 2013).

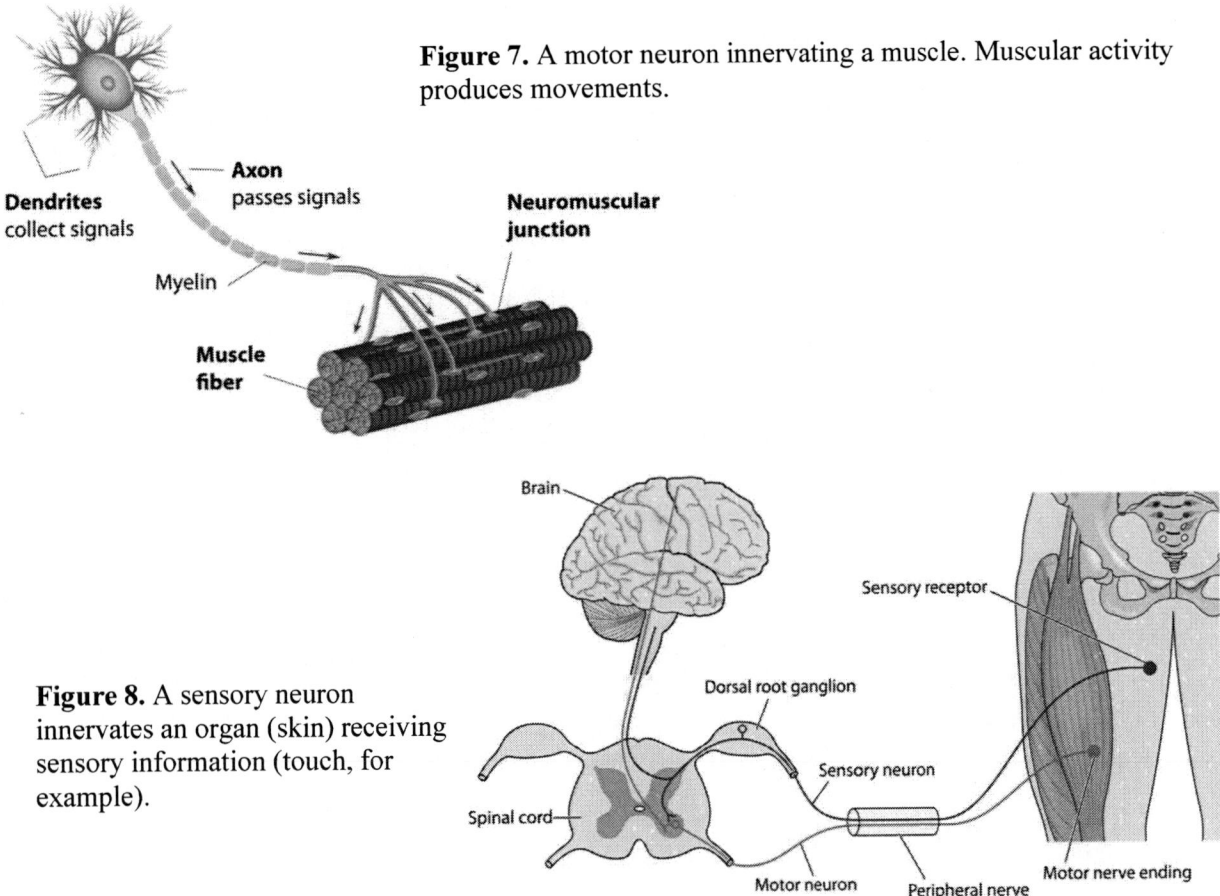

Figure 7. A motor neuron innervating a muscle. Muscular activity produces movements.

Dendrites collect signals

Axon passes signals

Myelin

Muscle fiber

Neuromuscular junction

Figure 8. A sensory neuron innervates an organ (skin) receiving sensory information (touch, for example).

Brain

Sensory receptor

Dorsal root ganglion

Sensory neuron

Spinal cord

Motor neuron

Peripheral nerve

Motor nerve ending

GLIAL CELLS

In addition to neurons, the nervous system contains **glial** cells, also called **neuroglia** or just **glia**. Glial cells also contain the cellular elements (mitochondria, nucleus, filaments, GA, ER, ribosomes, etc.) that we examined when we talked about neurons' **cytoarchitectonics,** which is cellular architecture. Glial cells have neither axons nor axon terminals. It seems that the glial cells and neurons are approximately equally represented in terms of their total number in the nervous system (Azevedo, 2009).

ASTROCYTES

Some glial cells look like stars, and that's why they are called **astrocytes** (translated from Latin, meaning "star cells"). Astrocytes are located in the *central* nervous system (Martini et al., 2012). Astrocytes perform functions like those listed below:

- Produce chemicals that neurons use for optimal functioning.

- Engage in the neurotransmitter **reuptake,** which is a process initiated by a neuron's presynaptic terminal that absorbs the neurotransmitters from the synaptic gap back into that terminal. Astrocytes are also involved in the **recycling** of neurotransmitters, a process that happens in the axon terminal of presynaptic neuron (Figley & Stroman, 2011).

- Connect to the blood capillaries, collecting glucose from blood, and breaking the glucose down into a chemical called lactate. Then, astrocytes release lactate into the extracellular fluid that surrounds neurons. These neurons take up the lactate and transport it to their mitochondria. The mitochondria transform lactate into neuronal energy used for executing all neuronal processes. Lactate is a fuel that neurons can process and use faster than glucose (Magistretti, Pellerin, Rothman & Shulman, 1999).

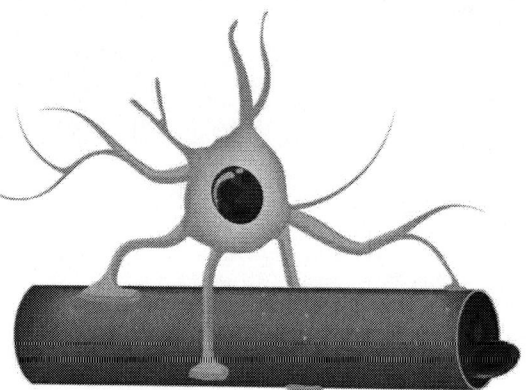

Figure 9. An astrocyte.

- Obtain **glycogen** (a carbohydrate) from the blood capillaries and break it down into glucose, which is further broken down into lactate. The breakdown of glycogen happens when neurons are very active, meaning they have a high *metabolic rate* (Brown & Ransom, 2007).

- Envelope synapses, isolating them. This synaptic isolation prevents the scattering of neurotransmitters so that these chemicals remain confined to a very particular synapse. Neurotransmitters can spillover from a synaptic cleft to neighboring synapses, where the neurotransmitters can stimulate or inhibit the post-synaptic neurons, interfering with the intended cellular communication. When there is a higher number of astrocytes isolating more synapses, the scattering occurs less, and the communication is improved. Fewer astrocytes means less isolation of synapses, and more communication errors, due to the scattering of neurotransmitters. Astrocytes modulate (increase or decrease) the synaptic activity through their ability to isolate more or fewer synapses (Piet, Vargova, Sykova, Poulain & Oliet, 2004).

- Create a scaffolding that holds neurons in place (Marieb & Hoehn, 2013).

- Assist olygodendrocytes (a type of a glial cell) in their creation of myelin. More specifically, when the electricity forms in neurons, it triggers a release of adenosine-three-phosphate (ATP). ATP causes astrocytes to secrete a protein (cytokine leukemia inhibitory factor or LIF) that stimulates the myelinating activity of oligodendrocytes (Ishibashi, Dankin, Stevens, Lee, Koslow, Stewart & Fields, 2006).

- Move throughout the central nervous system, locating dead neurons. Once astrocytes locate them, the dead neurons become engulfed by astrocytes digesting them. This process is called **phagocytosis** (phagein = to eat; kutos = cell) (Marieb & Hoehn, 2013).

- Divide when there are many dead neurons so that the division creates more astrocytes that can perform the phagocytosis of those neurons. After breaking down the dead neurons, astrocytes form scar tissue, walling off the area (Carlson, 2013).

- Control the amount of blood flow to different brain areas (Mulligan & Mac Vicar, 2004).

- Dilate blood vessels, bringing more nutrient-rich blood to highly-active brain areas (Filosa, Bonev, Straub, Meredith, Wilkerson & Aldrich, 2006).

- Eliminate dangerous levels of glutamate. High levels of glutamate release causes **neurotoxicity** (destruction of nervous system tissue). Astrocytes absorb and break down the excessive amount of glutamate (Kattenmann & Verkhratsky, 2011).

MICROGLIAL CELLS (OR MICROGLIA)

Microglia are the smallest type of glial cells in the *central* nervous system. With their extensions, they touch nearby neurons, monitoring their health. When microglial cells detect that neurons are not healthy, the microglia move towards those unhealthy neurons, engulfe them and phagocytize the neurons. The same process happens when microglia detect invading microorganisms (viruses, fungi, bacteria) in the nervous system—the organisms are engulfed and phagocytized. Many scientists consider microglia to be a part of the immune system that, with its army of cells (microglia being some of those cells), protects the health of the nervous system (Marieb & Hoehn,

2013). Microglia also release chemicals that destroy the unhealthy neurons and invade microorganisms. Many researchers believe that *excessive* production of these chemicals by microglia, may contribute to diseases, such as Alzheimer's, multiple sclerosis, stroke, and dementia (cognitive descent) (Sherwood, 2004).

Microglia are created during the **embryonic development** (when the child is still an embryo in the uterus) from the tissue that creates white blood cells (cells of the immune system). During the embryonic development, the microglia cells move to the central nervous system. Also, microglia release a chemical (**nerve growth factor**) that stimulates the growth and development of neurons and other glial cells (Sherwood, 2004).

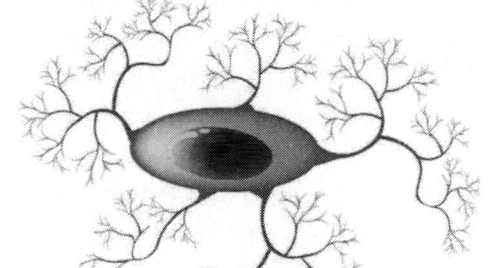

Figure 10. Microglia.

RADIAL GLIA

Radial glia play an important role in the **prenatal** development of the brain. These cells guide the **migration** of neurons during this early stage. Migration occurs in the following manner: neurons cling to radial glia that are like cables or wires supporting neuronal movement. Neurons must move, along radial glia, to reach specific positions in the nervous system so that they become localized in certain areas of the nervous system. Different neuronal areas influence different mental processes and behaviors (Kalat, 2013). Once this migration is complete during the prenatal period, then radial glia differentiate into neurons, astrocytes and oligodendrocytes (Pinto and Gotz, 2007)

SATELLITE CELLS

Satellite cells are glial cells confined to the peripheral nervous system (PNS), specifically to the ganglia (clusters of cell bodies within the PNS). Satellite cells surround neuron cell bodies in the ganglia and regulate the extracellular environment—levels of oxygen, carbon dioxide and neurotransmitter levels in the environment outside the neuron (Martini et al., 2012).

EPENDYMAL CELLS

Ependymal glial cells line the ventricles of the brain, as well as the central canal running through the spinal cord. Some ependymal cells in ventricles have cilia. These protrusions help move the cerebrospinal fluid (CSF) so that it circulates around the central nervous system. In some parts of the brain, ependymal cells secrete the CSF. In other parts of the brain, ependymal cells have a sensory function that monitors the composition of CSF. Some ependymal cells in the adult brain can produce new neurons, as well as other glial cells. Ependymal cells have extensions that connect with other glial cells. It is not clear what these connections accomplish, though. The CSF removes the waste material from the brain and the spinal cord. Also, the CSF allows the exchange of substances between the brain and blood vessels, as well as between the spinal cord and blood vessels. In addition, the CSF is a shock-absorbing fluid since it protects the brain from hitting the bones of the skull. It also protects the spinal cord from hitting the vertebrae. (Martini et al., 2012).

Figure 11. Ependymal cells.

OLYGODENDROCYTES AND SCHWANN CELLS

Previously in this chapter we explored olygodendrocytes (confined to the central nervous system) and Schwann cells (in the peripheral nervous system). Review the information regarding these glial cells.

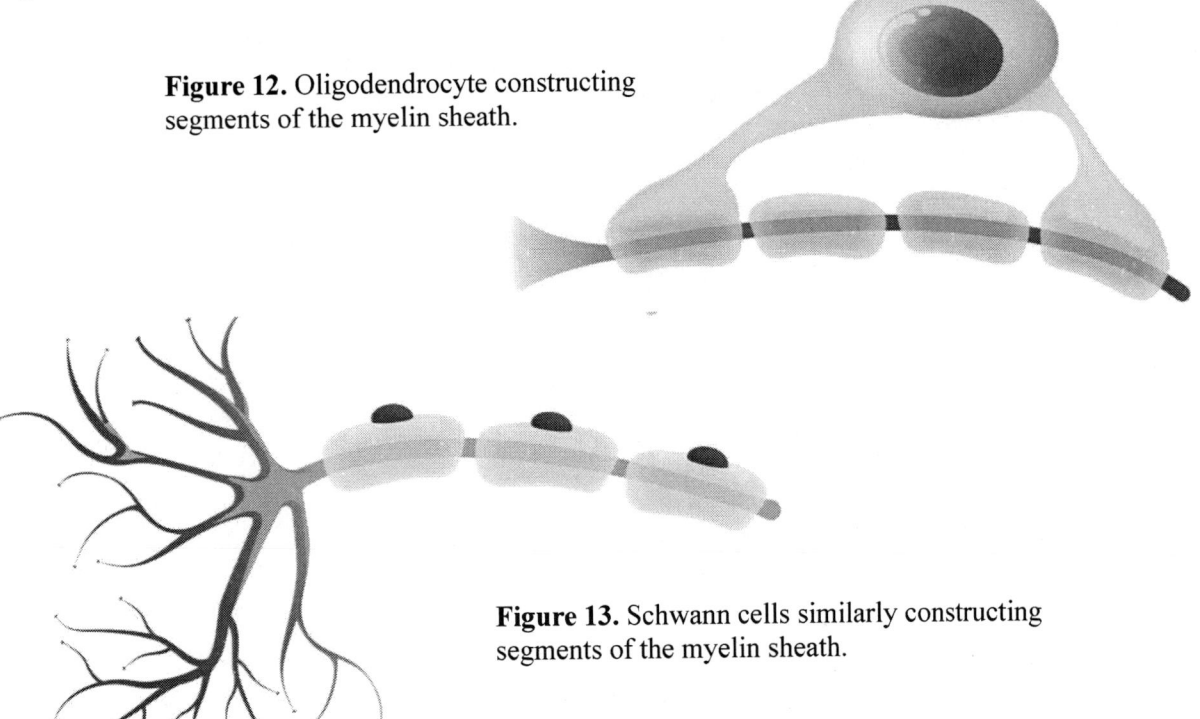

Figure 12. Oligodendrocyte constructing segments of the myelin sheath.

Figure 13. Schwann cells similarly constructing segments of the myelin sheath.

Properties of the neuronal membrane, as well as events that affect this membrane, are crucial for understanding how the nervous system operates. Think of the membrane as the cell's surface. A *positive* electrical charge (say +30 millivolts) exists in the upper portion of the membrane, the segment that borders the extracellular fluid. This positive charge is due to positively charged ions that can be found in the upper portion of the membrane. A *negative* electrical charge (say -100 millivolts), however, resides in the lower portion of the membrane, a region that borders the intracellular (inside cell) fluid. These two regions of the membrane (upper and lower) produce a *voltage* that is the *difference* between these two electrically charged areas. That's why this voltage is also called *potential difference*. That difference is around 70 millivolts (1 millivolt is 1/1000 of a volt), and it is also called **membrane potential**. This difference is marked -70 millivolts (Marieb & Hoehn, 2013).

The membrane is **polarized** since the membrane has two poles (like a battery): a positive pole is the upper portion of the membrane, and the negative pole is the lower portion of the membrane.

The extracellular space bordering the upper region of the membrane also has a positive charge, similar to the upper region of the membrane. The extracellular space above this region, however, is electrically neutral. The intracellular space bordering the lower region of the membrane is negatively charged, just like the lower region of the membrane. However, the intracellular space, further below that region, is electrically neutral (Marieb & Hoehn, 2013).

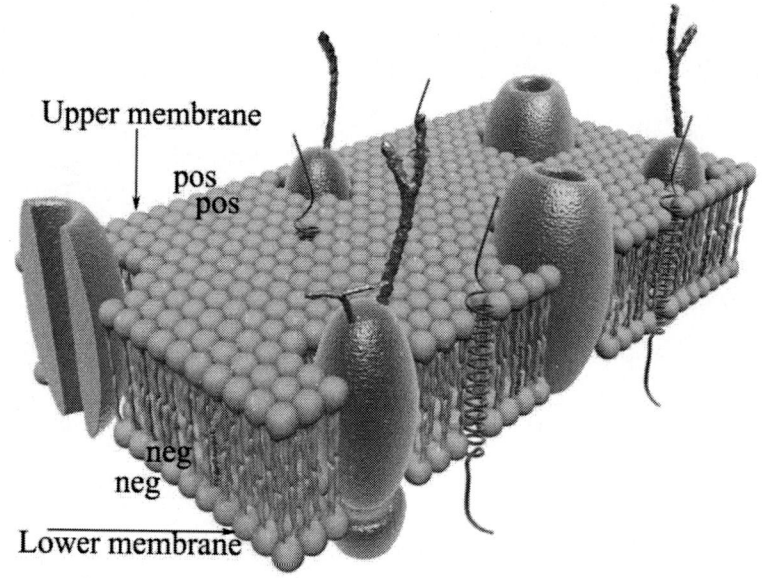

Figure 14. The distribution of charges within the lower membrane and its intracellular area, and the upper membrane and its extracellular region.

The aforementioned electrical differences between the upper portion of the membrane and the lower portion of the membrane can be measured with tools called **microelectrodes**. When both microelectrodes are positioned into the upper portion of the membrane, the measured electrical difference is zero since the tools are positioned in the identical environment. When both microelectrodes are positioned into the lower portion of the membrane, the electrical difference is zero as well. However, when a tip of one microelectrode is positioned into the upper portion of the membrane, while the tip of the other microelectrode sits in the lower portion of the membrane, the measurement discloses the (above-mentioned) -70 millivolts of electricity. This negative voltage of the membrane is called the **resting potential.** During this phase, the neuron neither generates electrical current nor releases neurotransmitters, so the neuron is not activated. However, the neuron has the likelihood or *potential* (potential energy) to become activated. (Marieb & Hoehn, 2013).

WHAT'S CAUSING THE RESTING POTENTIAL?

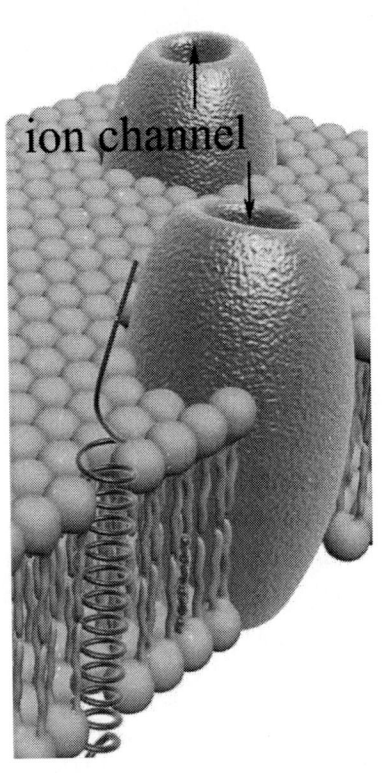

Figure 15. Ion channels.

The resting state or the inactivity of a neuron is accomplished through the movements of **ions** (positively or negatively charged atoms), their different amounts in the extracellular and intracellular fluid, and the membrane's **permeability,** which is the property of the membrane to let the ions through itself so that they can reach the extracellular and intracellular fluid. Let's examine the movements and distributions of sodium ions first. The resting state of a neuron (resting potential) is produced by an *unequal distribution* of sodium ions; specifically, more sodium ions accumulate *outside* the neuron, in the extracellular space bordering the upper region of the membrane. A smaller number of sodium ions accumulate inside the neuron in the area bordering the lower region of the membrane. There are openings or *pores* within the membrane, and these pores are protein-made *ion channels*. They allow ions to flow through them, getting to the inside and the outside of the cell. Some of these channels are *passive* (leakage), meaning they are always open. They do not contain a mechanism that closes and opens these pores. Since the membrane has *a few* of these passive channels for sodium ions, only a few sodium ions (positively charged sodium atoms) can get into the cell, and only a few can escape out of the cell. However, some of the membrane's ion channels are more active, meaning that they contain protein structures that, like *gates*, can open. But this opening of the channels happens only when a neuron becomes *stimulated* by a certain stimulus (we will talk about this stimulation later in the chapter). The resting state of a neuron is maintained as long as the neuron is not stimulated. When neurons are not stimulated, then gated ion channels are *closed*. When gated channels are closed, then sodium ions cannot substantially cross from the extracellular fluid to the intracellular fluid of the cell (Marieb & Hoehn, 2013).

There are two forces that push sodium ions from the outside of the cell towards the closed ion channels. Those forces are electrostatic pressure and concentration pressure. **The electrostatic pressure** (also called **electrostatic gradient**) is a force in nature dictating that the opposite electrical charges attract one another. Since the lower portion of the membrane has a negative charge, and sodium ions on the outside have a positive charge, these ions are attracted to the lower portion of the membrane. But, as you already know, the gated ion channels are closed. The passive ion channels exist in a small amount, so a few sodium ions leak into the cell. The majority of the sodium ions from the extracellular space (just above the upper surface of the membrane) wait "knocking on the closed door" (so to speak) of the gated ion channels. The **concentration pressure** (also called the **concentration gradient**) is yet another force that pushes sodium ions towards the (closed) ion channels. This gradient is a force that dictates that when particles are located within an area of high concentration, they will tend to move to the area of lower concentration (area with more space among them). Since the lower portion of the membrane has a smaller number of sodium ions, the sodium ions on the outside of the neuron have a tendency to go towards the intracellular fluid of the cell (Marieb & Hoehn, 2013).

Now is a good time to expand this entire picture and add another important "player" to this mix —potassium ions. In Latin, potassium is called Kalium, and the abbreviation is K. Potassium ions are *positively* charged. During the resting potential state of the neuron, there are more potassium ions inside the intracellular fluid than in the extracellular fluid. This imbalance is due to the passive channels that potassium ions use. Sodium ions, however, accumulate more on the outside of the cell passing through the passive channels too. Potassium ions get into the cell influenced by the electrostatic pressure that pushes positively charged potassium ions towards the negatively charged environment within the cell. There are *many more* potassium passive ion channels than sodium passive ion channels; therefore, more potassium ions get into the cell. Some potassium ions go out of the cell due to their concentration gradient (leave the intracellular area of high concentration and go outside the cell to lower concentration). However, the force that influences the positively charged potassium ions to stay inside the cell close to the lower membrane is the electrostatic pressure—the inside area close to the lower membrane is negatively charged, as you recall, and the positively charged ions of potassium move towards the negative charge. Even though a few potassium ions leak out into the extracellular space, and more potassium ions stay inside the cell along the lower region of the membrane, the few ions that leave the cell contribute to the negative charge of the lower part of the membrane and the neighboring intracellular fluid (Marieb & Hoehn, 2013).

Yet another factor plays a very important role in the maintenance of the resting potential. That factor is a set of protein structures called *transporters* (carrier proteins) embedded in the membrane. One type of transporter is the **sodium-potassium** pump, and it works like this: for every 3 sodium ions that the pump transports outside the cell, it transports 2 potassium ions into the cell from the extracellular fluid. Obviously, more positive charges (sodium ions) get out, and fewer positive charges (potassium ions) get in (Marieb & Hoehn, 2013).

In addition, large protein molecules that are *negatively* charged are a significant contributing factor to the negatively charged lower membrane and its bordering region of the intracellular space. These molecules are made within the cell, and they are so large that they cannot exit the cell through the membrane channels that have smaller openings. Negatively charged chloride ions are an additional contributing factor to the resting potential. More of these ions are located in the extracellular space bordering the upper membrane than in the intracellular space bordering the lower membrane. Electrical gradient drives chloride ions out of the cell since the intracellular space, close to the lower membrane, is negatively charged, and equal charges repel each other. The concentration gradient (more chloride ions on the outside), however, drives chloride ions inside the cell. The net result is that an equal number of chloride ions get in and out, but this maintenance of the negative chloride ions inside the cell contributes to the negative charge of the lower portion of the membrane (Marieb & Hoehn, 2013).

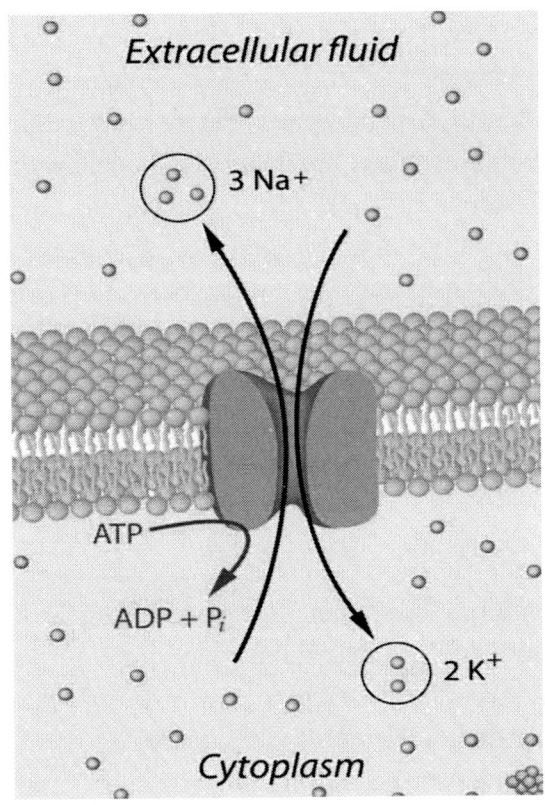

Figure 16. Sodium-potassium pumps bringing two potassium ions into the cell and transporting three sodium ions out of the cell.

EXCITATORY POST-SYNAPTIC POTENTIAL

To become active, a neuron needs to be stimulated during its resting state. Let's examine this stimulation. After a pre-synaptic neuron releases its neurotransmitters, they arrive shortly (in milliseconds; 1 millisecond is 1/1000 of a second) at the *receptor* on the post-synaptic neuron. Once a neurotransmitter attaches to the receptor, the receptor stimulates the opening of **chemically-sensitive channels,** which are protein structures in the membrane. These channels are gated and can be found predominantly on the *dendrites* and *the cell body*, although there are some channels on all other parts of the neuron. Channels are given this name because they *open* once a *chemical* (neurotransmitter) attaches to the nearby receptor. Once these channels open, then nearby sodium ions from the extracellular fluid enter the cell through the channels. So, just to emphasize this point, chemicals (neurotransmitters) stimulate the opening of the channels, but what gets through the channels are ions. Neurotransmitters that influence the opening of the channels are called **excitatory neurotransmitters,** but *receptors* (not neurotransmitters) determine whether the channels will open or not. This is to say that the same neurotransmitter can stimulate a receptor to open the channels, but on another receptor, the same neurotransmitter can be inhibitory (deactivating) if it does not stimulate the receptor to initiate the opening of the channels. For instance, depending on the *receptor*, the neurotransmitter dopamine can be an excitatory neurotransmitter, but it can also be inhibitory if it attaches to receptors that don't initiate the opening of the chemically-sensitive channels. Another example is the neurotransmitter acetylcholine. This transmitter is excitatory in most neuro-muscular and neuro-glandular junctions, but it is an inhibitory neurotransmitter when it binds to the heart receptors. So, the action of a neurotransmitter is dependent upon the receptor it binds to (Martini et al., 2012).

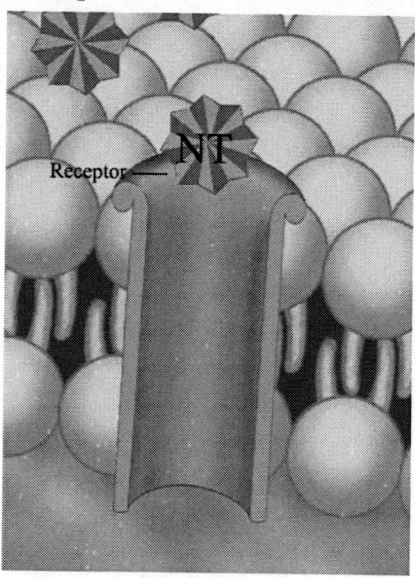

Figure 17. Receptors determine whether a neurotransmitter (N) is an inhibitory or excitatory. Ionotropic receptors and channels are integrated.

When the chemically-sensitive channels open (say on a dendrite), the sodium ions move (flow) through them, then through the membrane and into the cell's cytosol (intracellular fluid), located below the lower surface of the membrane. Then, these ions continue to flow through the cytosol, just below the membrane, in parallel with the lower surface of the membrane. This flow is in *both directions*, right and left from the point of entry into the cytosol. Why in both directions? These positively charged sodium ions are attracted to the negative charge that exists along the negatively charged lower region of the membrane as well as a part of the negatively charged cytosol adjacent to the lower portion of the membrane. The flow of ions is called **the signal**. However, the flow of sodium ions is a **graded signal** (or **decremental**), meaning that the flow of ions will decrease and fade out shortly, after a few millimeters. The graded signal has two aspects: local signal and electrotonic signal. **Local signal** is the vertical flow of ions through the chemically-sensitive channels towards the inside of the neuron. But, the **electrotonic signal** occurs when those same ions continue to move horizontally *along* the lower surface of the membrane and through the bordering intracellular fluid. As these ions move, they encounter *resistance* (an obstruction in their flow) from the

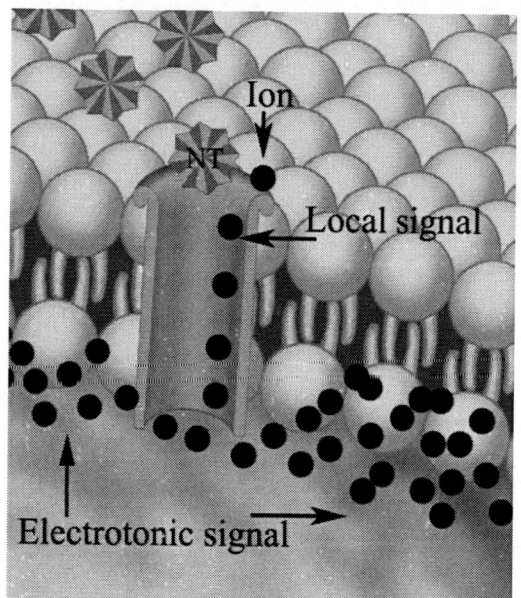

Figure 18. Local and electrotonic signals. Ions move horizontally through the lower membrane and cytosol.

material (discussed in chapter four) that makes up the membrane, as well as from the cytosol. The resistance they encounter slows them down and eventually stops their movement. Additionally, there are sodium passive channels in the membrane that allow some sodium ions to escape outside of the cell. For these reasons the signal is decremental. But, when *more* neurotransmitters open more chemically-sensitive channels for ions, some ions will stop, and some will continue moving further to the **axon hillock**, where the cell body meets the axon (Marieb & Hoehn, 2013).

The electrical signal is defined as the flow of sodium ions to the axon hillock. This signal is called the **excitatory post-synaptic potential (EPSP)**. It's called "excitatory" since this flow of ions "wakes up" the resting neuron and activates or excites it. As the sodium ions travel, they reduce the membrane's resting potential from -70 mv to about -60 mv. How did this shift to a less negative voltage happen? Remember, sodium ions are *positively* charged, and bringing that positive charge with them, they reduce the negative charge of the lower membrane and the bordering fluid (from -100 to -90 mv). This reduction in the membrane's voltage to -60 mv is absolutely crucial since that is the voltage point (or **threshold of excitation**) at which other types of channels, called the **voltage-sensitive channels,** open in the membrane. These channels are predominantly located on the membrane covering the axon, and they are different from chemically-sensitive channels since the voltage-sensitive channels open when they detect the afore-mentioned switch (from -70 mv to -60 mv) in the membrane potential. This switch from a negative voltage to a *less* negative one is called **depolarization**. So, depolarization creates the threshold of excitation, and at

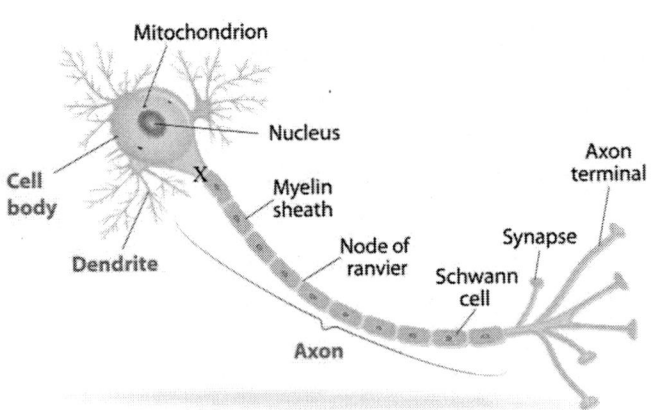

Figure 19. The axon hillock (X) is where the cell body meets the axon.

the threshold, the voltage-dependent channels open. As they open, the sodium ions waiting in the extracellular space above the upper membrane rush through the channels into the cell. Before we examine what happens next, let's consider the inhibitory post-synaptic potential or IPSP (Marieb & Hoehn, 2013).

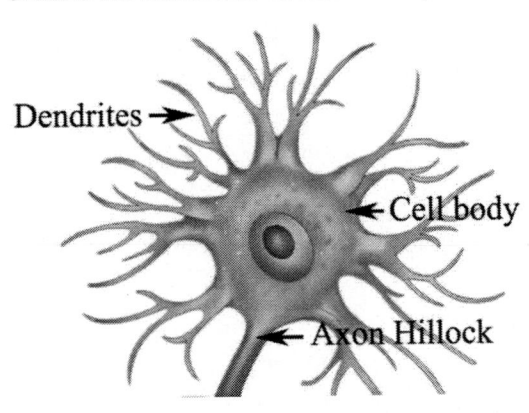

Figure 20. Chemically-sensitive channels are mostly located on dendrites and cell bodies. Voltage-sensitive channels are mostly found on the axon hillock and axon.

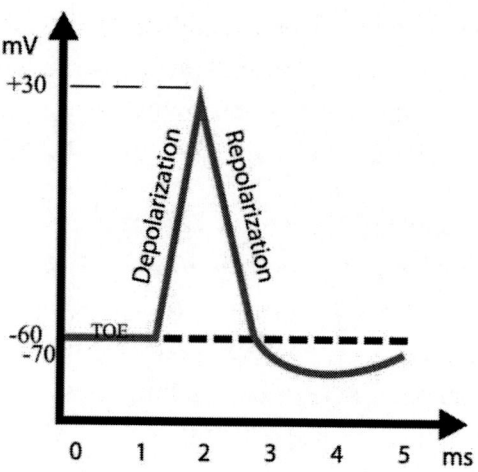

Figure 21. The depolarization phase includes the threshold of excitation (TOE). The vertical axis represents change in voltage, and the horizontal axis is the passage of time.

INHIBITORY POST-SYNAPTIC POTENTIAL

Consider a resting, post-synaptic neuron. When a neurotransmitter attaches to the neuron's receptor, the binding stimulates the receptor to open the chemically-sensitive channels to let *chloride* ions into the cell. These ions bring the negative charge with them. This **influx** (entering) of the negative charge makes the already negative voltage of the membrane even *more* negative. This exaggeration in the charge is called **hyperpolarization** (or amplified polarization). Hyperpolarization maintains the resting state of a neuron or it deactivates an active neuron. The neurotransmitter that initiates the hyperpolarization is called the **inhibitory** neurotransmitter. However, keep in mind that the receptor "decides" whether the chemically-sensitive channels will open for chloride or for some other ion. Other neurotransmitters can influence the opening of chemically-sensitive channels that let potassium ions out of the cell into the extracellular environment. This leaking out of the positively charged potassium ions depletes the cell from the positive charges, making the membrane's voltage even more negative than it is in the resting neuron. This is hyperpolarization again, and the neurotransmitter that initiates this process is also an inhibitory neurotransmitter. The flow of chloride ions *inside* the cell, or the flow of the potassium ions *outside* the cell, is called **the inhibitory post-synaptic potential (IPSP)** (Marieb & Hoehn, 2013).

TEMPORAL AND SPATIAL SUMMATION

At any given moment, a neuron makes thousands of synapses with other neurons. As a result, a post-synaptic neuron receives many EPSPs and IPSPs at the same time and very often. So, the neuron analyzes these signals and determines which signal type prevails. If there are more EPSPs, then the neuron will become activated. If there are more IPSPs, the neuron will maintain its resting state. The neuron has a mechanism in the axon hillock that allows these computations. EPSPs and IPSPs are graded potentials. So, EPSP can die out quickly if there are a *few* neurotransmitters influencing the opening of a few chemically-sensitive channels for sodium ions. However, if a post-synaptic neuron is stimulated by excitatory neurotransmitters and then *rapidly* the same neuron gets stimulated *again,* at the same location and with the same amount of the excitatory neurotransmitter, then the electrical charge of these EPSPs will combine. The combined signals will travel *further* than the first signal alone. This is called **temporal summation** since time plays a role here. However, if the time *between* these two signals is increased (not a rapid succession), then the combined signal does not travel as far as in the first scenario in which the first signal was *rapidly* followed by the second signal. The same principle holds true for IPSPs. Also, when a receptor at *location* A on a post-synaptic neuron, and a receptor on *location* B on the identical neuron are stimulated at the same time by neurotransmitters (binding to them), the EPSP signals will combine and travel further than when *only one location* is stimulated by the same number of neurotransmitters. This is called **spatial summation** since adding an additional location of simultaneous stimulation plays a role. The same principle holds true for IPSPs (Marieb & Hoehn, 2013).

BACK TO EPSP AT THE AXON HILLOCK...

Let's say that the EPSP was initiated at a dendrite. From there, these ions *decrementally* move and arrive at the axon hillock. That EPSP depolarizes the membrane, as you already know. Next, the *voltage-sensitive channels* open, and the sodium ions from the extracellular region start to rush into the cell, reaching the lower membrane and the intracellular fluid below it. Sodium ions that reach that region become attracted (due to electrostatic pressure) to the *negative* charge of the next *adjacent* area of the lower membrane that has not yet been depolarized. Then, sodium ions start to move in one direction towards those negative charges. That movement is away from the axon hillock towards the axon terminal. This movement of sodium ions further depolarizes the membrane, and the depolarization is a stimulus for the *adjacent* set of the voltage-sensitive channels to open so that more sodium ions rush in. As they rush into the cell towards the intracellular fluid, they depolarize the next set of the membrane's voltage-sensitive channels, and the process repeats. This depolarizing flow, or **current**, of sodium

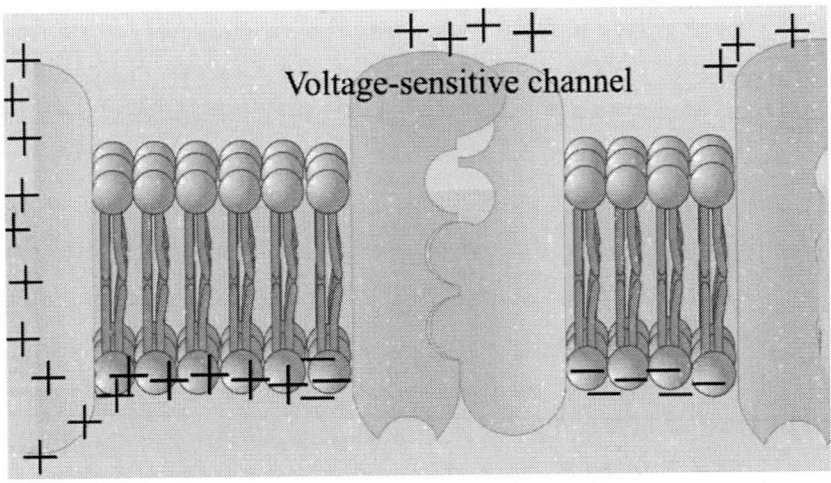

Figure 22. Sodium ions (+) enter the ion channel and move towards the negatively charged segment (-) of the membrane, causing depolarization. Depolarization opens an adjacent voltage-sensitive channel, which lets more sodium ions through (+). The process repeats.

ions through the lower membrane and through the intracellular fluid right below it is called the **action potential**. An action potential is not a single event; instead, the action potential is composed

141

of many action potentials that are generated at successive, adjacent segments of the membrane. An action potential "gives birth" to itself, which is a process called **self-propagation**. Utilizing the process of self-propagation, the action potential *moves* along the axon towards the axon terminal. The action potential lasts about 1 millisecond (1/1000 of a second). During the action potential, the membrane's **permeability** (gated and passive channels allowing ions to go through it) is about 1,000 times greater than during the resting potential. We mentioned a "rush" of sodium ions into the cell, and it is easy to make a mistake and create a mental image of a tremendous number of sodium ions moving from the extracellular space into the cell through the membrane. Surprisingly, only 0.012% (less than 1 percent!) of sodium ions (of the total number located in the intracellular fluid and outside the neuron) rush into the cell (Marieb & Hoehn, 2013).

POTASSIUM IONS AND ACTION POTENTIAL

During the action potential, its depolarizing nature opens the voltage-sensitive channels for sodium ions, as you know. As more of these ions enter the cell, a more positive charge is added to the negative charge of the lower membrane and the bordering cytoplasm. Due to these incoming positive charges, the membrane **reverses its polarity**. In the resting state the voltage was -70 mv (+30 upper membrane, -100 lower membrane). Now, it is -5 in the upper membrane and +35 in the lower. The difference (voltage) is +30 mv. After the membrane reverses its polarity, the voltage-sensitive channels for sodium ions start to *close* (approximately after 1 millisecond from the start of the action potential). At that point, the voltage-sensitive channels for *potassium* ions start to open and these ions exit the cell (**efflux**) to the extracellular fluid. This efflux is driven by the concentration gradient (too many potassium ions inside the lower membrane and the bordering intracellular fluid). Also, the electrostatic gradient drives potassium ions out into the extracellular space since the membrane's voltage is positively charged now. Potassium ions are positively charged, and the newly formed positively charged environment repels them (Pinel, 2014).

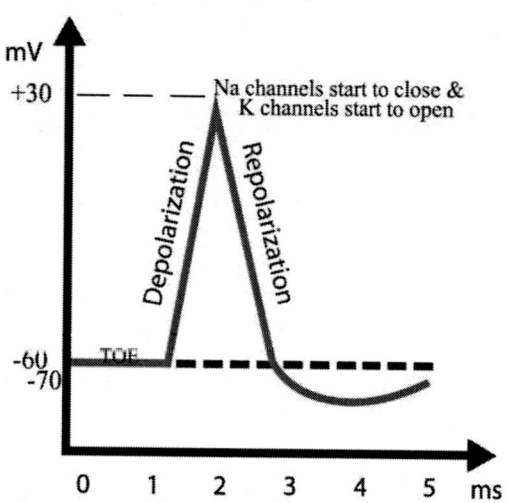

Figure 23. During repolarization the resting potential is re-established. Action potential includes depolarization and repolarization.

Since many potassium ions leave the cell, taking much of the positive charge with them, the **recovery state** or **repolarization** happens. During repolarization, the membrane's voltage gradually becomes more and more *negative*, and the resting potential state (-70 mv) is eventually re-established. After repolarization, sodium voltage-sensitive channels close completely, so no more positive charge comes into the cell. Positively charged potassium ions still leave the cell, though. This brief phase of positive charges leaving the cell and making the membrane's voltage even more negative (-90mv) than the original resting state (-

70mv) is called **hyperpolarization**. At the end of the hyperpolarization stage, the voltage-sensitive channels for potassium ions close completely too. After this phase, it is manageable for the sodium-potassium pump (3 sodium ions out, 2 potassium ions in) to restore the resting potential, considering that there are thousands of these pumps in the membrane (Marieb & Hoehn, 2013).

ACTION POTENTIAL AND REFRACTORY PERIODS

The **absolute refractory period** (1-2 milliseconds) refers to a period during which a neuron going through an action potential cannot generate an additional (new) action potential. This refractory period includes a depolarization period (from the threshold of excitation on) throughout the entire repolarization phase. Depolarization includes already opened voltage-sensitive channels for sodium, so a new arriving EPSP does not lead into an additional influx of sodium. During repolarization, the voltage-sensitive sodium channels start to close and shortly after become closed completely. Thus, the sodium ions cannot get through these channels and cannot depolarize the lower region of the membrane and the bordering intracellular fluid. Since the voltage-sensitive channels for sodium ions are closed, the action potential cannot go back towards the cell body. Thus, the absolute refractory period influences the action potential to move from the axon hillock to the axon terminal. An action potential moves in that direction for another reason too—voltage-sensitive channels are almost entirely absent from the cell body to the axon hillock. These channels are predominantly found in the membrane covering the axon. Voltage-sensitive channels for potassium ions, however, are opened during the repolarization stage, and potassium ions exit the cell, following the electrostatic pressure (Marieb & Hoehn, 2013; Kolb & Whishaw, 2003).

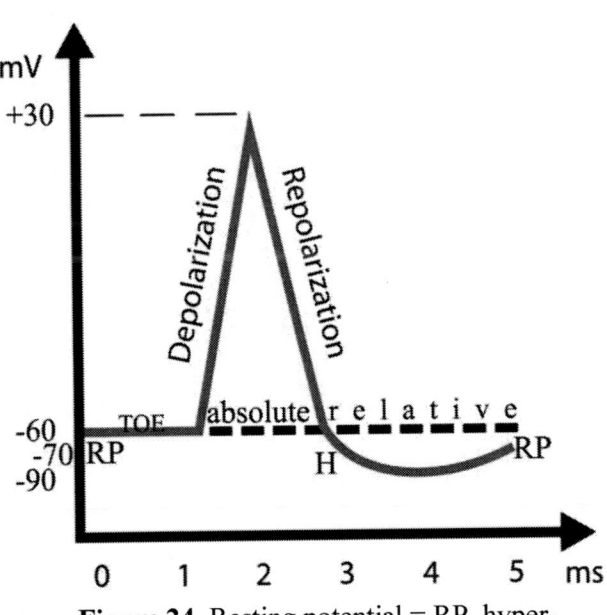

Figure 24. Resting potential = RP, hyperpolarization = H (from -70 to -90 to -70).

Immediately after the absolute refractory period, the **relative refractory period** (around 2 milliseconds) begins, which is the next phase of the neuron's activity. This is the phase when hyperpolarization happens. During this stage, the sodium voltage-sensitive channels are closed, but the voltage-sensitive channels for potassium ions are open, and the efflux of potassium ions generates hyperpolarization. During the relative refractory period, a stimulus that's stronger than a usual stimulus *can* initiate an action potential by opening the voltage-sensitive channels for sodium ions. In other words, during this phase, the membrane requires *more* sodium ions in the form of EPSPs (more depolarization) to replenish the positive charge that is lost, due to the potassium ions leaving the cell (Marieb & Hoehn, 2013; Kolb & Whishaw, 2003).

The all or none law states that all action potentials generated in a neuron are *identical*. Also, regardless of the number of neurotransmitters that lead to depolarization, the action potential will have the *same speed* and the *same intensity* (the amount of sodium ions flowing). The all or none law also posits that an action potential either happens (when a neuron reaches the threshold of excitation) or does not happen at all if the threshold is not reached (Marieb and Hoehn, 2013).

If action potentials are identical, do neurons send identical messages? How does the nervous system differentiate between these identical action potentials? The answer lies in the *frequency* (how often something happens) of action potentials. A strong stimulus (a higher number of neurotransmitters attaching to receptors) is represented as a *short* pause between action potentials. Hence, the action potentials representing a stronger stimulus occur more often (in a more rapid succession). A weak stimulus (fewer neurotransmitters binding with receptors), however, is represented as a *longer* pause between action potentials. In other words, a weak stimulus produces action potentials that occur less frequently (Marieb & Hoehn, 2013).

CONTINUOUS VERSUS SALTATORY PROPAGATION

Neuronal axons can be unmyelinated and myelinated. In unmyelinated axons, the propagation of the action potential happens continuously along every adjacent segment of the membrane from the axon hillock to the axon terminal. These action potentials travel at a speed of about two miles per hour or one meter per second (Martini et al., 2012).

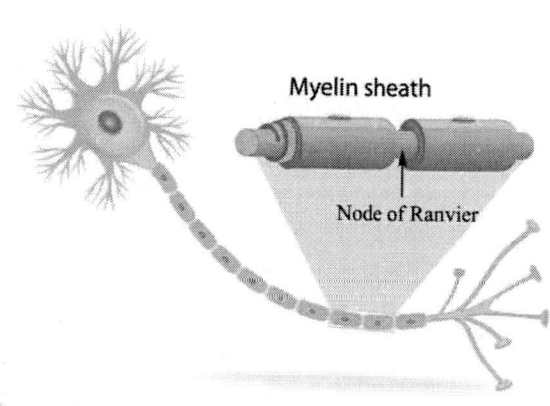

Figure 25. Some neurons are myelinated while others are not.

In myelinated axons, however, the speed of travel of the action potential is approximately 30 times faster. How? Myelin covers the axon except at the Nodes of Ranvier. The myelin wraps around the membrane preventing it from growing voltage-sensitive channels there. The channels exist *only* on the Nodes of Ranvier (segments without myelin). Furthermore, myelin is a barrier for the flow of ions, so myelin slows ions down. But, since there are not so many channels to open (in unmyelinated axons, however, ions must work excessively to open many adjacent channels), the ions in myelinated axons flow quickly along the membrane on the non-myelinated sections and depolarize those sections only (not the myelinated parts). Obviously, ions need to work less here since they don't have to bother with opening channels on the myelinated segments since the channels are absent. Ions, in other words, use less energy to flow along the lower surface of the membrane, which allows them to flow faster. Also, myelin segments are great *insulators* because they prevent the ions from leaking out from the cell, which contributes to their high number when they flow. This higher number of ions allows depolarization to happen more quickly. Since the depolarization at the Nodes of Ranvier influences action potential to occur, this situation resembles an action potential "jumping" from a Node to Node. But there is no real jumping, there is just a faster flowing of ions along the myelinated axon's sections that are not myelinated (Nodes of Ranvier). This type of conduction of sodium flow in myelinated axons is called the **saltatory** conduction or a **jump-like** conduction. As mentioned earlier, this saltatory conduction is about 30 times faster than the continuous conduction in unmyelinated axons (Marieb & Hoehn, 2013).

There are certain exceptions, however, to the rules of the action potential in some neurons of the brain. Specifically, many neurons fire all the time even without a stimulus (Lisman, Ragvachari and Tsien, 2007). Also, many brain neurons do not display action potentials, and even dendrites of some neurons conduct action potentials (Pinel, 2014). In addition, even though in most neurons an action potential starts at the axon hillock, in some it begins at the first Node of Ranvier (Kuba, Ishii & Ohmari, 2006).

CONDUCTION SPEED

The speed of the conduction of action potentials is determined by the *diameter* of an axon, and it has been observed that the larger diameter, the larger the speed. This is due to the fact that larger axons provide less resistance to the flow of the ions. Another factor is the amount of myelination; axons that are myelinated more, have fewer voltage-sensitive channels; thus, they conduct the impulse faster. **Group A fibers** are the largest in diameter and conduct impulses up to 150 meters per second (up to 335 miles per hour). These fibers are somatic motor and somatic sensory, and they innervate the skin, joints and skeletal muscles. They also have a thick myelin sheath that provides better insulation. **Group B fibers** have a medium size diameter; they are lightly myelinated and conduct impulses about 15 meters per second (35 miles per hour). These fibers can be found in the sympathetic and parasympathetic (motor) divisions that innervate visceral organs. These fibers are also found in the visceral sensory system, where they innervate the cardiac muscle and glands. Also, these fibers can be found in the somatic sensory regions conducting impulses from the skin (pain, pressure, temperature and touch). **Group C fibers** are not myelinated, and they have the smallest diameter. The speed of action potential here is about 1 meter per second (2 miles per hour) or even less. These fibers innervate the same regions as group B fibers (Marieb & Hoehn, 2013).

Multiple sclerosis is a condition characterized with a deterioration of the myelin. This damaged myelin blocks or reduces the axons' ability to conduct impulses. The myelin is attacked by the body's immune system for unknown reasons. Damaged myelin results in the following:

- numbness or weakness in one or more limbs (this usually affects one side of the body)

- muscle stiffness and spasms
- partial or complete vision loss, usually in one eye at a time, often with pain during eye movement
- prolonged double vision
- tingling or pain in body parts
- electric-shock sensations that occur with certain neck movements, especially bending the neck forward
- tremors, lack of coordination or unsteady gait
- slurred speech, fatigue and dizziness
- bowel and bladder function problems.

Multiple Sclerosis cannot be cured so that the person is completely healed from the condition; however, certain medications can slow down the progression of the disease and/or reduce the symptoms. This is accomplished by administering medications that block or reduce the activity of the immune system (Mayo Clinic Staff, 2015).

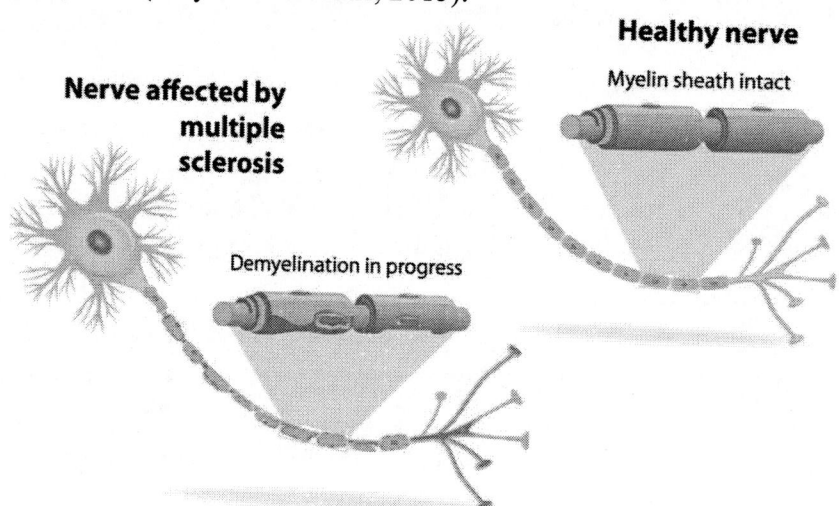

Figure 26. Myelin on healthy axons, and myelin affected by multiple sclerosis.

SYNAPSE

Synapse comes from a Greek word *syn*, and means to clasp or join. So, a synapse is a point of communication between or among neurons. Most neurons are at the same time both pre-synaptic (send messages to other neurons) and post-synaptic (receive messages from other neurons). Each neuron makes 1,000 to 10,000 synapses with other neurons! There are different types of synapses: **axodendritic,** an *axon* of one neuron synapses with the *dendrites* of another neuron; **axosomatic,** an *axon* of a neuron synapses with a *cell body* of another neuron; **axoaxonal,** an axon of one neuron synapses with an axon of another neuron; **dendrodentritic,** a dendrite of one neuron synapses with a dendrite of another; **somatodendritic**, a cell body of one neuron synapses with the cell body of another neuron (Marieb and Hoehn, 2013).

CHEMICAL SYNAPSES

A synapse is a fluid-filled space, about one millionth of an inch wide. Chemical synapses allow a pre-synaptic neuron to deposit neurotransmitters into a synapse so that these chemicals can bind to the receptor on the post-synaptic cell. The axon terminal of a pre-synaptic neuron contains vesicles, each containing thousands of neuro-

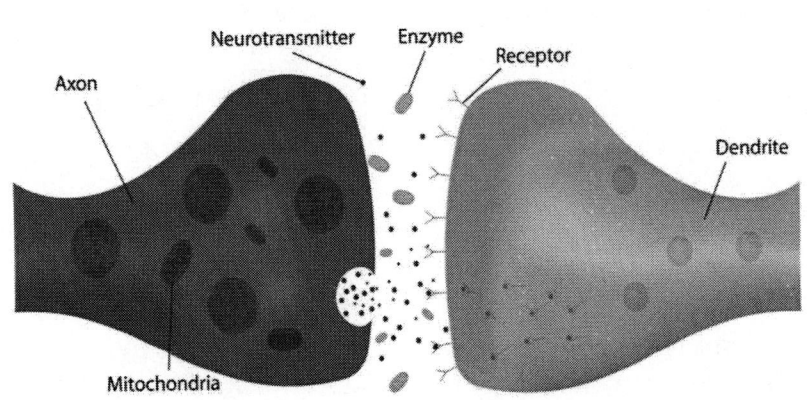

Figure 27. The pre-synaptic neuron (left) and post-synaptic neuron (right) in a directed synapse.

transmitters. Chemical synapses channel the neurotransmitters in *one direction* only (pre-synaptic to post-synaptic); also, these synapses are directed or non-directed. The **directed** synapses include a release of neurotransmitters from the pre-synaptic axon terminals onto the nearby post-synaptic receptors. This directed process can be imagined as a laser (a narrow beam). However, the non-directed synapses consist of a pre-synaptic neuron releasing neurotransmitters towards post-synaptic receptors that are not close, and, therefore, the release is more like a shower of neurotransmitters over a large area. In terms of the non-directed synapses, the neurotransmitters are in vesicles that exist within bulges along the axonal branches. These synapses are also called the **string-of-beads synapses** (Pinel, 2014).

SEQUENCE OF EVENTS AT A CHEMICAL SYNAPSE

When an action potential arrives at the axon terminal of a neuron, it opens the voltage-dependent channels for *calcium* ions. The next step is the entrance of calcium ions into the axon terminal. A calcium ion is positively charged, so it is driven by the electrostatic pressure into the negatively charged environment of the lower surface of the membrane and the bordering intracellular fluid. Also, the concentration pressure moves this ion; since calcium ions concentrate on the outside, they move to the area of lower concentration—inside the cell. In the axon terminal, there is a protein that detects the presence of calcium ions and binds with them. The protein interacts with another protein (SNARE protein) that stimulates the vesicles from the axon terminal to fuse with the membrane and release their stored neurotransmitters into the synapse. After this action, calcium ions are ejected from the cell via the *calcium pump* (a protein transporter). The remaining calcium ions are eliminated through absorption by mitochondria (Marieb & Hoehn, 2013).

Each action potential influences roughly 300 vesicles to fuse with the membrane and empty their neurotransmitters into the synapse. The more frequent the action potential is, the more vesicles fuse with the membrane; consequently, more neurotransmitters are released. After a few milliseconds of being attached to the post-synaptic receptor, the neurotransmitters are deactivated. The deactivation is conducted by the **enzymatic degradation** performed by enzymes located in the synapse and in the post-synaptic membrane. Some neurotransmitters simply diffuse from the synapse, and they become deactivated in that way. The deactivation can also happen through the **reuptake process,** which brings the neurotransmitters back to the pre-synaptic axon terminal and releases them again. The reuptake can also mean taking *parts* of the neurotransmitters that were degraded by enzymes back to the pre-synaptic terminal and using those parts to create a new neurotransmitter for future release. How do neurotransmitters or their degraded parts end up back into the pre-synaptic neuron? The reuptake process is completed by the protein transporters located on the membrane of the pre-synaptic terminal. The protein transporters have a mechanism to move the neurotransmitter, or its parts, from receptors back into the pre-synaptic neuron. Also, the reuptake can be done by astrocytes. In astrocytes, the neurotransmitters are either stored via enzymes for recycling and later use, or the neurotransmitters are broken down by the enzymes. The astrocytes can send the entire neurotransmitter, or parts of it, to the pre-synaptic terminal for future use (Kolb & Whishaw, 2003).

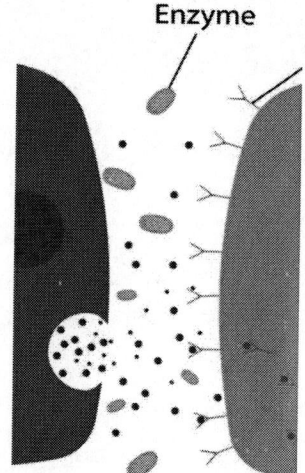

Figure 28. Enzymes sometimes conduct deactivation processes.

ELECTRICAL SYNAPSES

Picture a neuron with its membrane and its protein channels filled with cytoplasm. Now, picture another neuron with the same characteristics. Turn one of those neurons upside down and place its channels right on top of the other neuron's channels. The channels are called **connexins** (or connexons), and this arrangement allows the neuron's cytoplasm to be connected as well. This is an **electrical synapse.** But, there is still a small gap between these channels; they are not completely attached, in other words. However, the size of a chemical synapse is like a *lake* in comparison to the size of an electrical synapse. An electrical synapse is also called a **gap junction.**

Electrical synapses do not contain neurotransmitters, only *ions* and some small molecules. Hence, only ions influence depolarization of the membrane and the action potential. The speed of transmission via electrical synapses is very high and efficient, and much faster than the transmission via a chemical synapse. The transmission (involving the electrical synapse) can go in one direction from neuron A to B or even both directions from neuron A to B, and back from B to

148

A. The membranes (of two different neurons) are so close in electrical synapses that the ionic flow happening in one neuron can affect the membrane's voltage of the connecting neuron. Thus, when depolarization happens in the membrane of one neuron, the depolarization affects the other neuron's membrane as well. These synapses are rare and located in the hippocampus (a structure involved in the transfer of information from short-term memory to long-term memory), in the vestibular nuclei of the brain stem (influencing muscle tone and movement of the head, neck, trunk, arms, legs and eyes in order to maintain posture and balance as we move and stand) and in the ciliary ganglia (pair) of the parasympathetic system (influencing secretion of tears, movement of muscles for facial expressions and secretion of glands in the nasal cavity). The electrical synapses are also known to exist among some glial cells (Marieb & Hoehn, 2013; Martini et al., 2012).

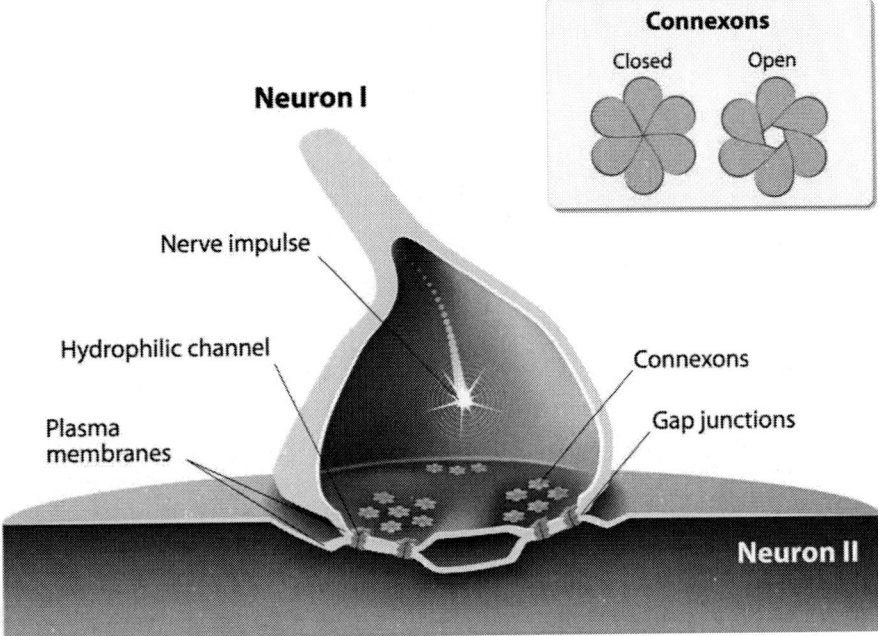

Figure 29. An electrical synapse between the pre-synaptic Neuron I and the post-synaptic Neuron II.

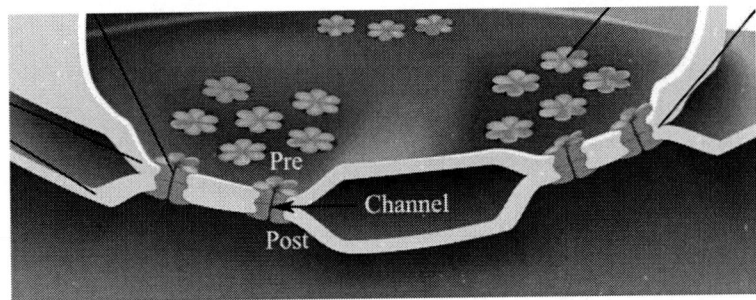

Figure 30. Aligned channels of the pre-synaptic neuron and the post-synaptic neuron create a single channel for the electrical synapse.

Myelinated axons exist both in the CNS and PNS. Also, nonmyelinated axons exist both in the PNS and CNS. **White matter** refers to the myelinated axons in the CNS. **Gray matter**, however, refers to cell bodies and unmyelinated axons in the CNS. The **cortex**, composed of the gray matter, is the bark or the surface of the brain. Each bump of the cortex is a gyrus, and each valley is a sulcus. The subcortical (below cortex) portion of the brain, is the white matter. However, there are some cell bodies and unmyelinated axons in the white matter, and some myelinated axons in the gray matter. Recall that the

"butterfly" shaped portion of the spinal cord is the gray matter. The surrounding tissue is white matter. Within the butterfly-shaped section are cell bodies and unmyelinated axons spreading out from those cell bodies. The white matter in the spinal cord is not exclusively white matter; instead, the white matter does contain, in places, some cell bodies and unmyelinated axons (gray matter elements). So, white matter versus gray matter distinction is not an absolute distinction with a clear cut border; instead, there are bits and pieces of gray matter *within* the white matter (Marieb & Hoehn, 2013).

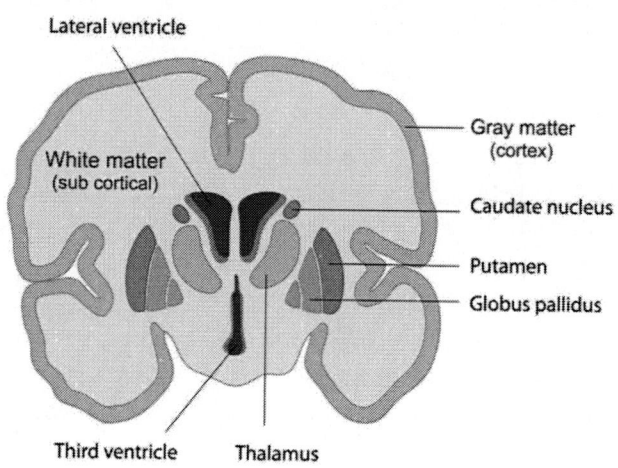

Figure 31. The white and gray matter of the brain (a cross-section).

REFERENCES

Azevedo, F. A., Carvalho, L.R., Grinberg, L.T., Farfel, J. M., Feretti, R. E., Leite, R. E. & Herculano-Houzel, S. (2009). Equal numbers of neuronal and nonneuronal cells make the human brain in isometrically scaled-up primate brain. *Journal of Comparative Neurology*, 513, 532-541.

Breedlove, S. M., Rosenzweig, M. R. and Watson, N. V. (2007). *Biological Psychology: an introduction to behavioral, cognitive, and clinical neuroscience* (5th ed.). Sunderland, MA: Sinauer Associates, Inc.

Brown, A. M., & Ransom, B. R. (2007). Astrocyte glycogen and brain energy metabolism. *Glia*, 55(12):1263-71.

Carlson, N.R. (2013). *Physiology of Behavior* (11th edition). Boston, MA: Allyn and Bacon.

Figley, C. R., and Stroman, P. W. (2011). The role(s) of astrocytes and astrocyte activity in neurometabolism, neurovascular coupling, and the production of functional neuroimaging signals. *European Journal of Neuroscience*. 33(4):577–588.

Ishibashi, T., Dakin, K., Stevens, B., Lee, P., Kozlov, S., Stewart, C., & Fields R. (2006). Astrocytes promote myelination in response to electrical impulses. *Neuron* 49 (6): 823–32.

Kalat, J.W. (2013). *Biological Psychology* (11th ed.). Belmont, CA: Wadsworth, Cengage Learning.

Kolb, B., & Whishaw, I. Q. (2003). *Human neuropsychology* (5th ed.). New York, NY: Worth Publishers.

Kettenmann, H., Verkhratsky, A. (2011). Neuroglia--living nerve glue. *Fortschr Neurol Psychiatr*, 79(10):588-97.

Marieb, E., & Hoehn, K. (2013). *Human anatomy and physiology* (9th ed.). Glenview, IL: Pearson Education.

Magistretti, P. J., Pellerin, L., Rothman, D. L., & Shulman, R. G. (1999). Energy on demand. *Science*, 283(5401):496-7.

Martini H. F., Nath, L. J., Bartholomew, F. E., & Ober, C. W. (2012). *Fundamentals of Anatomy and Physiology.* (9th ed.). San Francisco, CA: Pearson Benjamin Cummings.

Perea, G., Navarrete, M., & Araque, A. (2009). Tripartite synapses: astrocytes process and control synaptic information. *Trends in Neuroscience,* 32(8):421-31.

Piet, R., Vargová, L., Syková, E., Poulain, D., & Oliet, S. (2004). Physiological contribution of the astrocytic environment of neurons to intersynaptic crosstalk. *Proc Natl Acad Sci USA,* 101 (7):2151–5.

Pinel, P.J. (2014). *Biopsychology* (9th ed.). Boston, MA: Pearson Education.

Pinto L., Götz M. (2007). Radial glial cell heterogeneity – the source of diverse progeny in the CNS. *Progress in Neurobiology*, 83, 2-23.

Sherwood, L. (2004). *Human physiology: from cells to systems* (5th ed.). Belmont, CA: Thompson Learning.

Learning

Chapter Five

WHAT IS LEARNING?

Learning is a *change* in mental processes and behaviors resulting from experience or acquisition of new information. For example, a girl likes to play with her pet rabbit. But she eventually develops a fear of it. Her fear towards the rabbit is a change in the girl's behavior, since she did

not originally fear the rabbit. Thus, the girl *learned* to fear the rabbit. But how did the girl develop fear of something as adorable and seemingly harmless as a rabbit? One answer is that her fear was acquired through *classical conditioning*, a type of learning. This is not the only type of learning; other types of learning include cognitive, observational, instrumental, and subliminal. All of these types of learning will be discussed in this chapter.

Figure 1. How can anyone fear something as adorable as a rabbit? The answer lies in classical conditioning.

CLASSICAL CONDITIONING

Conditioning is synonymous with learning. The term "classical" signifies this type of learning as the oldest method scientifically investigated, dating back to the beginning of the 20th century. Before we examine the first experiment that pioneered the study of classical conditioning, let's look at a study from the mid-20th century in which researchers conditioned an 11-month-old boy, Albert, to fear a white rat. The goal of the study was to determine whether a boy could learn to fear an animal (in this case a rat) that he initially quite liked. Why would someone do something like this to a child? Researchers wanted to determine if people could develop a fear of things they did not fear before. This was a quest for a *mechanism* of how fears are learned. Ask yourself: What is something you fear? Where does that fear come from? Perhaps, without even knowing it, you were classically conditioned. But by whom? Surely not by researchers. Anyone can be conditioned through certain circumstances. Circumstances can occur in such ways that fears are learned and adopted. For example, a soldier in the midst of a battlefield sees his friends killed from a grenade

153

blast and at the moment glances at his watch. From that moment on he starts to fear watches. Unbelievable, right? But, classical conditioning serves to explain this type of fear. Examining the study of little Albert will shed some light on the mechanisms of classical conditioning.

CLASSICAL CONDITIONING: TERMINOLOGY

11-month old Albert played with a white rat. The rat, in the field of the classical conditioning, would be the **neutral stimulus** (NS), since on its own it does not produce fear in the boy. During the study a researcher hid behind a couch and smashed metal bars with a hammer, creating a loud and surprising sound that made Albert cry. This fearful response is called the **unconditioned response** (UR). It is called "unconditioned" since it is not learned. It did not emerge from experience, meaning that even a newborn would be fearful of such a loud sound. It is an inherent response. Any stimulus that triggers an unconditioned response is called an **unconditioned stimulus** (US). An unconditioned response is similar to an involuntary (reflexive) response, an action that is very difficult (probably impossible) to avoid. The next step in the little Albert study was to let the boy play with the rat while the loud sound (US) was being produced. The simultaneous presence (or *pairing together*) of NS and US is called an **association**. The association between the NS and the US was done for several days for a few minutes per day, but what eventually happened was extraordinary: the rat was brought to the Albert, the loud sound was *not* generated, yet the boy displayed the same fearful reaction to the rat *as if* the loud sound was present. The rat (the NS) now produced the fearful response (the UR). When this point is finally reached, the UR becomes the **conditioned response** (CR) (or the learned response). It is a learned response since it was not present from the beginning (it was not triggered by the rat initially). Instead, the response emerged as a result of the boy's *experience*. When the neutral stimulus (the rat) produced a response (fear) that it initially did not produce, that same stimulus is then called the conditioned stimulus (CS). The NS, in other words, *evolves* into a more powerful stimulus (CS), which then triggers a learned (or conditioned) fearful response (CR) previously triggered only by the loud sound (US). Sadly, Albert became fearful of any white, furry animal, and even of many white furry things such as Santa Claus's beard! (Ciccarreli & White, 2017).

Figure 2. Albert learned to fear white rabbits and the Santa Claus's beard.

A person responding with a CR to stimuli that are *similar* stimuli to the original CS (as Santa Claus's beard is similar to the furry animal Albert was conditioned to fear) is called *generalization*. This means that the response has generalized or spread to similar stimuli (Davidson et al., 2016). Luckily, these learned responses obtained via classical conditioning usually fade away. The time it takes for a response to fully disappear varies from person to person but usually fades after one to two years. A conditioned response fading away is called *extinction*. However, after the extinction there is often a *spontaneous recovery* effect, where the CS is reintroduced and the CR re-emerges, but this time weaker and briefer. This is seen in situations when, after several years, we run into an ex-boyfriend or ex-girlfriend, and we start to feel good about that encounter. But, the general positive feeling about this encounter is likely false because of this effect and therefore will be short lived (John & Pineno, 2015). Research indicates that certain CRs depend on a particular time-arrangement of the CS and US. For example, a puff of air (US) makes a research participant blink (UR). Light (NS) is then shone into that participant's eyes at 1/10th of a second before the air puff is administered. Light is shone into another participant for 4/10ths of a second before the air puff is administered. This latter scenario produces a *stronger* eye-blink (CR) to the light, suggesting that the participant was conditioned to respond to the source of light separated 4/10ths of a second from the puff of air. If , however, NS occurs one minute before the US (or more than one minute), the CR will either be weak or absent. So, the *interval* in between the NS and US is a very important factor to consider, and the optimal interval (for the strongest CR) varies across different types of CR. In another study, a person was given a substance (US) that induced nausea (UR). Apple pie (or another food known to not result in nausea in the subject) was given to the person *one minute* before the substance (US) was administered. After a sufficient number of pairings of NS and US, the person developed nausea to the apple pie, a phenomenon called *taste aversion* (Chance, 2003).

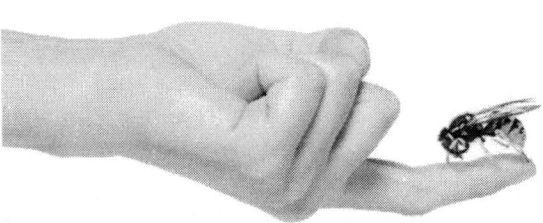

Figure 3. Is a bee sting a US or a NS or a CS? Why?

CLASSICAL CONDITIONING: APPLYING IT TO REAL LIFE

When classical conditioning occurs outside of a research lab, this authentic (real-life) situation can result in a CR that can last a lifetime. And, sometimes only one classical conditioning episode (or a trial) is enough to create a CR. An example of this is the soldier I mentioned before. A sight of blown up friends is a US, his fear is the UR, the watch he glances at is a NS. The US and NS became associated. Since that watch now makes him feel fear, the watch is the CS (not the NS any longer), and his fearful response to it is a CR. The sight of his friends being killed in battle and glancing at his watch became associated (Chance, 2003).

When a celebrity endorses a product (a car, for example), some people acquire a positive opinion about that product. But why? They *learned* to have a positive feeling about the *celebrity*, so the celebrity is a CS. The CR is a positive feeling people have about the celebrity, since they *learned* to like that celebrity (they are not born with that liking, in other words). Then, they may see the celebrity driving that car and the celebrity becomes *associated* with the product (NS). Due to this association, the car evolves from a NS to a CS, producing a positive feeling, which may persuade us to buy that same car since we have only positive associations with it. The repetition and abundance of advertisements increases the chance of the CR formation.

Figure 4. Why are celebrities or attractive people featured with commercial products?

Classical conditioning plays a role whenever a sexy model (US) is associated with some neutral stimulus (say a hamburger). The presence of a sexy model gives us a pleasant feeling (UR). When the gorgeous model starts eating a hamburger we are still feeling pleasant but now have another stimulus with which to associate the feeling (the hamburger). We may now buy that particular burger since seeing it on TV with a voluptuous model made us feel good.

Figure 5. Now that you know some secret mechanisms of how advertisements work you may never watch a commercial the same way again.

The examples in the previous paragraphs reflect an important concept within the framework of classical conditioning: *higher-order conditioning*. Once a CS is formed, that particular stimulus can be associated with a NS (but a different one from the original NS used to create that CS), so that this new NS result in a new CS. For example, how can one explain a person salivating when they see a McDonald's sign in the newspaper? The person was initially exposed to McDonald's food (the US), and that food stimulated their salivation (UR). Let's add that they were also inside a McDonald's *restaurant* (NS) while eating the food. After several visits to the restaurant the person begins to salivate (CR) just from seeing the McDonald's restaurant (CS). Later, while driving to the restaurant (CS), the person notices a McDonald's sign (NS) on the street. After driving to the restaurant on several occasions, the person starts to salivate (CR) from merely seeing the sign associated with food (CS) from McDonald's. *First-order conditioning* is when the person develops the first CS (seeing the *restaurant*), and the *second-order conditioning* was when the person develops the second CS (the *sign*). In order for the restaurant CS to be able to elicit a CR (salivation), the restaurant CS must be associated every now

156

and then with the US (food), otherwise the CR (salivation) will be lost, and the sign CS will not develop (Huffman & Sanderson, 2017).

CLASSICAL CONDITIONING: DROOLING DOGS AND BLINKING FROGS

Ivan Pavlov (1849-1936) was a Russian biologist. In an experiment he conducted at the beginning of the 20th century, Pavlov managed to condition dogs to salivate at the tone of a bell. Pavlov presented food (US) to a hungry dog, and the dog drooled (UR) out of reflex. Then, he paired the tone of a ringing bell with the presentation of the food. After a sufficient number of these pairings of the US and the NS, the dogs would drool (CR) at the tone of the bell (CS) (Huffman, 2017 in HUFFMAN). While this example of classical conditioning might not seem applicable to reality, it is indeed very important to understand since it reflects the *mechanism* of classical conditioning. Pavlov was the first researcher to publish research on classical conditioning, hence the term "classical" conditioning (classical meaning original, the first).

Figure 6. How would you classically condition this frog to blink when you show it a picture of Brad Pitt?

Understanding the basic concepts of classical conditioning allows us to understand why some people can't stand certain foods. They ate some food (US) that made them feel sick (UR). That sickness was then associated with some other food (NS). Now, they can't stand (CR) that other food (CS). *Taste aversion conditioning* is obvious in cancer patients who undergo drug therapy (chemotherapy). Chemotherapy (US) makes them feel nausea (UR). If a patient eats a certain food, say ice cream (NS), just before going to the chemotherapy and then feels sick after the therapy, the patient may feel sick (CR) when attempting to eat that type of ice cream (CS) at another time (Berteretche et al., 2004; Chance, 2003). Mechanisms discussed in this chapter also help explain what will happen when you go *hungry* on a date and you order food (US). The salivary glands in your mouth will go "crazy," shooting out saliva, hopefully not into the face of your date. It also explains how some of our fears can be triggered by certain classical conditioning situations. There are people who fear feathers, chalk, walls, cars, anything from rational to irrational. It is commonly though that this type of learning can explain the origin of many fears. Oppositely, people can be conditioned to be sexually attracted to almost anything. They only need to be exposed to a strong enough stimulus (say masturbation/US) that will trigger sexual arousal (UR). If masturbation occurs around balloons, it may happen (but not guarantee) that the person, after several masturbatory episodes, will develop sexual arousal at merely the sight of balloons! In the field of human sexuality research, it is recommended to not masturbate to *violent* pornography since the following scenario has been observed: masturbation (US) elicits sexual arousal (UR). Violent sex

(NS) is then associated with masturbation (US), and the person can develop sexual attraction to violent sex, which will be tolerated by porn actors, but not by many others.

Figure 7. How can an attractive person influence one's sexual attraction to balloons?

INSTRUMENTAL OR OPERANT CONDITIONING

Classical conditioning influences a subject to learn *involuntarily*. A person or an animal does not have a choice to acquire certain behaviors, since the unconditioned stimulus *automatically* triggers the unconditioned response, and the neutral stimulus links with the unconditioned stimulus without any conscious choice. **Instrumental conditioning** (or instrumental learning), however, is very different since a subject is *voluntarily* performing a behavior. The results or *consequences* of that intentional behavior determine whether the behavior happens again or happens less. Both classical and instrumental conditioning are considered to be *associative* types of learning. The associations being made in instrumental learning are between behavior and its consequences. Instrumental learning gets its name from the concept of using a *behavior* as our "instrument" to influence the environment. Instrumental learning is also called *operant learning* since we use our behaviors to *operate* and alter the environment. This type of learning refers to the processes of *reinforcement* for a behavior as well as the opposite process, the *punishment* for a behavior (Alexander et al., 2014).

Reinforcement is a process that allows an acceptable behavior to reoccur. This is accomplished through *positive* reinforcement. This means that an acceptable behavior is rewarded (a child behaves well and receives a cookie), which increases the chance that the behavior will be repeated, in anticipation of another reward. Reinforcement can be *negative* as well. In this sense a negative reinforcement is a behavior that *prevents* some bad outcome. We put a seat belt on *to avoid* getting injured in a car accident or receiving a ticket. This is called *negative reinforcement* since the behavior (putting on the seat belt) avoids/eliminates/*subtracts* (hence "negative") the probability of a bad event (a ticket or an accident). Conversely, the process of **punishment** is used to stop an undesirable behavior. So, punishment is entirely opposite from reinforcement. *Positive punishment* introduces a negative consequence (spanking a bad child, for example). It is called "positive" since we are *adding* a negative consequence. *Negative punishment* works as follows: a child misbehaves, and the parent *removes* (or *subtracts*—hence "negative") something that the child enjoys (the child may not be allowed to go to the park for two days) as a result of their misbehaving (Alexander et al., 2014). It is important to understand that the "negative" and "positive" aspects of instrumental conditioning refer to the addition or subtraction of allowances/rewards, not the value of the additions or subtractions themselves.

Figure 8. Before a party, a mother gives her child a cookie so that the child avoids misbehaving. This is an example of positive reinforcement.

WHICH IS MORE EFFECTIVE, REINFORCEMENT OR PUNISHMENT?

Which is more effective, reinforcement or punishment? Research has proven time and time again that the answer is reinforcement. Punishment, more often than not, creates fear, anxiety, anger, frustration, and hostility. Also, to escape punishment, an individual will usually avoid the punisher and will continue to misbehave. Similarly, an individual is very likely to lie in order to avoid punishment (Gershoff, 2010; Taylor et al., 2010). If the punishment is successfully avoided, after some time the bad behavior resurfaces (Cicarrelli, 2016). For example, when we get a traffic violation ticket, we swear we won't do it again, but after a while, we may repeat the same violation. Even with experiencing a punishment, the punishment usually does not have a long-term effect. Punishment also provides a behavior that may be later imitated by the punished individual (Larzelere, 1986). In addition, punishment does not have educational value since it does not indicate what an appropriate behavior is. Reinforcement, on the other hand, shows what the acceptable behavior is, so in that sense has an informative value.

In order for a punishment to be effective, it should immediately follow the bad behavior. If the punishment is administered later on, it will not be perceived as being directly related to the bad behavior. In addition, the punishment must be consistently applied. If parents want to punish their child for jumping on the bed, they should do so every time the child does so. The punishment should also be administered each time with consistent intensity. If a child is punished once with a spanking and the next time with only a scolding, the child will misbehave hoping for a mere scolding (it will gamble, hoping for the best). Punishment for misbehavior should be immediately followed with reinforcement of good behavior. For example, a child does not want to wear slippers in a house with cold tile flooring. The child is punished (can't watch TV for an hour) and told that when they start wearing the slippers they will get their TV privileges back as well as a cookie. When the child starts wearing the slippers, it is praised and given a cookie and the TV is turned on. The child learns that listening has its benefits (Cicarelli, 2017).

Well-researched concepts of operant learning include extinction, generalization, discrimination, shaping, and schedules of reinforcement. *Extinction* is not only a process in the domain of classical conditioning; it occurs in operant conditioning also, and refers to a removal of the reinforcement. Usually, when the reinforcement is removed, the behavior will slowly cease. But why would someone stop reinforcement? Imagine you are in a store with your child, and the little one throws

a tantrum since you don't want to buy her a toy. Next time, you want to avoid being annoyed by another tantrum and when your child asks for the toy you buy it for her. What you are doing is negatively reinforcing the child's behavior – to avoid a tantrum you buy her the toy, so you are reinforcing the child's behavior of requesting a toy next time too. Instead, it is recommended that you aid the extinction (stop the reinforcement) regardless of the child's tantrum. Eventually, the child will learn that they get neither your attention (reinforcement), nor the toy. *Generalization* occurs in the context of operant conditioning too. A child

Figure 9. How would you deal with a tantrum? Ignore the child? Punish the child?

who is learning to talk calls her father "Dada" and is rewarded (by the father) for that with a hug, kiss, smile, or praise. Soon the same child starts calling all men "Dada." However, the child soon starts to display *discrimination*, meaning they will continue saying "Dada" *only* to their father since only the father provides the positive reinforcement (not all other males). Learning via operant conditioning often does not happen immediately, but gradually over time, a process called *shaping*. This is especially evident in animals that are operantly conditioned to do certain tricks, like a gorilla that allows a person to brush its teeth. Initially the gorilla is rewarded (with food) for allowing a toothbrush to be near him. Next, it is rewarded for allowing a person to hold the toothbrush near the gorilla's face. Then, the gorilla is rewarded for allowing the person to put the toothbrush into his mouth. All kinds of complex behaviors are constructed in this way. Learning to tie shoelaces, for example. We may take it for granted but this behavior is very difficult for a child and every step deserves a reward.

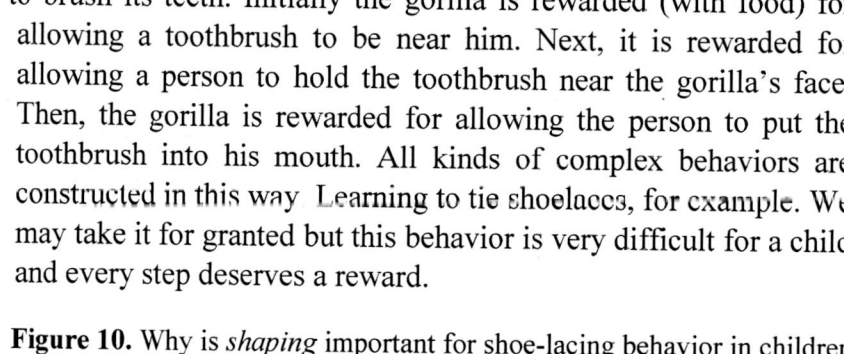

Figure 10. Why is *shaping* important for shoe-lacing behavior in children?

Learning via reinforcement happens fastest when the behavior is rewarded every time it happens (called *continuous schedule of reinforcement*). However, continuous reinforcement, once discontinued, leads to a rapid *extinction* or fading away of the learned behavior. Continuous reinforcement is not realistic, though, since in real life we are seldom rewarded every time we perform a good behavior. A more realistic type of reinforcement is *partial (intermittent) schedule of reinforcement*. This requires a behavior

160

being rewarded only from time to time. This reinforcement, when discontinued, leads to a slower extinction. This was demonstrated on pigeons that were placed in two groups. One group was given food every time they performed a certain behavior and the other was given food only occasionally after they performed the same behavior. Once the food reward stopped, pigeons that were rewarded continuously lost the learned behavior pretty quickly. The group of pigeons that were only occasionally rewarded lost the learned behavior much slower (Skinner, 1956). How does this apply to humans? One example is gambling. People who gamble only win sometimes. This is a partial reinforcement scenario. When a gambler loses, they still gamble, since they know that they must win again at some point. This observation is consistent with what Skinner discovered with pigeons (Strange et al, 2016). *Primary reinforcer* and *secondary reinforcer* are two terms important to operant conditioning. A primary reinforcer is a reward whose value we do not need to learn, such as human touch, food, water, shelter, etc. Secondary reinforcers include money, for example, since we need to learn that money can be used to buy things.

PIONEERS OF OPERANT CONDITIONING

During the first decade of the 20th century, Edward Thorndike (1874-1949) realized that rewarding a cat with food helped the cat learn to press a lever, open a gate and find its way out of its cage. Thorndike was the first researcher to articulate that learning depends on a connection between behavior (in this case pressing a lever) and its effects or consequences (food after pressing the lever). He termed this observation the *law of effect;* if a behavior is followed by pleasurable effects then it will be repeated, and if it is followed by unpleasant effects, it will decrease (Thorndike, 1911). In the 1930s, B.F. Skinner (1904-1990) continued the work of Thorndike, but Skinner eliminated certain terms such as "pleasant" and "unpleasant," arguing that psychology should focus only on the *observable* behavior, while the terms pleasant/unpleasant are subjective mental processes that cannot be objectively verified. In addition, Skinner coined the terms "operant conditioning" and "reinforcement" and dedicated his career to designing numerous experiments in the field of instrumental learning. *Skinner's box*, a famous term in psychology, refers to a cage with a lever in which a rat presses that lever to get a reward (food) or to avoid an electric shock. The benefit of the cage is that it provides an environment that can be controlled by a researcher.

Figure 11. Thorndike's famous experiments were with cats, Skinner's with rats and pigeons.

A real problem in psychology, continuing even today, is completing a research study and not being able to account for unknown factors, factors out of the hands of researchers. Skinner's cages, however, were small environments that provided the researchers with an ability to control the research environment to an unprecedentedly high extent (Cicarelli, 2017; Huffman & Sanderson, 2017).

In the 1930s it became apparent that learning also occurs through the utilization of cognitive (thinking) processes. Edward Tolman (1886-1959) demonstrated that rats, through experience, could form (learn) a *cognitive map* – a mental representation of a spatial layout — even without reinforcement. How was this demonstrated? Tolman formed three groups of rats that performed a task for 16 days. Group A was placed in a maze, and every time a rat would find the way out, it would be reinforced with food. Group B rats were not initially rewarded for finding the way out of the maze; however, beginning on day 10 they were rewarded with food each time they found the maze's exit. Group C was never rewarded for finding the way out. According to the operant learning approach, Tolman reasoned that Group A would learn how to solve the maze fastest due to consistent rewards; group B would start learning how to get out of the maze only after they were rewarded for finding the exit; and group C would be the slowest at learning, since they were not externally motivated at all. The results of the experiment supported the predictions regarding groups A and C. And, surprisingly, group B learned how to navigate the maze much faster than expected after they were given a reward. Tolman offered an explanation: Rats from group B *learned* about the layout of the maze during the beginning nine days without being rewarded. So, during those nine days they did still learn the layout even without being reinforced. But the lack of reinforcement meant they did not have a reason to display what they learned. When the reinforcement finally occurred, however, the rats wanted to find the way out faster in order to receive more of the pleasurable reward. While the reinforcement was important in motivating their behavior, it was not the only factor influencing their learning. The cognitive map was formed even before the reinforcement; the map was simply passive or dormant knowledge (called *latent learning*) that manifested when there was a reason for it – food. Tolman's study about acquiring of a cognitive map is a prime demonstration of cognitive learning (Tolman & Honzik, 1930).

Figure 12. Rats can form cognitive maps even before their behavior is reinforced.

In 1915, Wolfgang Kohler (1887-1967) showed that when presented with a problem, chimpanzees could have an *insight*, a rapid perception of how elements are related. This mental process was not reached through a mere trial-and-error process; instead, Kohler observed chimpanzees' behavior suggesting *reflections* on the problem. For example, a chimpanzee was given the opportunity to eat a banana, but the banana was hanging from a rope too high for the chimp to reach. The chimp looked at the nearby boxes, then at the banana, and back to the boxes. Then, the chimp stacked boxes on top of each other to grab and eat the banana. This behavior, suggesting a sudden realization of how the problem could be solved, was an indication of an *insight* (Kohler, 1925). The mental process of an insight is very important in learning how to solve problems.

Another famous study demonstrated the power of expectations or learned mental processes. In this classic study, dogs were classically condition to fear a tone (an electric shock was the US, fear was the UR and a tone was the NS). During this conditioning they were trapped and not allowed to escape. But, when they were placed in a situation that resembled the conditioning situation in which they suffered but this time with a way out, yet they did not even try to escape. It seemed that they surrendered and just waited for the painful electric shocks to stop. In the same study another group of dogs escaped immediately and easily when they felt the first electric shock. Martin Seligman (1942-), who conducted this study in the 1960s, argued that the dogs that did not escape believed (expected) that they could not escape. They acquired this expectation on the basis of the previous setting to which they were exposed. Their belief in not being able to escape was so

inflexible that they did not even try to get away. The dogs learned to be helpless (that's why this behavior is called *learned helplessness*). This has a tremendous application in our human life—many times people endure suffering believing that they cannot overcome it, when in fact they have only been conditioned to think this way.

Figure 13. How would animals with learned helplessness behave in this situation? They would simply wave in the wind, not even attempting to escape.

Cognitive learning is very much used in an academic environment where we use cognitive processes to comprehend, memorize, solve problems, and make decisions about what to study, what not to study, and how to study.

OBSERVATIONAL LEARNING

Learning can also happen via *observational learning*, a process that includes various cognitive and motivational processes. This type of learning refers to a person observing and imitating a behavior of someone who *models* the behavior. An observational learning approach would support the claim that watching a violent movie influences a person to be violent. In the 1960s Albert Bandura (1925-) designed a study consisting of two groups of preschool children. One group observed an adult playing with a large, inflatable doll. The other group observed an adult kicking and punching the doll. Then, one by one, each child was brought into a room with the doll. The children who were exposed to the aggressive adult model mimicked that same aggressive behavior, while the children who observed the non-violent model acted non-violently towards the doll (Bandura, 1961). Other studies confirmed the hypothesis that exposure to violence can lead to aggressive verbal and physical behavior as well as aggressive thoughts and emotions. Conversely, observing a helpful behavior decreases aggressive behavior in the observer (Anderson et al., 2014). There are several

163

processes that must occur in order for observational learning to take place: first, one must pay *attention* to the model's behavior; then, the learner needs to *memorize* that behavior; the behavior needs to be *imitated* by the learner, and the learner needs to be *motivated* to engage in all these mental processes again.

BIOLOGY OF LEARNING

Cognitive processes such as paying attention, decision-making, problem-solving, planning, self-discipline, cause and effect analysis, and language are mostly processed by the *prefrontal cortex.*

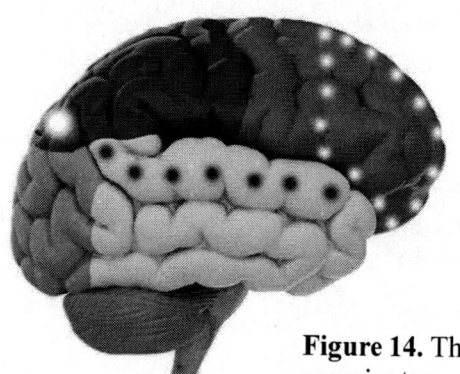

Another cognitive process is imagination (or our ability to visualize elements of reality). It is largely processed by the areas that process vision – occipital and temporal cortex (Ganis et al., 2004; Weller et al., 2012). In addition to the prefrontal cortex, attention is also processed by the *parietal cortex,* specifically, the inferior aspect of the right hemisphere. Damage to this area produces an inability to pay attention to anything located to the left of one's body.

Figure 14. The right inferior parietal area (white dot) and the right superior temporal area (black dots). White dots encompass the prefrontal cortex.

The *temporal cortex,* specifically the superior aspect of the right hemisphere, is also responsible for maintaining attention. Damage to this area produces an inability to pay attention to the left side of seen *objects* (Hillis et al., 2005). The superior longitudinal fasciculus, which connects the right posterior parietal cortex to the prefrontal cortex, influences the ability to pay attention to the *left side* of what one sees (Ptak & Schnider, 2010).

As we study, we engage in *language comprehension* (understanding the material) and *language production* tasks (reviewing the material). Even in the 19th century, derived from studies on individuals suffering from brain damage, it was determined that the following areas (see figure 15) encompassing the left hemisphere process language:

- *Primary visual cortex* allows us to receive an image of the letters we read
- *Angular gyrus* transforms the visual image of the word into the auditory format and passes it along to the Wernicke's area
- *Wernicke's area* (in the temporal cortex) facilitates our comprehension of words and transmits the message to Broca's area (in the prefrontal cortex)
- *Broca's area, arcuate fasciculus* (connects the Warnicke's area and Broca's area) and the *primary motor cortex.* These structures are involved in the production of speech (Gerschwind, 1970).

However, while modern research confirms the observation from the 19th century, it also reveals that there are *additional* language-supporting areas that complement those mentioned above (McDermott, Watson & Ojemann, 2005; Damasio et al., 1996). Also, while the left hemisphere *dominates* in language processing, the right hemisphere also shows considerable activity during language tasks (Bevelier et al., 1997). Further, in conducted studies, different research participants displayed significant differences in the *pattern of activity* in language areas, as well as differences in the brain *locations* that process language (Casey, 2003; Schlaggar et al., 2002).

Memory also plays an important role in cognitive learning, and there will be an entire chapter dedicated to memory and its diverse localization in the brain.

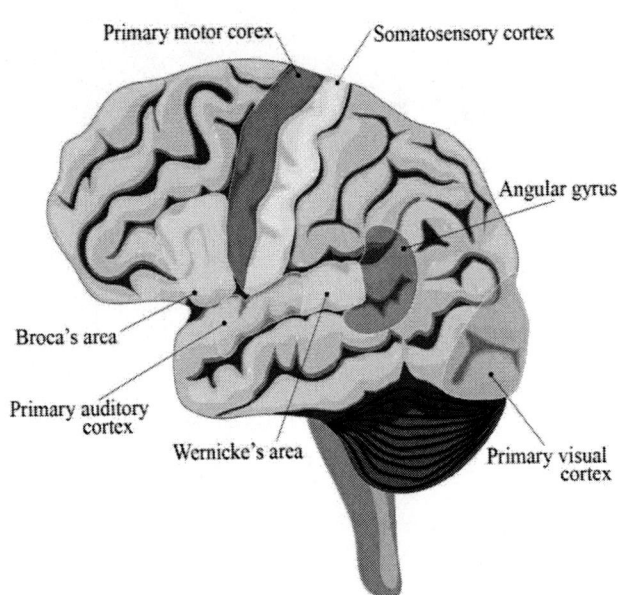

Figure 15. Language processing areas.

OBSERVATIONAL LEARNING

Observational learning refers to the process of acquiring new experiences by observing others and mimicking (imitating) their behavior. Others exhibiting their behaviors for us are called "models" in the context of observational learning. This type of learning is mostly employed when we acquire a skill or learn how to do a particular task, like riding a bicycle. Due to the observational component inherent in the name, *perception* plays a prominent role in observational learning. Another factor in observational learning are *mirror neurons*—neurons that become active once we observe and/or imitate another person's behavior in a particular situation (including an emotional response, like disgust). Mirror neurons (see figure 16) reside in the *premotor cortex* (Rizzolatti & Sinigaglia, 2010), making connections with the *posterior parietal cortex* (Buccino et al., 2004; Molenerghs et al., 2012). Mirror neurons from the posterior parietal cortex send their axons back to the premotor mirror neurons (Carlson, 2013). These premotor and parietal neurons in turn receive axons from the superior temporal sulcus (Carlson, 2013), where more mirror neurons may reside. Research indicates that mirror neurons may also exist in the right somatosensory cortex, a region that influences one's perception of particular emotions in another person (Adolphs et al., 2000; Hussey & Safford, 2009). Through mirror neurons we are able to observe and imitate others, thus allowing ourselves to empathize with them (to relate and understand how they feel) (Carr et al., 2003) and to learn how to comprehend their *intentions* (Iacoboni, et al., 2005), and to *cooperate* with others (Ocampo & Kritikos, 2011).

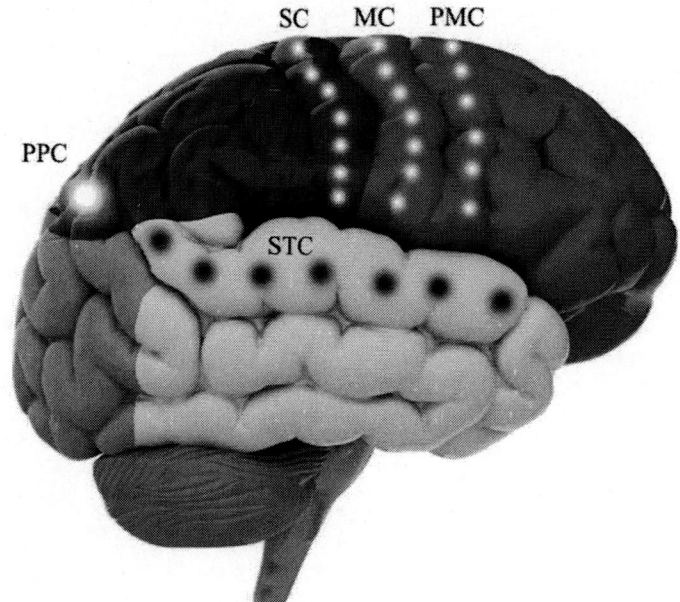

Figure 16. Mirror neurons are located in the posterior parietal cortex (PPC) and the premotor cortex (PMC). They may also reside in the right somatosensory cortex (SC) and the superior temporal sulcus (the valley below the STC). STC and black dots are superior temporal cortex. The motor cortex is labeled MC.

INSTRUMENTAL LEARNING

Instrumental learning is composed of a person's perception of a *stimulus* and their *response* to it. In the context of negative reinforcement, when a person anticipates a bad event (the stimulus), that person behaves (responds) in ways to avoid that event. In the context of positive punishment, however, if an individual misbehaves and is consequently deprived of a valuable possession (stimulus), that person does not engage (their response) in the same bad behavior in the future in order to secure their valuable possession. When a person behaves well and is rewarded (a stimulus) for that behavior, they tend to repeat the behavior (response) in the future in attempts be rewarded again. Perception of a stimulus depends on the *sensory systems* (vision, hearing, taste, etc.). These systems process our *initial* contact with the stimulus. For example, taste stimuli are processed by our frontal, temporal and parietal cortex; smell stimuli by the frontal and temporal cortex; hearing stimuli by the frontal, temporal and parietal cortex; touch stimuli by the parietal cortex, and so on. Each sensory system also involves a variety of *subcortical* brain regions that process sensory stimuli, but our *awareness* of stimuli occurs in the cortical regions. Sensory systems allow us to become aware of some *basic* aspects of a stimulus (our initial contact with it), but our perception of that stimulus is a more detailed interpretation of it, involving various cognitive processes.

Behavioral *responses*, since they require an action, involve the motor system, starting in the motor cortex in the frontal lobe. The activation of the skeletal muscles via the cranial and spinal motor neurons then follows. Thus, we can say that instrumental learning relies on the neural connections between the sensory and motor systems.

The information acquired through instrumental learning flows through the connections between the cortical sensory and motor systems. Likewise, the sub-cortical *hippocampus* plays a role in the instrumental learning. During the process of learning to *repeat* a particular behavior (via reinforcement) or to *eliminate* a particular behavior (via punishment), the hippocampus transfers the information that is being learned to the long-term memory (LTM) distributed throughout the cortex (Carlson, 2013; Kalat, 2013). The LTM is a storage place for learned or memorized material; similarly, the LTM storage *consolidates* material. The information from the cortical (motor and sensory) connections and from the LTM storage is shared with the subcortical *basal nuclei*. Basal nuclei process the *automatic* (or routine) aspect of the learned behavior; the information at the basal nuclei level is such that we do not have to learn it any longer: it is already learned, and can become incorporated as a routine (naturally and often unconsciously) into our daily behavior. For example, putting on our seatbelt when we enter a car, performing a handshake when we

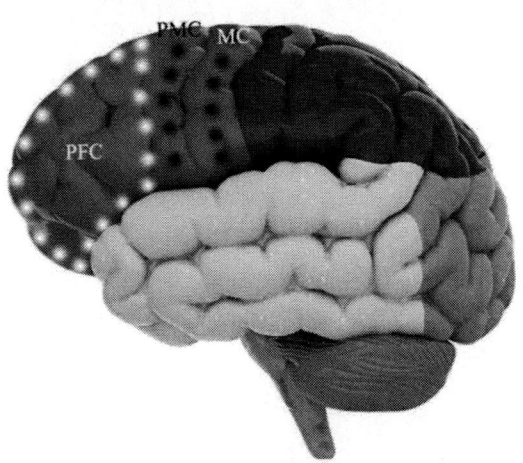

Figure 17. The prefrontal cortex (PFC), premotor cortex (PMC) and motor cortex (MC).

greet someone, and not sticking our fingers in electrical outlets are all automatic behaviors. From the basal nuclei, information is sent to the frontal lobe's *motor cortex*, specifically to the premotor cortex for the *planning* of the action, and then to the primary motor cortex for the *execution* of the action (Martini et al., 2012; Marieb & Hoehn, 2013).

Reinforcement allows us to learn what acceptable behaviors are. Engaging in appropriate behavior makes us feel good; this is because of the reward that follows that behavior (positive reinforcement). But from where is this good feeling originating, biologically speaking? When we experience a reward, the *prefrontal cortex* sends its axons that release glutamate to the cells of the *ventral tegmental area* of the midbrain (Gariano & Groves, 1998). Glutamate stimulates the ventral tegmental cells to release dopamine onto the cells of the *nucleus accumbens* of the basal forebrain. Dopamine release into the cells of the ventral tegmental area has been associated with pleasurable experiences (Knutson et al., 2001; Aharon et al, 2001). It is reasonable to assume that negative reinforcement also utilizes the same mechanism since we also feel good when we prevent a bad thing from happening. Interestingly, dopamine is released in the nucleus accumbens not only as a result of reinforcement, but also as a result of *punishment* (Salamone, 1992).

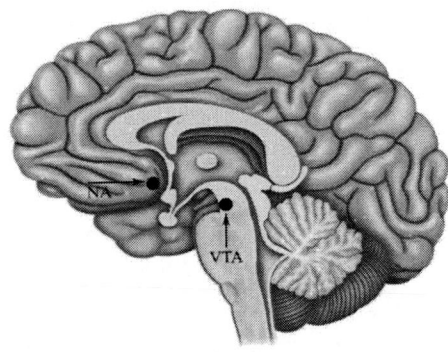

Figure 18. The nucleus accumbens (NA) and ventral tegmental area (VTA).

This is a logical process once we understand the fact that the *receptors* (receiving dopamine) determine the *meaning* of the dopamine release. In other words, when binding to one receptor, dopamine has a mood-lifting effect (when our behavior is rewarded), but when it acts on a *different* receptor, dopamine can have a negative effect (when we receive punishment).

LEARNING: HABITUATION AND SENSITIZATION

Through the process of *habituation* we learn to *decrease* our responses to stimuli that are repetitive. For example, in a room with a ticking clock, we pay less and less attention to the ticking as time progresses. *Sensitization*, on the other hand, is the completely opposite process—through **sensitization** we learn to *increase* our response to a stimulus that we encounter again after some previous exposure to it. If a child is tickled, then they laugh. Next time, when someone merely begins to tickle the child, they laugh even more than the first time (Kalat, 2013).

Figure 19. Aplysia the snail.

These phenomena were investigated in a sea snail called Aplysia. The snail was an excellent subject, due to its small number of large neurons, so scientists could easily see what was going on. Let's consider habituation first. It was observed that when the body of the snail was repeatedly touched, the snail initially withdrew that part of the body. But, after a sufficient number of repetitions, the snail eventually did not care about being touched—it habituated. What happened biologically speaking? When the snail's body was touched (stimulus), the stimulus was registered by the snail's sensory neuron. When the touch was repeated, however, then this stimulus influenced many voltage-sensitive calcium channels to remain *closed*, and the production of the action potentials *decreased* so that the motor neurons were not sufficiently stimulated to initiate the withdrawal of the touched body part. However, in terms of the sensitization of the snail, the story went like this: a body part of the snail was stimulated with the electricity—that stimulus was *aversive* (uncomfortable). The snail forcefully withdrew that body part. After the aversive stimulus was administered, the body part was gently touched. It was observed that the snail withdrew (response) that body part with *more force* compared to the situation when the snail was *initially* gently touched without the aversive stimulus. Biologically, the aversive stimulus influenced the closing of *potassium* channels (on the sensory neuron) so that potassium ions remained in the cell for a longer period, which prevented them from leaking out. Since the potassium ions could not leak out, that prevented the establishment of the sensory cell's resting potential. Thus, the cell was active longer (generating more action potentials) which led to more influx of calcium ions into the sensory axon terminal. This produced a prolonged release of neurotransmitters onto the motor neurons responsible for the withdrawal response. This prolonged release of the neurotransmitters caused their accumulation on the post synaptic receptors, which produced a more vigorous withdrawal response lasting from minutes to hours (Kolb & Whishaw, 2004). Similar mechanisms may play a role in habituation and sensitization in humans.

What is the biological basis of classical conditioning? In a series of studies a rabbit was exposed to puff of air (US), which made the rabbit blink (UR). Influence from the cells located in a nucleus of the *cerebellum* (lateral interpositus nucleus) conditioned the rabbit to *blink* (CR) at the sound of a certain *tone* (NS) (Clark & Lavond, 1993; Krupa Thompson & Thompson, 1993). Humans with damage to their cerebellum develop a weak conditioned response when researchers attempted to classically condition these individuals to blink when they heard a tone (Gerwig et al., 2005). These results are supported in cases in which unconditioned and conditioned stimuli are presented at about the same time. However, in classical conditioning studies in which NS ceases before the onset of US (requiring the individual to form a memory of NS), the basal nuclei, in addition to the cerebellum, become involved in the conditioning (Flores & Disterhoft, 2009). In other classical conditioning studies, animals are conditioned to emotionally respond to a stimulus, (to fear a tone, for example). In these studies, cells in the region of the *amygdala* (lateral nucleus) register the US (an electric shock to the foot) and the NS (a tone) (Rumpet et al., 2005; Migues et al., 2010). A damaged amygdala in humans has proven to prevent formation of a CR. For example, in a study anxiety (UR) was triggered by a very loud sound (US). Later, the US was presented along with a picture (NS), but the participants did *not* develop increased sweating (CR) to the picture (CS). Since the formation of a CS depends on an association between a US and an NS, the link (US/NS) could not be created due to the amygdala's damage (Carlson, 2013).

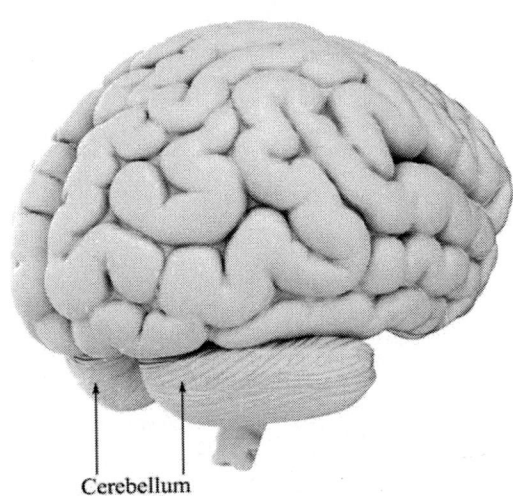

Cerebellum

Figure 20. The basal nuclei, amygdala and cerebellum are known to be involved in classical conditioning.

LEARNING: STRENTHENING OF THE SYNAPSES VIA LONG TERM POTENTIAION

Learning can be understood as a *change* in our behavior. Initially, we do not possess a certain behavior, and then, as a result of learning, we come to possess that behavior—this is an obvious example of a change. A fundamental observation about the biology of the learning process is that there is a certain change that happens at the level of a *synapse*. That synaptic change represents learning. Specifically, presynaptic neurons and postsynaptic neurons cooperate via their synapses, and through this mutual activity, the synapses become *increasingly* more *effective*. Synapses that are more active will become strengthened, and synapses with less activity will be weaker or even lose their effectiveness. This efficiency results from the co-occurring activity/use (reverberation) of the pre-synaptic and post-synaptic neurons. The synapses with increased effectiveness (more activity) are called Hebbian synapses since Donald Hebb (1949) hypothesized their existence even before they were discovered. Let's examine a pattern of synaptic activity influencing certain neuronal changes. This pattern may be a biological mechanism of learning.

Consider a pre-synaptic neuron synapsing with a post-synaptic neuron. A thin wire (the electrode) is placed in the pre-synaptic neuron. A *weak* electrical stimulus is administered through the wire stimulating the pre-synaptic neuron. This weak stimulus results in a *few* released neurotransmitters creating a barely noticeable EPSP (response) on the post-synaptic neuron. Next, a *strong* stimulus (100 pulses that last 1 second each) applied to the pre-synaptic neuron, produces a release of many more neurotransmitters and a much stronger EPSP in the post-synaptic neuron. Several weeks later, a much *weaker* electrical stimulus is administered to the pre-synaptic neuron; however, this weaker stimulus produces, surprisingly, an enhanced (stronger) EPSP in the post-synaptic neuron as if the stimulus to the pre-synaptic neuron is strong again. This is because the *post-synaptic* neuron is *potentiated*, or more responsive to a weaker input, due to the previous strong stimulation. This phenomenon of a weaker stimulus being administered to a pre-synaptic neuron and influencing an enhanced response in the post-synaptic neuron is called *long-term potentiation* (LTP) (Kalat, 2013; Pinel 2014).

In order to explain LTP biologically, we must revisit the strong stimulus being applied to the pre-synaptic neuron. When this happens, the pre-synaptic neuron releases glutamate. This transmitter crosses the synapses and binds to the dendrites of the post-synaptic neuron, specifically to the glutamate receptors NMDA and AMPA (receptors are located close to each other). When glutamate binds to the NMDA receptor, glutamate is prevented from further action since there is a magnesium ion in the NMDA receptor blocking the activity of glutamate. The magnesium, however, is displaced through the following process: when glutamate binds to the AMPA (not NMDA)

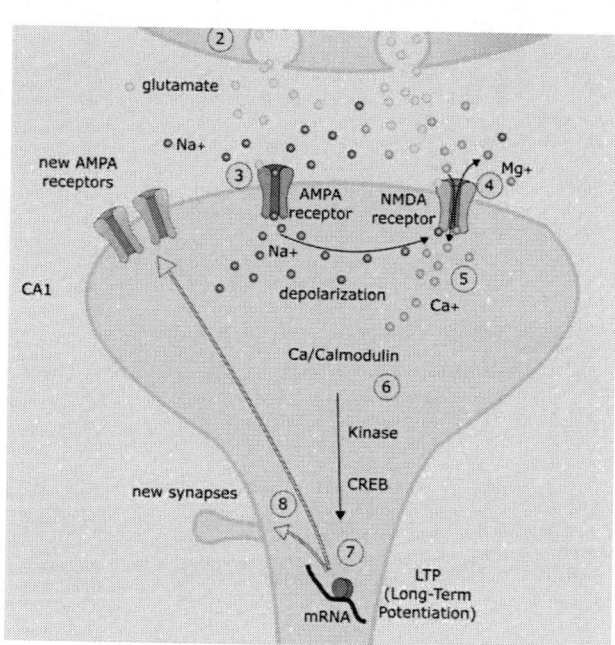

Figure 21. AMPA and NMDA receptors.

receptor, the depolarization of the dendritic membrane occurs. This depolarization affects the NMDA receptor as well and leads to a displacement of the magnesium ion that was preventing the activity of the glutamate. Once the magnesium ion is displaced, glutamate gets into the NMDA receptor and influences the opening of the chemically sensitive channels within the NMDA receptor, and the sodium and calcium ions rush through the ion channel into the cell (Kalat, 2013; Pinel 2014).

Calcium ions have a very special role in this process since they activate certain cellular proteins that further activate certain genes within the cell. The result of the activation of these proteins and genes are *changes* in the above-mentioned *dendrites* of the postsynaptic neuron (Kuczewski et al., 2008; Minichiello, 2009; Silva et al., 2009). These dendritic lead to receptors that are more responsive to weaker input. This is the fundamental aspect of the LTP. These dendritic changes consist of the following:

- Dendrites synthesize more AMPA receptors and rearrange already existing receptors in better positions so that they can receive more glutamate (Poncer & Malinow, 2001; Takahashi, Svodoba & Malinow, 2003).
- Dendrites generate more branches and spines, which allow the pre-synaptic neuron to form more synapses with branches and spines belonging to the post-synaptic neuron (Engert & Bonhoeffer, 1999; Xu et al., 2009).
- Certain chemicals bind to AMPA receptors making them more susceptible to glutamate than before. Dendrites also create more NMDA receptors (Grosshans et al., 2002).

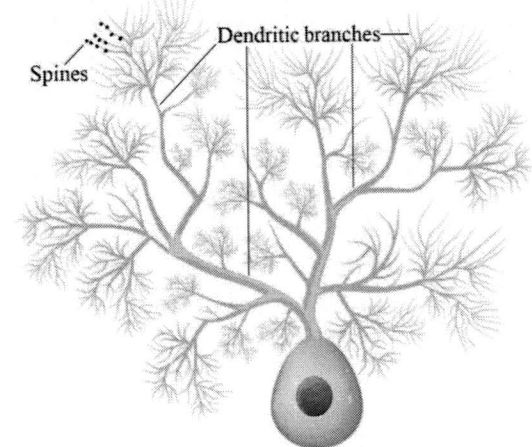

Figure 22. Dendritic branches and their spines.

So far we have talked of LTP being influenced by changes happening at the post-synaptic level, but LTP results from pre-synaptic changes as well. These pre-synaptic changes are not the only factor influencing LTP; sometimes the pre-synaptic changes occur in addition to post-synaptic (dendritic) changes. The pre-synaptic changes occur with the release of nitric oxide from the post-synaptic neurons. Nitric oxide travels back to the pre-synaptic neuron, diffusing into it and influencing the following changes:

- The pre-synaptic neuron *decreases* its threshold of excitation so that action potential can happen with less depolarization (Ganguly, Kiss & Poo, 2000).
    - This occurrence means that fewer ions are needed to trigger the action potential. So, even though a weaker stimulus will trigger a smaller EPSP on the pre-synaptic neuron, the smaller amount of flowing ions (comprising the EPSP) will still be sufficient to trigger the action potential.
- The pre-synaptic neuron releases *more* neurotransmitters even though the stimulus is weaker (Zakharenko, Zablow & Siegelbaum, 2001).
    - The presynaptic neuron releases neurotransmitters from additional locations along the axon (Reid et al., 2004). Releasing neurotransmitters from additional locations increases their chance to bind to post-synaptic receptors; in addition, more locations of release increase the amount of the released neurotransmitters.

LTP is stronger if *more axons* stimulate the post-synaptic neuron *at the same time*, and LTP is weaker if only one axon stimulates the post-synaptic neuron (Kalat 2013; Kerchner & Nicoll, 2008). LTP has been observed in the hippocampus and amygdala as well as other parts of the brain (Carlson, 2013; Pinel 2014; Kalat 2013). So, how is LTP related to learning? Learning involves change, and LTP reflects changes in the pre-synaptic and/or post-synaptic neurons as a result of synaptic use/activity. It seems that LTP represents a biological mechanism for learning. LTP is similar to sensitization, but LTP lasts longer (weeks) and it is more complex biologically.

171

Long-term depression (or reduction of activity) refers to a long-lasting *weakening* of a synapse due to lower activity of the presynaptic neuron. This lowered activity of the pre-synaptic neuron influences changes in the post-synaptic dendrites, such as retraction of the AMPA receptors (Collindgridge et al., 2010). The lowered activation of the pre-synaptic neuron influences a reduction in its stimulation of the post-synaptic neuron. Long-term depression is useful when we try to understand the *extinction* of what is learned. Extinction is well known in classical conditioning; several years after the conditioning has ended, the learned response (the conditional response) is lost, most likely due to the drop in use (activity) of the synapses between unconditioned stimulus neurons and neutral stimulus neurons. It is very likely that LTD plays a role in many other processes, where we observe the loss or a reduction (in the intensity) of certain learned behaviors.

REFERENCES

Adolphs, R., Damasio, H., Tranel, D., & Cooper, G. (2000). A role for somatosensory cortices in the visual recognition of emotion as revealed by three-dimensional lesion mapping. *Journal of Neuroscience*, 20, 2683-2690.

Aharon, L., Etcoff, N., Ariely, D., & Chabris, C. F. (2001). Beautiful faces have variable reward value: fMRI and behavioral evidence. *Neuron*, 2001, 32, 537-551.

Alexander, P., & Yakel, D. (2014). Psychology Exploring Our Universe Within (4th ed.). Boston, MA: Pearson Education.

Alexander, J. F., Waldron, H. B., Robbins, M. S., & Neeb, A. A. (2013). Functional family therapy for adolescent behavior problems (pp. 11-128). Washington, DC: American Psychological Association.

Anderson, C. A., Bushman, B. J., Donnerstein, E., Hummer, T. A., & Warburton, W. (2015). SPSSI research summary on media violence. *Analyses of Social Issues and Public Policy*, 15(1), 4-19.

Bailey, C. H., Giustetto, M., Huang, Y.-Y., Hawkins, R. D., & Kendel, E. R. (2000). Is heterosynaptic modulation essential for stabilizing Hebbian plasticity and memory? *Nature Reviews Neuroscience*, 1 (13), 11-20.

Bandura, A., Ross, D., & Ross, S. A. (1961). Transmission of aggression through imitation of aggressive models. *Journal of Abnormal and Social Psychology*, 63, 575-582.

Berteretche, M. V., Dalix, A. M., Cesar d'Ornano, A. M., Bellisle, F., Khayat, D., & Faurion, A. (2004). Decreased taste sensitivity in cancer patients under chemotherapy. *Supportive Care in Cancer,* 12(8), 571-576.

Buccino, G., Riggio, L., Melli, G., & Binkofski, F. (2005). Listening to action-related sentences modulates the activity of the motor system: A combined TMS and behavioral study. *Cognitive Brain Research*, 24, 355-363.

Carlson, N. R. (2013). *Physiology of behavior* (9th ed.). Boston, MA: Allyn and Bacon.

Carr, L., Jacoboni, M., Dubeau, M. C., & Mazziotta, J. C. (2003). Neural mechanisms of empathy in humans: A relay from neural systems for imitation to limbic areas. *Proceedings of the National Academy of Sciences*, 100 (9), 5497-502.

Ciccarelli, S. & Noland White, J., (2017). Psychology (5th ed.). Boston, MA: Pearson.

Clark, R. E., & Lavond, D. G. (1993). Reversible lesions of the red nucleus during acquisition and retention of a classically conditioned behavior in rabbits. *Behavioral Neuroscience*, 114 (9), 707-712.

Collingridge, G. L., Peineau, S., Howland, J. G., & Wang, Y. T. (2010). Long-term depression in the CNS. *Nature Reviews Neuroscience*, 11(7), 459-73.

Damasio, H., Grabowski, T. J., Tranel, D., Hichwa, R. D., & Damasio, A. R. (1996). A neural basis for lexical retrieval. *Nature,* 380, 499-505.

Engert, F. & Bonhoeffer, T. (1999). Dendritic spine changes associated with hippocampal long-term synaptic plasticity. *Nature*, 399 (13), 66-70.

Ganguly, K., Kiss, L., & Poo, M. (2000). Enhancement of presynaptic neuronal excitability by correlated presynaptic and postsynaptic spiking. *National Neuroscience*, 3(10), 1018-26.

Ganis, G., Thomspon, W. L., & Kosslyn, S. M. (2004). Brain areas underlying visual mental imagery and visual perception: An fMRI study. *Cognitive Brain Research*, 20 (2), 226-41.

Gariano, R. F., & Groves, P. M. Burst firing induced in midbrain dopamine neurons by stimulation of the medial prefrontal and anterior cingulate cortices. *Brain Research,* 1988, 462, 194-198.

Gershoff, E. T. (2010). More harm than good: A summary of scientific research on the intended and unintended effects of corporal punishment on children. *Law and Contemporary Problems*, 73(31), 31-56.

Geschwind, N. (1970). The organization of language and the brain. *Science*, 170, 940-944.

Grosshans, D. R., Clayton, D. A., Coultrap, S. J., & Browning, M. D. (2002). LTP leads to rapid surface expression of NMDA but not AMPA receptors in adult rat CA1. *Nature Neuroscience*, 5 (13), 27-33.

Hillis, A. E., Newhart, M., Heidler, J., Barker, P. B. (2005). Anatomy of spatial attention: Insights from the perfusion imaging and hemispatial neglect in acute stroke. *Journal of Neuroscience*, 25, 3161-3167.

Huffman, K., & Sanderson, C. A. (2017). Real World Psychology, 2nd edition. Bognor Regis: John Wiley & Sons, Inc.

Hussey, E., & Safford, A. (2009) Perception of facial expression in somatosensory cortex supports simulationist models. *Journal of Neuroscience*, 29, 301-302.

Iacoboni, M., Molnar-Szakacs, I., Gallese, V., & Buccino, G. (2005, February 22). Grasping the intentions of others with one's own mirror neuron system. *PLoS Biology*, Retrieved from http://journals.plos.org/plosbiology/article?id=10.1371/journal.pbio.0030079.

Kalat, J. W. (2013). *Biological psychology* (11th ed.). Belmont, CA: Wadsworth, Cengage Learning.

Kerchner, G. A., & Nicoll, R. A. (2008). Silent synapses and the emergence of a postsynaptic mechanism for LTP. *Nature Reviews Neuroscience*, 9 (11), 813-25.

Knutson, B., Adams, C. M., Fong, G. W., & Hommer, D. (2001). Anticipation of increasing monetary reward selectively recruits nucleus accumbens. *Journal of Neuroscience,* 21, RC159 (1-5).

Köhler, W. (1925,1992). *Gestalt psychology: An introduction to new concepts in modern psychology (reissue)*. New York: Liveright.

Krupa, D. J., Thompson, J. K., & Thompson, R. F. (1993) Localization of a memory trace in the mammalian brain. *Science*, 260 (13), 989-991.

Kuczewski, N., Porcer, C., Ferrand, N., Fiorentino, H., Pellegrino, & C., Kolarow, R.(2008). Backpropagating action potentials trigger dendritic release of BDNF during spontaneous network activity. *Journal of Neuroscience*, 28 (13), 7013-7023.

Larzelere, R. (1986). Moderate spanking: Model or deterrent of children's aggression in the family? *Journal of Family Violence,* 1(1), 27-36.

Marieb, E., & Hoehn K. (2013). Human anatomy and physiology (9th ed.). Glenview, IL: Pearson Education.

Martini, H. F., Nath, L. J., Bartholomew, F. E., & Ober, C. W. (2012). Fundamentals of Anatomy and Physiology (9th ed.). San Francisco, CA: Pearson Benjamin.

McDermott, K. B., Watson, J. M. & Ojemann, J. G. (2005). Presurgical language mapping. *Current Directions in Psychological Sciences*, 14, 291-295.

Minichiello, L. (2009). TrKB signaling pathways in LTP and learning. *Nature Reviews Neuroscience*, 10 (13), 850-860.

Molenberghs, P., Cunnington, R., & Mattingley, J. B. (2012). Brain regions with mirror properties: A meta analysis of 125 human fMRI studies. *Neuroscience and Biobehavioral Reviews*, 36, 341-349.

Ocampo, B., & Kritikos, A. (2011). Interpreting actions: The goal behind mirror neuron function. *Brain Research Reviews*, 67, 260-267.

Pinel, P. J. (2014). Biopsychology (9th ed.). Boston, MA: Pearson Education.

Poncer, J. C. & Malinow, R. (2001) Postsynaptic conversion of silent synapses during LTP affects synaptic gain and transmission dynamics. *Nature Neuroscience*, 4, 989-996. (13)

Ptak, R., & Schnider, A. (2010). The dorsal attention network mediates orienting toward behaviorally relevant stimuli in spatial neglect. *Journal of Neuroscience*, 30 (14), 12557-12565.

Reid, C. A., Dixon, D. B., Takahashi, M., Bliss, T. V., & Fine, A. (2004). Optical quantal analysis indicates that long-term potentiation at single hippocampal mossy fiber synapses is expressed through increased release probability, recruitment of new release sites, and activation of silent synapses. *Journal of Neuroscience*, 24 (14), 3618-26.

Rizolatti, G., & Sinigaglia, C. (2010). The functional role of the parieto-frontal mirror circuit: Interpretations and misinterpretations. *Nature Reviews Neuroscience*, 11, 264-274.

Salamone, J. D. (1992). Complex motor and sensorimotor function of striatal and accumbens dopamine: Involvement in instrumental behavior processes. *Psychopharmacology*, 107, 160-174.

175

Sanderson, C., & Huffman, K., (2017) Real World Psychology (2nd ed.) USA: John Wiley & Sons.

Schlaggar, B. L., Brown, T. T., Lugar, H. M., Visscher, K. M., Miezin, F. M., & Petersen, S. E., (2002). Functional neuroanatomical differences between adults an school-age children in the processing of single words. *Science, 296*, 1476-1479.

Silva, A. J., Zhou, Y., Rogerson, T., Shobe, J. & Balaji, J. (2009). Molecular and cellular approaches to memory allocation in neural circuits. *Science, 326* (13), 391-395.

Skinner, B. F. (1956). A case history in the scientific method. *American Psychologist, 11*, 221-233.

Strange, M., Graydon, C., & Dixon, M. J. (2016). "I was that close": Investigating players' reactions to losses, wins, and near-misses on scratch cards. *Journal of Gambling Studies, 32*, 187-203.

Taylor, C., Manganello, J. A., Lee, S. J., & Rice, J. C. (2010). Mothers' spanking of 3-year old children and subsequent risk of children's aggressive behavior. *Pediatrics, 125*,1057-1065.

Tolman, E. C., & Honzik, C. H. (1930). Introduction and removal of reward and maze learning in rats. *University of California Publications in Psychology, 4*, 257-275.

Xu, Y., Padiath, Q. S., Shapiro, R. E., Jones, C. R., Wu, S. C., & Saigoh, N. (2005). Functional consequences of a CKrd mutation causing familial advanced sleep phase syndrome. *Nature, 434*, 640-644.

Zakharenko, S. S., Zablow, L., & Siegelbaum, S. A. (2001). Visualization of changes in presynaptic function during long-term synaptic plasticity. *National Neuroscience, 4* (7), 711-7.

Memory

Chapter Six

WHAT IS MEMORY?

Memory is the mental process of *storing* and *retrieving* information, mental processes and behaviors. There are various types of memory, such as sensory, short-term, long-term, episodic, semantic, procedural, explicit, implicit, hypermnesia, flashbulb memory, and false memories.

Information needs first to be encoded before the storing takes place. *Encoding* refers to the input of information into our mind. Let's say you need to memorize the term "hippocampus." To encode it, you need to focus your *attention* on that word (called selective attention). Encoding can have different *formats*, and some facilitate better memory than others. For example, you can repeat the word "hippocampus" many times, hoping that it becomes engrained into your mind and remains there (storing). This is an *auditory format* since one relies only on how the word sounds (not yet focusing on understanding the word). There is a much better chance that the word will not be stored if the encoding process relies on sound alone. Similar is the *visual format* – if you focus only on the appearance of the letters (h, i, p, p, etc.), the word won't be stored for a long time. A more effective format is one that incorporates *cognitive-sensory elaboration*. You need to *elaborate* on the term "hippocampus" in order to create associations that help your mind store the word. Upon elaborating the term

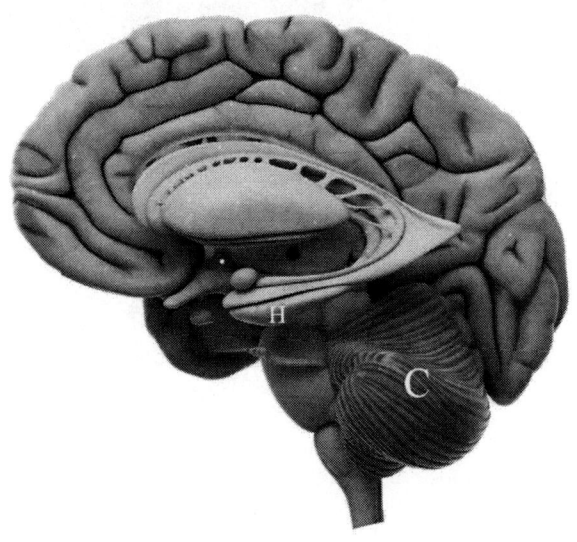

Figure 1. The hippocampus (H) is located deep within the brain (one half of the surface of the brain is not shown.

"hippocampus," we can come to contextualize it as a brain structure that helps us form memories (without the hippocampus, we would not be able to remember new information!). Let's elaborate even further: the hippocampus is a Latin term that means "a seahorse." How is a seahorse going to help in memorizing hippocampus, you may ask. Let's continue to elaborate by breaking the word "hippocampus" into two more *meaningful* words: "hippo" and "campus." This is an important step since it is easier to memorize smaller bits of meaningful information than larger amounts of meaningless information (Schlichting & Preston, 2014). The next level of elaboration is creating a mental movie featuring all of what we said about the hippocampus. Additionally, let's add some sensory information too: in your mind's eye *picture* a hippo walking through your campus.

Picture the hippo with a flash-drive USB hanging around its neck and a tattoo in the shape of a seahorse. Studies suggest that these mental movies should be as *strange* as possible, for the sake of standing out, thus being easier to remember. With that in mind let's blow up our hippo to gargantuan proportions. We'll picture it sitting in the campus. It has also been proved that information that is related to *ourselves* is easier to memorize than information that is irrelevant to us (Leblond et al., 2016), thus picture yourself riding on the back of this hippo, like a cowboy or a cowgirl. This exceptionally elaborate image should also include as much additional *sensory* information as possible, so smell the scent of the hippo
— this will make the image more realistic and more memorable. In your mind, it is totally fine to even yell a long "yeehhawww," like a real cowboy or a cowgirl, since you want to include *auditory* information as well to make the scene as realistic as possible in your mind. The reality of the scene is inconsequential; all that matters is that the scene is memorable to you, the individual memorizing "hippocampus." After this thorough elaboration you will probably never forget the scene of riding a gigantic, aromatic hippo through your campus, with a flash-drive USB around its neck and seahorse tattoo. From now on the term hippocampus will remain with you forever. The process we followed here was adding as many cognitive and sensory layers of elaboration possible. In other words we engaged in multiple *levels of processing of information* so that the information can be encoded. You can now apply this encoding approach to any term or concept you wish to memorize.

Figure 2. Howdy partner! Did you enjoy the ride?

SENSORY MEMORY

As previously mentioned, there are various types of memory. *Sensory memory* lasts very briefly, up to about a second. The most researched sensory memories are *visual* and *auditory*. Visual sensory memory, also called the *iconic memory*, allows us to absorb visual information from the environment. Whatever can fit into our visual field becomes our sensory memory, but if we do not *attend* to that information, it will most likely be lost from our memory in up to one second (Cicarelli, 2017). Some rare individuals have a gift to prolong their visual sensory memory, so they can maintain the visual information in their mind. This ability is also called the *photographic memory* (Stromeyer & Psotka, 1971), but what causes this is poorly understood.

Let's consider a famous study. George Sperling (1934 -), showed to his subjects 12 letters (three rows of four letters) extremely briefly -- for 1/20ths of a second. He asked them to recall the letters and found that subjects could only recall four or five out of the 12. But Sperling wanted to find out whether they actually maintained more letters in their visual sensory memory. He showed them the same set of 12 letters and, at the same time, played a high-pitched tone. The tone was the signal that the subjects were to recall only the uppermost level of three letters. This time the subjects were able to recall the top level of letters, even though the presentation was for only 1/20ths of a second. Sperling repeated the same procedure but with a *low* tone, signaling the subjects to recall the lowermost level of letters. And, again, the same results as the last tone. The procedure was then repeated with a *middle* tone, and the subjects recalled all letters in the middle level. Sperling concluded from this that his subjects did in fact keep *all* 12 letters in their sensory memory, but *consciously* recalled only those that they attended to. But, when he presented the letters and waited for one second to sound one of the three tones, the subjects could not recall all letters from any given level (Sperling, 1960). So, memory fades with the passage of time. It seems that the visual sensory memory allows us to preserve the information that's in front of us, but we need to focus on a certain segment of the scene (and recognize it as important) in order to recall it. Intuitively this makes sense, since paying attention to a segment of reality allows us to disregard the less important stimuli. We respond quickly to the most important information, in less than a second, and if the information is not perceived as important, it fades from our memory relatively quickly. *Echoic sensory* memory stores sounds for two-four seconds (Erviti et al., 2015). Important sounds are attended to and stored for a longer amount of time, irrelevant sounds rapidly fade away. The capacity of this memory is what can be heard at any one moment (Schweickert, 1993).

Figure 3. Playing in a band requires maximum synchronicity of a variety of sounds (rhythm, instruments, vocals). Without instantaneously hearing what others members play, the music may fall apart and sound awful.

SHORT-TERM MEMORY

Short-term memory (STM) processes new, incoming information. There are two types of STM: *working memory* and *non-working memory*. Working memory is when we *rehearse* the information to which we are exposed. By rehearsing it, we actively work on that new information. Say someone gives you a phone number, but you have nowhere to record the number. Yet Mr. Right or Ms. Right is giving you their phone number. You simply need to maintain it in your mind by rehearsing it (whether in your head or out loud). This is called *maintenance rehearsal*, an aspect of working memory. The information will remain in your STM as long as you can rehearse it, so STM's *duration* has no limit, but STM's *capacity* does: its limit being anywhere from three to five *pieces* of information (Cowan et al., 2005; Palva et al., 2010). What is meant by "pieces" of information is as follows: the phone number 562-938-4322 can be broken down into pieces such that 562 is piece number one, the piece number two is 938, and piece three 4322. We are talking about three *chunks* of information. Be aware that this rehearsal relies on the auditory format. However, elaborative rehearsal based on meaning has proved to make memorization easier, for example: when I was 5, I had 6 cousins, 2 of them are now doctors. Non-working memory is a passive type of STM, since a person does not rehearse the information. In this situation we are just passive recipients of information. The duration of the non-working aspect of STM ranges anywhere from 12 - 30 seconds (Atkinson & Shiffrin, 1968; Peterson & Peterson, 1959). For example, I was once staying in a hotel in Las Vegas with my wife. I stepped out for a few minutes, but before I left the floor I made sure I spent a few seconds rehearsing the number on the door of my hotel room. I thought I had it memorized—it was a simple 5-digit number—and stopped rehearsing. So, from that point on I was at the mercy of my non-working STM. Alas, non-working memory lasts only up to half a minute, so it is no wonder that very soon I had absolutely no idea in which room I was staying. I did not take my ID, and the receptionist refused to look under my name in the system, saying it was for my own protection. To make the things even more absurd, when I asked if a security officer could help me, they said there were none available, even though

it was one of the major hotels (later I learned that the receptionist just began working for the hotel, and did not know how to help lost souls like myself). I will let you guess how the story ends. Hint: it pays to have a rescuing wife.

Figure 4. What happens in Vegas does not always stay in Vegas (sometimes it ends up in a textbook).

LONG-TERM MEMORY

When behaviors, habits, emotional reactions, and information are stored in our mind to the point where they are automatically available for retrieval, we can say that those contents (behaviors, etc.) are then aspects of our **long-term memory** (LTM). How old are those aspects of our LTM? In other words, did they end up in our LTM a few days ago or a few decades ago? There is no specific time frame, really. As long as a memory does not have to be rehearsed, but can be recalled on command, it is a long-term memory. Thus, long-term memories can be a day, five days, several months, a year, or even several decades old. How long do these memories last? They can last as long as we live.

Certain factors influence our *retrieval* of LTM. Memory retrieval is better if the conditions under which a memory is formed are the same to the conditions in which retrieval occurs. In accordance with this principle you are more likely to perform better on a test if the classroom in which you are taking the test is the same in which you learned the material. This is called *context-dependent memory* (Tulving & Thompson, 1973; Gao et al., 2016). Likewise, memories formed during a particular *state of mind* will be likely retrieved when the person is in the same mental state. For example, when you are in a good mood you will tend to retrieve memories that are associated with your previous positive mood. Intoxicated individuals retrieve information from a previous episode

180

of intoxication. When they are sober, however, they may not easily retrieve the positive information from that previous euphoric experience. This is called *state-dependent memory* (Hunt & Barnet, 2016). A technique that helps us form a LTM is called a *mnemonic*. Elaborative rehearsal (see the "hippocampus" example) is one such technique. There are other mnemonics as well, such as *acronyms*. A famous acronym in psychology is OCEAN, for storing and retrieving people's major personality characteristics such as Openness, Conscientiousness, Extraversion, Agreeableness and Neuroticism.

LTM (as well as STM) can be *declarative* and *non-declarative*. Declarative memories are those that we can state (or declare) in words easily, such as what we had for breakfast. Since this is an episode from our personal life, this type of declarative memory is called *episodic*. *Semantic* memories are declarative memories for facts and general knowledge (accessible to all people) such as: "Paris is the capital of France." There are memories that cannot be easily articulated (or not at all) such as how to play an instrument, how to dance, and how to do tasks. Those are non-declarative memories. *Implicit memories* are ones that we cannot formulate how they were obtained despite clear and undeniable possession of them. Damage of brain structures such as the temporal lobe, can turn our normal memories into implicit memories. *Explicit memories*, conversely, are those that we know exactly how, where, and when we obtained them (Kalat, 2016).

Figure 5. Dance choreography is a procedural memory. It includes a lot of moves and body positions that are difficult to put in words.

FORGETTING

The inability to retrieve information that we could previously recall is known as *forgetting*. But, why and how does it happen? Ebbinghaus (1885) showed that forgetting meaningless material (a list of words like XOL, PUY, JOF) is common. One hour after learning these syllables, subjects remembered 44 percent of them, one day later 35 percent, and one week later 21 percent. He concluded that most forgetting occurred during the first hour. The ability to recall still declined but not as dramatically as in the first hour after learning. Ebbinghaus first employed meaningless material, but after having his subjects memorize more meaningful content the process of forgetting became slower and much less total (Conway et al., 1992). Research shows that spacing out studying sessions (called *distributed practice*) produces less forgetting than studying material in a compacted amount of time, "cramming" (*mass practice*). For example, students often have a habit of studying only the day before an exam, and as a result they do not do well on the exam. Had they instead studied every day for a week leading up the exam for about 30 minutes to an hour, their scores would have improved since more information would have been retained (Capeda et al., 2006; Donovan & Radosevich, 1999). When we do not pay attention to information (called *encoding failure*), memory is not even initiated, so we cannot say that forgetting happens rapidly since in order to forget something we first need to have stored information in our mind. Forgetting, instead, is explained via a view that if memory is not being used, the information will decay due

181

to the lack of use. Memories are a pattern (also called a *trace*) of an electrical current in a network of brain cells, and if we do not do anything to refresh memories and stimulate the passage through the brain cells (utilize the memorized information through retrieval) the current will weaken or stop, and memories will become inaccessible or fade away completely. This *trace decay view* of forgetting is a "use it or lose it" view (Bjork & Bjork, 1992). However, we sometimes do not rehearse or refresh some memories for decades and yet they may miraculously pop into our consciousness one day. The trace decay view has a hard time explaining this observation.

Perhaps another explanation, the *interference view*, can complement the trace decay view. Some memories may be forgotten due to interference with other, competing bits of information (Anderson & Neely, 1995). For example, picture a person who drives a car with automatic transmission. Then, this person moves to another country where only manual transmission cars exist. The individual now needs to learn to drive an unfamiliar type of car. What will happen? At first, her legs and arms will instinctually do all the things that are associated with driving an automatic car. That procedural memory will interfere with her learning how to drive the manual car. This tendency for an old memory (procedural memory of driving an automatic car for years) to interfere with the retrieval of a *new* memory (procedural memory of driving a stick-shift car in a new country) is called *proactive interference*. There is *retroactive interference* too, where newly learned information interferes with retrieving an *old* memory. People, who move from their homeland to a new country, after living in the new country for years and speaking an adopted language, often have trouble remembering words and phrases from their native tongue. Their speech may sound like a mixture of two languages when they go back to the homeland and attempt to return to their original language (Cicarelli, 2017).

Figure 6. Calling your significant other by the name of an old significant other can be blamed on proactive interference.

Information can be registered (encoded) in one's sensory memory, but if it does not receive necessary attention it will not reach the STM storage – it will be forgotten (Blake et al., 2015). For example, do you recall the Apple's logo? It is an apple right? But is it a bitten or whole apple? Where does the petal point, to the left or right? And what about the stop sign when we drive? You see them every day on the streets, but is it a circle or some other shape? Is the word STOP outlined in red or white or black? These details likely reached your sensory memory, but never got into your STM since you did not pay attention to them. They are certainly not in your LTM either.

There is another factor at work as well – *motivated forgetting*. This means that sometimes we are motivated to not be able to retrieve information. This may occur when we witness a traumatic event. Our mind may be driven by some subconscious mechanisms to relocate the troubling information from consciousness into the subconscious mind. Forgetting is also influenced by a *serial-position effect*, which states that we remember the information we heard first and the information we heard last, yet the middle information is not remembered as well. For example, this happens at job interviews when many applicants are interviewed. Employers will remember the best the applicants who were closer to the beginning of the interview process and those who came last, but will not remember as well those in the middle. This happens since the ones at the beginning were rehearsed in STM (by those who conducted the interviews) without interference from too many sources of information, which occurs when the middle interviewees became involved. Those who were interviewed last, since they occurred most recently, will be remembered better than those that interviewed earlier. That's why we say that the serial position effect is composed of *primacy effect* (those who were heard first), the *recency effect* (those who were heard last), and the *middle effect* (ones in the middle who were not remembered well at all) (Bjork & Whitten, 1974; Murdock, 1962).

Yet another factor can stimulate forgetting – the *misinformation effect* states that false information happening *after* the event we witnessed can alter the original memory of the event so that we no longer remember the original event. For example, research participants were asked to view an arrangement of items within a room. They were then taken to another room. One group of these subjects was asked: "was there a telephone in the room?" The majority of the subjects answered correctly, saying that there was not a telephone. However, when another group was asked: "what color was the telephone in the room?", 98 percent of them guessed a color, falsely remembering the telephone that didn't exist (Morgan et al., 2013).

Figure 7. Sometimes interviewers can be tough, cold and intimidating. After interview, we feel that we failed. If other candidates interviewed better than us, how can the serial positioning effect work to our advantage?

Forgetting is sometimes influenced by *stress*. For example, two groups of participants were exposed to a movie. One group saw an ending where a man was shot in the face, and the other group saw the same movie with a non-violent ending. The group that saw the more stressful version of the movie had a harder time recalling 16 other aspects from the movie (Loftus & Burns, 1982)

FALSE MEMORY

False memory is memory of an event that did not occur in reality. People who have false memories are not lying about their recollections, but they firmly believe that their memories reflect something that actually happened, even though they do not. In a study, participants were provided with three stories (one of which was about being lost in a shopping mall). They were told that the researchers contacted their parents and that the parents confirmed that these events happened. Then, the participants were asked to rate the clarity of those three events. 25 percent of the participants remembered being lost in the shopping mall (some remembered it more clearly than others); however, that story was made-up. The researchers had parents confirm that it did not happen to the participants (Loftus & Pickerell, 1995). A woman, Elizabeth, had a tragedy in her family – her mother drowned in a pool when Elizabeth was around 14. Her relative misinformed her years later that she was the one who discovered her mother's body in the pool, and, from then on, Elizabeth started to vividly remember that tragic event. It haunted her. Years later, several other of her relatives told her that it was not Elizabeth who discovered the body, but instead her aunt. The Elizabeth anecdote is an example of a false memory due to the aforementioned misinformation effect. The Elizabeth here is none other than Elizabeth Loftus (see the previous reference of the study on being lost in the shopping mall), an authority on false memory research (Huffman, 2016).

Figure 8. People can falsely remember being lost in a shopping mall when sufficiently prompted.

False memories can stimulate erroneous *eyewitness testimony*. False memories caused more wrongful convictions than all other causes combined (Loftus, 2002). When researchers examined 40 cases of prisoners who were later found to be empirically innocent it turned out that 90 percent of them were convicted on the basis of inaccurate eyewitness testimony (Wells, 1998). Research has shown that eyewitness accounts can be inaccurate due to the *expectations* and *bias* of a witness. Another factor that can negatively influence the eyewitness testimony is the way in which the witness is questioned. For example, a detective should ask: "what was he wearing?" But, if the detective asks: "what kind of a hat was he wearing," the witness may be influenced to create a false memory of someone wearing a hat, and later identify a person who wears a black hat (Loftus, 1996). When a witness faces a line-up of suspects, the witness will usually pick someone from the line-up even if the culprit is not in the line-up. They are likely to identify a suspect who resembles their memory of the suspect closest. This leads to an innocent individual pegged as the culprit (Rubenzer, 2002). Sometimes a witness will identify a person from a line-up after recognizing that person from a totally different context than the crime at hand (Haw et al., 2007). For example, in the 1980s there was a famous case of child abduction in Las Vegas. However, it turned out that several witnesses who identified the man as the kidnapper did so solely based off the fact that they saw him in the same hotel as the kidnapped boy. But correlation (association of man and the boy) does not imply causation (the man kidnapping the boy). Later, it was established that they initially reported seeing a completely different man with the boy, but they forgot those initial recollections and unintentionally altered them.

False memory can also result from our tendency to fill in memory gaps with information that makes sense for us personally. For example, participants were read a story. Some aspects of the story were meant to not make sense at all. After the story was read, participants were asked to recall the story. Many participants did not recall the nonsensical parts. Instead, they recalled their own, logical versions of the story. This process of filling the gaps with the information that makes sense is called *confabulation* (Loftus & Loftus, 1980). This and other studies mentioned thus far demonstrate that memory is not a synonymous with a snapshot or video recording of reality;

184

instead, memory is our *reconstruction* of reality. Another factor that can influence creation of false memories is *hypnosis* (Frenda et al., 2014). During hypnosis, a hypnotist suggests certain scenarios to an individual, and may accidentally suggest events that never happened. The client is suggestible, and will absorb the truth of the suggestions as if the events really occurred. After regaining consciousness, the individual could recall false memories, believing they are real. Hypnosis also promotes an easier recall of real memories (Bowman, 1996). The term "recall" has been mentioned several times so far. *Recall* is a process of retrieving relatively *full* information out of LTM (an example would be an essay exam). This is different from *recognition*, which is a process of matching the information from one's memory with the presented information. Recognition is simpler than recall since recognition does not require pulling out information from memory (an example could be working on a multiple choice exam). Recall and recognition are different types of *retrieval*.

False memories are formed from plausible pieces of information that are suggested to research participants. False memories are usually not formed when implausible information is suggested. For example, children were presented with several scenarios. They were informed that all scenarios truly happened to them; however, some were plausible (getting lost), and others were implausible (getting a rectal enema). Children remembered the plausible events, but could not remember the implausible ones (Pezdek & Hodge, 1999). Research on adults confirms the notion that if information is presented as plausible, it is good material for influencing a false memory. Usually, the trick is to inform participants that an implausible event happened to other people, only then the event becomes more plausible to the participants (Mazzoni et al, 2001). Personality is another

factor influencing one's susceptibility to false memories. Some people have a higher tendency to form false memories than others. A study showed that people who recall being abducted by aliens have a higher tendency to recall and recognize more false information (false memories) in other tasks than people without alien abduction experience. Higher false recall and false recognition quotients are also observed in people who are more susceptible to hypnosis and depression (Clancy et al., 2002).

Figure 9. What factors influence the creation of false memories?

REPRESSED MEMORY

Repressed memory refers to memories that at first are not consciously available, and then suddenly resurface, causing the individual to remember the event or information. Research shows that this type of memory is not a myth – it does exist (Dalenberg, 1996). A study recorded 129 women who were sexually abused. Physicians and social service agencies confirmed the fact of their abuse; however 38 percent of these women could not recall their abuse 17 years later (Williams, 1996). Another study recapitulated that many women could not recall their sexual abuse, even though the traumatic events were confirmed by other people who knew the victims (Summers-Feldman &

Pope, 1994). And yet another study showed that rape victims were less apt to recall the traumatic event than non-rape victims tasked with recalling some other bad memories (Schachter, 1996). Still, it is a common pattern for traumatic events to be remembered for a long time (i.e. not repressed).

FLASHBULB MEMORY

For most information to get into LTM, it has to be rehearsed in STM. But there are memories that do not have to go through STM to end up in LTM. Memories that are emotionally significant for an individual can surpass the STM stage. Both extremely tragic and extremely wonderful events immediately end up in LTM, and remain there for a long time. Additionally, these memories are often remembered exceptionally clearly. Since it is like a flashbulb, which attracts attention when it is lit in the darkness, this type of memory is called a *flashbulb* memory. However, even flashbulb memories can decay with the passage of time and a variety of previously mentioned influences. This observation was made in a study that involved university students who saw the September 11th terrorist attack event on TV. One group was tested for memory accuracy 1 week after the event, another group after 6 weeks, and a third group after 32 weeks. It was found that their flashbulb memories were no more accurate than their non-flashbulb, episodic memories (Talarico & Rubin, 2003). While some other studies support this finding, additional studies did find a great deal of accuracy of flashbulb memories over time (Neisser & Harsch, 1992). Even though there are obviously mixed results about the accuracy of false memory, it is safe to say that flashbulb memories can be altered, at least in some people more susceptible to memory alteration, just like other memories.

Figure 10. Flashbulb memories are also prone to fading away.

BIOLOGY OF MEMORY

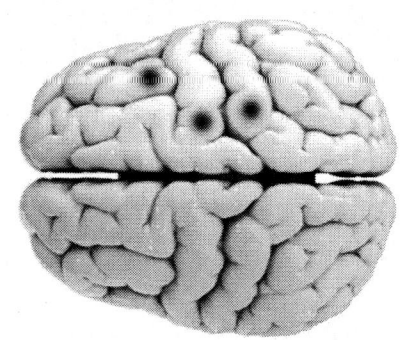

Figure 11. Rogue tissue (black dots) is removed through epilepsy surgery (H.M.'s rogue tissue is not shown here).

To understand what aspects of the nervous system are involved in the human memory, let's focus on the case study of Henry Molaisson. He suffered from epilepsy, a condition characterized with recurring *seizures* (fits or attacks). His seizures resulted in Molaisson collapsing to the floor and experiencing *convulsions,* involuntary, spastic movements of his body. These seizures occurred multiple times per day, disrupting Molaisson's daily functioning. The seizures were produced by malfunctioning neurons—neurons not producing normal, healthy levels of electricity, but instead abnormally high levels of electrical activity. In many patients, seizures can be reduced significantly with medication, but some patients are not responsive to medication. In this case seizures can be reduced or even completely eliminated through brain surgery. These surgeries are designed to extract the rogue brain tissue containing neurons that overproduce the electrical currents (Pinel, 2014; Kalat, 2013).

ANTEROGRADE AND RETROGRADE AMNESIA

Molaisson had his *hippocampus, amygdala,* and adjacent *cortex* removed. Collectively, these three areas are called the *medial temporal lobe*. The surgery was a bilateral lobectomy; brain tissue was removed from both the right and left temporal lobes. The surgery was very successful since, post-operation, Molaisson only experienced a few seizures *per year*; however, the surgery had devastating consequences on his memory faculties.

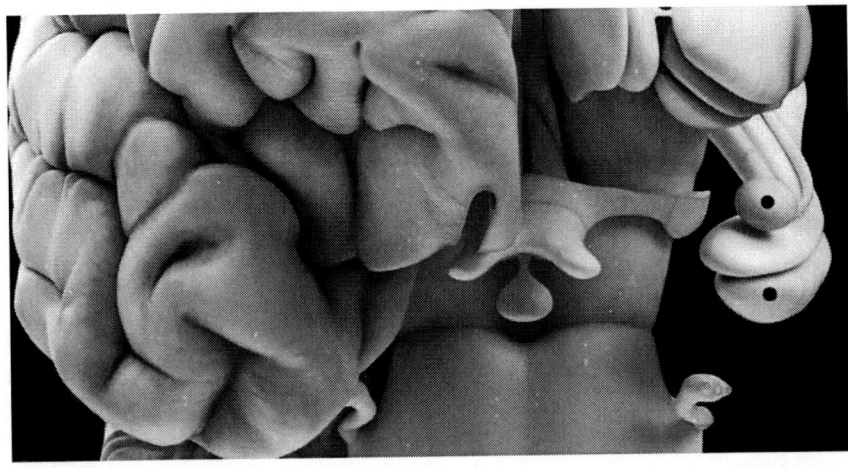

Figure 12. The medial temporal lobe includes the amygdala (upper black dot), temporal cortex (left) and hippocampus (lower black dot).

Molaisson suffered from anterograde amnesia, a memory disturbance in which a patient *cannot form new memories*. So, as a result of the surgery, Molaisson would not remember any new individual with which he came into contact, or any new event he witnessed. The medial temporal lobectomy influenced his inability to form *new* long-term memories, recollections from hours, days, months, or years before that would otherwise have been consolidated. A memory is consolidated when it is transferred into the long-term storage, existing embedded in the brain tissue, even when a person does not attend to it (Pinel, 2014; Kalat, 2013).

The hippocampus is an area responsible for transferring memories into long-term storage in the brain (Eldrigde, et al., 2005). Thus, removal of the hippocampus greatly affects a person's ability to form new long-term memories (as in Molaisson's case), since memories cannot be moved to the brain areas that host long-term memories. However, it must be emphasized that the hippocampus is not the only brain structure involved in the transfer of information from short-term to long-term storage. At least one other structure seems to contribute to this transfer — the *neocortex* (the surface of the brain) (Allen et al., 2006).

Molaisson also suffered from retrograde amnesia—a memory deficit in which a person has problems recalling events that took place *before* the responsible brain damage (Molaisson's surgery, in this case). His retrograde amnesia was mild, affecting only the two years prior to the surgery. All events that occurred approximately more than three years before the surgery could still be remembered. But how is this possible if his hippocampus was completely removed? This is most likely due to the fact that long-term memories are also stored throughout the *cortex*, not solely in the hippocampus (Pinel, 2014).

Transient Global Amnesia is a condition characterized by temporary (usually up to 10 days) severe anterograde amnesia and moderate retrograde amnesia. This condition is induced by a *stroke* (rupturing of a blood vessel) damaging the hippocampus (Hunter, 2011). This condition indicates that the hippocampus not only plays a role in memory consolidation, but also influences the recall of consolidated memories (Eldrigde, et al., 2005).

THE HIPPOCAMPUS AND OTHER MEMORY STRUCTURES

The hippocampus is also involved in *spatial memory*—memory of locations (where certain streets are, for example) and their physical relationships to one another (which streets are parallel) (Kumaran & Maguire, 2005; Morgan, MacEvoy, Aguirre and Epstein, 2011). London taxi drivers have proved to posses larger than average hippocampi, and accordingly exhibit superbly accurate senses of direction (Maguire et al., 2000). The hippocampus is also involved in the processing of memory *details* (Pinel, 2014).

Further, damage to the hippocampus is often associated with impairments in *episodic memory* (memory for episodes of personal experience (Kalat, 2013). The hippocampus is also involved in visual memory, memory of objects an individual has seen (Bussey and Saksida, 2005; Mumby, 2001). The medial temporal cortex (specifically, the entorhinal cortex, perirhinal cortex and parahippocampal cortex) is also involved in the processing of episodic and object memory (Pinel, 2014).

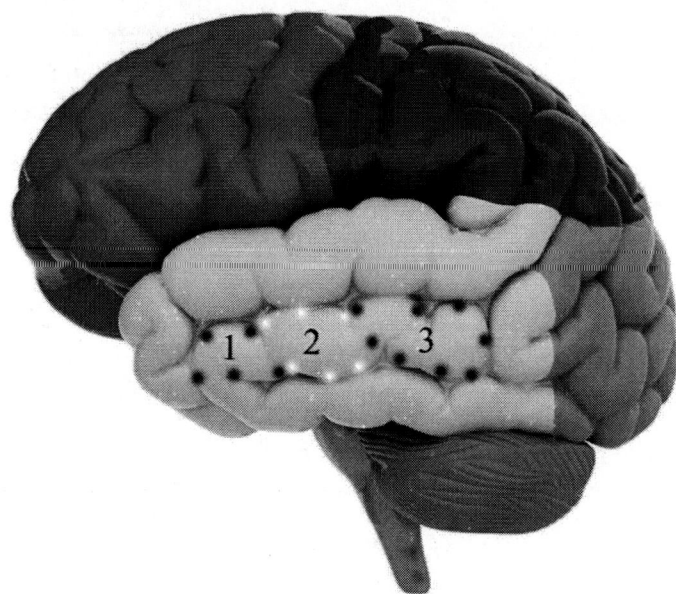

Memories of visual information are stored in the *inferior temporal cortex* (inferotemporal cortex) and the adjacent *perirhinal cortex* (Bussey & Saksida, 2005; Naya, Yoshida & Miyashita, 2001). The amygdala facilitates the strengthening of emotional memories that are located in parts of the brain other than amygdala. (Paz et al., 2006; Roozendaal, McEwen & Chattarji, 2009).

Figure 13. The medial temporal cortex includes entorhinal area (1), perirhinal area (2) and parahippocampal area (3). The inferotemporal cortex is below 1, 2 and 3 areas.

Significant deficits in semantic memory (memory for facts and knowledge, ex: "Paris is the capital of France") result from *bilateral* damage to the anterior and inferior temporal cortex, though these are not the only areas hosting semantic memory. People who suffer from this type of damage cannot remember colors of fruits and vegetables, and what certain concepts (a rabbit, for example) stand for (Ralph, Cipoloti, Manes & Patterson, 2010). Individuals who have damage to only one hemisphere of the temporal cortex exhibit normal semantic recall (Pinel, 2014).

PROCEDURAL MEMORY

Henry Molaisson was still capable of forming new *procedural* long-term memories (memories of carrying out tasks, like riding a bike or playing an instrument). He successfully memorized how to complete a mirror-drawing task, in which the subject needs to trace a star-shape by hand. The task is considered relatively difficult since the star shape can only be seen in a mirror but Molaisson was no less capable of completing it. Molaisson's ability to carry out the task means that he did not have anterograde amnesia for procedural memory. This is because the cerebellum hosts long-term procedural memories, and Molaisson's cerebellum was not surgically removed. (Gao, van Beugen & De Zeeuw, 2012*)*. The caudate nucleus and the putamen nucleus store memories for well-practiced (or automatic) behaviors such as *habits* and *skills* (Laubach, 2005; Schultz, Tremblay & Hollermar, 2003; Carlson, 2013).

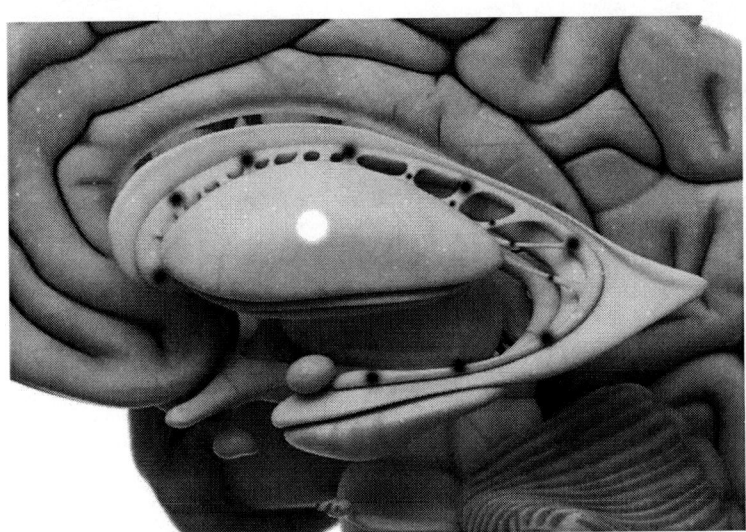

Figure 14. Basal nuclei: Caudate (black dots) and putamen (white dot).

Explicit memories are those of which we are conscious and know *when* and/or *how* they were obtained. Molaisson could not remember how or when he learned a skill (like the mirror-drawing task) after the surgery, which is a deficit in explicit memory. But, he had an intact *implicit memory,* which is evident in individuals, like Molaisson, who learn to do a task, but are not aware that they know how to do it since they cannot remember when or how they acquired the skill. Implicit memories are associated with basal nuclei, and explicit memories are located throughout the cortex, most densely in the temporal cortex (Kalat, 2013; Pinel 2014).

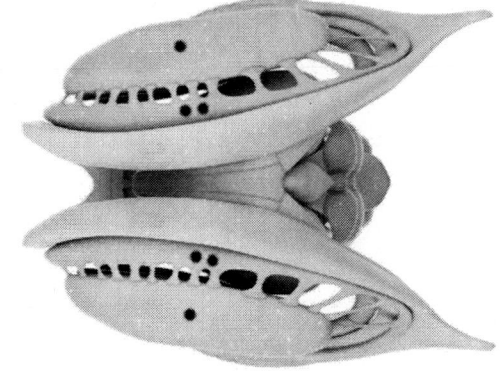

Figure 15. Caudate (dot pairs) and putamen (one dot) are bilaterally represented in the brain.

Molaisson's short term memory was largely preserved as well. Short-term memory is comprised of non-working and working memory. Non-working memory refers to our ability to retain information without rehearsing it. Typically, people can hold information in their non-working memory for up to one minute. Working memory, on the other hand, is our ability to remember through repetition and rehearsal information to which we are attending. When Molaisson was given a task to memorize digits, he was able to rehearse them (maintain them in his mind) just like a person with healthy memory faculties. Molaisson's working memory was spared, due to his intact *prefrontal cortex,* known to be responsible for this type of memory (Kimberg, D'Esposito & Farah, 1998; Smith, 2000). The prefrontal cortex is also involved in the memory for the *temporal* order of events. Damage to the prefrontal cortex may result in an inability to recall the chronology of events that took place before the injury (retrograde amnesia) as well as after the injury (anterograde amnesia) (Stuss & Alexander, 2005).

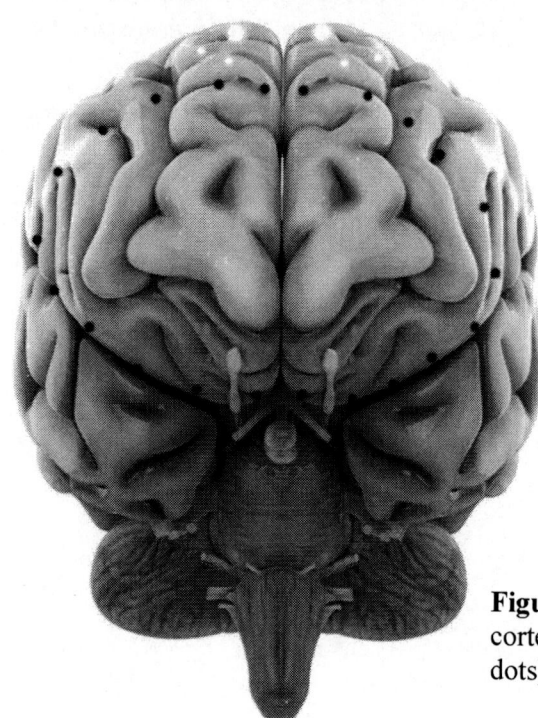

Figure 16. The prefrontal cortex (black dots), premotor cortex (small white dots) and motor cortex (larger white dots).

Korsakoff's Syndrome is a disorder characterized by:

- Apathy (lack of interest)
- Confusion
- Personality changes
- Memory loss:
    o Anterograde amnesia
    o Retrograde amnesia
- Spared implicit memory
- Deficits in episodic memories:
    o Confabulation (filling in memory gaps with guesses) of episodic memory.

This syndrome is caused by a deficiency of vitamin B1 (thiamine) due to a lack of a proper and sufficient diet. It can also result from alcoholism, as vitamin B1 intake is not present during alcohol consumption. The insufficient amounts of this vitamin may lead to neuronal loss and malfunctioning. The areas damaged are the thalamus (medial nucleus or dorsomedial nucleus), mammillary bodies (located at the base of the brain, adjacent to hypothalamus), the hippocampus, the cerebellum, and the cortex (Pinel, 2014; Fama, Pitel & Sullivan, 2012; Kril & Harper, 2012; Savage, Hall & Resende, 2012; Van Tilborg et al., 2011; Oudman et al., 2011). Treatment consists of breaking the alcohol addiction as well as the administration of glucose and proper nutrition containing vitamin B1 (Carlson, 2013).

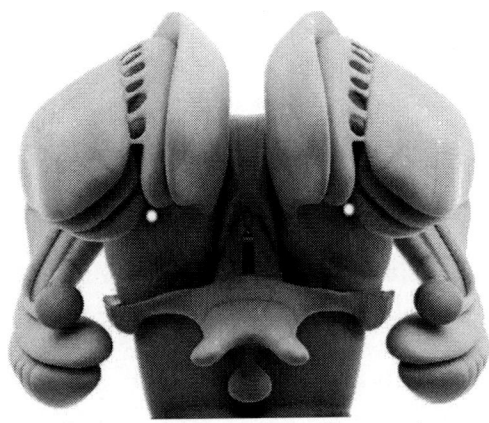

Figure 17. The thalamus has many nuclei, dorsomedial is one of them (white dots).

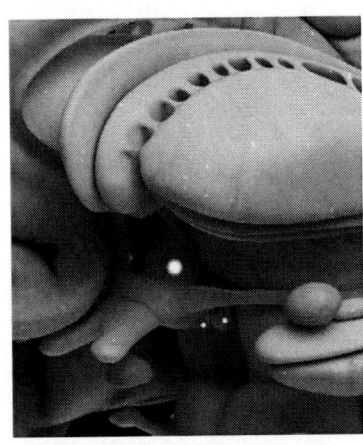

Figure 18. Mamillary bodies (small white dots) and the hypothalamus (large white dot).

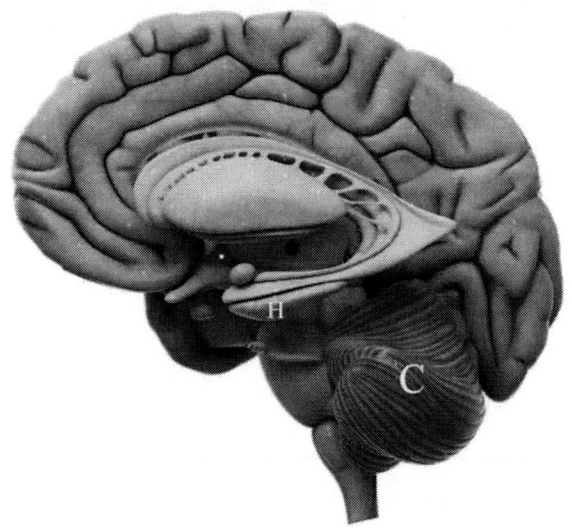

Figure 19. The thalamus (black dot), hypothalamus (white dot), hippocampus (H), and cerebellum (C).

ALZHEIMER'S DISEASE

Alzheimer's disease (AD) manifests as the following:

- Deficits in procedural and declarative memory (explicit memory)
- Major anterograde and retrograde amnesia
- Short-term memory problems

- Confusion
- Hallucinations
- Delusions:
  - Delusions, memory loss, confusion and hallucinations are collectively called dementia
- Restlessness
- Depression
- Sleeplessness
- Loss of appetite (Pinel, 2014; Kalat, 2013).

The cause of AD is the malfunctioning and loss of neurons. The malfunctioning of neurons is influenced by errors in several genes. Some of these genes influence the development of early onset AD (apparent in people younger than 40). Yet, another gene influences the emergence of this disease in people who are 65-74. 50% of people older than 80 develop a non-gene-related type of AD (Bertram and Tanzi, 2008; St George-Hyslop, 2000). These malfunctioning genes synthesize a protein called *amyloid beta*. The protein has an error too since it accumulates both inside and outside of neurons. This accumulation damages dendritic spines, decreases synaptic input and decreases the brain's ability to adapt and repair itself (Wei, Nguyen, Kessels, Hagiwara, Sisodia & Malinow, 2010). Amyloid accumulation also damages axons and dendrites. These damaged parts cluster together creating tissue called *plaque*. The accumulation of plaque causes damage to the brain stem regions, basal forebrain, amygdala, hippocampus and cortical regions (especially the temporal and prefrontal areas).

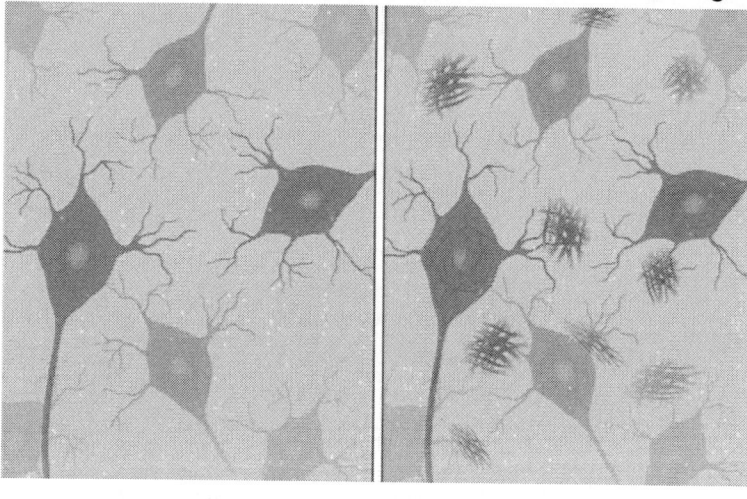

Figure 20. Healthy brain environment (left) and abnormal brain tissue with plaques (right).

The accumulation of amyloid beta protein influences changes in yet another protein—tau proteins. These proteins are the building blocks of microtubules. When the structure of tau protein changes, these altered proteins start to accumulate in cell bodies and their dendrites. This accumulation disrupts the flow of substances along the microtubules, and the cell eventually dies. Accumulated tau protein remains; this abnormal tissue is called *tangles* (Carlson, 2013; Pinel, 2014; Kalat, 2013; Itner and Gotz, 2011). Tangles damage the same areas that are affected by plaques. Therapy for AD consists of administering medications that attach to Acetylcholine (Ach) receptor and stimulate or prolong Ach release. This treatment, however, only slows down the progression of the disease. Within the Indian spice *turmeric* is a substance, *curcumin,* which has proved to be a promising treatment; in studies it has blocked amyloid beta accumulation and structural changes caused by tau proteins (Hamaguchi, Ono & Tamada, 2010).

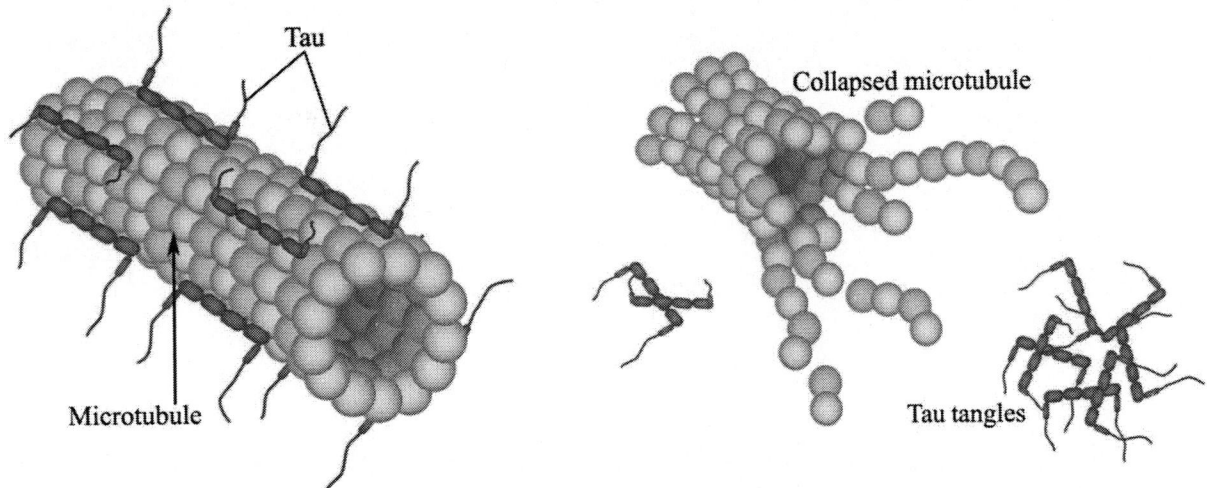

Figure 21. Healthy microtubule, where tau protein provides structural support for microtubules.

Figure 22. Unhealthy microtubule.

REFERENCES

Allen, J. S., Tranel, D., Bruss, J., & Damasio, H. (2006). Correlations between regional brain volumes and memory in anoxia. Journal of Clinical and Experimental Neuropsychology, 28, 457-476.

Anderson, M. C., & Neely, J. H. (1996). Interference and inhibition in memory retrieval. In E. L. Bjork & R. A. Bjork (Eds.). Handbook of perception and cognition, Memory, (2nd ed.), 237-313. San Diego, CA: Academic Press.

Bertram, L., & Tanzi, R. E. (2008). Thirty years of Alzheirmer's disease genetics: The implications of systematic meta-analyses. Nature Reviews Neuroscience, 9 (13), 768-778.

Bjork, R. A., & Bjork, E. L. (1992). A new theory of disuse and an old theory of stimulus fluctuation. In A. Healy, S. Kosslyn, & R. Shiffrin (Eds.), From learning processes to cognitive processes: Essays in honor of William K. Estes (Vol. 2, pp. 35-67). Hillsdale, NJ: Erlbaum.

Bjork, R. A., & Whitten, W. B. (1974). Recency-sensitive retrieval processes in long-term free recall. Cognitive Psychology, 6, 173-189.

Blake, A. B., Nazarian, M., & Castel, A. D. (2015). The Apple of the mind's eye: Everyday attention, metamemory, and reconstructive memory for the Apple logo. The Quarterly Journal of Experimental Psychology, 68, 858-865.

Bowman, E. S. (1996). Delayed memories of child abuse: Part II: An overview of research findings relevant to understanding their reliability and suggestibility. Dissociation: Progress in the Dissociative Disorders, 9, 232-243.

Bussey, T. J., & Saksida, L. M. (2005). Object memory and perception in the medial temporal lobe: An alternative approach. Current Opinion in Neurobiology, 15, 730-737.

Carlson, N. R. (2013). Physiology of behavior (9th ed.). Boston, MA: Allyn and Bacon.

Ciccarelli, S. & Noland White, J., (2017). Psychology (5th ed.). Boston, MA: Pearson.

Stromeyer, C. F., III, & Psotka, J. (1971). The detailed texture of eidetic images. Nature, 237, 109-112.

Clancy, S. A., McNally, R. J., Schacter, D. L., Lenzenweger, M. F., & Pitman, R. K. (2002). Memory distortion in people reporting abduction by aliens. Journal of Abnormal Psychology, 111(3), 455-461.

Conway, M. A., Cohen, G., & Stanhope, N. (1992). Very long-term memory for knowledge acquired at school and university. Applied Cognitive Psychology, 6, 467-482.

Cowan, N., Elliott, E. M., Saults, J. S., Morey, C. C., Mattox, S., Hismjatullina, A., & Conway, A., & Conway, A. R. A. (2005). On the capacity of attention: Its estimation and its role in working memory and cognitive aptitudes. Cognitive Psychology, 51(1), 42-100.

Dalenberg, C. J. (1996). Accuracy, timing and circumstances of disclosure in therapy of recovered and continuous memories of abuse. The Journal of Psychiatry and Law, 24(2), 229-275.

Donovan, J. J., & Radosevich, D. R. (1999). A meta-analytic review of the distribution of practice effect: Now you see it, now you don't. Journal of Applied Psychology, 84, 798-805.

Ebbinghaus, H. (1885). Memory: A contribution to experimental psychology. New York, NY: Dover Publications.

Eldrigde, L. L., Engel, S. A., Zeinech, M. M., Bookheimer, S. Y., & Knowlton, B. J. (2005). A dissociation of encoding and retrieval processes in the human hippocampus. Journal of Neuroscience, 25 (13), 3280-3286.

Eriviti, M., Semal, C., Wright, B. A., Amestoy, A., Bouvard, M. P., & Demany, L. (2015). A late-emerging auditory deficit in autism. Neuropsychology, 29, 454-462.

Fama, R., Pitel, A.-L., & Sullivan, E. V. (2012). Anterograde episodic memory in Korsakoff's syndrome. Neuropsychology Review, 22, 93-104.

Frenda, S. J., Patihis, L., Loftus, E. F., Lewis, H. C., & Fenn, K. M. (2014). Sleep deprivation and false memories. Psychological Science, 25(9), 1674-1681.

Gao, Z., Gao, Q., Tang, N., Shui, R., & Shen, M. (2016). Organization principles in visual working memory: Evidence from sequential stimulus display. Cognition, 146, 177-288.

Gao, Z., van Beugan, B. J. & De Zeew, C. I. (2012). Distributed synergistic plasticity and cerebellar learning. Nature Reviews Neuroscience, 13, 619-635.

Hamaguchi, T., Ono, K., & Yamada, M. (2010). Curcumin and Alzheimer's disease. CNS Neuroscience and Therapeutics, 16 (13), 385-297.

Haw, R. M., Dickinson, J. J., & Meissner, C. A. (2007). The phenomenology of carryover effects between show-up and line-up identification. Memory, 15, 117-127.

Hunt, P. S., & Barnet, R. C. (2016). Adolescent and adult rats differ in the amnesic effects of acute ethanol in two hippocampus-dependent tasks: Trace and contextual fear conditioning. Behavioural Brain Research, 298(Part A), 78-87.

Hunter, G. (2011). Transient global amnesia. Neurologic Clinics, 29, 1045-1054.

Ittner, L. M., & Gotz, J. (2011). Amyloid-beta and tau--a toxic pas de deux in Alzheimer's disease. Nature Reviews Neuroscience, 12 (3), 67-72.

Kalat, J. W. (2013). Biological psychology (11th ed.). Belmont, CA: Wadsworth, Cengage Learning.

Kimberg, D. Y., D-Esposito, M., & Farah, M. J. (1998). Cognitive functions in the prefrontal cortex -working memory and executive control. Current Directions in Psychological Science, 6, 185-192.

Kril, J. J., & Harper, C. G. (2012). Neuroanatomy and neuropathology associated with Korsakoff's syndrome. Neuropsychology Review, 22, 72-80.

Laubach, M. (2005). Who's on first? What's on second? The time course of learning in corticostriatal systems. Trends in Neuroscience, 28 (10), 509-511.

Leblond, M., Laisney, M., Lamidey, V., Egret, S., de La Sayette, V., Chetelat, G.,... Eustache, F. (2016). Self-reference effect on memory in healthy aging, mild cognitive impairment and Alzheimer's disease: Influence of identity valence. Cortex., 74, 177-190.

Loftus, E. F., & Burns, T. E. (1982). Mental shock can produce retrograde amnesia. Trends in Cognitive Science, 6, 299-305.

Loftus, E. F., & Loftus, G. R. (1980). On the permanence of stored information in the human brain. American Psychologist, 35, 409-420.

Loftus, E.F., & Pickerell, J. E. (1995). The formation of false memories. Psychiatric Annals, 25, 720-725.

Loftus, E. F. (1996). Repressed memory litigation: Court cases and scientific findings on illusory memory. Washington State Bar News, 50, 15-25.

Loftus, E. F. (2002). Memory faults and fixes. Issues in Science and Technology, 18, 41-59.

Maguire, E. A., Gadian, D. G., Johnsrude, I. S., & Good, C. D. (2000). Navigation-related structural change in the hippocampi of taxi drivers. Proceedings of the National Academy of Sciences USA, 97, 4397-4403.

Mazzoni, G. A. L., Loftus, E. F., & Kirsch, I. (2001). Changing beliefs about implausible autobiographical events: A little plausibility goes a long way. Journal of Experimental Psychology: Applied, 7(1), 51-59.

Morgan, C. A., Southwick, S., Steffian, G., Hazlett, G. A., & Loftus, E. F. (2013).

Misinformation can influence memory for recently experienced, highly stressful events. International Journal of Law and Psychiatry, 36, 11-17.

Morgan, L. K., MacEvoy, S. P., Aguirre, G. K., & Epstein, R. A. (2011). Distances between real-world locations are represented in the human hippocampus. Journal of Neuroscience, 31 (13), 1238-1245.

Murdock, B. B., Jr. (1962). The serial position effect in free recall. Journal of Experimental Psychology, 64, 482-488.

Naya, Y., Yoshida, M., & Miyashita, Y. (2001). Backward spreading of memory-retrieval signal in the primate temporal cortex. Science, 291, 661-664. Lancet, 2000, 355, 39-40.

Neisser, U., & Harsch, N. (1992). Phantom flashbulbs: False recollections of hearing the news about Challenger. In E. Winograd & U. Neisser (Eds.), Affect and accuracy in recall: Studies of "flashbulb memories" (pp. 9-31). New York: Cambridge University Press.

Oudman, E., Van der Stigchel, S., Wester, A. J., Kessels, R. P. C., & Postma, A. (2011). Intact memory for implicit contextual information in Korsakoff's amnesia. Neuropsychologia, 49, 2848-2855.

Palva, J. M., Monto, S., Kulashekhar, S., &Palva, S. (2010). Neuronal synchrony reveals working memory networks and predicts individual's memory capacity. Proceedings of the National Academy of Sciences, USA, 107(16), 7580-7585.

Paz, R., Pelletier, J. G., Bauer, E. P., & Pare, D. (2006). Emotional enhancement of memory via amygdala-driven facilitation of rhinal interactions. Nature Neuroscience, 9, 1321-1329.

Peterson, L. R., & Peterson, M. J. (1959). Short-term retention of individual items. Journal of Experimental Psychology, 58, 193-198.

Pezdek, K., & Hodge, D. (1999) Planting false childhood memories in children: The role of event plausibility. Child Development, 70, 887-895.

Pinel, P. J. (2014). Biopsychology (9th ed.). Boston, MA: Pearson Education.

Ralph, M. A. L., Cipolotti, L., Manes, F., & Patterson, K. (2010). Taking both sides: Do unilateral anterior temporal lobe lesions disrupt semantic memory? Brain, 133 (13), 3243-3255.

Roozendaal, B., McEwen, B. S. & Chatterji, S. (2009). Stress, memory, and the amygdala. Nature Reviews Neuroscience, 10, 423-43.

Rubenzer, S. (2002). Eyewitness identification: challenging a confident witness and common misconceptions, Voice for the Defense, 1-3.

Sanderson, C., & Huffman, K., (2017) Real World Psychology (2nd ed.) USA: John Wiley & Sons.

Savage, L. M., Hall, J. M., & Resende, L. S. (2012). Transitional rodent models of Korsakoff syndrome reveal the critical neuroanatomical substrates of memory dysfunction and recovery. Neuropsychology Review, 22, 195-209.

Schacter, D. L. (1996). Searching for memory: The brain, mind and the past. New York: Basic Books.

Schlichting, M. L., & Preston, A. R. (2014). Memory reactivation during rest supports upcoming learning of related content. Proceedings of the National Academy of Sciences of the United States of America, 111, 15845-15850.

Schultz, W., Tremblay, L., & Hollermar, J. R. (2003). Changes in behavior-related neuronal activity in the striatum during learning. Trends in Neurosciences, 26, 321-328.

Schweickert, R. (1993). A multinomial processing tree model for degradation and redintegration in immediate recall. Memory and Cognition, 21, 168-175.

Smith, E. E. (2000). Neural bases of human working memory. Current Directions in Psychological Science, 9, 45-49.

Sperling, G. (1960). The information available in brief visual presentations. Psychological Monographs, 74, 1-29.

St George-Hyslop, P. H. (2000). Genetic factors in the genesis of Alzheimer's disease. Annals of the New York Academy of Sciences, 924 (13), 1-7.

Stuss, D. T., & Alexander, M. P. (2005). Does damage to the frontal lobe produce impairment in memory? Current Directions in Psychological Science, 14, 84-88.

Summers-Feldman, S., & Pope, K. S. (1994). The experience of "forgetting" childhood abuse: A national survey of psychologists. Journal of Consulting and Clinical Psychology, 62(3), 636-639.

Talarico, J. M., & Rubin, D. (2003). Confidence, not consistency, characterizes flashbulb memories. Psychological Science, 14(5), 445-461.

Tulving, E., & Thomson, D. M. (1973). Encoding specificity and retrieval processes in episodic memory. Psychological Review, 80, 352-373.

Van Tilborg, I. A. D. A., Kessels, R. P. C., Krujit, P., Wester, A. J., & Hulstijn, W. (2011). Spatial and nonspatial implicit motor learning in Korsakoff's amnesia: Evidence for selective deficits. Experimental Brain Research, 214, 427-435.

Wei, W., Nguyen, L. N., Kessels, H. W., Hagiwara, H., Sisodia, S., & Malinow, R. (2010). Amyloid beta from axons and dendrites reduces local spine number and plasticity. Nature Neuroscience, 13 (13), 190-196.

Wells, G. L., Small, M., Penrod, S., Malpass, R. S., Fulero, S. M., & Brimacombe, A. E. (1998). Eyewitness identification procedures; Recommendations for lineups and photospreads. Law and Behavior, 22(6), 1-39.

Williams, M. R. (1996). Suits by adults for child sexual abuse: Legal origins of the "repressed memory" controversy. Journal of Psychiatry and the Law, 24, 207-228.

Cognition

Chapter Seven

WHAT IS COGNITION?

Cognition equates to thinking. But thinking and mental processes can be broken down into several sub-processes such as perception, attention, problem-solving, decisions, memory, and creativity. Intelligence is also an aspect of cognition, a notion we will address as well.

PERCEPTION

Perception is a process of selecting, organizing, and interpreting our sensations. Since we are overwhelmed with stimuli every moment of our waking life (our peripheral vision remains aware of the myriad objects and occurrences around us), we need to focus on a narrow range of these incoming stimuli. Otherwise, we would be overloaded with information, and we would be unlikely to function effectively. We focus on specific aspects of reality by *selecting* that segment of reality. Selective attention is a process of focusing our mental effort on a limited range of stimuli and filtering out the rest. But these stimuli are not randomly selected; they need to be deemed *important* enough to warrant our focus. Therefore *relevance* is the predominant criterion (Rosner et al., 2015).

Imagine you are engaged in a conversation with someone at a party. Then, from another part of the room, you hear your name. Immediately, you will try to find out who mentioned your name and why. This "cocktail party phenomenon" demonstrates how we select information that is important to us (like our name). Our selective attention is helped by a process called *feature detection*. Within the brain, there are cells that specialize in detecting specific features of a stimulus; some of these cells respond to motion, some to shape, some to the length of stimuli, some to both shape and length. Some brain cells detect more complex patterns such as faces. An inability to recognize

Figure 1. The cocktail party phenomenon often occurs in social situations.

faces is called *prosopagnosia*. This condition results from damage to *any* of the following regions: the inferior temporal cortex, occipital cortex, anterior temporal cortex, prefrontal cortex, and fusiform gyrus. When the gyrus is damaged, a patient is unable to form clarity in identifying details

201

(having difficulties judging dogs in dog shows, distinguishing cars, etc.) (Kalat, 2013). Thus, cells within these regions of the brain, when they are healthy and undamaged, help us detect complex stimuli like faces and other details, so **that** we can pay attention to them.

When we experience unchanging or repetitive information, we learn to ignore that information: a process called *habituation*. Conversely, *change* will attract our attention, so we tend to cognitively select that change. In addition to change, stimuli that grab our attention are those that are intense, unfamiliar, moving, and contrasting (Sanderson & Hufmann, 2017).

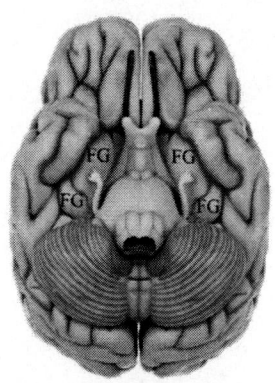

Figure 2. The location of the fusiform gyrus (FG) at the bottom of the temporal cortex.

PERCEPTION: ORGANIZING STIMULI

In addition to selection of information, our perception also refers to *organizing* stimuli. When it comes to visual perception, we organize sensory information in terms of *form, depth,* and *constancy*. Gestalt psychologists (mentioned in chapter one) noticed that our mind organizes sensory information into a *gestalt* (a "form" or "whole"). The goal of this pattern-driven organization allows us to connect parts of a stimulus into a unit as opposed to being attracted to every single detail and perceiving them as distinct, disconnected parts. Organizing saves us time and effort, and provides a broader perspective of reality entailing connected elements. There are several principles that our mind uses to organize form:

Figure-ground principle:

- We perceive an object (the figure) as *separate* from the ground (surroundings or the background), like black letters on white paper. Sometimes, however, when both the figure and background are meaningful forms, we can alternate our selective attention and focus on grounds, which become figures, and vice versa.

Figure 3. Focus on the vase and you will see it. Focus on the outlining faces and you will see them instead.

Proximity:
- We focus on objects that are physically *close*, and our mind perceives them as belonging together in a group. Thus, we see the following symbols as two groups of six circles (as opposed to 12 separate circles): oooooo   oooooo.

Continuity:

202

- Our mind perceives elements that create *patterns* of belonging, not separating elements. In this example, we do not perceive each diamond and triangle as separate or disconnected from the rest of the pattern.

Figure 4. Continuity.

Closure:
- We perceive a *complete unit* (the largest triangle), even though the stimulus has many empty spaces/breaks.

Figure 5. Closure.

Similarity
- Our mind *groups similar* objects together. For example, we see dots of similar colors comprising a number as opposed to perceiving those dots as separate units without a meaningful symbol (the number).

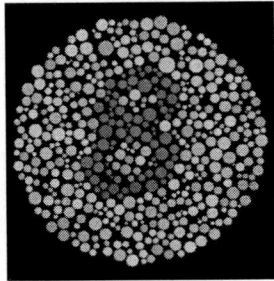

Figure 6. Similarity.

Contiguity:
- Similar principles exist for our perception of sound. Contiguity, for example, is our tendency to perceive *sounds* as belonging together in a group when they rapidly *follow one another* in time. Also, figure-ground distinction exists in perception of sound too. Whenever we hear a number of sounds, we focus only on some that are of primary interest; the rest are pushed to the background (as in the cocktail party phenomenon) (Sanderson & Huffman, 2017)

PERCEPTION: DEPTH

We also organize visual sensations by perceiving the *depth* of a visual scene. If we did not perceive depth, we would experience a two-dimensional world as if we lived on a surface of a painting containing only two dimensions: height and width. Our depth perception is highly influenced by *binocular* and *monocular* effects. Binocular effects are *retinal disparity* and *convergence*. Retinal disparity, an image ending in two different locations on the retina, is evident when we focus on an object and close our left eye. However, once we open the left eye and close the right eye, we notice that the image has slightly shifted from one condition (closed left eye) to the other condition (closed right eye). How is this possible? This slight movement of the image is due to the image ending in different locations (due to the two different viewing conditions) on the retina. Yet, when we open both eyes (and keep focusing on the same object) our brain corrects this difference in localization of the image, and the brain blends two images into only one, thus creating a sense of depth. This process of reconciling the disparity is called *stereopsis*. *Convergence*, on the other hand, refers to eyes' focus moving inward, towards the nose. When an object is closer to us, there is more strain on our eyes since they move more inward. For farther objects, there is less convergence. However, these binocular effects do not help us much when we need to judge distances longer than 100 yards. The binocular effect has this name since both eyes interact to influence depth perception. Monocular effects, however, rely on the activity of only one eye to contribute to depth perception. In other words, we can perceive depth via monocular effects if we close one eye. Monocular effects include:

- Linear perspective:
    - Parallel lines (like the edges of the pool in Figure 7) appear to converge as they recede into the distance (though they remain parallel in reality).
- Interposition:
    - Objects that overlap other objects are perceived as closer (trees obscuring the façade in Figure 7).

Figure 7. The Taj Mahal in India.

- Relative size:
    - A known object (like a human being in Figure 7) appears smaller than usual which suggests that it is farther away.
- Texture gradient:
    - Objects that are closer have more detailed textures than distant ones.
- Atmospheric perspective:
    - Distant objects appear hazy and blurred (due to more air particles between the viewer and the object) compared to closer objects.
- Light and shadow:
    - Brighter objects are perceived as closer than the darker ones.
- Relative height:
    - Objects positioned higher in our field of vision are perceived as farther away.

Some additional monocular effects for depth perception are accommodation of the lens and motion parallax. *Accommodation* refers to certain modifications of the lens (within our eye). For perceiving near objects the lens thickens, for perceiving far objects, it flattens. These activities of our lens are produced by muscles attached to the eye. The brain receives messages about the lens' modifications and interprets them as our distance and depth experience. *Motion parallax* means that close objects appear to move very fast, and objects that are farther away appear to move slower or even remain located in one place. In reality, the travelling speed of objects near and far may be identical (Sanderson & Huffman, 2017).

Depth perception has been observed in infants as young as six months old. In visual cliff type studies, infants are encouraged by their parent to crawl over a glass-covered steep drop; however, very few infants complete the crawl, suggesting that they can perceive the depth of the abyss below the glass (Gibson & Walk, 1960). Are they born with this ability to perceive depth, or is six months sufficient time to learn how to perceive depth? This is uncertain, but it is likely that infants have a genetically determined capacity that interacts with their learning about depth as their experience unfolds. Once this capacity and the environmental influence mix, the product may be the successful perception of depth.

PERCEPTION: CONSTANCIES

We organize our world by relying on our *perceptual constancies,* or an ability to perceive stabilities of objects' size, color, brightness, and shape even when these features *appear* to be changing. *Size constancy* is our ability to perceive stability of size of objects even though their distance changes. For example, the glasses in Figure 8 appear large since they are closer to the viewer, but in reality we know that they remain smaller than the trees behind them. *Color constancy* is our ability to perceive a color even when the illumination changes. If we saw these same glasses at night, we would know that they did not miraculously change color, but that their color just appears different due to the reduced exposure to light. *Shape constancy* is our ability to perceive the same shape of these glasses even though we can change the angle we are looking at them.

Figure 8. Size constancy.

PERCEPTION: INTERPRETATION OF STIMULI

In addition to selecting and organizing the stimuli that affects us, we *interpret* them via our perceptual ability. For example, in a video game that has various stages or levels, there is usually a pattern: some kind of portal or task that takes you from the entrance to each level's final boss (a monster you need to defeat). Once we are done with that level and see a portal in the next level, we interpret the signifier to mean that it will take us straight to the next boss. How do we know this when we did not even complete the level? Experience from the previous level helps us create an *expectation*. Processing given information based on perceptual expectation is called *top-down processing* since expectation (something in our mind which is the top of our development) is applied to interpret a given detail (in this case, a portal and its function). However, in video games (just like in life), sometimes we are presented with a situation for which we do not have an expectation. We simply need to analyze *elements* of a situation and try to interpret what they are and how they operate. For example, your avatar comes to a level where you face, for the first time, three pyramids that you must rearrange (but they can only move in one way) to produce a particular pattern that opens a door to another level. What to do here? How do we interpret what is required from us? This would be a *bottom-up processing*, where we do not rely on expectations (since we lack them due to the unprecedented situation). Rather, in this case, one must rely on a trial and error approach. We figure out a rule of how pyramids (or other elements) move. We analyze these elements and their properties. The distinction between the top-down and bottom-up processing, however, should not be seen as exclusive and opposed. From the video game example, it is clear that top-down and bottom-up processing can be used simultaneously or interchangeably. In order

Figure 9. Playing Zelda and the Wind-waker (highly recommend).

to move the pyramid, we need to have an expectation that things can even move. Without that basic expectation, we would not even try to move the object (Cave & Kim, 1999).

Expectations can be helpful, but they can also make us less safe. For example, people have a tendency to drive, bike, or ski *faster* (increasing chance of injury) when wearing a helmet. They interpret the situation as less dangerous since they can rely on the protective headgear, yet their increased speed on makes the situation more dangerous. When we wear protective gear, we expect we are safer, and therefore feel that we can engage in more risky behaviors (Gamble & Walker, 2016). Now, consider the drawing of a fork. There is something odd happening with this picture, right? When this type of drawing is presented to some tribes that are not accustomed to seeing a three-dimensional picture (such as Figure 10), they do not see a problem and can draw it in two dimensions. But, many viewers do have a problem perceiving it since we are used to three-dimensional images, and we perceive a discrepancy here. For us, drawing this fork is impossible since we will try to do it in three-dimensions. Thus, culture, too, plays a role in shaping our perceptions (Deregowski, 1999).

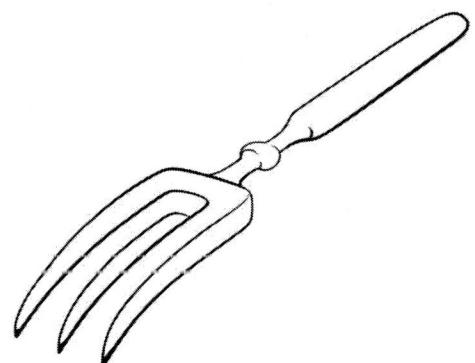

Figure 10. How does culture influence our perception?

Confusion abounds when it comes to differentiating between hallucinations and illusions. An *illusion* is a perception of reality, but one not accurately capturing reality. A *visual hallucination*, however, is an *unreal* sensory experience where we see things that are not there at all. Where do visual hallucinations come from if they are not rooted in reality? Our brain creates them. And where do illusions come from? They come from an interaction of our mind and reality, but this interaction creates a distorted reality.

Let's analyze some well-known illusions. The Hermann grid illusion is such that we perceive shadows appearing and disappearing in the locations where white lines intersect (left image in figure 11) as well as in white circles (right image in figure 11). When straight edges are made with a slight curvature, however, the illusion disappears. This tells us that straight edges are necessary for an illusion to take place. Biologically speaking, there are cells in our visual cortex that respond to the intersecting straight edges. Black backgrounds and white intersecting lines also stimulate these cells. These stimulations create our perceptions of appearing and disappearing shadows (Geier et al., 2008).

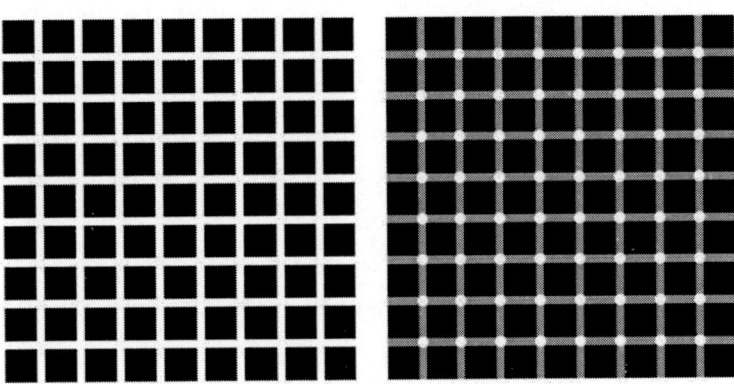

Figure 11. The Hermann grid illusion.

Figure 12. Motion illusion.

This circular image in Figure 12 seems to have aspects that move, yet in reality the image is totally static. What influences our perception of this illusion? If you focus your eyes and keep them steady on any segment of the picture, you will likely be able to stabilize that part. Thus, it would seem that when we don't focus hard enough, our eyes can still move, creating micro-movements (micro-saccades), a factor contributing to the perception of movement (Kuriki et al, 2008). In addition, this particular repetitive pattern composed of specific degrees of brightness stimulates certain cells within our visual cortex. Those cells respond to the stimulation by perceiving movement. Now, ask yourself: since these patterns (the Hermann grid and moving circle) of reality can interact with our eyes to easily trick us and induce misperceptions of reality (or illusions), how do we know that everything else we see is not an illusion too? Perhaps, reality is something slightly or totally different from what we see.

Subliminal information is a stimulus presented to a person in such a way that he/she is not consciously aware of it, yet it influences the person's response. How can a stimulus be presented subliminally? The stimulus becomes subliminal when it is presented so fast, for a fraction of a second, that a person does not consciously detect it. Research supports the notion that subliminal stimuli exist and are effective. Consider the following study: research participants were placed in two groups and exposed to photographs of a woman. Each photograph depicted a different situation such as: the woman getting into a car, walking through the front door of her apartment, walking on a sidewalk, grocery shopping, sweeping a floor, and studying. Immediately before each photograph, however, a subliminal image (different for each photo of the woman) was presented to only one group. The subliminal stimuli included: a child with a Mickey Mouse doll, a pair of kittens, smiling men wearing tuxedos, and others. What these subliminal images had in common were that they were about something emotionally positive. These positive images were subliminally presented randomly. The other group, however, was presented with negative subliminal images, such as an image of a skull, a bloody shark, a bucket of snakes, and a corpse on a bed. These images were also presented randomly. After the participants saw all the photographs of the woman, their task was to decide whether she was friendly or not, how cruel or kind, how honest or dishonest, how selfish or unselfish, how polite or rude. For each of these categories there was a scale for response (zero meaning not at all, up to seven meaning extremely). Those who were exposed to the negative subliminal images perceived the woman in a more negative light, while those who were exposed to the positive subliminal images perceived her in a more positive light. It is not known how exactly subliminal information influences our perception, only that its influence is undeniable (Krosnick et al., 1992).

Other studies support the claim that subliminal stimuli do exist and influence our perception (Merikle, 2001). Williams (1938) presented to research participants images of a circle, triangle, or square at a fraction of a second. When they were asked to determine what geometric figure they saw, they performed much better than the level of chance (guessing), indicating that their mind perceived the image though not at the conscious level. Furthermore, when pictures of fearful faces are presented to people in such ways that they cannot consciously see these (subliminal) faces, the brain scanning technology detects the amygdala's heightened

Figure 13. An expression of fear.

activity (the amygdala is famously activated when we consciously observe a fearful face or fear-provoking stimuli) (Whalen et al., 1998). How does the brain register fearful faces when the participant does not consciously perceive the faces? Well, they did perceive the faces, but at the subliminal, or subconscious, level.

In another study, researchers presented the word "flake" as a subliminal stimulus. Subjects reported not seeing any word. Then, they were asked to complete a word starting with "fla" and 36 percent of the participants came up with the word "flake." However, in a condition without any subliminal stimulus (in which "flake" was not presented), only 4 percent of subjects came up with "flake". Thus, those who were subliminally exposed to the word were influenced to come up with that same word (Mack & Rock, 1998). In addition, some individuals with brain damage do not perceive information presented in their visual field located on the opposite side of the damage. So, if damage is sustained in the right parietal lobe, then the patient will not perceive a stimulus presented in the left visual field. Patients will still attend to the stimulus, even though they are not consciously seeing it. However, when a subliminal stimulus is presented in the left visual field, patients attend to the area *faster* than when the subliminal stimulus is not presented. Thus, subliminal stimuli seem capable of influencing perception (Danziger et al., 1998). Many additional studies have shown that subliminal stimuli can influence perception (Merikle et al., 2001).

INTELLIGENCE

Intelligence is the ability to learn from one's experience, acquire knowledge, and use resources effectively in adapting to new situations or solving problems (Sternberg & Kaufman, 1998). Let's have a look at several views regarding what specific aspects comprise intelligence.

Figure 14. Intelligence contains different "pieces," or aspects. It is not comprised of a single mental process.

Spearman (1904) suggested that intelligence has two factors, *g-factor* and *s-factor*. G-factor refers to the ability to reason and solve problems. S-factor refers to specific abilities such as music, business, writing, art, reading, etc. We employ s-factors to accomplish g-factors. Gardner (1993) expanded this view and suggested that there are at least nine types of intelligence:

- Verbal
  - Ability to utilize language, specifically reading comprehension and vocabulary
- Musical
  - Ability to compose or perform music
  - Ability to create and adhere to tempo, rhythm and identify sounds
- Logical/mathematical
  - Ability to think by using rules of logic and solve mathematical problems
- Visual/Spatial

- o Ability to understand how objects are oriented and related in space
- Movement
  - o Ability to coordinate and control one's body motions
- Interpersonal
  - o Sensitivity to others and understanding what drives them
  - o Ability to communicate and interact with others
- Emotional
  - o Ability to understand one's emotions and how they guide actions

- Naturalist
  - o Ability to recognize patterns in nature (farmers, biologists, landscapers, etc.)
- Existentialist
  - o Ability to see the big picture of the human life by asking questions about the origin of life, death, and the purpose of living.

Figure 15. What type of intelligence does an astronaut display?

There is no consensus on whether all these aspects are different types of intelligence or just different abilities reflecting general intelligence (Waterhouse, 2006a, Gardner & Morgan, 2006). Sternberg (1988a) argued that there are three types of intelligence:

- Analytical
  - o Ability to break down problems into parts in order to solve them
- Creative
  - o Ability to come up with new ways of solving problems
- Practical
  - o Ability to be tactful, manipulate situations, and use information to one's advantage

A criticism of Sternberg's view is that it is difficult to accurately assess creative and practical intelligence (Gottfredson, 2003). Catell, Horn, and Caroll (CHC) proposed their own view of intelligence, which incorporates aspects we have already mentioned and adds some new ones. According to their view, intelligence is comprised of:

- Quantitative knowledge
  - o Ability to solve math problems
- Comprehension
  - o Ability to understand information

210

- Reading and writing
  - Ability to read and write
- Domain specific knowledge
  - Ability to have breadth and depth of knowledge in a domain of interest
- Fluid reasoning
  - Ability to adapt to new situations and solve new problems
- Short-term memory (STM)
  - Ability to maintain information in STM
- Long-term memory (LTM)
  - Ability to store information in LTM and later retrieve it
- Visual processing
  - Ability to sense and perceive visual information
- Auditory processing
  - Ability to sense and perceive sounds
- Olfactory processing
  - Ability to sense and perceive smells
- Tactile processing
  - Ability to sense and perceive stimuli via sense of touch
- Kinesthetic abilities
  - Ability to locate one's body in space (like localizing one's stretched out arms while keeping eyes closed)
- Psychomotor abilities
  - Ability to move various part of the body (such as dance)
- Reaction speed
  - How fast we respond to stimuli
- Decision speed
  - how fast we make decisions
- Psychomotor speed
  - how fast we perform psychomotor abilities

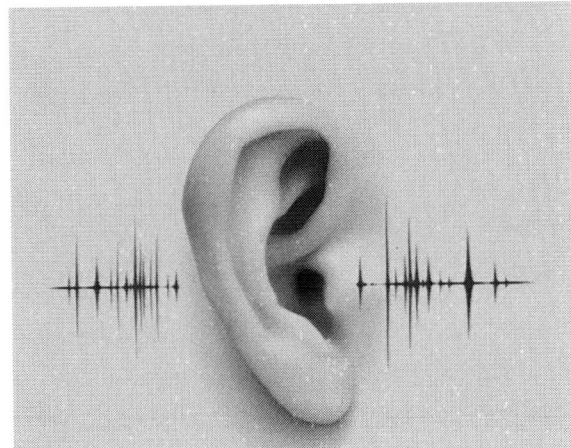

Figure 16. Auditory processing is an important aspect of intelligence.

It seems that the CHC view is the most researched and most supported by evidence (Schneider & McGraw, 2012; Flanagan & Dixon, 2013). In addition, Goleman (1995) proposed that there is an *emotional intelligence* consisting of the following abilities:

- To accurately perceive emotions of others and respond to them adequately
- To understand and express one's own emotions
- To control and regulate (increase or decrease) one's own emotions
- To use emotions in order to stimulate thinking and motivation

Figure 17. Anger-management is an important aspect of emotional intelligence.

When comparing people with high emotional intelligence to people with high non-emotional intelligence, research indicates that people with higher emotional intelligence are usually more effective leaders and adapt better in various workplace scenarios (Goleman, Boyatzis & McKee, 2002).

ASSESSMENT OF INTELLIGENCE

In 1904, The French Ministry of Education asked Alfred Binet, a French psychologist, to create a test that would identify children who were unable to learn as quickly as their peers, so that they could be properly helped. Binet and his colleague, Theodore Simon, designed such a test discovering that fast learners gave correct answers performing as older children, and that slower learners performed as younger children (Binet & Simon, 1916). Then, William Stern (1912), a German psychologist, derived a formula for an *Intelligence Quotient* (IQ). A quotient is a number resulting from dividing one number with another number, in this case: *Mental age* divided by *Chronological age* = IQ. Mental age is an average age at which children can successfully answer a particular level of questions. Chronological age is the actual age of a child. For example, a child who is 10 yet answers questions as a 15 year old would answer, would equate to 15/10, or 1.5. Stern multiplied the obtained number by 100 to eliminate decimal points (1.5 times 100 = 150 IQ). In 1916, Lewis Terman, a researcher at Stanford University, translated this test into English and revised it. From then on the test was known as the *Stanford-Binet Intelligence Scale* (Roid, 2003). However, the test only measures intelligence in *children*. It does not apply well to adults since somebody who has a mental age of 30 and actual age of 50 would be considered disabled when that may not be the case at all. Adults reach a mental maturity where intelligence does not continue to increase much further. A different test is used for assessing intelligence in adults – The *Wechsler Intelligence Scale* created by David Wechsler, an American psychologist, in 1936.

In Wechler's test (Wechler's Adult Intelligence Scale, or WAIS) the intelligence score is reflected in the amount that an individual's score *deviates* from the *average* score. This test does not rely on dividing mental age by chronological age. Wechler also did not believe that a single score captures the full extent of intelligence. His test contains several sub-tests and their individual scores are ultimately combined. The sub-tests are:

- Verbal comprehension
  - Similarities
    - In what ways are a door and window alike?
  - Vocabulary
    - General test of vocabulary
  - Information
    - What is an atom made of?
- Perceptual Reasoning
  - Block Design
    - After you look at a pattern, try to arrange small cubes in the same pattern.
  - Matrix Reasoning
    - After looking at an incomplete matrix pattern or series, select an option that completes the matrix series.
  - Visual Puzzles
    - Look at a completed puzzle and select three components from a set of options that would recreate the puzzle, all within a specified time limit.
- Working Memory
  - Digit Span
    - Recall lists of numbers, some forward and some backward, and recall a mixed list of numbers in correct ascending order.
  - Arithmetic
    - Four men divided 20 balls equally among themselves. How many balls did each man receive?
- Processing Speed
  - Symbol Search
    - Visually scan a group of symbols to identify specific target symbols, within a specified time limit.

  - Coding

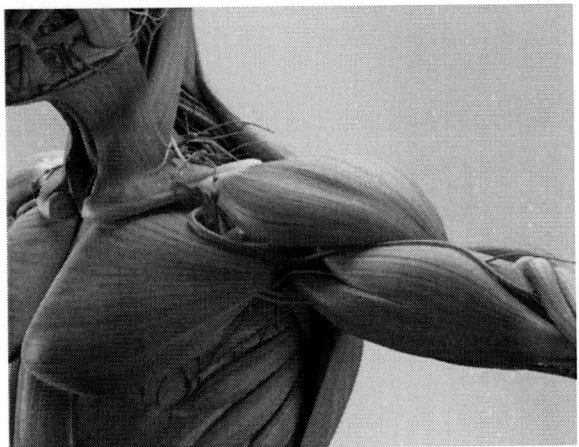

Figure 18. What is a pterodactyl? A type of muscle?

- Learn a different symbol for specific numbers and then fill in the blank under the number with the correct symbol.

Wechsler also designed tests assessing intelligence in children such as the Wechsler Intelligence Scale for Children (WISC) and the Wechsler Preschool and Primary Scale of Intelligence (WPPSI). All of Weschler's tests are still frequently used today (Kaplan & Sacuzzo, 1989).

INTELLIGENCE: FAIRNESS OF IQ TESTS AND STEREOTYPE THREAT

There is an argument that IQ scores do not accurately measure intelligence. Imagine this scenario: you are in a society that's very different from yours: different language, different values, different view of the world, different clothing style, different manners, practices, and beliefs. Imagine the big boss of this hypothetical society gives you their IQ test to determine whether you live or are thrown into the ocean to the sharks. In this hypothetical society you would most likely fail the IQ test miserably. IQ tests must be adjusted so that the test taker is *familiar* with the items on the test. Oftentimes, as research shows, that is not the case, and people perform worse on IQ tests due to this lack of familiarity with the test content. When members of one race are tested, the test should be adjusted to the cultural/social circumstances with which they are familiar. For example, if a Chinese American individual's experiences are rooted predominately with other Chinese Americans, but the intelligence test mostly reflects situations typical for Caucasians in America, the Chinese-American test-taker would fail. The Chinese American individual may not be familiar with such content (Cicarelli, 2017). So, only once an IQ test has been adjusted to be *fair* towards the test taker can say that the score accurately reflects intelligence.

Figure 19. Asking people who live in a community without money about situations in restaurants or stores puts them at an unfair disadvantage on intelligence tests.

There is another concern known as the **stereotype threat** – anxiety that people feel when performing on a test for which they believe may confirm a negative belief about their racial/cultural/economic *group*. The stereotype threat reduces short-term memory, heightens susceptibility to distractions, reduces confidence, and undermines motivation (Forbes & Schmader, 2010). For example, women perform worse on tests for which they believe that men outscore women. If a test is presented as non-evaluative (instead for fun), however, then they will likely achieve the same scores as men (Schmader et al., 2008). When individuals are informed about the negative effects of stereotype threat prior to an examination, their performance significantly improves (Johns et al., 2005). These findings regarding the stereotype threat should be taken into consideration when people take intelligence tests. Gender roles may also play a role in inducing the stereotype threat. *Gender role* is a societal expectation of a gender's behavior. For example, female students may create an expectation of performing worse on math tests than male students. In a research study, females were told that usually males outperform females on math. A test was administered and female participants scored worse than males. However, in the same study another group of female and male students did not receive any information regarding who usually scores better. The result was very different – females and males performed at the same level. Thus, when gender roles were not stimulated, the scores became equal (Spencer, Steel & Quinn, 1999). This is a demonstration of the *self-fulfilling prophecy effect* – our expectations are like prophecies that can embody themselves in reality.

INTELLIGENCE: NATURE VERSUS NURTURE

Is intelligence rooted in genetic or environmental influences? Do both factors influence intelligence? Observing twins can help us better understand. Identical twins have the same genetic material since they develop from the same fertilized egg cell while fraternal twins come from different fertilized eggs, so their genetic material is less similar than in the case of identical twins. Non-twin siblings have a very similar extent of genetic similarity as fraternal twins. Now, consider the following discoveries: Identical twins raised *together* have high levels of similarity on their IQ scores. Identical twins raised *apart* have less similar IQ scores. In comparison to identical twins, *fraternal* twins, when raised together, have less similar scores, and fraternal twins raised apart even

less. Non-twin siblings raised together have even less similarity in IQ scores, and siblings raised apart even less. If genetics plays the only role in shaping IQ scores, then people of the same genetics (like identical twins) should have the same IQ scores. Since that is *not* the case, the environment must also play a role in influencing IQ scores. The environment having an important influence is also apparent from the finding that identical twins raised together have different IQ scores than identical twins raised apart. Although, since identical twins have the most similar IQ scores than other types of siblings, it seems that

Figure 20. Which type of identical twin pair would you expect to have the most similar IQ score, those raised apart or raised together? Why?

genetics plays a significant role in influencing IQ scores (Bouchard et al., 1997b; McGue et al., 1993; Grissom et al., 2016). It is clear that both genetics *and* the environment play a role in influencing the intelligence. How can the environment influence IQ scores? Lower IQ scores can be influenced by: poor nutrition negatively affecting brain development (Noble et al., 2013; Noble et al., 2012); a mother's intake of drugs and alcohol during pregnancy; less breast feeding during infancy (Mortensen et al., 2002); lower amounts of education (Ceci, 1999); a lack of reading as a child (Grissom et al., 2016).

Across all ethnicities average IQ scores are significantly lower among children from lower social classes. Children raised in low-income environments have fewer books, less privacy to study, and less parental supervision, all likely contributions to their lower IQ scores (Lott, 2002; Seifer, 2001; Ceci, 1997). European Americans tend to have higher IQ scores than African Americans, but when African American children from disadvantaged homes become adopted into middle- and upper-class European families, they show a considerable increase in their IQ scores, which points to a significant influence of the environmental factors. Asian Americans show higher average IQ scores than European Americans (Alexander, 2014). Stevenson (1992) suggests that Asian American cultures emphasize perseverance and hard work – values that may influence higher IQ scores.

IQ SCORES, GIFTEDNESS AND DISABILITY

If the entire population of any given country were tested, it would be discovered that 68 percent (the vast majority) would have an IQ score of 85 – 115, which is considered normal. The average score is 100. Further, 14 percent of people would score in the range of 115 -130, 14 percent in the range of 70 – 85, 2 percent higher than 130 (1 percent score higher than 150), and 2 percent lower than 70. Let's now turn to the extreme highs and lows. Those who score above 130 are considered "gifted." Those who have IQ scores above 135 are considered gifted and geniuses. However, some people believe that gifted people and geniuses are eccentric, problematic, maladjusted, or even insane (imagine a mad scientist). This turns out to be, largely, a myth. Terman (1925) performed a longitudinal study (conducted over many years) on 857 gifted boys and 671 gifted girls. In 1947, children were considered young adults, and in comparison to the general population, most were socially well-adjusted, skilled leaders, above average in

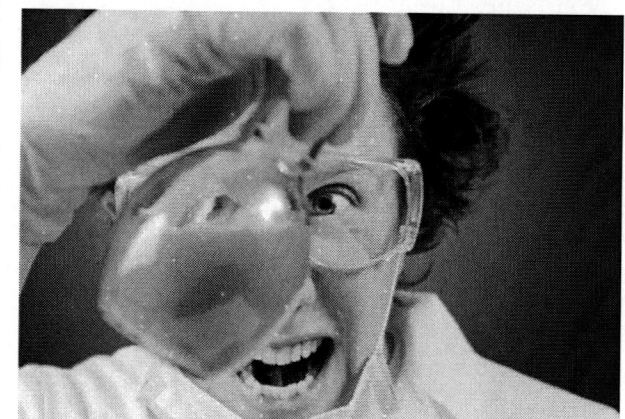

Figure 21. Geniuses tend to be eccentric, with weird manners, strange haircuts, living in isolation, socially inept, and even poor, since they don't care about money. Is this view correct?

height, weight, physical attractiveness, and more resistant to mental illness (Terman & Oden, 1949). Only those with the highest IQ scores (180 and above) exhibited behavioral problems when they were *children* (though not as adults) (Janos, 1987). Further, the vast majority of these gifted individuals obtained higher degrees and more financial success than the rest of the population (Cramond, 2001). Terman's study, however, is criticized for being flawed on several levels. One such criticism was that the gifted individuals were not randomly selected from the population, but were handpicked by their schoolteachers. This can be a problem because of the possibility that the teachers selected gifted children with the least problematic behavior. This leads to possibly unrealistic data. If they selected those with the worst behavior, on the other hand, those individuals could have ruined this beautiful picture of the success of the gifted (Leslie, 2000).

In 1959, Terman analyzed the two groups: participants who earned the most money, had careers with the most prestige, were the healthiest, were less likely to divorce, had the lowest level of alcoholism, and those who had poorer performance in the same variables. Terman discovered that IQ scores between these two groups did not differ, though, which indicates that intelligence was not the ultimate factor that helped the first group to be more successful. He dug deeper and found that the most successful participants were more goal-oriented, more persevering in pursuing goals, and more confident (Terman & Oden, 1959). Were these tendencies something that caused or resulted from their success? This is uncertain. Another longitudinal study of 210 gifted and non-gifted children discovered that when the gifted children are *forced* to achieve (by their parents or teachers), many grow up to become disappointed adults (Freeman, 2001). Torrance (1993) conducted another longitudinal study on the success of gifted individuals, and discovered that their success is associated with factors that Terman already mentioned. But Torrance noticed additional factors: high energy levels and enjoying one's work. However, the same issue persists: were these factors causing success or resulting from it? Therefore, we cannot talk about true causation, only correlation.

The 2 percent of individuals who score below 75 are considered *intellectually disabled* (mental retardation is now an outdated term). 85 percent of this population become self-sufficient, marry, have families and have full-time jobs in occupations that require minimal skill. 10 percent are moderately intellectually disabled. They can perform simple, low-skilled tasks, and, to some extent, care for themselves. 3-4 percent are considered severely disabled. They may learn basic communication skills, follow daily routines, but supervision is often needed. 1-2 percent of the severely disabled can only perform very simple tasks such as walking, eating, and saying a few phrases.

Figure 22. Derek Paravicini is an intellectually disabled person who can play thousands of songs extremely proficiently by heart.

The many causes include: genetic abnormalities, prenatal exposure to alcohol and other drugs (cocaine, methamphetamine), extreme neglect by caretakers in early childhood, and brain damage from physical trauma (car accidents, bike accidents). In some cases, the cause is unknown (or idiopathic) (Miller et al., 2016; Treffert, 2014; Sanders & Huffman). However, as previously stated, some intellectually disabled individuals are considered *savants* who excel in other areas.

Creativity, in the broadest sense, refers to the ability to make something new, original, and socially useful. It includes coming up with novel ways for solving a problem. In *convergent* ways of thinking, there is one solution to a problem that we arrive at by using previous knowledge and logical reasoning (Ciardiello, 1998). For example, a convergent way of answering the question, "how are a door and window similar?" would be, "they both open and allow contact with the outside world." *Divergent thinking*, which is often used in creative processes, refers to generating many different solutions to one problem. For example, how can a window be used? It can be decorated with prisms and crystals to bend light, opened to dry a towel, blocked with a curtain for privacy, and it can even be used as an exit. Creative people are known to engage in divergent thinking when they do some other behavior that is well automated, like driving. While engaging in an automated behavior, they tend to think about a problem from many different perspectives while focusing only minimal amounts of attention on the well-practiced task, (Goleman, 1995). A friend of mine, a musician, listens to his songs while driving, analyzing them and coming up with better versions as he is commuting to and from work. There are stories of famous creative individuals who came up with their most original work while taking a shower, swimming, or walking (all automated behaviors).

Divergent thinkers are less prone to certain processes that block our problem-solving ability. For example, a common problem-solving issue is *functional fixedness*, which refers to thinking of objects just in terms of their typical use. If you can't find a screwdriver to tighten a screw, eventually you discover that you can use a dime. *Confirmation bias* is another process that blocks our ability to solve a problem. This refers to our tendency to look for evidence that confirms our opinion and disregard evidence that doesn't. For example, in the 19th century, Franz Gall founded *phrenology*, a view that touching the bumps and valleys on the surface of the scalp could help us evaluate someone's personality.

Figure 23. Touching the scalp to assess personality was once a popular practice proposed by phrenologists.

Phrenologists believed that bumps and valleys on the surface of the brain indicated reductions and increases in mental processes. They also thought that the bumps and valleys would be visible on the scalp. The basis of phrenology, however, was found to be inaccurate since there is no true relationship between the surface of the scalp and the surface of the brain, but Gall focused only on data that supported his idea and disregarded the myriad data that rejected it, leading to a false science.

Having a broad range of knowledge about a variety of subjects, especially in one's area of interest, can stimulate creativity (Einstein published over 248 papers, for example) (Yakel, 2014). A knowledge base is like a foundation. Pieces of information are building blocks that the creative person combines in unique ways. As Sir Isaac Newton said, the only reason he can see farther than others is because he stands on the shoulders of giants (meaning he relied on previous findings of others). Creative people use mental imagery: the ability to generate image-like representations of reality in the mind. Also, creativity is stimulated by not being afraid to be different and by being open to new experiences. Creative people tend to value their independence, and are unconventional in their work Furthermore, creative people are able to recognize unique patterns and make new connections. These individuals are motivated by curiosity, a desire to help humanity, enjoyment, and much less or not at all by money. Creative people seek environments that spark their divergent thinking (Csikzentmihalyi, 1997).

It is often believed that creative people score above average on intelligence tests. This is, however, a misguided belief. Many highly creative people have, in fact, very low IQ scores. *Savants* are a good example of this. They are individuals who have serious deficits in various areas of functioning (communication with others, language production, inability to dress or tie shoe laces, etc.) and exhibit low IQ scores, yet they excel in specific areas such as math or memory or demonstrate a high level of creativity in drawing, painting or playing music (Ramachandran & Blakeslee, 1998; Sacks, 1985). Further, Williams Syndrome manifests itself as low IQ scores and deficits in motor and spatial abilities, but high proficiency in verbal and writing skills as well as a high level of an ability to dramatically express stories by varying the vocal pitch (corresponding to different characters as needed) (Alexander, 2014).

REFERENCES

Abdulla, A. M., & Cramond, B. (2017). After Six Decades of Systematic Study of Creativity: What Do Teachers Need to Know About What It Is and How It Is Measured? Roeper Review, 39, 9-23.

Alexander, P., & Yakel, D. (2014). Psychology Exploring Our Universe Within (4th ed.). Boston, MA: Pearson Education.

Binet, A., & Simon, T. (1916). The development of intelligence in children. Baltimore: Williams & Wilkins.

Bouchard, T. J., Jr., (1997). IQ similarity in twins reared apart: Findings and response to critics. In R.J. Sternberg & E. Grigorenko (Eds.), Intelligence, heredity, and environment (pp. 479-502). New York: Cambridge University Press.

Caroll, J. B. (2005). The three-stratum theory of cognitive abilities. In D. P. Flanagan & P. L. Harrison (Eds.), Contemporary intellectual assessment: Theories, tests, and issues (2nd ed., pp. 69-76). New York, NY: Guilford Press.

Cave, K. R., & Kim, M. (1999). Top-down and bottom-up attentional control: On the nature of interference from a salient distractor. Perception & Psychophysics, 61, 1009-1023.

Ceci, S. J. (1999). Schooling and Intelligence. In S. J. Ceci & Wendy M. Williams (Eds.) The nature-nurture debate: The essential readings. Essential Readings in Developmental Psychology (pp. 168-175). Oxford: Blackwell.

Ceci, S. J., & Williams, W. M. (1997). Schooling, Intelligence, and Income. American Psychologist, 52, 1051-1058.

Ciardiello, A. (1998). Did you ask a good question today? Alternative cognitive and metacognitive strategies. Journal of Adolescent & Adult Literacy, 42, 210-219.

Ciccarelli, S. K., White, J. N. (2017). Psychology, 5th edition. Pearson Education, Inc.

Csikzentmihalyim M. (1997). Finding flow: The psychology of engagement with everyday life. New York: Basic Books.

Danziger, S., Kingstone, A., & Rafal, R. D. (1998). Orienting to extinguished signals in hemispatial neglect. Psychological Science, 9, 119-23.

Deregowski, J. B. (1969). Perception of the two-pronged trident by two- and three- dimensional perceivers. Journal of Experimental Psychology, 82, 9-13.

Flanagan, D. P., & Dixon, S. G. (2013). The Cattell-Horn-Carroll theory of cognitive abilities. In C. R. Reynolds, K. J. Vannest, & E. Fletcher-Janzen (Eds.), Encyclopedia of special education (pp. 368-382). Hoboken, MJ: John Wiley & Sons.

Forbes, C. E., & Schmader, T. (2010). Retraining Attitudes and Stereotypes to Affect Motivation and Cognitive Capacity under Stereotype Threat. Journal of Personality and Social Psychology, 99(5), 740–754.

Freeman, J. (2001). Gifted children grown up. London: David Fulton.

Gamble, T., & Walker, I. (2016). Wearing a bicycle helmet can increase risk taking and sensation seeking in adults. Psychological Science, 27, 289-294.

Gardner, H. (1993). Multiple intelligence: The theory in practice. New York: Basic Books.

Geier, J., Bernáth, L., Hudák, M., & Sára, L. (2008). Straightness as the main factor of the Hermann grid illusion. Perception, 37(5), 651-665.

Gibson, E. J., & Walk, R. D. (1960). The "visual cliff." Scientific American, 202, 67-71.

Goleman, D. (1995). Emotional intelligence. New York: Bantam.

Goleman, D. (1995). Emotional intelligence: Why it can matter more than IQ. New York: Bantam Books.

Goleman, D., Boyatzis, R. E., & McKee, A. (2002). Primal leadership: Realizing the power of emotional intelligence. Boston: Harvard Business School Press.

Gottfredson, L. (2003). Dissecting practical intelligence theory: Its claims and evidence. Intelligence, 31, 343-397.

Grissom, J. A., & Redding, C. (2016). Discretion and Disproportionality: Explaining the Underrepresentation of High-Achieving Students of Color in Gifted Programs, AERA Open, 2(1), 1-25.

Huffman, K., & Sanderson, C. A. (2017). Real World Psychology, 2nd edition. Bognor Regis: John Wiley & Sons, Inc.

Janos, P.M. (1987). A fifty-year follow-up of Terman's youngest college students and IQ-matched agemates. Gifted Child Quarterly, 31, 55-58.

Johns, M., Shcmader, T., & Martens, A. (2005). Knowing Is Half the Battle: Teaching Stereotype Threat as a Means of Improving Women's Math Performance. Psychological Science, Vol 16, Issue 3, 175 – 179.

Kalat, J. W. (2013). Biological psychology (11th ed.). Belmont, CA: Wadsworth, Cengage Learning.

Kaplan, R. M., & Saccuzzo, D. P. (1989). Psychological testing: Principles, applications, and issues. Pacific Grove, CA: Brooks/Cole.

Krosnick, J. A., Betz, A. L., Jussim, L. J., & Lynn, A. R. (1992). Subliminal Conditioning of Attitudes. Personality and Social Psychology Bulletin, Vol. 18, Issue 2, 152 – 162.

Kuriki, I., Ashida, H., Murakami, I., & Kitaoka, A. (2008). Functional brain imaging of the Rotating Snakes illusion by fMRI. Journal of Vision, 8(10), 16 11-10.

Leslie, M. (2000, July/August). The vexing legacy of Louis Terman. Stanford Magazine. Retrieved August 12, 2010, from http://www.stanfordalumni.ord/news/magazine/2000/julaug/articles/terman.html.

Lott, B. (2002). Cognitive and behavioral distancing from the poor. American Psychologist, 57, 100-110.

Mack, A., & Rock, I. (1998). Inattentional blindness. Cambridge, MA: MIT Press.

McGue, M., Bouchard, T. J., Jr., Iacanom, W.G., & Lykken, D. T. (1993). Behavioral genetics of cognitive ability: A life-span perspective. In R. Plomin & G.E. McClearn (Eds.), Nature, nurture, and psychology (pp, 59-76). Washington, DC: American Psychological Association.

Merikle, P. M., Smilek, D., & Eastwood, J. D. (2001). Perception without awareness: perspectives from cognitive psychology. Cognition, Volume 79, Issue 1, 115-134.

Miller, J. L., Saklofske, D. H., Weiss, L. G., Drozdick, L., Llorente, A. M., Holdnack, J. A., & Prifitera, A. (2016). Issues related to the WISC-V assessment of cognitive functioning in clinical and special groups. In L. G. Weiss, D. H. Saklofske, J. A. Holdnack & A. Prifitera (Eds.), WISC-V assessment and interpretation: Scientist-practitioner perspectives (pp.287- 343). San Diego, CA: Elsevier Academic Press.

Mortensen, E. L., Michaelsen, K.F., Sanders, S.A., & Reinisch, J. M. (2002). The Association Between Duration of Breastfeeding and Adult Intelligence. JAMA, 287(18), 2365-2371.

Noble, K. G., Engelhardt, L. E., Brito, N. H., Mack, L. J., Nail, E. J., Angal, J., Barr, R., Fifer, W. P., Elliot, A. J., & collaboration with the PASS Network (2015). Socioeconomic Disparities in Neurocognitive Development in the First Two Years of Life. Developmental Psychobiology, 57(5), 535–551.

Noble, K. G., Houston, S. M., Kan, E., Sowell, E. R. (2012). Neural correlates of socioeconomic status in the developing human brain. Developmental Science, 15, 516-527.

Noble, K. G., Korgaonkar, M. S., Grieve, S. M., & Brickman, A. M. (2013). Higher Education is an Age-Independent Predictor of White Matter Integrity and Cognitive Control in Late Adolescence. Developmental Science, 16(5), 653–664.

Ramachandran, V. S., & Blakeslee, S. (1998). Phantoms in the brain: Probing the mysteries of the human mind. New York: Morrow.

Roid, G. II. (2003). Stanford-Binet intelligence scales (5th ed.). Itsasca, IL: Riverside.

Rosner, T.M., D'Angelo, M.C., MacLellan, E., & Milliken, B. (2015). Selective attention and recognition: Effects of congruency on episodic learning. Psychological Research, 79, 411-424.

Schmader, T., Johns, M., & Forbes, C. (2008). An Integrated Process Model of Stereotype Threat Effects on Performance. Psychological Review, 115(2), 336–356.

Schneider, W. J., & McGrew, K. S. (2012). The Cattell-Horn-Carroll model of intelligence. In D.P. Flanagan & P.L. Harrison (Eds.), Contemporary intellectual assessment: Theories, tests, and issues (3rd ed., pp. 99-144). New York, NY: Guilford Press.

Seifer, R. (2001). Socioeconomic status, multiple risks, and development of intelligence. In R. J. Sternberg & E. L. Grigorenko (Eds.), Environmental effects on cognitive abilities (pp, 59-82), Mahwah, NJ: Erlbaum.

Spearman, C. (1904). "General intelligence" objectively determined and measured. American Journal of Psychology, 15, 201-293.

Spencer, S. J., Stelle, C. M., & Quinn, D. M. (1999). Stereotype threat and women's math performance. Journal of Experimental Social Psychology, 35, 1-28.

Stern, W. (1912). The psychological methods of testing intelligence (G. M. Whipple, Trans.) (Educational Psychology Monograph No. 13). Baltimore, MD: Warwick & York, Inc.

Sternberg, R. J. (1986). A triangular theory of love. Psychological Review, 93, 119-135.

Sternberg, R. J., & Kaufman, J. C. (1998). Human abilities. Annual Review of Psychology, 194, 526-531.

Stevenson, H. W. (1992). Learning from Asian schools. Scientific American, 267, pp.6, 70-76.

Terman, L. M. (1925). Mental and physical traits of a thousand gifted children (I). Standord, CA: Stanford University Press.

Terman, L. M., & Oden, M. H. (1947). The gifted child grows up: 25 years' follow-up of a superior group: Genetic studies of genius (Vol. 4). Stanford, CA: Stanford University Press.

Terman, L. M., & Oden, M. H. (1959). The gifted group at mid-life, thirty-five years follow-up of a superior child: Genetic studies of genius (Vol. 3). Stanford, CA: Stanford University Press.

Torrance, E. P. (1993). The Beyonders in a thirty-year longitudinal study of creative achievement. Roeper Review, 15(3), 131-135.

Treffert, D. A. (2014). Savant syndrome: Realities, myths and misconceptions. Journal of Autism and Developmental Disorders, 44, 564-571.

Waterhouse, L. (2006). Inadequate evidence for multiple intelligences, Mozart effect and emotional intelligence theories. Educational Psychologist, 41(4), 247-255.

Whalen, P. J., Rauch, S. L., Etcoff, N. L., McInerney, S. C., Lee, M. B., & Jenike, M. A. (1998). Masked presentations of emotional facial expressions modulate amygdala activity without explicit knowledge. Journal of Neuroscience, 18, 411-418.

Williams Jr., A. C. (1938). Perception of subliminal visual stimuli. Journal of Psychology, 6, 187-199.

Consciousness

Chapter Eight

Consciousness is awareness of the external world of our surroundings and our inner world of thoughts, emotions, needs, and intentions. Consciousness manifests in *states*. These states of consciousness include dreaming, a hypnotic state, a meditative state, day dreaming, wakefulness, a drug-induced state of consciousness, and so on. States of consciousness can be *altered* as well as *unaltered*. Unaltered states occur naturally and spontaneously; we can easily trigger them by behaving in a very typical, everyday way. For example, we become wakeful after we wake up in the morning, experience dreams when we fall asleep, and daydream at our will. However, altered states of consciousness are not something that we can naturally, spontaneously induce; instead, altered states are triggered by utilizing certain behavioral techniques, gadgets, substances, or elaborate procedures such as meditation or hypnosis.

Figure 1. Driving on auto-pilot.

Consciousness comes in states, but also in *levels*. For example, after driving to work or school time after time, our mind downshifts to "auto-pilot" and we seemingly miraculously end up where we are supposed to be. While I drive to work, I listen to podcasts on physics, psychology, anthropology. At these times my attention is focused more on the complexities of the podcasts than on the road. Obviously, my consciousness is less *concentrated* on driving, but heightened on educational content. Yet, I continue to arrive at work every day, almost never late. This shows us that we tend to pay less attention to a behavior we have performed many times, once it becomes an *automated* operation. In the language of psychology, we are engaged in an *automatic processing*. Attention being fully focused on an aspect of reality such as a class lecture is called *controlled processing*—in these instances our awareness is highly focused on certain stimuli. Wakefulness is intensely involved when we are trying to learn and retain something (a lecture), but poorly involved during an automated behavior (driving to work). This illustrates different levels of consciousness.

During a 24-hour period, we are awake some of the time, and then, at other times, say at night, we fall asleep. This alternation of wakefulness and sleep during a 24-hour period is called the circadian rhythm. This rhythm is not exclusive for wakefulness and sleep, though; the *circadian rhythm* also affects our temperature, mood, and eating and drinking habits. Because of circadian rhythms, our body temperature is lower during the day, and then increases during the night; similarly, our mood improves from morning up until around 5 pm, and then progressively decreases for the rest of the day (Murray et al., 2009). Of course, there are always exceptions, people who feel better later in the day, but this is not the pattern for the *majority*. The term "biological clock" refers to inner (endogenous) mechanisms that control our circadian rhythm. One such mechanism is within the *suprachiasmatic nucleus* (SCN) of the hypothalamus. This nucleus controls the sleep-wake cycle and temperature fluctuation in the body (Refinetti & Menaker, 1992). The suprachiasmatic nucleus is innervated with axons from ganglion cells of the retina. The cells include melanopsin, a photopigment stimulated by light, so are considered photoreceptors like the rods and cones of the retina (Kalat, 2013).

Light messages (processed by the ganglion cells of the eye) arrive at the SCN and stimulate its activity through axons projected into the hypothalamus (the preoptic nucleus and the dorsomedial nucleus). The axons to the preoptic nucleus *inhibit sleep* while the axons to the dorsomedial nucleus *promote wakefulness* (Sapper et al., 2005). The activity of these axons is high during the day (when we are awake) and low during the night (when we are typically asleep) (Carlson, 2013). There *may* be another mechanism allowing the SCN to control the sleep-wake cycle as indicated by research on fruit flies; the SCN contains proteins, whose concentrations rise during the day and reach the highest amount at night when the tested fruit flies get tired. In the morning, these proteins' levels decline, and the fruit flies awaken. In humans, similar proteins exist and it is known that

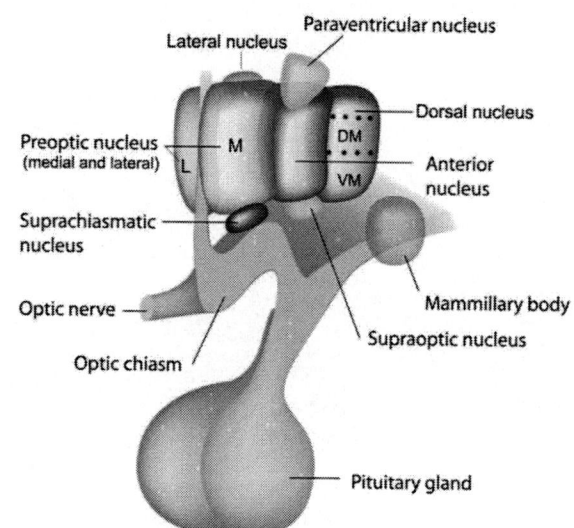

Figure 2. Hypothalamic nuclei involved in states of consciousness are the preoptic, suprachiasmatic, and dorsomedial/DM.

mutations in genes producing these proteins lead to skewed sleep cycles (i.e. becoming sleepy early in the evening and waking up too early in the morning) (Xu et al., 2005). It seems that these proteins play a significant role in the sleep-wake cycle.

Also, the SCN controls the sleep-wake cycle by influencing the brain's pineal gland to release the hormone *melatonin*. Melatonin is released mainly during the night and influences us to feel sleepy. Two to three hours before we fall asleep, melatonin secretion increases, influencing drowsiness (Haimov & Lavie, 1996). However, it seems that melatonin's influence is not as prominent as once thought; melatonin's influence on our sleepiness seems to only be *minor,* judging by the results of 17 studies on the effects of melatonin (Brzezinski et al., 2005).

CONSCIOUSNESS, UNCONSCIOUSNESS, AND STATES IN BETWEEN

Brain death is a state without any sign of brain activity. Stimuli do not receive any response. A person usually needs to be brain dead for 24 hours before they are pronounced dead. A *comatose* state, on the other hand, is the absence of consciousness. A coma is not a deep sleep since, during this state, oxygen consumption is below the levels typical of deep sleep (Marieb & Hoehn, 2013). A person in a comatose state has a low level of brain activity and minimal or no response to external stimuli (even painful stimuli). If patients do exhibit movements, they are unintentional and non-reactionary. Recovery from a coma must happen within a few weeks to avoid death. A *vegetative state* is an alternation between sleep and arousal, but, during arousal, the individual is still unaware of the stimuli. A painful stimulus can produce an increase in heart rate, an increase in breathing, and an increase in sweating (all autonomic functions). No speaking or response to speaking occurs, and there is no intentional activity. However, some cognitive activity still seems to exist (Guerit, 2005). A *minimally conscious state* entails brief periods of purposeful actions and some speech comprehension. This state can occur for anywhere from months to years (Kalat, 2013).

STAGES OF SLEEP

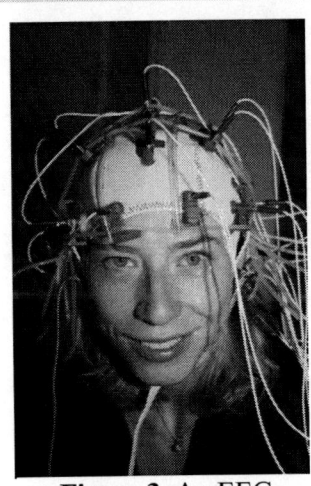

Figure 3. An EEG.

Wakefulness and sleep are characterized by particular patterns of electrical activity in the brain tissue. This electrical activity is measured through an *electroencephalography* procedure consisting of electrodes placed over many different areas on the scalp. The electrodes are connected to a machine that receives the electrical activity. The electrical activity represents the overall (average) brain activity detected by the electrodes. Different stages of sleep, just like different states of wakefulness, have *characteristic patterns* of electrical activity. The pattern for an individual who is *wakeful* and *relaxed* is called *alpha activity,* consisting of waves of electrical activity of eight-12 cycles per second. These alpha waves are more prevalent when our eyes are closed, but still happen when our eyes are open. *Beta activity* (waves of 13-30 cycles per second) refers to a pattern of the brain's electrical activity during wakefulness when we are engaged in daily activities employing attentiveness without relaxation. In a beta state, many different neurons are actively processing information, so we say that their activity is *desynchronized.* Synchronized activity occurs when neurons work as one; in beta activity, however, this is not the case. Beta activity waves have shorter amplitude (manifesting as peaks and valleys in the electrical data) than the alpha waves, meaning that they have a lower voltage. Beta waves are also more common (occur in a higher frequency) than alpha waves (Kalat, 2013).

Stage one of the sleep cycle is a transition from wakefulness to sleep; thus, stage one is not full sleep quite yet. In stage one, the electrical activity of the brain is similar to that of wakefulness, but stage one is characterized by occasional *theta activity* (3.5 – 7.5 cycles per second). This theta activity has a lower frequency (occurs less often) than the alpha and beta activity of wakefulness. Theta activity also implies that the activity of many neurons is more *synchronized* than during wakefulness. The amplitude of this activity is higher, so this electrical pattern has more voltage than the pattern for wakefulness. In *Stage two* of sleep, the activity is again similar to wakefulness, but also contains periods of theta activity as well as bursts of *sleep spindles* and *K-complexes*. A sleep spindle is a short burst of 12-14 cycles per second occurring several times per minute. Sleep spindles occur during this stage, as well as in stages three and four. Spindles seem to play a role in *memory consolidation*, the process of memory strengthening. People tend to be more intelligent when they have more sleep spindles. A K-complex is a burst of electrical activity involved in memory consolidation and suppression of cortical stimulation by outside stimuli (Cash et al., 2009). A K-complex is recorded as a single peak and a single valley. A K-complex happens once per minute. Amplitude of the electrical activity in stage two is higher than the previous stage, which signifies that this activity has more voltage than stage one. In *Stage three* sleep, the activity is similar to stage two, but 20-50% of stage three is characterized by *delta activity*, which is a pattern of high voltage activity happening infrequently (less than 3.5 cycles per second). Sleep spindles are present during this stage as well.

Figure 4. Stage five (or the REM stage) is associated with dreaming.

In *Stage four* is composed of more than 50% delta activity. The voltage of this electrical pattern is the highest of all the stages, and the frequency is low (less than 3.5 cycles per second). Again, sleep spindles happen during this stage. Stages three and four are both called *slow-wave sleep*. Stage four is the deepest stage of sleep, in which only loud noises or other excessive stimuli could awaken a person. When a person is awakened from stages three or four, they may report a presence of a thought, an image, or some emotion, but a coherent *story-like* dream is rarely remembered. However, even though story-like dreams rarely occur during stages three and four, these stages (especially stage four) are known for the horrible nightmares that take place within (Fisher, Byrne, Edwards & Kahn, 1970). Approximately 45 minutes after the start of stage four, stage five begins. Stage five starts approximately 90 minutes after the beginning of the first sleep stage. *Stage five* resembles stage one in terms of its electrical activity; high frequency electrical activity is characterized with low voltage, all of which signifies cellular *de-synchronization*. The eyeballs, under the closed eyelids, start to move rapidly (Kalat, 2013).

Due to these fast movements of the eyes, stage five is known as the *rapid eye movement* or REM stage. The electrical activity of the movements of the eyeballs is recorded by an *electro-oculogram (EOG)*, a method consisting of electrodes positioned on the skin near the eyes. At the same time, an *electromyogram* (EMG) records the muscle tone via electrodes placed on the person's chin. The EMG indicates a substantial loss of muscle tone (i.e. paralysis) during this stage. Most spinal and cranial motor neurons controlling neuromuscular junctions for the limbs, head, and neck movements are paralyzed, but those controlling breathing and eye movements are not. Due to this inhibition of neuromuscular junctions, an individual is unable to move during the REM phase, which is important for preventing physical behavioral expressions of the dream content. However, during the REM stage, brain activity increases and resembles the level found in wakefulness; oxygen consumption by brain cells and blood flow through the brain's blood vessels is just as high as during wakefulness. Mild penile erections and vaginal lubrications occur, but are often not associated with any sexual dream content (Schmidt & Schmidt, 2004).

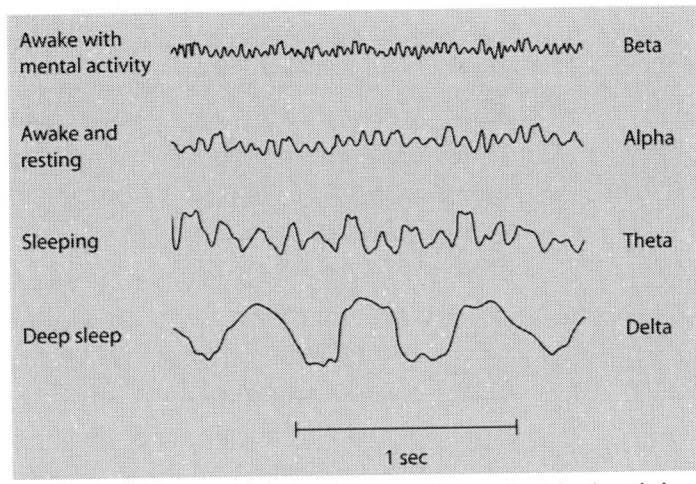

Figure 5. A visual representation of the electrical activity during sleep stages.

During the REM stage, an individual does not react to noises but does react to other meaningful stimuli, like his or her name. When awakened from REM, a person is attentive and alert, and can report a story-like dream. During REM, the activity of the prefrontal cortex, the region involved in planning, ordering of events in time, differentiating reality from illusion, is low, thus, all such functions are poorly performed in our dreams (Braun et al., 1998; Hobson, 1998). If a dream involves speaking and listening, those regions of the brain are especially active in the dream (Hong et al., 1996). The association visual cortex is very active, which suggests hallucinations, yet the primary visual cortex has a much lower activity, which signifies an absence of visual input (Carlson, 2013). If a dream involves movement, then the cortical and subcortical areas controlling movement are active (McCarley a& Hobson, 1979). Sleep containing the REM stage is called REM sleep, and sleep without an REM stage (sleep containing only stages one through four) is non-REM sleep. REM sleep manifests in episodes, meaning there are about four to five episodes of REM, approximately 20-30 minutes of each, during a typical eight hour period of sleep. About 80 percent of awakenings from REM sleep result in the sleeper reporting a story-like dream, while only 7 percent of awakenings from a non-REM sleep result in a reported dream (McNamara et al., 2010). Individuals that claim they do not dream still experience REM sleep and will report dreams when they are awakened during the REM stage (Goodenough et al., 1959).

Adults spend about 20 percent of sleep time in the REM stage and 80 percent in non-REM stages. It is incorrect to think that sleep stages always progress in numerical order. A more correct pattern is as follows: stage one, stage two, stage three, stage four, stage three, stage two, stage three, stage four, REM stage. We normally spend about 90 to 120 minutes in REM sleep each night, with each REM session divided into 15 to 60 minute periods. We spend 15 to 60 minutes in each non-REM sleep stage (Mahowald & Ettinger, 1990 in ALEXANDER).

SLEEP DISORDERS

REM Sleep Disorder is a condition in which a dreamer's muscles are not inhibited (not paralyzed) while in asleep; thus, the sleeper moves according to the story of the dream, enacting parts of whatever may be happening. Neurons in pons send their axons to the spinal cord and from there, synapse with the neurons that inhibit the motor neurons innervating limbs. This mechanism influences us to not be able to move when we dream (physically enacting our dreams while asleep would be dangerous for ourselves and others). However, genetic errors and/or brain damage of the mentioned pons area, will induce this disorder (Schenck, Hurwitz & Mahowald, 1993; Culebras & Moore, 1989). This condition occurs predominantly in older men who develop Parkinson's disease (Olson et al., 2000). REM sleep disorder is treated with benzodiazepine tranquilizers (such as clonazepam) that are GABA (a neurotransmitter) agonists (stimulate its activity). These medications enhance GABA (inhibitory) activity on GABA receptors. After the GABA transmitter binds to this receptor, the receptor increases the chloride channel opening. This influences the resting state of the neuron so that neuromuscular junctions remain un-activated, and movement does not occur (Riss et al., 2008).

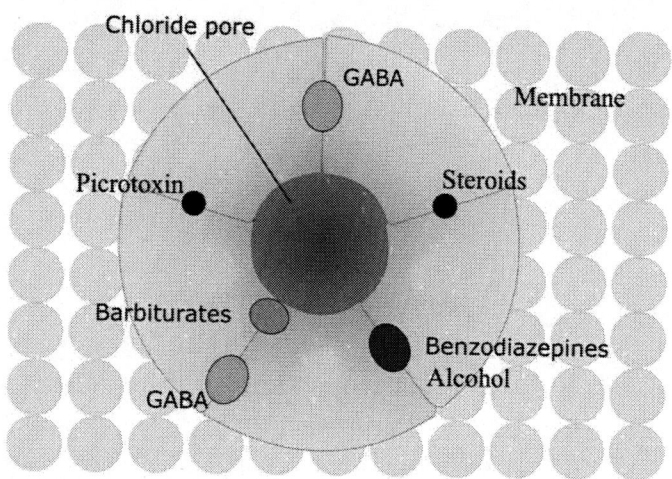

Figure 6. A GABA receptor (embedded in the neuronal membrane) viewed from above. Notice the binding sites for a variety of chemicals, including two binding locations for GABA.

Narcolepsy is a condition that manifests as an unexpected *attack of sleep* (sometimes REM), *cataplexy* and *sleep paralysis*. The sleep attack (lasting anywhere from two-15 minutes) happens at when a person would not normally be sleeping, during periods of alter consciousness (while walking down the street, eating, etc). Exceptionally non-stimulating situations usually trigger this sleep attack. Cataplexy refers to a sudden loss of muscle tone (becoming paralyzed), while the individual is fully awake. This event can last for a few seconds or a few minutes. Stimuli triggering cataplexy attacks are events causing strong emotion (such as intense joy or anger) and abrupt physical effort (Wise, 2004). Sleep paralysis is another symptom of narcolepsy, characterized by one's inability to move shortly *before* falling asleep or shortly *after* waking up. The paralysis is often accompanied with intrusions of REM into the state of wakefulness. These intrusions include hallucinations (unreal sensory experiences) where people may see shadowy figures, hear buzzing sounds, see flashes and beams of light, or feel that they are floating in the air (Carlson, 2013). Sleep paralysis happens when the pons generates REM sleep while the biological mechanisms for wakefulness are still in effect. The pons also inhibits our spinal nerves, so the affected individual cannot move their arms, legs, or neck muscles (Kalat, 2013). When sleep paralysis occurs on its own and not as a part of narcolepsy, it does not have to be diagnosed as a condition as long as it does not impair normal daily functioning.

Only 25 percent of the formation of narcolepsy is attributed to genetics, 75 percent to unknown environmental factors (Raizen, Mason & Pack, 2006). Narcolepsy is caused by faulty receptors for the neurotransmitter *orexin* (produced in the lateral hypothalamus) (Lin et al, 1999), insufficient amounts of orexin in orexin-producing neurons (Nishino et al., 2000), and an extremely low amount of neurons producing orexin (Peyron et al., 2002). Some studies suggest that during an individual's adolescence, a faulty immune system can attack and destroy orexin-producing neurons (Fontana et al., 2010). In a healthy person, orexin is released onto the reticular formation in the brainstem, influencing wakefulness (Luppi et al., 2010; Mignot, 2013). In the treatment of narcolepsy, a stimulant drug, Modafinil/Provigil, is administered to patients. This drug stimulates wakefulness by acting on the remaining orexin-producing neurons in the hypothalamus, activating their production of orexin. The drug seems to also act on some additional mechanisms promoting wakefulness, since it reduces symptoms even in patients who have lost all orexin-producing neurons (Nishino, 2007; Scammell et al., 2000). There are many other medications used in the treatment of narcolepsy, all agonists for the neurotransmitters that influence wakefulness.

Insomnia refers to the inability to fall asleep and/or maintain sleep. The inability to fall asleep is often due to the withdrawal effects of ending sleeping medications. When an individual stops using those medications, they are unable to fall asleep without them. The same effect can be observed in people who use alcohol to fall asleep. (Kales, Scharf & Kales, 1978). Some other triggers of insomnia are stress, pain, uncomfortable temperatures, epilepsy, Parkinson's disease, brain tumors, depression, and anxiety (Horne, 1992). Insomnia with sleep maintenance problem is often associated with sleep apnea that causes this form of insomnia. Sleep apnea refers to periods of cessation of breathing during sleep. This results in disturbances during wakefulness, such as depression, attention deficits, heart problems, sleepiness, poor impulse control, and learning and reasoning deficiencies (Beebe

Figure 7. Insomnia.

& Goxal, 2002; Macey, et al., 2002). This condition stems from the impairment (due to the unavoidable aging process) of brainstem areas responsible for breathing, genetics, and obesity. Obesity produces tissue-swelling and consequent narrowing of breathing airways. Due to this narrowing, the individual needs to breathe forcefully and often. This cannot be maintained during a sleeping state, so interruptions in breathing are experienced (Mezzanotte, Tangel & White, 1992). Therapy for this condition consists of staying away from alcohol and sleeping pills since both agents prevent breathing muscles from working properly. Also, losing weight is important for obese patients. Surgery can be utilized to remove tissue that blocks the breathing passage, and administration of a mask that blows air forcefully into the mouth can transfer air through the breathing passage (Kalat, 2013).

Sleepwalking refers to the execution of behaviors during sleep that are normally reserved for the wakeful state such as eating, dialing phone numbers, cooking, rearranging furniture, and even driving (Gunn & Gunn, 2007). Sleepwalking, however, is not considered an abnormality unless it starts to disturb the everyday life of an individual displaying this behavior. Sleepwalking does not

usually occur during REM since during this stage muscles are paralyzed (Usui et al., 2007). This behavior most often happens in sleep stages three and four. In a sleepwalker, some parts of the brain are awake while other parts remain asleep—this is how we can explain the relatively complex behaviors mentioned above that take place (Kalat, 2013). Sleepwalking usually spontaneously disappears with age—it mostly affects children until they are teenagers *Night terrors* (waking up fearful, sometimes screaming) also sometimes affect children who, in most cases, outgrow this pattern by adulthood (Carlson, 2013).

Figure 8. It is a misconception that sleepwalking occurs as it is depicted here.

FUNCTIONS OF SLEEP

Many studies have examined the role of *sleep* without breaking it into its slow-wave or REM constituents. The following functions of sleep are well-known: resting muscles, rebuilding the proteins in the brain tissues (Kong, 2002), and synaptic reorganization. A sufficient amount of sleep (seven to eight hours per night) is associated with less vulnerability to physical and mental

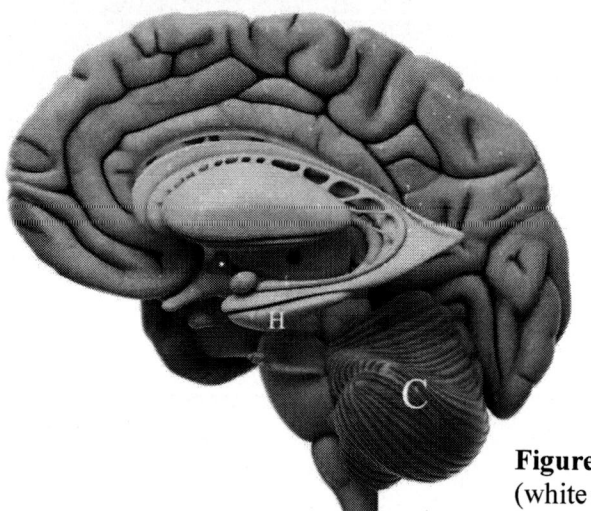

illnesses (Wulff et al., 2010) and better attention and focus (Chee et al., 2008). Information obtained before sleep is remembered significantly better after sleep (Korman et al., 2007; Hu, Stylos-Allan & Walker, 2006; Ji & Wilson, 2007; Euston, Tatsuon & McNaughton, 2007). Sleep spindles represent the flow of information between the thalamus and the cortex; after learning new information, sleep spindles increase (Eschenko et al., 2006).

Figure 9. Thalamus (black dot), hypothalamus (white dot), hippocampus (H) and cerebellum (C). The wrinkled tissue is the cortex.

Sleep deprivation studies (in which subjects sleep three or four hours less than normal) illustrate how people display more sleepiness, negative moods, and lower vigilance when not allowed sufficient sleep (Pinel 2013). If people are sleep deprived for 24 consecutive hours, they display a lower level of innovative thinking and ability to update plans and strategies with newly acquired information (Killgore, Balkin & Wesensten, 2006). People sleeping less than eight hours per night are more likely to develop cold symptoms on a regular basis (Cohen et al., 2008).

In a 10-year study examining over a hundred thousand participants, it was found that people who sleep five to eight hours per night have lower mortality rates than people who sleep less or more than that. In that study, the lowest number of death rates were evident in people who slept *seven* hours per night; slightly higher death rates were found in people who slept 6 hours, slightly more in those that slept 5 hours and even more in those who slept 8 hours per night (Tamakoshi & Ohno, 2004).

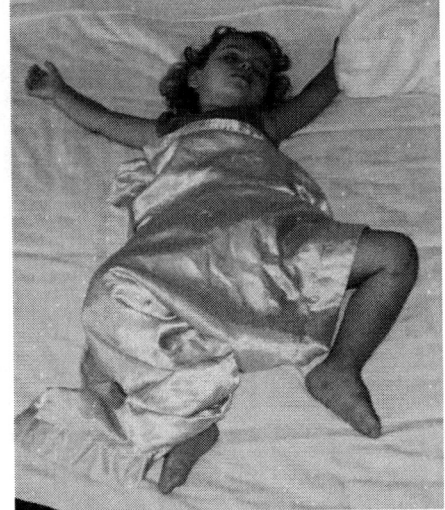

Figure 10. Sleeping like a baby.

FUNCTIONS OF SLOW-WAVE SLEEP

Why is slow-wave sleep (stages three and four) important? It seems that these stages of sleep serve to *rest* and *rebuild* brain regions. Let's look at the resting function a bit more closely. The brain regions that show the highest activity during wakefulness display the highest number of delta waves (activity patterns indicating *reduced* work by cells) (Huber, 2004; Huber, 2006; Carlson, 2013). The regions displaying the highest number of delta waves also show the *lowest* amount of *metabolic activity* (synthetizing and degrading processes) and the *lowest* amount of blood flow. These observations indicate that slow-wave sleep has a resting function since the abovementioned functions are significantly reduced in comparison to wakefulness.

Now let's examine the *rebuilding* function of the slow-wave sleep. During wakefulness, metabolic changes in the brain take place at a high rate. This metabolism influences cells to produce free radicals—chemicals that destroy cells. Due to the reduced metabolic activity in slow wave sleep, the cells within brain regions are able to utilize their restoration processes to destroy free radicals (Siegel, 2005).

It is also important to mention studies that show how slow-wave sleep influences the strengthening of *declarative memories* (memories that can be stated in words, such as what we had for breakfast this morning or recalling the capital of France). In typical studies, participants learn a declarative task (attempting to memorize pairs of words) and a *procedural* task (a task that a person cannot easily put in words, such as playing an instrument). Then, they are allowed to sleep but only during slow-wave stages. Participants show better performance in the *declarative task* the next morning, while their ability to perform the procedural task is not affected at all (Tucker et al., 2006).

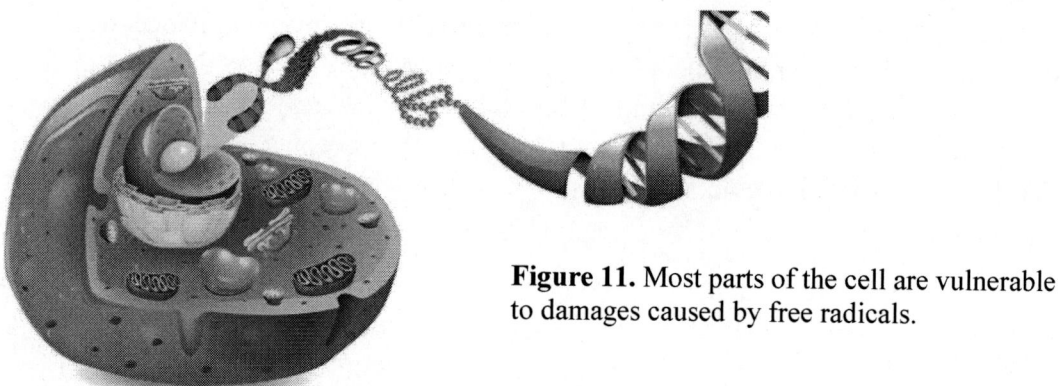

Figure 11. Most parts of the cell are vulnerable to damages caused by free radicals.

FUNCTIONS OF REM SLEEP

When research participants experience *REM sleep deprivation* (being prevented from experiencing REM sleep), they display a *rebound phenomenon*—they spend significantly more time in REM the following night when they are no longer sleep deprived. This phenomenon indicates that our body requires a certain amount of REM sleep (Carlson, 2013). REM sleep is also important for brain development. This notion is evident when comparing different species. For example, humans and ferrets are born with immature nervous systems and spend much more time in REM sleep as infants than species that are born with more developed nervous systems such as cattle and pigs (Jouvet-Mounier, Astic & Lacote, 1970).

Also, it seems that human adults need REM sleep since it facilitates learning (just as slow-wave sleep does). REM sleep influences the consolidation of procedural memory (also called non-declarative memory), memory for skills used to perform tasks (Mednick, Nakayama & Stickgold, 2003).

However, there are some studies that do not show any significant impact of REM sleep on memory consolidation (Vertes, 2004; Siegel, 2005). One study illustrates that when REM sleep is blocked with certain antidepressant medications, the participants' memory of a verbal (declarative) task was not impacted at all, while the memory of a motor task (procedural memory) was actually improved (even though REM sleep was absent), which casts doubt on the importance of REM for memory consolidation (Rasch et al., 2008). At best, these findings on REM sleep should be perceived as mixed and therefore inconclusive.

HYPNOSIS

Hypnosis is a procedure aimed at triggering a hypnotic state of consciousness. A hypnotic state is characterized by the following:

- Narrowed or highly focused attention (tuning out competing stimuli)
- Hallucinations
- Increased use of imagination

- Decreased responsiveness to pain
- Greater willingness (heightened suggestibility) to perceive proposed changes such as: "this marker is a burning cigarette" (Polito et al., 2014; Robertson, 2013).

Hypnosis is sometimes used to reduce pain in surgeries, cancer treatments, and severe burns (Jansen & Patterson, 2014; Iserson, 2014). Hypnosis helps people relax and experience less pain during childbirth and dentistry procedures (Bebe, 2014; Madden et al., 2012). Hypnosis can also help an individual lose weight, stop smoking, and improve studying (Iglesias & Iglesia, 2014; Robertson, 2013). Hypnosis can reduce nausea and vomiting caused by chemotherapy. It can reduce surgical bleeding and improve postoperative recovery time (Bernstein et al., 2006). Can hypnosis influence a person to murder another person? Not if that behavior is against someone's system of values. Can hypnosis influence people to be hypnotized against their will? No, hypnosis depends on one's willingness to participate. A subject will not be hypnotized if they do not want to be. When someone is hypnotized, can they suddenly possess superhuman strength? No. Under hypnosis, can people recover memories about their past life, birth or some repressed memories (such as an alien abduction experience)? It seems that the mind under hypnosis becomes sufficiently stimulated to generate *confabulations* (filling in memory gaps with stories that make sense, but did not actually happen). Hypnosis is often associated with generating false (imagined) memories (Huffman & Dowdell, 2017; Barrios, 2009). For this reason, hypnosis is unreliable in uncovering memories (Bernstein et al., 2006).

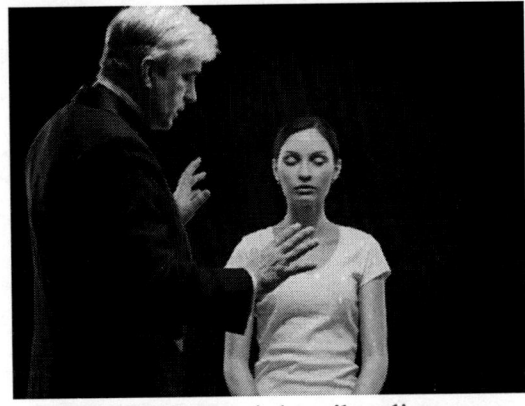

About 15 percent of the population can be easily hypnotized, and about 10 percent are very difficult to hypnotize. Good subjects for hypnosis include children and individuals with vivid imaginations (those who are normally easily absorbed into a movie or a book), open to cooperation, can readily focus their attention, have positive expectations of hypnosis (Hockenbury & Hockenbury, 2006).

Figure 12. Hypnosis heavily relies on the suggestibility of the subject.

The term "hypnosis" derives from the Greek god of sleep Hypnos. Since hypnotized people often have their eyes closed it appears that they may be asleep, but assessment of brain activity during hypnosis strongly suggests that the hypnotic state of consciousness is merely a relaxed wakefulness (not sleep). How is hypnosis conducted? A hypnotist establishes *trust* with the clients by presenting him/herself as genuinely concerned about the clients, providing some expert information on hypnosis, dressing appropriately for the occasion, and providing clients with some type of a certificate or diploma related to the hypnosis. After this the clients should be *relaxed*, which helps them become more open to suggestion.

Next, a *focal point* (a point of focus) is introduced on which a client focuses in order to reduce other distractions and narrow attention only on the hypnotist's direction. Next, the hypnotist *suggests* changes that the client will experience, ultimately suggesting an altered frame of mind or perception of reality to the client (Alexander et al., 2014).

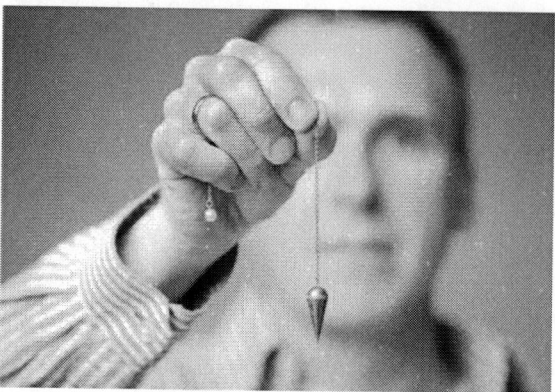

Figure 13. A swinging pendulum can be used as a hypnotic focal point, but can be replaced by a finger, paper, one's voice, or many other objects.

MEDITATION

Meditation is a procedure that induces a meditative state of mind. There are different forms of meditation, each with different goals. *Concentrative meditation* consists of narrowing one's attention to a mantra (a word or phrase) or one's breathing until one stops thinking about other stimuli. The idea is to allow distracting thoughts and feelings to disappear without actively trying to suppress them. The goal of this concentrative effort is to become fully aware of the present moment instead of being distracted by the past or future. Distracting thoughts, sensations, and feelings may still happen, but the goal is to be aware of them and gently (without self-criticism) return to the point of focus. (Bernstein et al., 2006). Another type of meditation is *a mindfulness meditation,* which does not necessitate focusing on anything in particular; rather, the meditator's goal is to become aware of *everything* in the present moment, including all thoughts, sensations, needs, and feelings manifesting in one's mind. All aspects of the present moment are to be treated with equal indifference. A person should neither cling to them nor try to actively avoid them, similarly avoiding passing judgment (Blackmore, 2004). *Gratefulness* meditation aims at focusing on aspects of life that the meditator is grateful for achieving. Within this meditation, a person expresses gratitude to various natural processes (a mantra like: "thank you heart for bringing blood to my brain, muscles…") and people, including one's enemies who are perceived as individuals who taught us some valuable lessons (thus, deserving our gratitude).

What is accomplished by attaining these meditation goals? This is an important question since it is not clear what these different meditations actually accomplish other than exceptional concentrative effort, open awareness, and heightened gratitude. But meditation has been proved **to** reduce insomnia, anxiety, high blood pressure, headaches, and back pain. Meditation improves one's social openness, self-esteem, creativity, attention, immune system, and mental health (Sumter et al., 2009; Ding et al., 2014; Goyal et al., 2014). A decrease in activity in the parietal lobe has been observed during meditation. Feelings of timelessness and absence of space (feeling connected with the rest of the universe) may be attributed to this decreased activity in the parietal lobe, which is involved in spatial and temporal tasks (Flemons, 2005). During meditation there is also an increase of activity in the frontal lobe, a brain area responsible for maintaining one's attention (Bernstein et al., 2006).

Figure 14. You do not have to be a monk to enjoy the benefits of meditation.

DRUG-INDUCED STATES OF CONSCIOUSNESS

There are many different types of drugs that produce different states of consciousness. How are drugs classified?

Depressants suppress (or depress) nervous system activity. Some depressants, such as alcohol, however, both stimulate the activity of some cells and depress activity of other cells. For example, alcohol attaches to the receptor for glutamate (a neurotransmitter) and blocks the receptors. The result is no production of glutamate, which leads to relaxation, and impairments in learning and memory. Here, alcohol acts as an *antagonist*. An antagonist is a substance that attaches to a cell's receptor and prevents the neurotransmitter from binding to this receptor, which maintains the cell's resting state. However, alcohol also acts as an *agonist* on other receptors. For example, alcohol binds with GABA receptors and, by doing so, increases the activity of GABA neurotransmitters (when attached to their binding site on the GABA receptor), a process that maintains the resting state of the cell. In this way, alcohol lowers (blocks) people's inhibitions, making people more talkative and sexual impulses more difficult to control. Alcohol also stimulates GABA-producing cells to release this transmitter, which influences a reduction of anxiety, muscle relaxation, and inhibition of cognitive and motor skills. In the meso-limbic pathway (from the midbrain to the limbic system), alcohol increases the release of dopamine, leading to a feeling of pleasure. Also, alcohol binds with opiate receptors (which receive endorphins, morphine, opium and heroin), resulting in a pain-killing effect and relaxation (Carlson, 2013; Garrett, 2011).

Additional depressants are benzodiazepines and barbiturates. *Benzodiazepines* (Valium, for example) bind to GABA receptors, influencing an easier binding of GABA transmitters. By doing this, benzodiazepines stimulate sleep, induce muscle relaxation, and reduce seizures and anxiety. *Barbiturates* (such as phenobarbital) bind to yet another site on GABA receptors, thus making them more sensitive to GABA transmitters. In low doses, barbiturates induce relaxation, but, in higher doses, they produce difficulty in walking and talking, and can also lead to comas and death (Carlson, 2013; Breedlove, 2007).

Stimulants stimulate or activate cells of the nervous system. Stimulants block *reuptake* (a mechanism that brings neurotransmitters back from the synapse into the axon terminal for recycling and release), so the neurotransmitter remains in the synapse stimulating the receptor

237

longer. Examples of this occurrence are amphetamines, methamphetamines, and cocaine. These drugs block the reuptake mechanism of dopamine primarily in nucleus accumbens (of the basal forebrain), which makes it more available in the synapse. This produces euphoria (pleasure).

Amphetamines and methamphetamines also block the reuptake of serotonin and norepinephrine. In low doses, these drugs can increase attention. High doses yield feelings of euphoria while attention and learning capabilities may be impaired. Ritalin (methylphenidate) is a dopamine agonist since it blocks dopamine reuptake. The effect of Ritalin is a gradual increase in concentration, if taken as a pill, but if injected into the vein directly (in a higher dose than a pill), it produces euphoria similar to that of cocaine (Pinel, 2014).

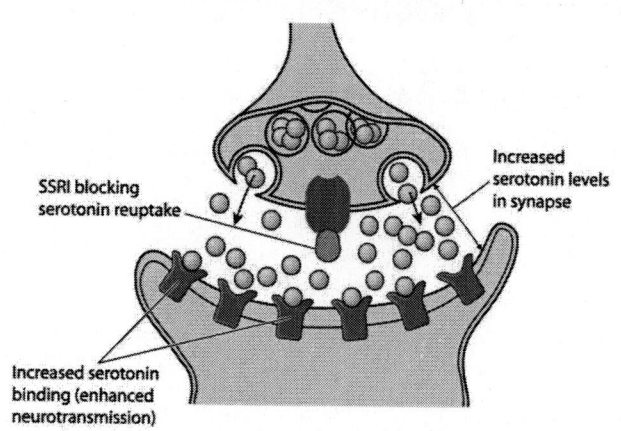

Figure 15. Serotonin's reuptake system is very similar to the dopamine's.

Nicotine (a compound found in tobacco) binds to nicotinic receptors for Acetylcholine (a neurotransmitter, ACH) in the nucleus accumbens (in the basal forebrain). These receptors are located on cells that also produce dopamine, so this binding increases the release of dopamine in the area. The effect is an experience of relaxation, pleasure, alertness, and happiness (Kalat, 2013).

Drugs called *opiates* have a single representative, *opium*. Opium's derivatives are morphine and heroin. The brain contains opiate receptors to which these drugs bind. Opiate receptors are primarily located in the limbic system (especially in hypothalamus) and in the periaqueductal gray area of the brainstem/midbrain. When these receptors are stimulated by opiates, they produce *analgesia* (a reduction of pain) and pleasure. Heroin is a synthetic (lab-created) opiate that binds to the aforementioned receptors and induces analgesia. Other heroin-like opiates have been developed in labs as well; some are much safer than heroin and are even used in hospitals. Naloxone is a blocker of opiate receptors. It is a synthetic drug that attaches to these receptors and prevents heroin (and other opiate drugs) from binding with them. This is important for the process of drug rehabilitation, when drugs like naloxone are used to help prevent heroin from binding to the receptors, which can prevent an overdose (Martini et al., 2012; Carlson, 2013).

Opioids (substances like opiates) are neurotransmitters that are produced within our body. Since they are natural to the human body, they are also called *endogenous opiates*. They bind to the same receptors as opiates. Endorphins are endogenous opiates that control pain by blocking it via an inhibition of a neurotransmitter called the Substance P. They also induce feelings of pleasure by inhibiting GABA that inhibits cells producing dopamine (North, 1992). This inhibition of an inhibition results in the excitation of dopamine cells. There are different types of endorphins, such as beta endorphins, located in the thalamus, hypothalamus, brain stem, and the retina of the eye.

Endomorphins are located in the thalamus, hypothalamus, and basal nuclei. Dynorphins are located in the hypothalamus, midbrain, and medulla oblongata. Enkephalins are located in the hypothalamus, basal nuclei, pons, medulla oblongata, and the spinal cord. (Martini et al., 2012; Carlson, 2013).

Figure 16. The opium drug is extracted from the seeds of the opium flower.

Hallucinogens (also known as psychedelics) are drugs that produce hallucinations. An example is the drug Ecstasy (MMDA or 3-methoxy-4,5-methylenedioxyamphetamine). In lower doses, ecstasy attaches to post-synaptic dopamine receptors and stimulates dopamine release, hence inducing excitement, alertness, elevated mood, and decreased fatigue. These effects are similar to stimulants. In higher doses, however, Ecstasy attaches to post-synaptic serotonin receptors stimulating serotonin release, which is associated with hallucinations. Another example is LSD (lysergic acid diethylamide), which is, structurally, very similar to serotonin. LSD attaches to serotonin receptors and remains attached for a longer period than serotonin. The effect of this prolonged stimulation is an increased release of serotonin manifesting as an LSD "trip" characterized by hallucinations (Kalat, 2013).

THC (tetrahydrocannabinol), a compound found in marijuana leaves, binds to cannabinoid receptors (for the endogenous neurotransmitter anandamide). The effects of THC binding to the cannabinoid receptor include euphoria, sedation, analgesia (pain reduction), stimulation of appetite, reduction of nausea, relief of asthma attacks, reduction of eye pressure for people suffering from glaucoma (an eye-disease), reduction of uncontrollable movements (such as tremors), alterations of visual and auditory perception, distortion of time perception, impairment of concentration, and memory impairment. THC binding with the anandamide receptor in the hippocampus is responsible for memory disturbances. THC attaches to *auto receptors* (on the pre-synaptic neuron) and influences a reduction in the release of glutamate (producing an impairment in learning and memory). In addition to glutamate, THC binds to the GABA auto receptor, CB1, and reduces the release of GABA in the ventral tegmental area (midbrain). This area also contains dopamine cell bodies that send axons to nucleus accumbens where dopamine is released. Thus, a reduction in the activity of the inhibitory transmitter GABA *activates* dopamine cells to produce more dopamine. This process of dopamine release (via GABA inhibition) explains the sensations of pleasure after the intake of cannabinoids (such as THC). In the hypothalamus and hippocampus,

THC binds to the serotonin auto receptors, which, in turn, reduces the release of serotonin. Reducing the release of serotonin increases appetite and decreases nausea. THC effects are reminiscent of both depressants (reducing the release of glutamate and GABA) as well as stimulants (increasing the release of dopamine) (Carlson, 2013).

ADDICTION

Plasticity refers to changes affecting the nervous system's tissue. In this chapter, we will examine plasticity by considering addiction. People can develop addictions to certain substances (heroin, cocaine, alcohol, nicotine, methamphetamine, etc.) or activities (sex, gambling, etc.). Addiction refers to a complex, behavioral pattern that is composed of aspects such as *cravings, tolerance,* and *withdrawal*. A craving is a persistent urge to satisfy a *want* by engaging in certain behaviors.

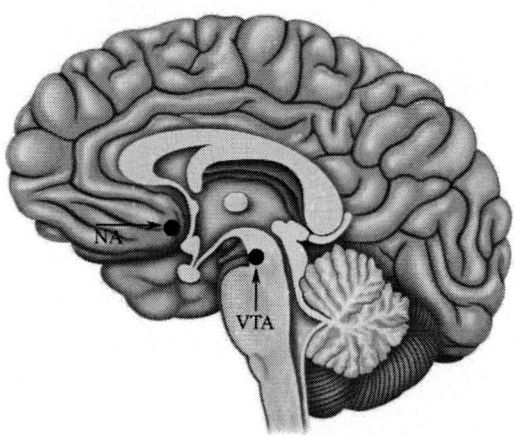

Figure 17. NA: the nucleus accumbens; VTA: the ventral tegmental area.

When we have a craving for something sweet, for example, we buy a chocolate bar. People who have a craving for cocaine will try to obtain that drug. Biologically speaking, alcohol, cocaine, and nicotine *alter* receptors in the nucleus accumbens of the mesolimbic dopamine pathway (and other brain regions responsible for rewards) causing the receptors to become more responsive to the substance and less responsive to other rewarding stimuli. The nucleus accumbens becomes "hijacked" by addiction (Kalat, 2016). A drug-seeking habit is a repetitive behavior orchestrated by neurons in basal nuclei, specifically caudate and putamen. The ventral tegmental area sends its axons to the nucleus accumbens and the basal nuclei. The connection between these regions comprises a pathway involved in addiction. Hypothalamic neurons that produce orexin also reach the nucleus accumbens. Orexin contributes to the rewarding effects of dopamine in the same area. When the release of orexin is blocked in the nucleus accumbens, the drug-seeking behavior is seriously reduced or even blocked. Similarly, the peptide MCH (melanine concentrating hormone) is produced in the hypothalamus and released into the nucleus accumbens of the neurons that contain receptors for MCH and dopamine. MCH increases the rewarding effects of dopamine. Addiction has a reinforcing effect not only through positive reinforcement, but also as a negatively reinforcing behavior—one uses drugs to avoid negative experiences, such as stress or depression (Carlson, 2013).

ADDICTION: TOLERANCE AND WITHDRAWAL

Why can't drug addicts snap out of their patterns and control the dangerous urge to use drugs? Repetitive use of drugs reduces the activity of the prefrontal cortex, an area known to help us control impulses. This region goes through significant maturation (development towards full functionality) during adolescence, which means that it is not fully functional at that time, so it is no surprise that 50 percent of drug addictions begin during that fundamental period (Carlson, 2013; Kalat, 2016). After repeated exposure to a drug, the user develops a tolerance, experiencing fewer pleasurable effects with the same amount of drug intake. Regular users take more drugs each time to obtain the same effect equal to the previous usages (Kalat, 2016).

What biological changes create drug tolerance? First of all, it is important to understand that there are metabolic and functional types of tolerance. *Metabolic tolerance* refers to our organs (the liver, for example) becoming more proficient at eliminating the drug before it impacts the brain tissue. Thus, a higher dosage is then needed; the liver will metabolize (break down) a portion of the higher dosage, yet some remaining portion will still reach the brain. *Functional tolerance*, however, affects the brain tissue directly. When the drug is used

Figure 18. The experience of a certain amount of a drug ceasing to have an effect is called tolerance.

repeatedly, cells reduce their membrane receptors (called *down-regulation*) since they are over-stimulated by the constant presence of the drug. Since there are now fewer receptors, and therefore less stimulation of the cells, the brain tissue needs *more* of the drug to stimulate cells that have not yet initiated down-regulation. A larger amount of the drug is consumed in order to reach the same effect previously accomplished with a lesser amount of the drug acting on receptors (before their retraction). Similarly, when a drug is available on a continuous basis, receptors become less sensitive to it. Hence, the drug cannot bind any longer to those receptors as efficiently as it did before. The drug has a reduced *affinity* for the receptors. Thus, more drug use is needed to stimulate those de-sensitized receptors in order to reach the same effect as before the de-sensitization took place. In addition, due to a constant presence of the drug, the receptors may reduce efficiency in their opening of ion channels. So more of the drug is needed to stimulate inefficient receptors to properly open ion channels. This can result in an *overdose*, which sometimes results in death (Pinel, 2014). *Withdrawal* refers to a lack of drug intake. The body reacts to the absence of a drug (heroin, for example) via withdrawal symptoms such as anxiety, sweating, vomiting, and diarrhea. Other withdrawal symptoms (in alcohol addiction, for example) include irritability, fatigue, uncontrollable shaking, sweating, and nausea. More severe symptoms could include hallucinations, convulsions, fever, and cardiovascular problems. Withdrawal symptoms are usually opposite of whatever were the drug's pleasurable effects. For example, some pleasurable effects of heroin are euphoria and relaxation; however, the withdrawal symptoms are depression and agitation.

Figure 19. Depression is often a symptom of withdrawal.

Sleeping pills that induce sleep, when withdrawn, often cause insomnia. It seems that the neural changes that happen as a result of drug withdrawal are signs that the body was used to the presence of the drug, and when the drug is no longer available, the body "rebels" to that absence by producing withdrawal symptoms (Pinel, 2014). It would appear that the body develops addictions in order to avoid withdrawal symptoms. However, this cannot be the only explanation for addiction since many people, once they overcome the withdrawal symptoms, will *relapse* (use the drug again) sometime later. Thus, in addition to avoiding the withdrawal symptoms, addiction must provide a way of reducing one's stress and dissatisfaction with life (Kalat, 2016). Of course, people do not realize that true addiction leads to even more stress and dissatisfaction later in life. Similarly, another cause of addiction may be the user's search for the rewarding/euphoric effects of drugs (positive reinforcement) (Pinel, 2014).

ADDICTION: RISK FACTORS

There are certain risk factors that make someone more susceptible for developing addiction. In twin siblings, if one twin suffers from alcoholism, the other twin has a higher chance for developing it compared to non-twin siblings. Individuals who have a family history of addiction have a higher chance of developing it themselves. For example, individuals whose fathers are alcoholics show less than average intoxication levels after drinking a moderate amount of alcohol. They also have more than a 60 percent chance of developing alcoholism than individuals with a non-alcoholic parent. Alcohol may seem to decrease stress, and this effect is amplified in most children of alcoholics. This suggests that genetics plays a role in behaviors related to alcohol intake. Several genes have attracted considerable attention in this research. One such gene controls the sensitivity of a dopamine receptor (D4 subtype). People who have this genetic pattern report higher cravings for alcohol. Researchers believe that people who suffer from alcoholism seek more alcohol to compensate for a lack of pleasure due to the reduced sensitivity of the dopamine receptor. Also, there is a gene that breaks down an enzyme that metabolizes dopamine after its release. People with a more active type of this gene tend to be more impulsive (less able to control urges) and more prone to alcohol intake than others who do not have the form of this gene (Kalat, 2016).

Environmental influences on addiction are similarly well known. For example, if a mother drinks alcohol during pregnancy, the chance that the child will develop alcoholism later in life increases.

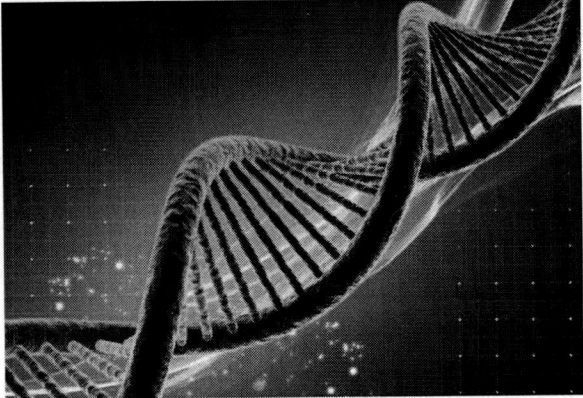

However, the amount of alcohol a mother drinks later on in life as the child is growing up does not seem to have an effect on the outcome for the child (Kalat, 2016). Remaining in a physical setting where a person previously used drugs can trigger drug cravings in that person. Higher susceptibility toward addiction has been found in individuals who experience family breakups, poor relationships with parents, presence of an antisocial sibling, and peer groups that use drugs (Breedlove, 2007).

Figure 20. A gene is a segment of the DNA molecule (shown here).

TREATMENTS FOR ADDICTION

One medication used to combat alcoholism is disulfiram (Antabuse). It blocks an enzyme in the liver involved in converting alcohol into acetic acid, which the body uses as energy. By blocking this enzyme, disulfiram produces sickness after alcohol ingestion. The idea behind this approach is that if alcohol use will produce sickness in a person, then that person will not drink any longer. The effectiveness of the treatment is moderate. Nausea-producing drugs that do not act on alcohol can accomplish a similar effect. Once people take alcohol with this drug, sickness will follow. These drugs are involved in the production of a *conditioned response* (through classical conditioning) in which people learn to dislike alcohol once it is associated with nausea. Further, the medications naloxone and naltrexone block opiate receptors (the receptors to which alcohol binds) and reduce pleasure obtained from alcohol. These drugs are also moderately effective. Heroin and morphine addiction are treated with different drugs. The drug methadone is very similar to heroin and morphine, binding to the same receptors producing the same effects. However, it acts slowly since it is taken orally. The effects begin slowly as opposed to morphine and heroin, which are injected through veins. Since methadone slowly reaches the brain, the effects are not meant to suddenly disrupt daily activities. And since methadone leaves the body slowly as well, withdrawal symptoms are much more tolerable. These factors work to make it is easier to break the addiction (Kalat, 2016). In smokers, nicotine addiction can be treated with a transdermal patch that releases nicotine through skin. This maintains high levels of nicotine in the brain, which decreases the craving. The dose of nicotine in the patch can be progressively reduced to wean the individual off cigarettes. This approach has the best effect if coupled with psychotherapy or counseling (Carlson, 2013).

Since our brain tissue conforms to the principle of *plasticity* (being prone to alteration or change), drugs can modify the brain tissue in a detrimental way. Alcohol, for example, disrupts NMDA receptor and interferes with long-term potentiation, which translates into learning deficits. It also interferes with the function of hippocampal cells. This process can influence memory deficits. When alcohol blocks the pre-synaptic NMDA receptor for a long amount of time, the post-synaptic NMDA receptors proliferate (up-regulation), seeking glutamate (which is scarce since the pre-synaptic neuron does not release glutamate). When a person stops

Figure 21. How does one restore beauty, clarity, and serenity to a life affected by addiction? A pharmacological approach may be a good start.

using alcohol, this is especially dangerous since there are suddenly so many open receptors. When they are stimulated by available glutamate, the cell becomes over-stimulated, thus bringing excess ions into the cell. These overabundant ions prevent mitochondria from normal functioning, resulting in *apoptosis*, cell death. This situation can lead to seizures and convulsions. Negative effects of alcohol are also visible in children born to mothers who used alcohol during pregnancy. Some of these children develop *fetal alcohol syndrome*, a condition that manifests itself as heart problems, difficulties maintaining attention, irritability, poor impulse control, learning problems, motor deficits, and mental delays. In children alcohol also impairs *neurogenesis* (creation of new neurons), *neuronal migration* (movement to target locations prenatally), neuronal maturation, and synaptic transmission. Korsakoff's syndrome is yet another devastating disorder caused by alcohol consumption (see chapter six) (Kalat, 2016; Carlson, 2013). Some studies have shown that THC molecules in marijuana impair hippocampal activity by binding to its numerous THC receptors and excessively stimulating them. This can lead to memory problems (typical in marijuana users) such as an inability to keep track of a particular topic or losing the thread

Figure 22. Poor impulse control can be a symptom of fetal alcohol syndrome.

of a conversation (Carlson, 2013). However, most studies indicate that these are only short-term memory deficits (Pinel, 2014). Methamphetamines can damage axon terminals of serotonin-producing cells and cause cell death in the cortex, hippocampus, caudate, and putamen. Damage to these areas can manifest into longer-lasting memory deficits, other cognitive problems, and movement abnormalities. Cocaine, amphetamine, and methamphetamine, influence decreased dopamine axon terminals in caudate and putamen nuclei, which increases the risk for developing Parkinson's disease as the user ages. Hallucinations and delusions that result from frequent use of these drugs likely result from blocking the reuptake of dopamine. The resulting increased amount of dopamine over-stimulates dopamine receptors in the meso-limbic system. These psychotic symptoms cease, in most cases, when the person stops using these drugs. MDMA or "Ecstasy," a derivative of amphetamine, seems to influences a reduced binding of serotonin to its cortical receptors (Carlson, 2013). This change can influence memory disturbances and depression (Carlson, 2013), which may be experienced long term (Pinel, 2014).

Figure 23. Auditory hallucinations.

REFERENCES

Alexander, P., Flint, W. R., Flome, R., Hakala, C., Hayashi, C., Jones, J., July, W., Nguyen, B., Patry, M., Shobe, E., Sweetman, A., Thomas, B., Vukov, B., Wark, V., & Yakel, A.D. (2014). *Psychology: exploring our universe within* (4th edition). Boston, MA: Pearson Custom Publishing.

Barrios, A. (2009). *Understanding Hypnosis: Theory scope and potential.* Hauppauge, NY: Nova Science Publishers.

Beebe, D. W., & Gozal, D. (2002). Obstructive sleep apnea and the prefrontal cortex: Towards a comprehensive model linking nocturnal upper airway obstruction to daytime cognitive and behavioral deficits. *Journal of Sleep Research*, 11 (9), 1-16.

Beebe, K. R. (2014). Hypnotherapy for labor and birth. *Nursing for Women's Health, 18,* 48-59.

Bernstein, D., Penner, L., Clarke-Stewart, A., & Roy, E. (2006). *Psychology* (7th ed.). Boston: Houghton Mifflin.

Blackmore, S. (2004). *Consciousness. An introduction.* New York. Oxford University Press.

Braun, A. R., Balkin, T. J., Wesensten, N. J., & Gawdry, F. (1998). Dissociated pattern of activity in visual cortices and their projections during human rapid eye movement sleep. *Science*, 279, 91-95.

Breedlove, M. S., Rosenzweig, M. R., & Watson, N. V. (2007). *Biological psychology* (5th ed.). Sunderland, MA: Sinauer Associates.

Breedlove, M. S., Rosenzweig, M. R., & Watson, N. V. (2007). *Biological psychology* (5th ed.). Sunderland, MA: Sinauer Associates.

Brzezinski, A., Vangel, M. G., Wurtman, R. J., Norrie, G., Zhdanova, I., Ben-Shushan, A., & Ford, I. (2005). Effects of exogenous melatonin on sleep: A meta-analysis. *Sleep Medicine Reviews*, 9, 41-50.

Carlson, N. R. (2013). *Physiology of behavior* (9th ed.). Boston, MA: Allyn and Bacon.

Carlson, N.R. (2013). *Physiology of behavior* (9th ed.). Boston, MA: Allyn and Bacon.

Cash, S. S., Halgren, E., Dehghani, N., Rosssetti, A. O., Thesen, T., & Wang, C. M. (2009). The human K-complex represents an isolated cortical down-state. *Science*, 324 (9), 1084-1087. (9)

Chee, M. W. L., Tan, J. C., Zheng, H., Parimal, S., Weissman, D. H., & Zagorodnov, V. (2008). Lapsing during sleep deprivation is associated with distributed changes in brain activation. *Journal of Neuroscience*, 28 (9), 5519-5528.

Clayton, E. C., & Williams, C. L. (2000). Glutamatergic influences on the nucleus paragigantocelularis: Contribution to performance in avoidance and spatial memory tasks. *Behavioral Neuroscience*, 114 (9), 707-712.

Cohen, J. (2007). Relative differences: The myth of 1%. *Science*, 316, 1836.

Culebras, A., & Moore, J. T. (1989). Magnetic resonance findings in REM sleep behavior disorder. *Neurology*, 1989, *39*, 1519-1523.

Damasio, H., Grabowski, T. J., Tranel, D., Hichwa, R. D., & Damasio, A. R. (1996). A neural basis for lexical retrieval. *Nature*, 380, 499-505.

Deadwyler, S. A., Porrino, L., Siegal, J. M., & Hampson, R. E. (2007). Systemic and nasal delivery of orexin-Λ (hypocretin-1) reduces the effects of sleep deprivation on cognitive performance in nonhuman primates. *Journal of Neuroscience*, 27, 14239-14247.

Ding, X., Tang, Y. Y., Cao, C., Deng, Y., Wang, Y., Xin, X., & Posner, M. I. (2014). Short-term meditation modulates brain activity of insight evoked with solution cue. *Social Cognitive and Affective Neuroscience*. Advance online publication.

Eschenko, O., Molle, M., Born, J., & Sara, S. J. (2006). Elevated sleep spindle density after learning or after retrieval in rats. *Journal of Neurophysiology*, 26, 12914-12920.

Fisher, C., Byrne, J., Edwards, A., & Kahn, E. A. (1970). Psychophysiological study of nightmares. *Journal of the American Psychoanalytic Association*, 1970, *18*, 747-782.

Flemons, D. (2005). Hypnosis and relaxation scripting. In G. P. Koocher, J. C. Nocross, & S. S. Hill (Eds.), *Psychologists desk reference* (pp. 332-337). New York: Oxford University Press.

Fontana, A., Gast, H., & Reigh, W. (2010). Narcolepsy: Autoimmunity, effector T cell activation due to infection, or T cell independent, major histocompatibility complex class II induced neuronal loss? *Brain*, 133, 1300-1311.

Goodenough, D. R., Shapiro, A., Holden, M., & Steinschriber, L. (1959). A comparison of "dreamers" and "nondreamers": Eye movements, electroencephalograms, and the recall of dreams. *Journal of Abnormal and Social Psychology, 59,* 295-303.

Goyal, M., Singh, S., Subinga, E. M., Gould, N. F., Rowland-Seymour, A., Sharma, R., … Haythornthwaite, J. A. (2014). Meditation programs for psychological stress and well-being. A systematic review and meta-analysis. *JAMA International Medicine, 174,* 357-368.

Guérit, J. M. (2005). Neurophysiological patterns of vegetative and minimally conscious states. *Neuropsychological Rehabilitation, 15,* 357-371.

Gunn, S. R., & Gunn, W. S. (2007). Are we in the dark about sleepwalking's dangers? In C. A. Read (Ed.), *Cerebrum 2007: Emerging ideas in brain science* (pp. 71-84). New York: Dana Press.

Haimov, I., & Lavie,P. (1996). Melatonin – A soporific hormone. *Current Directions in Psychological Science, 5,* 106-111.

Hobson. J. A. (1988). *The Dreaming Brain.* New York: Basic Books.

Hockenbury, D., & Hockenbury, S. (2006). *Psychology* (4th ed.). New York: Worth Publishers.

Horne, J. A. (1992). Sleep and its disorders in children. *Journal of Child Psychology & Psychiatry & Allied Disciplines, 33,* 473-487.

Hu, P., Stylos-Allan, M., & Walker, M. P. (2006). Sleep facilitates consolidation of emotional declarative memory. *Psychological Science*, 17, 891-898.

Huber, R., Ghilardi, M. F., Massimini, M., & Tononi, G. (2004). Local sleep and learning. *Nature*, 430, 78-81.

Huber, R., Ghilardi, M. F., Massmini, M., & Ferrarelli, F. (2006). Arm immobilization causes cortical plastic changes and locally decreases sleep slow wave activity. *Nature Neuroscience, 9,* 1169-1176.

Huffman, K., Dowdell, K. (2015). Psychology in Action. Hoboken, NJ: John Wiley & Sons.

Iglesias, A., & Iglesias, A. (2014). Hypnosis aided fixed role therapy for social phobia: A case report. *American Journal of Clinical Hypnosis, 56,* 405-412.

Iserson, K. V. (2014). An hypnotic suggestion: Review of hypnosis for clinical emergency care. *The Journal of Emergency Medicine, 46,* 588-596.

Ji, D. & Wilson, M. A. (2007). Coordinated memory replay in the visual cortex and hippocampus during sleep. *Nature Neuroscience,* 10, 100-107.

Jones, B. E.(1990). Influence of the brainstem reticular formation, including intrinsic monoaminergic and cholinergic neurons, on forebrain mechanisms of sleep and waking. In *The Diencephalon and Sleep,* edited by M. Mancia and G. Marini. New York: Raven Press.

Jouvet-Mounier, D., Astic, L., & Lacote, D. (1978). Ontogenesis of the states of sleep in rat, cat, and guinea pig during the first postnatal month. *Developmental Psychobiology,* 2, 216-239.

Kalat, J. W. (2013). *Biological psychology* (11th ed.). Belmont, CA: Wadsworth, Cengage Learning.

Kalat, J. W. (2013). *Biological psychology* (11th ed.). Belmont, CA: Wadsworth, Cengage Learning.

Kales, A. Scharf, M. B., & Kales, J. D. (1978). Rebound insomnia: A new clinical syndrome. *Science,* 201, 1039-1041.

Killgore, W. D. S., Balkin, T. J., & Wesensten, N. J. (2006). Impaired decision making following 49 h of sleep deprivation. *Journal of Sleep Research,* 15, 7-13.

Kong, J., Shepel, P. N., Holden, C. P., Mackiewicz, M., Pack, A. I., & Geiger, J. D. (2002). Brain glycogen decreases with increased periods of wakefulness: Implications for homeostatic drive to sleep. *Journal of Neuroscience,* 22, 5581-5587.

Korman, M., Doyon, J., Doljansky, J., Carrier, J., Dagan, Y., & Karni, A. (2007) Daytime sleep condenses the time course of motor memory consolidation. *Nature Neuroscience,* 10, 1206-1213.

Luppi, P. H., Clement, O., Sapin, E., Gervasoni, D., Peyron, C., Leger, L., Salvert, D., & Fort, P. (2011). The neuronal network responsible for paradoxical sleep and its dysfunctions causing narcolepsy and rapid eye movement (REM) behavior disorder. *Sleep Medicine Reviews,* 15, 153-163.

Macey, P. M., Henderson, L. A., Macey, K. E., Alger, Jr. R., Frysinger, R. C., & Woo, M. A. (2002). Brain morphology associated with obstructive sleep apnea. *American Journal of Respiratory and Critical Care Medicine,* 166, 1382-1387.

Madden, K., Middleton, P., Cyna, A. M., Mathewson, M., & Jones, L. (2012). Hypnosis for pain management during labour and child birth. *Cochrane Database if Systematic Reviews,* 11.

Marieb E., & Hoehn K. (2013). Human anatomy and physiology (9th ed.). Glenview, IL: Pearson Education.

Marieb, E., & Hoehn K. (2013). Human anatomy and physiology (9th ed.). Glenview, IL: Pearson Education.

Martini, H. F., Nath, L. J., Bartholomew, F. E., & Ober, C W. (2012). *Fundamentals of anatomy and physiology* (9th ed.). San Francisco, CA: Pearson Benjamin Cummings.

Martini, H. F., Nath, L. J., Bartholomew, F. E., & Ober, C. W. (2012). Fundamentals of Anatomy and Physiology (9th ed.). San Francisco, CA: Pearson Benjamin.

McCarley, R. W. (2007). Neurobiology of REM and NREM sleep. *Sleep medicine*, 8, 302-330.

McDermott, K. B., Watson, J. M. & Ojemann, J. G. (2005). Presurgical language mapping. *Current Directions in Psychological Sciences*, 14, 291-295.

McNamara, P. Johnson, P., McLaren, D., Harris, E., Beauharnais, & C., Auerbach, S. (2010). REM and NREM sleep mentation. *International Review of Neurobiology*, 92, 69-86.

Mednick, S., Nakayama, K., & Stickgold, R. (2003). Sleep-dependent learning: A nap is as good as a night. *Nature Neuroscience*, 6, 697-698.

Mezzanotte, W. S., Tangel, D. J., & White, D. P. (1992). Waking genioglossal electromyogram in sleep apnea patients versus normal controls (a neuromuscular compensatory mechanism). *Journal of Clinical Investigation,* 89, 1571-1579.

Mignot, E. (1998). Genetic and familial aspects of narcolepsy. *Neurology,* 50, S16-S22.

Nishino, S. (2007). Clinical and neurobiologcal aspects of narcolepsy. *Sleep Medicine*, 8, 373-399.

Nishino, S. Ripley, B., Overeem, S., & Lammers, G. J. (2007). Hypocretin (orexin) deficiency in human narcolepsy. *Sleep Medicine*, 2007, 8, 373-399.

Olson, E. J., Boeve, B. F., & Silber, M. H. (2000). Rapid eye movement sleep behavior disorder: Demographic, clinical, and laboratory findings in 93 cases. *Brain*, 123, 331-339. (9)

Peyron, R., Laurent, B. & Garcia-Larrea, L. Functional imaging of brain responses to pain: A review and meta-analysis. *Neurophysiology Clinics*, 2000, 30, 263-288.

Pinel, P. J. (2014). *Biopsychology* (9th ed.). Boston, MA: Pearson Education.

Polito, V., Barnier, A. J., Woody, E. Z., & Connors, M. J. (2014). Measuring agency change across the domain of hypnosis. *Psychology of Consciousness: Theory, Research, and Practice, 1,* 3-19.

Ptak, R., & Schnider, A. (2010). The dorsal attention network mediates orienting toward behaviorally relevant stimuli in spatial neglect. *Journal of Neuroscience*, 30 (14), 12557-12565.

Raizen, D. M., Mason, T. B. A., & Pack, A. I. (2006). Genetic basis for sleep regulation and sleep disorders. *Seminars in Neurology*, 5, 467-483.

Rasch, B., & Born, J. (2008). Reactivation and consolidation of memory during sleep. *Current Directions in Psychological Science*, 17, 188-192.

Refinetti, R., & Menaker, M. (1992). The circadian rhythm of body temperature. *Physiology & Behavior, 51,* 613-637. (9)

Riss, J., Cloyd, J., Gates, J., & Collins, S. (2008). Benzodiazepines in epilepsy: pharmacology and pharmacokinetics. *Acta Neurologica Scandinavica* 118 (2), 69–86.

Robertson, D. (2013). *The practice of cognitive-behavioural hypnotherapy: A manual for evidence-based cinical hypnosis.* London: Karnac Books.

Schenck, C. H., Hurwitz, T. D., & Mahowald, M. W. (1993). REM-sleep behavior disorder: An update on a series of 96 patients and a review of world literature. *Journal of Sleep Research,* 2, 224-231.

Schmidt, M. H., & Schmidt, H. S. (2004). Sleep-related erections: Neural mechanisms and clinical significance. *Current Neurology and Neuroscience Reports*, 2004, 4, 170-178.

Sumter, M. T., Monk-Turner. E., & Turner, C. (2009). The benefits of meditation practice in the correctional setting. *Journal of Correctional Health Care.* Vol. 15, No. 1, 42-57.

Tamakoshi, A., & Ohno, Y. (2004). Self-reported sleep duration as a predictor of all-cause mortality: Results from the JACC study, Japan. *Sleep*, 27, 51-54.

Tucker, M. A., Hirota, Y., Wamsley, E. J., & Lau, H. (1985). A daytime nap containing solely non-REM sleep enhances declarative but non procedural memory. *Neurobiology of Learning and Memory*, 86, 241-247.

Usui, A., Matsushita, Y., Kitahara, Y., Sakamoto, R., Watanabe, T., & Motohashi, N. (2007). Two cases of young adults sleepwalking. *Sleep and Biological Rhythms,* 5, 291-293.

Vertes, R. P. (2004). Memory consolidation in sleep: Dream or reality? *Neuron*, 44, 135-148.

Wise, M. S. (2004). Narcolepsy and other disorders of excessive sleepiness. *Medical Clinics of North America,* 99, 597-610.

Wulff, K., Gatti, S., Wettstein, J. G., & Foster, R. G. (2010). Sleep and circadian rhythm disruption in psychiatric and neurodegenerative disease. *Nature Neuroscience*, 11, 589-599. (9)

Xu, Y., Padiath, Q. S., Shapiro, R. E., Jones, C. R., Wu, S. C., & Saigoh, N. (2005). Functional consequences of a CK*x*d mutation causing familial advanced sleep phase sundrome. *Nature, 434*, 640-644.

Developmental Psychology

Chapter Nine

Development is a process of an individual becoming more complex. Increasing complexity of our mental processes, behaviors, and physiological processes is influenced by biological makeup (or **nature**), environmental factors (or **nurture**), and time. What do we mean by the **environmental influence** or nurture? By the environmental influence we mean *information* that we learn from our family, relatives, friends, school, media (radio, tv, film, internet), society, religious institutions and culture. By "information" we mean instructions for how to live life, what our values should be, how to perform a certain skill, how to think, how to read, what to feel in a certain situation, how to make sense of the world, etc. So, our environment nurtures us (raises us) via these messages.

What do we mean by **biological makeup**? Biological makeup means our anatomical structures and their physiological processes present at birth, before any environmental influence has left any mark on us. These structures are made of cells and physiological processes are functions that these cells perform. Genes heavily influence the creation of our anatomy and physiology. But what are genes? DNA (deoxyribonucleic acid) is contained within each one of our cells (and there are billions and billions in our body). Segments of the DNA are chemicals called genes. Genes create proteins (chains of amino acids), and these proteins influence the creation and work of our anatomical structures and their processes. Our anatomy and physiology also involves lipids (fats) and other non-protein substances, but proteins heavily influence the creation and work of those other substances too. Therefore, genes are fundamental to our biological makeup. Anatomical structures and their physiological processes allow our behaviors, mental processes, and reflexes to occur. For example, one cannot move arms and legs without neurons (nervous system cells) making our muscles move. Mental processes are created by the nervous system cells too. Reflexes are automatic, involuntary simple behaviors (they just happen, without our will). Our life as a newborn starts with biological makeup that gives us reflexes (instead of some

Figure 1. Time, biological makeup, and environment are factors influencing our development.

more complicated behaviors) and various other simple mental processes. The purpose of this chapter is to examine how those simple aspects become more complex over time.

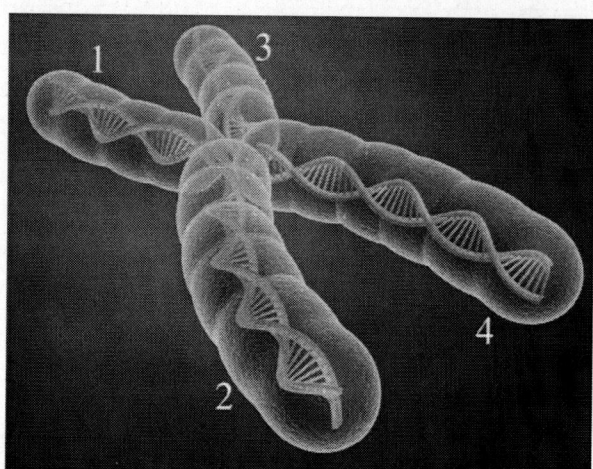

Figure 2. A chromosome is composed of 2 chromatids (1 and 2). The adjacent chromosome is composed of its chromatids 3 and 4. Chromosomes contain the DNA (twisted ladder) molecule. A gene is a segment of the DNA. One chromosome comes from our mother, and the other from our father. Each cell has 23 pairs of chromosomes. Only reproductive cells have 23 chromosomes.

Time is significant factor in our development. Let us illustrate with an example. In the 1970s, a girl--Genie--was discovered in the suburb of Los Angeles. She was 13.5 years old but she looked as if she was 7.5 (she was tiny). Once she was discovered by the authorities, she did not know to talk or walk, she still used diapers, and she sniffed things like an animal. How can this strange behavior be explained? She was severely neglected by her parents. They did not teach her anything, fed her only enough to survive, kept her in a tiny room with almost no light, kept her tied to a potty chair, did not allow her to have friends, did not allow her to watch TV, and continued this treatment for over 13 years. After being discovered by the authorities, she was taken away from her parents. She found new homes at both a foster home and UCLA where psychologists provided her with caretakers (environmental influence) sensitive and responsive to her needs. She soon learned manners, how to dress, how to use the bathroom, and how to walk. She learned words, but she could not put them into sentences longer than two or three words, never mastering grammar (rules of language). She could create very simple sentences by stringing two or three words, but she could not do more than that, and even those simple sentences were sometimes constructed in an awkward way. Scientists became aware that she missed a **critical period** – a time frame during which someone needs to speak to us, so that we learn to use language. Obviously, language development depends heavily on the environmental influence. If that critical time frame is missed, the person cannot learn to speak language, just like Genie could not (Baird 2010; Raaska et al., 2013; Curtis, 1977).

Figure 3. "Genie" is a nickname, actually. She emerged from isolation into the world, just like a Genie from a hidden magic lamp.

For some aspects of development, like speaking language, time is an important factor. For other aspects--like walking, learning manners--time does not seem to be important, allowing us to learn these skills later without any problems. What would have happened if Genie did not have a healthy brain (biological makeup), but she was exposed to a proper environmental influence? Likely, she would not develop language skills either, since the brain contains regions for language processing (in the left frontal lobe and left temporal lobe), and if those regions are not functioning properly, the environmental input cannot be processed by the brain. Language development reflects an *interaction* between the biological makeup and the environmental influence.

But is environmental influence always that important? Certain aspects of the mind seem to not depend in a major way on the environmental influence. Gender identity (a sense of being a female versus a male) seems to be one such aspect. In the 1960s, baby Bruce was born. When the circumcision (removal of the foreskin) was performed, it went terribly wrong and Bruce's penis was severely damaged. The penis had to be removed and female genitals were created instead. The shocked parents were instructed to raise the boy as a girl and that everything would be fine since the environment is so significant that it can overpower the genetics of a male. The parents raised the boy in such way, starting by renaming him Brenda. But at puberty, the girl rejected her female gender and declared that she was male. Even before puberty, Brenda *occasionally* rejected feminine clothing and toys, but at puberty her gender identity became apparent and enduring (Colapinto, 2000). A similar situation was observed in 25 genetic boys (males) who were born without penises and raised as girls. 14 of them embraced the masculine gender instead (Meyer-Bahlberg, 2005; Reiner, 2005).

COGNITIVE DEVELOPMENT

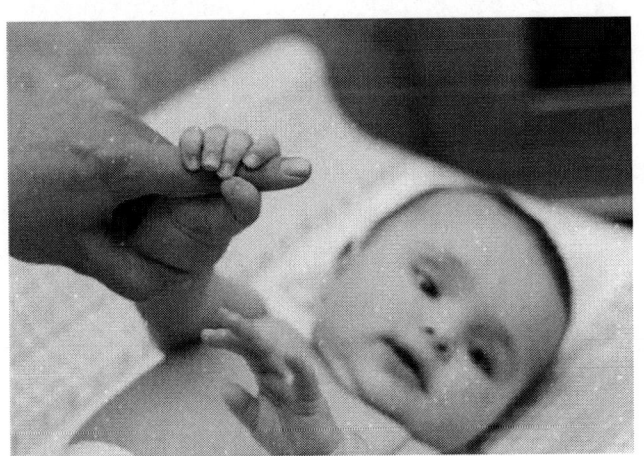

Figure 4. The grasping reflex.

Jean Piaget (1896-1980), a Swiss psychologist, proposed a view of how children develop cognitively. He suggested several stages of development: sensorimotor, preoperational, concrete operational and formal operational. A child in the **sensorimotor** stage (birth to 2 years old), interacts with the world initially by relying on its **reflexes** which are inborn (not learned, present at birth) involuntary responses occurring automatically in the presence of a stimulus. For example, *rooting reflex* is the child's turning of the head towards a stimulus that touches its cheek. This reflex likely exists to help a child with food intake. *Sucking reflex* refers to a child sucking on a stimulus that touches its lips, which also helps food intake. The *gag reflex* exists to clear the child's throat to prevent choking. *Stepping reflex* is when the child kicks with its legs when lifted up in the air. This reflex prepares a child for walking later on in life. Reflexes are inborn automatic actions--or products of our biological makeup without the influence of the environment--since these reflexes are present at birth.

During the sensorimotor stage, the next pattern of responses emerges: a child *combines and coordinates* two (or more) separate reflexes, like grasping something and sucking on it. The next emerging pattern is *repeating* certain responses for the sake of enjoyment, like repeatedly sucking the pacifier or thumb. This is followed with the child starting to suck repeatedly on *many objects*, not only the pacifier. Next, the child starts to move from directing its activities to self to directing activities *to others*. This is evident in children's vocalizations (gu-gu, ga-ga), as they attempt to communicate with others. This tendency to engage others is also indicated in children's imitations of sounds others make. Then, a child starts to *conduct experiments*, throwing toys and objects to see what happens. These experiments give rise to an anticipation of events (e.g. the toy will make a certain sound if I throw it in a certain way). Then, the anticipation becomes a basis for the emergence of *mental representation*, which is an ability to imagine things. For example, a child who is about 9-12 months old will look for a toy hidden behind a barrier, meaning that the child has developed the **object permanence** concept. A younger child does not look for a hidden toy, indicating that it has not yet developed this concept. In a nutshell, the main patterns that occur within the sensorimotor stage are children's *motor behaviors* (movements of arms, legs, and body in general) that stimulate sensory experiences. These sensory-motor aspects influence the emergence of cognition.

EVALUATING PIAGET'S SENSORIMOTOR STAGE

A usual criticism of Piaget's view is that he overemphasized motor development driving the cognitive development. Those motor aspects are reflexes, repetitive actions, and the use of arms and legs to experiment with the environment. However, research shows that children born without arms and legs still have a normal cognitive development even without motor interaction. This indicates that sensation and perception play a significant role--if not prominent role--in the cognitive development at this stage (Butterworth, 1999). Research also indicates that object permanence is formed in children much earlier than 9-12 months. In those studies, an infant who is 3 ½ month old is presented with a toy block. Then the block is hidden behind a curtain. A toy truck runs along the tracks, hits the hidden block, and stops moving in front of the block. The child then sees the same toy truck moving towards the block (still behind the curtain) while the block is secretly removed, and the truck "miraculously" runs through "the block" without stopping. Children stare at this "impossible" event longer than at the possible event where the toy was stopped by the block. This longer stare is interpreted by researchers as a sign of

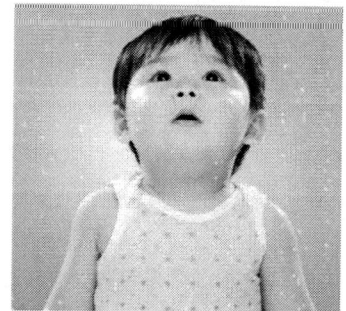

Figure 5. Facial expressions convey an infant's surprise.

surprise, meaning that the child expects the solid object (block) to stop the truck from moving. It seems that the object permanence concept (the idea that the block still exists behind the curtain) is indeed formed earlier than Piaget thought (Hespos & Baillargeon, 2008).

Children from Ivory Coast, Africa reach various developmental aspects of the sensorimotor stage earlier than children from the US and Canada. However, Piaget believed that the sensorimotor stage changes occur with the same time frame across all societies (Tamis-LeMonda et al., 2012). Furthermore, Piaget spoke of development as a transition from one activity to another. For example, at first the child sucks on one object, then only later it sucks on additional objects as well. Or the child experiments with toys and only later it forms the object permanence concept. However, it seems that a child develops several capabilities simultaneously (at once). Also, a child may use one good strategy to accomplish a goal today, and tomorrow it may use a much less effective strategy towards the identical goal. Therefore, there is a lot of "back and forth" development too, as opposed to a stage-like progression where every next stage is cognitively more complex and more sophisticated (Siegler, 2012).

PIAGET'S PREOPERATIONAL STAGE AND ITS CRITICISM

According to Piaget, several significant developmental changes occur during the **preoperational stage** (from ages 2–7) which encompasses the *preschool years*. During this stage, children develop their ability to *create concepts*. For example, they demonstrate the concept of an elephant when they know that many different types of elephants (yellow, blue, red with polka dots, elephant with wings, etc.) are still elephants. Also, children within this stage employ *symbolic thinking* which is evident in their use of words that symbolize (represent) segments of reality. For example, the word "mouse" represents a real mouse. During this stage, language develops significantly, also helping the development of thinking (Feldman, 2014). Within this stage, *centration* is the dominant way of thinking. Centration is focusing on an aspect of a stimulus disregarding the stimulus as a whole. For example, if an adult places a mask of a horse on a teddy bear, the child will believe the object is a horse, not the teddy bear.

Figure 6. Would a child in the preoperational stage say that this is a man or an elephant?

They also cannot perform *conservation,* which is an understanding that a certain *amount* of stuff does not change if it is distributed in differently shaped vessels. For example, a child is presented with a bottle of juice. Placing that juice in a very thin vessel does not change the amount of liquid, but the child will think there is more juice since the vessel is taller than the juice bottle (Feldman, 2014). *Egocentrism*--or viewing the world from one's perspective--is another typical thinking style during this stage. For example, a child

257

is talking to her mother on the phone showing her wonderful shoes she got today from daddy, assuming that her mother can see. Also common during this stage is *animistic thinking,* or when children think that the moon, sun, trees, and rocks behave, think, and feel like people. But why is this stage called "preoperational?" *Operations* are cognitive functions such as logic and analysis of event causes. During this stage, children have not yet developed these operations ("pre" meaning before) (Huffman & Dowdell, 2015).

In terms of evaluating Piaget's view, research has shown that conservation happens in many children around the age of 3 (Brandone et al., 2012; Izard et al., 2009), and that children can be taught to conserve (Ping & Goldin-Meadow, 2008), especially if tasks include objects with which children are familiar (Steinberg at al., 2011). Research on egocentrism shows that children are not egocentric across all tasks; for example, a child (let's call her Jessa) is shown a box with a photograph of crayons printed on the outside. When Jessa opens the box, she is completely surprised to realize that pencils are in there instead. Then, Jessa observes another child facing an identical situation (a box appearing to be the crayon box). Jessa is asked by the researchers, "What will the other child think is inside?" Jessa displays egocentrism if she says "pencils," since-- according to egocentric thinking--what she knows should be known by others as well. If Jessa is 3 years old, then this is exactly what happens. A child who is 4 however, would say "crayons" since it understands another child's point of view and knows that the other child will likely be tricked by the picture. Egocentrism can be overcome on some tasks (such as this one) earlier than Piaget thought (Barr, 2006).

PIAGET'S CONCRETE OPERATIONAL STAGE AND ITS CRITICISM

The **concrete operational stage** lasts from ages 7–12, a period encompassing school years. During this stage, children use appropriate reasoning, being able to conserve and show much less centration. They also show *reversibility,* which is an understanding that a certain change of an object can be reversed. For example, a ball of Play-Dough can be turned into a pancake, and the pancake can become a ball again. During this stage, children are known to stop believing in Santa Claus, since they realize that it is unrealistic for Santa Claus and his helpers to deliver presents to all the children in the world. Children start to use logic during this stage, but this operation is concrete. This means they think about tangible, observable reality (people, animals, objects) while not engaging in abstract thinking (like reflections on truth, justice, and beauty). What causes this switch to logical thinking? Most likely the switch is influenced by children's increasing experience of the world. Through this exposure to the world, they learn

Figure 7. How can so many children in the world receive presents? It must be magic.

258

how the world works. Their brains also become increasingly more functional, partly due to genetics influencing the development of brain structures and processes important for logic, and in part due to the mentioned experience that stimulates the brain to develop (Feldman,2014; Huffman & Dowdell, 2015). A usual criticism of Piaget's view is that concrete operational thinking emerges before the age of 7 in some children, especially if children are trained to perform cognitive functions of the concrete operational stage (Dasen, Ngini & Lavelle, 1979). Culture also plays a role: when children from non-Western societies are approached with cognitive tasks that they are familiar with, those children are more likely to master them than when they are approached with tasks designed for children from Western societies (Maynard, 2008).

PIAGET'S FORMAL OPERATIONAL STAGE AND ITS CRITICISM

According to Piaget, **formal operational stage** (ages 12-18) is characterized with abstract thinking (pure logic). For example, a child who has developed through this stage might think that if all mice know to dance and Ratatouille is a mouse, then Ratatouille knows how to dance. Even though this is wrong (since mice do not know to dance), children of this stage detect the logical *rule* and go along with that rule to arrive at a correct conclusion. Younger children however, would say that mice do not know to dance and would not even consider the rule. Their conclusion would be that mice do not know to dance, and that is that. Furthermore, Piaget thought that children of this stage become preoccupied with themselves feeling unique, special (like "nobody knows how it feels to be heartbroken as I am"), and misunderstood by others. During this stage a *new form of egocentrism* appears: a belief that one is at the center of the *criticism* of others. This leads to confrontation with authority figures like parents and teachers. Such conflicts are also fueled by the development of cognition which allows children to notice flaws and inconsistencies in the behavior of adults.

A major criticism of Piaget's formal operational stage is that real life is often not based on some clear-cut rules of logic, since logic may not apply in various situations. Consider this logic: if problems in Sandy's and Bob's relationship accumulate sufficiently, then they will break up.

Figure 8. Sandy's cat is obviously perplexed by the complexities of human life.

Problems in their relationship accumulated sufficiently. Therefore, they will break up. This reasoning makes sense in terms of pure logic only, but real life does not work like that. Imagine if Bob becomes suddenly ill, having fallen from a tree trying to rescue Sandy's cat. Sandy cannot leave him since he was next to her when she was ill in the past, plus now he tried to save her beloved cat. Now, in the process of Sandy taking care of him, they rediscover love. Due to that emotion, they put aside their differences and decided to forgive each other and focus on similarities instead, living with the ups and downs ever after. The point is that life is much more complex and unpredictable than logic, and formal operational thinking cannot often help a person navigate through real life, since life has many more factors to consider. It seems that Piaget's emphasis on formal operations should be seriously de-emphasized, and children should be taught how to think by taking into account various factors of life, instead of just relying on rules of logic (Labouvie-Vief, 2009).

What cognitive processes would assist this type of learning? A cognitive process that would help shape this approach would be broadening of one's perspective where people are not divided into good and bad, but perceiving every person as having good and bad qualities. Also, what is perceived as true in one society, is not something that is necessarily valued in another. In other words, different sets of values can be equally valid. In addition, many times we accomplish something by considering what others told us. Sometimes this can change our way of thinking which leads to our improved lives. A skill should be taught about how to argue for a position and how to create a counter argument so that many options are considered. One can learn that different views are not necessarily exclusive, but they can be equally valid and peacefully coexisting (Perry, 1981). Children should be taught to think in that way (in an age-appropriate manner, of course). The mentioned cognitive framework can bring about an understanding that an authority figure can sometimes be wrong, or that a parent still does care very much but does not know how to show it, or that both the teenager and the parents can be right simultaneously.

PIAGET'S VIEW OF DEVELOPMENT

Piaget saw development as an interplay among *schemas, assimilation,* and *accommodation.* A schema is a pattern of activity. For example, a child throwing a toy on the floor to produce a sound is a schema. The child then continues doing it since it likes the sound. Next, the child wants to hear sounds that other objects make. The schema is now assimilating (involving) other objects. Since the child starts breaking things in the house by performing the action, the schema needs to be modified to involve only objects that are allowed to be thrown. Modification--or an adjustment of a schema--is called accommodation. A schema can also be a pattern of feeling (or thinking). For example, a child fears a particular clown. Then the child starts to fear all clowns (assimilation). Then the child realizes that clowns are not real people but actors and stops fearing clowns (schema is adjusted/accomodated). The criticism of Piaget's view was that he was often merely descriptive and not explanatory, meaning he *described* that a schema exists (say animism), but he did not provide an *explanation* of what caused it to emerge. For example, current understanding is that

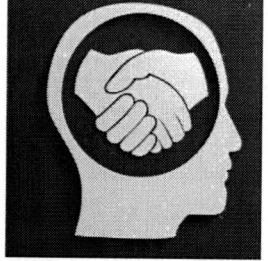

egocentrism in the formal operational stage originates from **pruning**, or the elimination of unnecessary connections among brain cells, specifically within the frontal lobe. Picture connections as a handshake between two hands, one hand is one cell, the other hand is another participating cell.

Figure 9. Development strives towards an optimal amount of cellular connections.

This elimination significantly reduces the number of connections (handshakes), and therefore reduces the number of cells. Due to these changes, the brain is unstable for a few years and mood swings are common, as well as poor control of impulses such as unprotected sex, fast driving, drug use, driving under the influence, uncontrollable outbursts of anger, and difficulties seeing the world from another person's perspective (Bunge & Toga, 2013; Pokhrel et al., 2013). These research findings became available after Piaget's death; perhaps he would have taken this new evidence into consideration.

VYGOTSKY

Lev Vygotsky (1896-1934), a Russian developmental psychologist, criticized Piaget for not focusing more on social and cultural forces that shape children's development. Vygotsky saw children as *apprentices* who cognitively progress due to adults providing consistent instruction, help, and stimulation. Apprentices need to be supervised by masters, and at some point they become independent, which is how Vygotsky saw the children's cognitive development. Related to this notion of the apprentice-master relationship is the concept of the **zone of proximal development**, which is Vygotsky's view that children should be encouraged to actively engage with a task alone until they cannot complete that task on their own. Only when a child gets stuck should adult intervention be needed via warm assistance and encouragement. Proximity means closeness, not that adults should do everything for a child. This is summarized very well by a saying I noticed on my daughter's homework folder the other day: "if you do everything for me, it just means that I cannot do it as good as you can." Vygotsky could not agree more with this realization, indicating a negative effect of doing too much for a child.

Scaffolding is a term that Vygotsky used for assistance, implying that it provides *support* for a child's progress. This support should be understood as providing help in terms of *tools* needed for completing a task (if a child wants to draw, the adult provides paper, paints, crayon, etc.), *cognitive framework* (such as language skills, math skills, etc.) and *motor* skills (such as showing the child how to use parts of the body to paint, draw, play an instrument, etc.). Culture plays a role in scaffolding since children need to be assisted with tools, cognitive frameworks, and motor skills that make sense within the child's culture. Otherwise, the child cannot relate to the offered help (Norton & Ambrosio, 2008; Blewitt et al., 2009).

After hearing these many criticisms of Piaget's views, shall we simply dismiss his observations? The answer is absolutely not, since he remains to be a great contributor. Piaget has provided a groundwork for cultivating many research hypotheses that have been tested ever since, thus his impact in generating research studies is tremendous. Also, the vast majority of the concepts that he proposed are accurate except that his timeline was off (as mentioned previously). The major criticism is about his stage-like view, or

Figure 10. How is an everyday scaffolding similar to Vygotsky's.

the idea that the vast majority of children complete a stage and *only then* move to the next one "without looking back." That is not accurate (as you learned already). A more precise picture is that a child who is in one stage still makes mistakes on some cognitive aspects of the previous stages, yet is able to perform well on the cognitive aspects of the stages that follow.

DEVELOPMENT OF ATTACHMENT

Attachment refers to a positive emotional bond between an infant and its caretaker. How is this bond formed? A psychologist, Harry Harlow (1905-1981) discovered that it may be genetically based. Specifically, he removed baby monkeys from their mothers shortly after being born so that they were raised in social isolation. Harlow then presented these monkeys (one at the time) with a choice: a cold wired replica of a monkey holding the bottle of milk, or a furry replica of the monkey mother not holding the bottle of milk. Where would the monkey go? The hypothesis was to the wired replica having food, but researchers were wrong. Monkeys went to the furry replica. It seems that they wanted to touch that fur and be touched by it. Some monkeys climbed on the furry replica and reached for the bottle of milk, suggesting that the monkeys used the furry object as a safety base. Monkeys were calmer and braver when near the furry replica (Harlow & Harlow, 1966). Likewise, when I was a surgery patient, I felt a very strong need to be touched on my hand. It seemed that my wife was thousands of miles away while she was in the waiting room and not allowed in the operating room, so I had a plan… to kindly ask the nurse for a simple touch. I felt a huge hole inside of me, a terrifying gaping void that had to be filled with a simple human touch. I voiced that wish, but the nurse felt uncomfortable and alas, she did not place her hand over mine. I was absolutely crushed and learned (in a hard way) how essential touch is.

John Bowlby (1905–1999), a British psychologist, continued Harlow's work, noticing that a child needs safety and forms an attachment with a caretaker from who it is provided. Once the child is ready to become more independent, it starts to explore the environment independently, knowing that the safety base always awaits with the mentioned caretaker. In fact, the safety base is a very foundation for independence. Mary Ainsworth (1913 –1999) continued Bowlby's theoretical work by introducing a method to scientifically study his ideas. She created a situation that was aimed at provoking signs of attachment in one-year-old children, specifically signs of different *patterns* (types) of their attachment. This means that different children have different attachment forms. Ainsworth's so-called "strange situation" consisted of several steps:

1. The mother and her child come into an unfamiliar room.

2. The child explores the room while the mother sits and waits.

3. A stranger walks into the room, first talking with the mother and then with the child.

4. The mother exits the room, leaving the child with the stranger.

5. The mother comes back and comforts the baby. The stranger leaves.

6. The mother leaves again.

7. The stranger returns.

8. The mother comes back and the stranger leaves.

Figure 11. Attachment is an emotional bond.

A child who is *securely attached* rushes to the mother when she comes back. The child may be upset or not for being left, but it quickly becomes consoled by the mother and continues to play. Most children in the U.S. have this pattern of attachment. A child with an *avoidant attachment* pattern however, does not get upset when the mother returns, seemingly showing indifference. About 20 percent of children have this type of attachment. *Ambivalently attached* children show a great distress when the mother leaves, but when she comes back, they rush to her but push her away, kick, and hit at the reunion. 10-15 percent of children have this style of attachment (Cassidy & Berlin, 1994). A child with *disorganized-disoriented attachment* pattern appear calm when the mother returns and then burst into tears, or they rush to the mother without looking at her. These children show a great deal of inconsistency in seeking closeness and maintaining contact with their mother. 5-10 percent of children have this style of attachment (Bernier & Meins, 2008). But why is this important? Why study attachment? These attachment patterns are important since they have an impact on later development. For example, adult romantic relationships tend to mimic the type of the attachment style during infancy. Also, securely attached children are more emotionally and socially adjusted than the children showing other attachment patterns. These children also have less psychological problems when they are older than children showing other attachment patterns (Bergman, Blom & Polyak, 2012; MacDonald et al., 2008). Furthermore, securely attached children are the most sociable, enthusiastic, cooperative, persistent, competent, curious, and aware of their own emotions and emotions of others (Thompson, 2013; Friedman et al., 2013). It is also important to say that *many* children with non-secure attachment patterns (the remaining three types) experience healthy lives as adults, and *some* securely attached infants have problems later on in life (Lewis, Feiring & Rosenthal, 2000; Fraley & Spieker, 2003).

ATTACHMENT AND PARENTING STYLES

For a child to develop a secure attachment, its caretaker should recognize the child's needs and strive to fulfill them. For example, when a child cries, the caretaker should respond fast with warmth and a comforting, understanding attitude, attempting to find the cause as to why the child is upset in an effort to ultimately eliminate that cause (for example, feeding the child if it is hungry).

This responsiveness applies to needs for food, shelter, sleep, dry clothing, emotional needs, social needs, and health needs. Also, caretakers should be *consistent* in how they interact with their children. For example, the caretaker should not be responsive one day and the next day spend hours on the cell phone while the child is crying and seeking attention. Children with avoidant attachment pattern usually have parents who are distant and detached. A parent who alternates between affection and indifference usually shapes the ambivalent attachment pattern. Abusive and neglectful parents usually shape the disorganized-disordered attachment pattern (Higley, 2008; Volker, 2007).

Parenting styles can also be categorized. For example, *permissive-neglectful* parents are those who make few demands, provide minimal monitoring and structure, and show minimal interest and emotional responsiveness. Their children usually tend to have poor social skills and are demanding and disobedient. Then, there are *permissive-indulgent* parents who have very few demands but are highly involved emotionally with their children. Their children often disrespect others, are impulsive, out of control, and immature. The next category is an *authoritarian* parent, who are inflexible and punishing, display low level of warmth, and show low responsiveness. They are the "my way or highway" type. Their children are easily upset, aggressive, and have poor communication skills. Finally, there is an *authoritative* parent who sets high demands and has firm rules, but also is very much involved, emotionally supportive, and tender. Their securely attached children are high achievers, emotionally stable, content, goal oriented, friendly, rely on themselves, and exhibit self-control (Baumrind, 2013; Celada, 2011; Topham et al., 2011).

Figure 12. Authoritative or authoritarian parents? What parenting style captures the image?

Do mothers and fathers differ in their attachment with children? The answer is yes. When infants are very upset, injured or ill, they usually go to their mothers to be soothed (Yu et al., 2013; Schoppe-Sullivan et al., 2006). Also, mothers more often nurture children by feeding them, bathing them, and dressing them up, while fathers more often play with their children. Also, when fathers play they do it in a more physical, rough way, while mothers engage with their children in hide-and-seek type of games and games involving language elements (Paquette, Carbonneau & Dubeau, 2003). These patterns have been noticed cross culturally (Hewlett & Lamb, 2002).

ATTACHMENT ACROSS CULTURES

Does attachment differ across cultures? In Germany, it seems that most infants develop avoidant pattern of attachment. In Israel and Japan, less children are securely attached in comparison with the U.S. (Rothbaum et al., 2000; Kiefer, 2012). Secure attachment is visible earlier in societies that nurture independence, and it becomes apparent later in societies that place an emphasis on social cohesiveness (Rothbaum, Rosen & Ujiie, 2002). This suggests that the environmental input influences the development of attachment. However, further research is needed to understand how this influence happens.

LANGUAGE DEVELOPMENT

During the first few months of life babies display gurgles, grunts, murmuring, cries, and breaths (Onishi & Vouloumanos, 2012). Cooing and laughing occurs from 3-5 months. Babbling (consonants and vowels) appears from 5-7 months. Babies babble by using syllables like ba-ba, ma-ma, ga-ga, gu-gu from 7-8 months. Babbling reflects sounds of the language to which the baby was exposed (Blake & Boysson-Bardies, 1992). First words appear from 10-12 months. During this time, babies use words to indicate aspects of their environment (doggy, kitty), action words (such as come, go, down), words signifying amounts (more, gone), words used for communication (hi, bye), and words indicating mental states (hurt, boo-boo). When the child is 16-24 months old, there is a dramatic increase in vocabulary from approximately 50–400 words (McMurray, Aslin & Toscano, 2009). Stringing two words together into a sentence (Dog bark, all gone) happens around 18 months of age (Rossi et al., 2012). Children employ *overregularization* around this time which refers to a tendency to overapply syntax or rules of grammar. For example, "she runned" is not a correct use of the word ran, but it shows that a child uses a rule of language even though it has never heard anyone saying "runned." Another example is that my daughter (5 years old) says "guyses" as plural for guys. By age 6, children polish these inaccuracies and their language is pretty similar to that of an adult (Marcus, 1996).

Where is this skill for language coming from? Definitely, in part, from hearing others when they speak. Also, it seems that genetics plays a prominent role. For example, babies prefer a language that was spoken to them when they were still developing *prenatally* (inside of their mother). When a child babbles, it produces the sounds of all language on the planet, indicating that babies possess a genetic foundation for learning all languages (Byers-Heinlein, Burns & Werjerm 2010).

SENSORY DEVELOPMENT

A newborn can see up to 20 feet with accuracy, yet an adult can see that same material with same accuracy from 200 feet, meaning that newborn vision is about 1/10th of the adult vision (Haith, 1991). Minutes after birth, newborns prefer to look at curves versus straight lines, human faces to non-faces, their mother's face versus other people's faces, and three-dimensional figures to two-dimensional figures. Since this pattern is present shortly after birth, it seems that genetics play a significant role in forming these preferences (Gliga et al., 2009). By about 2 months, infants can distinguish between blue, green, and red (Teller, Morse, Borton & Regal, 1974). By the 14th week, seeing depth and motion develops (by combining the images from both eyes). By 6 months, an infant's vision is identical to an adult's vision (Corrow et al., 2012).

What about hearing? Even in the womb, the baby responds to sounds from the outside, and newborns are born preferring certain combinations of sounds (Trehub, 2003; Pundir et al., 2012). Infants are poor at sound localization which allows one to determine where is the sound coming from, but at around the age of 1, they improve to the point of adult-level hearing (Clifton, 1992; Fenwich & Morrongiello, 1998). At 6 month of age, infants can distinguish particular notes and react to changes in rhythm (Phillips-Silver & Trainor, 2005). Infants as young as 1 month old can tell the minute difference between sounds "pa" and "ba" (Miller and Eimas, 1995). By the age of 5 months, infants can distinguish between very similarly sounding passages of Spanish and English (Kuhl, 2006). Newborns prefer to listen to their mother's voice than that of other people, but

Figure 13. When her brother is born, he will most likely prefer his mother's voice over other people's.

newborns do not show preference for their father's voice over other males. How could this be? It appears that it is because newborns are used to their mother's voice since the mother was reading, singing and talking to them during the prenatal period. In fact, melodies that a mother sings to her unborn baby are preferred melodies for that newborn (Kisilevsky et al., 2009).

In terms of smell and taste, infants prefer the taste of liquids that their mothers drank while they were pregnant (Mennella, 2000). Infants also prefer sweetness over other tastes and they find the scent of butter pleasant (Pomares, Shirrer & Abadie, 2002).

What about pain? Newborns respond to a painful stimulus (like injection with a needle for blood drawing) with crying, but only several seconds after the stimulus was administered. However, several months later, their response is immediate. Why is this so? Most likely it is due to an underdeveloped nervous system that cannot transmit fast pain messages before the child is several months old (Puchalski & Hummel, 2002). In the past, it was believed that newborns and infants

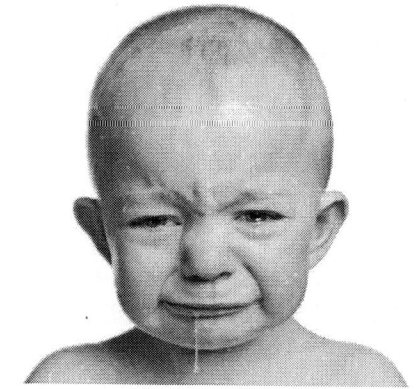

Figure 14. Why do newborns respond to a painful stimulus only several seconds after the stimulus is administered?

do not respond to pain or that they respond in a reduced way to it; however, the current view is that painkilling medications are appropriate for these ages (Taddio et al., 2002). The sense of touch is very well developed in newborns. For example, rooting reflex cannot be stimulated if there is no touching of the newborn's mouth. The newborn only seeks the object to suck on when the newborn is touched on the mouth (Haith, 1986). Touching an infant via massage initiates a production of brain chemicals that stimulate growing (Field, Diego & Hernandez-Reif, 2009).

What is the role of environment in the development of senses? To an untrained eye, it seems that sensory development happens due to the natural development of the nervous system programmed by genetics (brain, spinal cord, and nerves), and that the environment does not play a role. However, research has shown that the environmental input (visual information, for example) stimulates the brain cells to function and develop. In other words, the brain is a "use it or lose it" organ, meaning if it is not stimulated sufficiently by the environmental stimuli (sights, sounds, smells, tastes, etc.), the cells that make up the brain are going to literally die, which can impair the functioning of the senses (Kalat, 2013).

MORAL DEVELOPMENT

Treating others with respect and care, as well as treating ourselves in this same way, constitutes morality. We can express morality through actions, thoughts, and feelings. When we do something that deviates from the definition of morality, we feel embarrassed, guilt, and shame. These are moral emotions. When we make a decision to act morally, we are in the mode of moral reasoning (moral cognition). But, does morality develop? It seems so. Consider a scenario where a man has a sick child. If he does not steal a drug that he cannot afford, his daughter will die. Morally speaking, what is he supposed to do? At the **preconventional** level of development of morality, the father will consider *punishments* and *rewards*. There are options that he can choose. An option is that he will steal to avoid punishment. He will steal it since people will blame him (punishment) for letting his daughter die. Or he will not steal to avoid being punished, like being thrown into jail or feeling guilty and feeling worry that the police will find out about his crime. However, the father will consider rewards as well, such as that his daughter will survive and the judge--if the father is caught--will understand the situation and reduce the sentence (Kohlberg, 1969).

The next level of moral development is **conventional** morality. At this level, the father considers the approval or disapproval of the members of his *community*. He may think that if he does not steal, his neighbors and friends will turn their backs on him for being weak and letting his loved ones die. Or, the father considers an option that neighbors and friends will not trust him any longer if he steals. So he thinks of another way to save his child without stealing. Or he may think that if he steals it, the community members will approve that act considering the extraordinary circumstances. Thus, we are still talking about punishments and rewards, but coming from one's community. The conventional morality also includes a perspective that a behavior that breaks the law is an immoral behavior, since the society is an organized whole protected by the legal system. So, the father may decide to not steal since stealing undermines the integrity of the society (Kohlberg, 1969).

Postconventional morality stems from a *morality principle* or an ideal valued above any societal laws, or punishments and rewards coming either from an individual or that person's community.

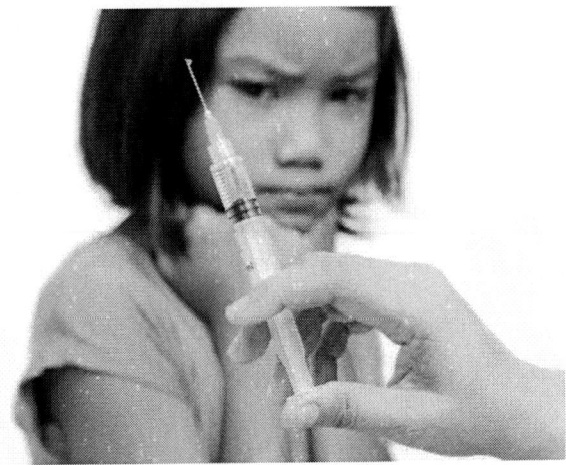

Figure 15. How do different stages of morality influence one's moral dilemma?

267

For example, the father may say to himself that life is sacred and that a law can be broken to save a life. That would constitute a moral thinking, and going along with the law and the opinions of others would be immoral. The ultimate judge is not the one in the court, but one's own sense of morality. When one lets down his/her own morality principle, then guilt results, and that guilt is one's ultimate judge of what is moral versus immoral. The preconventional and conventional levels occur during school age until adolescence, and the postconventional morality within the period following the adolescence (Kohlberg, 1969).

It seems that Kohlberg's view is more adequate for non-Western less-industrialized societies. This is so since some of these non-Western societies do not possess government institutions that dictate laws. So, conventional level in these societies does not usually encompass laws imposed by the government (Fu et al., 2007).

PHYSICAL DEVELOPMENT

When an **ovum** (egg cell) is released from an ovary, it reaches the fallopian tube where it becomes fertilized by a sperm cell. When the fertilized ovum (now called zygote) reaches the uterus, it

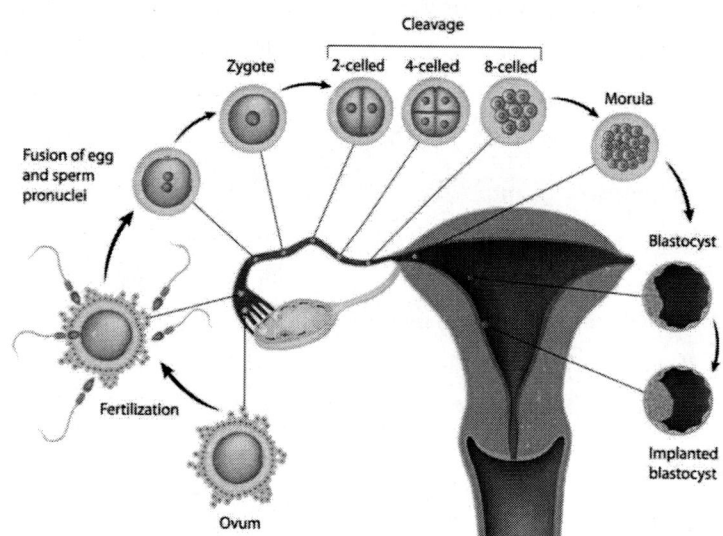

implants into the uterine wall and it is known as an **embryo**. This period from ovulation (released egg cell) until the implantation is called the *germinal period* (until the second week of the development). Then comes the *embryonic period* (from the implantation to eight weeks). At eight weeks the major organs become visible. From eight weeks until birth is the *fetal period*. At four months all body parts are visible and continue to develop until birth.

Figure 16. Ovum released from the ovary is fertilized by a sperm cell, and becomes a developing zygote.

Figure 17. Only one sperm cell performs the fertilization of the ovum.

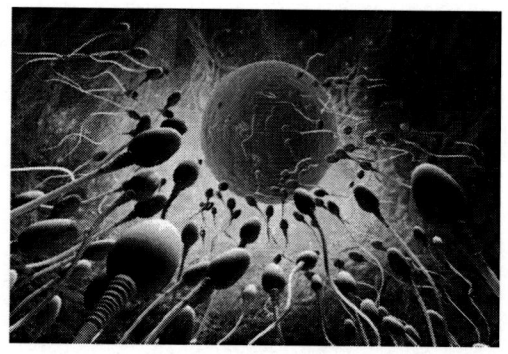

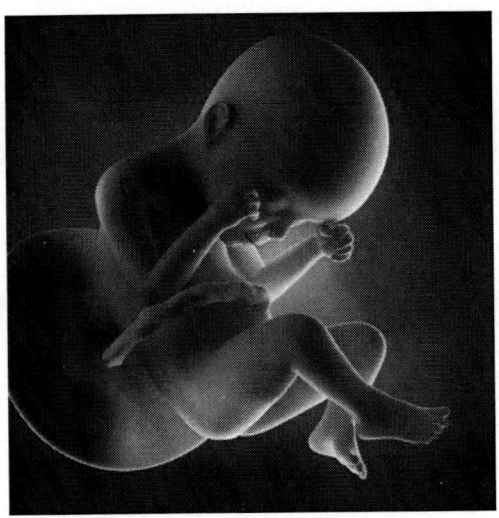

Figure 18. Fetus at week 24.

Teratogens (Greek "teras" means malformation) are substances from the environment that can damage the prenatal development. Smoking tobacco and drinking alcohol usually results in premature birth, low-birth-weight infants, fetal deaths, increased behavioral and cognitive problems, and adolescent obesity (Sickman et al., 2014; Popova et al., 2014). Children of older fathers may be at higher risk for attention deficit, bipolar disorder, autism, and schizophrenia (Carey, 2014; McGrath et al., 2014). Exposure to alcohol during pregnancy can cause fetal alcohol syndrome (FAS) characterized with facial abnormalities and poor growth, hyperactivity, learning disabilities, depression, and psychosis (Warren & Murray, 2013).

The brain is the fastest growing organ during the prenatal development and the first two years of life. This is due to neuronal growth as well as to the increase and development of axons, dendrites, and synapses (Bornstein et al., 2014). Motor (or movement) development begins with the presence of reflexes and it is followed with the lifting up of the chin (2.5 months old). This is followed by rolling over (3 months old), sitting with the support of others (3 months old), sitting alone (6 months old), standing holding furniture (6 months old), walking holding while holding someone's hand (9 months old), standing alone (11.5 months old), walking alone (12 months old), and walking up the steps (17 months old)[for this passage, decide whether to spell out numbers or use the numeral] (Adolph & Berger, 2012; Bornstein et al., 2014; Mitchell & Ziegler, 2013).

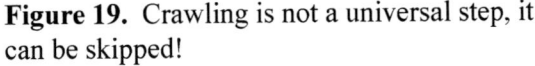
Figure 19. Crawling is not a universal step, it can be skipped!

Adolescence can be divided into early (11-14 years old), middle (14-16 years old) and late (16-18 years old) stages. The early stage is characterized by the beginning of the pubertal changes, the middle stage with pubertal changes nearing completion, and the late stage with an achievement of adult appearance and an anticipation of assumption of adult roles (Berk, 2014). During **early adolescence** or **puberty** (11-14 years old; 11 for girls, 13 for boys), a child experiences a *growth spurt* marked with a rapid increase in height, weight, and bone growth. Boys start their growth spurt around 12 and girls around 10. Girls are taller than boys until 13, but then boys become taller than girls (Cratty, 1986). The growth spurt is stimulated by the pituitary gland releasing its growth hormone (GH) and a thyroid-stimulating hormone. GH influences growth of all tissues, and thyroid-stimulating hormone influences the thyroid gland to release thyroxin which assists GH in its effect. During puberty, primary and secondary sex characteristics develop in males and females. **Primary sex characteristics** refer to reproductive organs (for example, prostate gland and penis in males; ovaries, uterus and vagina in females). **Secondary sex characteristics** are sexually related but not necessary for reproduction. These characteristics are pubic hair appearance, breast enlargement, underarm hair, and facial hair (in males) (Lemonick, 2000, The Endocrine Society, 2001).

During puberty, the male testes release **testosterone** (an androgen) that stimulates muscle growth, body and facial hair growth, voice deepening, and an increase in the body size. Testosterone secretions also influence the development of testes, scrotum, penis, and an onset of the first ejaculation. **Estrogen** released (from testes) in a male body (yes, males produce estrogens too!) influence an increase in bone density and stimulation of GH release from the pituitary gland (Cooper, Seyer & Dennison, 2006; Styne, 2003). In females, there is a rapid development of ovaries, uterus, vagina, feminine proportions, breasts, a characteristic feminine pattern of fat distribution, and the beginning of menstruation. These changes are influenced by estrogen released from ovaries. In females, the underarm hair, pubic hair, and height spurt are influenced by androgen hormones (one of which is testosterone!) released from adrenal glands on top of both kidneys.

On the image below, you noticed the hormones *gonadotropins* that are released from the pituitary gland into the blood in order to reach the testes and ovaries. What is the significance of gonadotropins? They can be divided into two categories: *follicle-stimulating hormones* (FSH) and *leutenizing hormones* (LH). FSH functions by stimulating: the secretion of **estrogen** from the ovaries; cells in the testicles (seminiferous tubules) to promote creation and maturation of sperm cells; the increase in testosterone level in testicles (promoting the creation of sperm cells); and the development of a follicle (which is a sac containing an immature egg cell). Each month, one mature follicle ejects one egg from an ovary in a process called ovulation.

PITUITARY GLAND

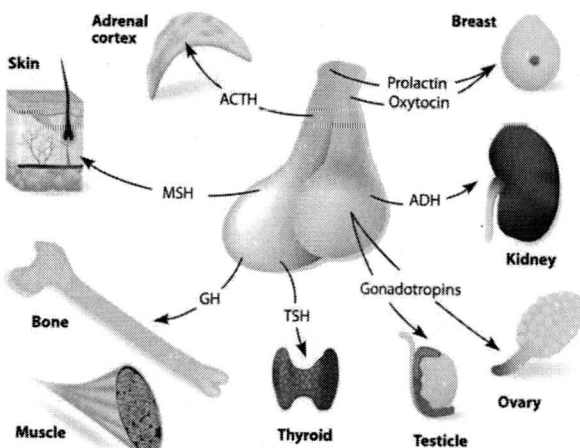

Figure 20. Pituitary gland and its targets.

Another gonadotropin hormone is the leutenizing hormone (LH), and it works by stimulating ovulation, working together with FSH to stimulate the release of estrogen by the ovaries, preparing the body for pregnancy, and stimulating cells in the testes to produce testosterone and estrogens. LH is called the *interstitial cell-stimulating hormone* (ICSH) in males. It stimulates the production of the androgens hormones (sex hormones) by the interstitial cells of the testes (Martini et al., 2012; Marieb & Hoehn, 2013). Anger and annoyance are typical for boys, and anger and depression for females.

270

Why adolescents have mood swings? It may be due to hormonal surges (Fujisawa & Shionohara, 2011).

In **adulthood** (18 and up; especially ages 20-40), we lose muscle mass, eyesight, hearing, and bone density. The frontal part of the brain shrinks slowing down the speed of storing and retrieving memory information. However, some adults live longer, experience an income raise which helps them live in safer neighborhoods, have better health care and eat better, experience more happiness and have less risk for psychological disorders, have more emotional satisfaction (in women), higher sexual satisfaction (in men), and have more money. What can explain these wonderful developments in the life of adults? The answer is marriage. Most married people experience the mentioned positive effects (Waite, 1995). But the number of people who marry decline in industrialized societies, and people marry later in life in those societies (Grossmon, 2005). If marriage can be so good, having children

Figure 21. Why do the adolescents have mood swings?

must be nearly as good, right? Wrong! Couples with adolescent children report less marital satisfaction than couples without children. There is an idea that having a baby makes the relationship stronger. The reality is very different--raising children increases stress in a relationship (children do not reduce it) (Belsky, 1990).

You have probably heard of **menopause**. It refers to the cessation of the menstrual cycle in women who are in their late thirties to late fifties, although the most usual age is 45-55 (Rossi, 2005). About 40% of women experience a sensation of less stimulation of their genitals, less vaginal lubrication, reproductive organs shrinking in size, loss of bone mass, and a reduction in the skin's elasticity (Lindau et al., 2007; Walsh & Berman, 2004). About half of the women experience mood changes (fluctuations) and hot flashes (sweating, warmth sensation with a rise in body temperature and redness in neck, face and chest) (Nelson, 2008). But these mood changes and hot flashes are manageable, and not experienced on a daily basis in most women. All mentioned changes seem to be influenced by a drop of estrogen, a phenomenon associated with menopause (Berk, 2014). Low daily doses of estrogen can significantly help with some mentioned changes, but these medications can have serious side effects such as heart attack, stroke, blood clots, breast cancer, and lung cancer (Marjoribanks et al., 2012). Antidepressants and the medication *gabapentin* (migraine headache medication; used to diminish hot flashes) are usually prescribed (Gutusso, 2012; Thacker, 2011). It seems that culture plays a role in menopause experience. For example, Mayan women do report hot flashes and other changes but welcome them since these changes mark the time of no more pregnancies! Mayan women marry as teenagers and have many pregnancies, so menopause is perceived by them as a break from childrearing (Mahady, 2008). Greek women view their menopausal changes as temporary and pay no attention to them, similarly

271

to women in Japan (Melby, Lock & Kaufert, 2005; Mahady et al., 2008). Research has yet to show why there are such diverse attitudes towards menopause across cultures.

The amount of semen diminishes in men after 40, but men can father children throughout their life. Testosterone production declines with age, but sexual activity stimulates cells to produce testosterone, so the drop is minimal in those men. More stimulation is needed to reach an erection due to reduced blood flow (erection is caused blood engorgement of penile tissue). Erectile problems (gaining and maintaining erections) are visible in about 35% of the US men by the age of 60 (Shaeer & Shaeer, 2012). In late adulthood (55 and above), the cardiovascular and sensory systems are mostly affected. Arterial walls gradually become more thick and stiff which influences blood pressure to rise. Hearing, visual sharpness, and depth perception decrease. Memory and other cognitive abilities do not usually decline significantly with age, but in late adulthood the memory *speed* (retrieval of information) becomes reduced (Whitbourne & Whitbourne, 2014). Thus, it comes as no surprise that many elderly students perform better or the same academically compared to much younger classmates. The speed of memorizing seems to be related to a large memory data bank that enlarges as we age (as a result of more experience), so it becomes more difficult to search through that "ocean" of information. Perhaps you did not know that studies show that as people age their mood, well-being, and satisfaction with life improve (Cartensen et al., 2011; Kern et al., 2014), so an image of the elderly as being lonely, depressed, ill, and scared is a myth and a reflection of prejudice and ignorance.

Figure 22. It is a myth that elderly are usually lonely, depressed, ill and scared.

What is the biological explanation for why we age? Two theories are taken as providing solid explanations: *telomere theory* and w*ear-and-tear theory*. Telomeres are structures on the tips of the chromosomes. Each time a cell divides, the telomeres shorten. When telomeres shorten too much, the cell cannot divide any longer. Cell division is a mechanism of cell's reproduction, so when that reproduction stops, the cells die or their functions become impaired. Having dead or malfunctioning cells means that organs are losing their capacity to be renewed. The other theory--wear-and-tear--states that our organs, due to wear and tear, accumulate damages that cannot be repaired indefinitely (Broer et al., 2013; Martin & Buckwalter, 2001).

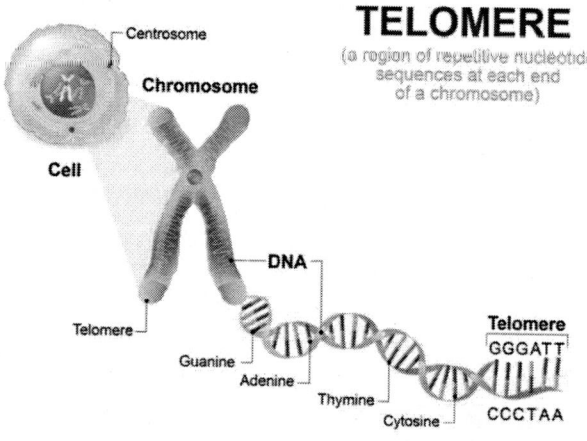

Figure 23. Telomeres are located on the chromosomes.

Temperament consists of *reactivity* (response) to stimuli and of *self-regulation* of that reactivity. Let's explain these terms. Reactivity refers to the level of motor activity (movement of arms, legs, trunk, head), length of showing an interest in a stimulus (also called attention span), distress (irritability and fear), positive mood (happiness and pleasure), and rhythmicity (does an individual do certain activities regularly or irregularly, like going to the bathroom, sleeping, eating, etc.). Self-regulation, on the other hand, refers to one's ability to voluntarily decide to suppress a response in order to plan and deliver a better (more adaptive) one. Self-regulation is visible when we manage a negative emotion--like fear--without being overwhelmed and paralyzed by it. Our ability to control impulses (for example, an urge to hit someone who irritates us), is another example of self-regulation. (Rothbart & Bates, 2006).

Temperament is usually observable very early in infancy, when a newborn "bundle of joy" arrives home. For that reason, it seems that temperament is influenced heavily by genetics. Even though infants come to the world with a particular temperament, their temperament can be modified (more on that later). Temperament is typically assessed (evaluated or measured) by relying on parents' reports, but the best way of studying it is in a lab (since parents can be subjective and a lab is not biased). In a typical study, an infant is brought to the lab by a parent, and then researchers present the infant with a *novel* (new) stimulus (say a Jack-in-the-box toy). The infant will be pleasantly surprised by this new toy since the Jack-in-the-box is an adorable toy, right? Wrong! Many infants like the toy, but many will not. In fact, many would be distressed (crying, fussing) after seeing this frightening or frustrating toy. A presentation of a novel stimulus is used to provoke temperament. In order to provoke temperament in a lab, an infant can be presented with a different stimulus, like one that presents a *barrier* so that a child is prevented from obtaining a desired stimulus (a puppet, for example). Researchers can evaluate all aspects of the temperament in this way, including the motor activity (some children will have very smooth, relaxed and leisurely movements of their body, and yet other children will have jerky and rapid movements). If a child starts to cry, how long does it take it to calm itself down? Can it do it on his/her own or is an adult intervention necessary? If it can calm itself down, the child scores higher on self-regulation.

Self-regulation is very important since the children's scores (in early childhood) can predict their future behaviors. For example, children with higher scores show more persistence, task mastery, academic accomplishment, cooperation, moral maturity (concern about wrongdoings and willingness to apologize), sharing and helpfulness, and resistance to stress (Eisenberg, 2010; Posner & Rothbart, 2007; Valiente et al., 2010; David & Murphy, 2007).

Research has shown that children's temperamental patterns can be classified into these three categories:

- *Easy* children who quickly learn regular routines in infancy. They are generally cheerful and adapt easily to new experiences. Their emotions are low to moderate in intensity, and they are curious about their environment.

- *Difficult* children who are irregular in daily routines, slow to accept new experiences, withdraw from a new stimulus, and react negatively and intensely.

- *Slow-to-warm-up* children who are inactive, show mild, calm reactions to environmental stimuli, are negative in mood, withdraw from new stimuli, and adjust slowly to new experiences.

Out of 100 percent of researched children, 40 percent are easy, 10 percent are difficult, 15 percent are slow-to-warm-up and the remaining 35 percent are children who display a mixture of these three patterns. But why are these categories (easy, difficult, etc.) important? It turns out that children with a difficult temperament are at risk of exhibiting aggressive behaviors, anxiety, and social withdrawal in early and middle childhood (Ramos et al., 2005; Bates, Wachs & Emde, 1994). Also, slow-to-warm-up children are at a risk of becoming excessively fearful around peers in the late preschool and school years (Schmitz et al., 1999). Fortunately, temperament is not set in stone; it can be modified. Stability of temperament is low in infancy and toddlerhood, and it is only moderately stable from preschool years onward (Putnam, Samson & Rothbart, 2000). Thus,

Figure 24. To me this toy looks creepy. Makes me think that children would be afraid of it, right? Not really, many would like it actually, but many would be afraid.

in order to modify temperament, interventions from the environment (caretakers, for example) are recommended. The optimal time frames for these interventions are infancy and toddlerhood (since temperament has the lowest stability during these periods). Children spontaneously improve their self-regulation around the age of 3 when their prefrontal cortex becomes more mature allowing them to control better their urges (Rothbart & Bates, 2006).

In addition to these spontaneous improvements, adult help is important in creating a good fit between child's temperament and a childrearing environment. An adult intervention consists of being sensitive, positive (as opposed to being angry at a child and stressed out), supportive and affectionate. It also includes setting firm, clear, and reasonable expectations. These positive adult behaviors can help children increase their self-regulation (controlling their urges and negative emotions) by the age of 3. Parents should also be patient but insistent in encouraging their children to not withdraw from stimuli that (children) interpret as threatening. A parent who displays anger, stress, is cold, and is intrusive can only intensify the negative aspects of temperament. The same parental attitude is advised when interacting with all

Figure 25. Parental anger usually brings about negative aspects of temperament.

274

remaining temperamental patterns (Feldman, Greenbaum & Yirmia, 1999; Cipriano & Stiter, 2010; Kochanska, Philibert & Berry, 2009).

Different temperaments are influenced by our biology. Research has shown that difficult and slow-to-warm-up children have a higher heart rate than the easy temperament, and their heart rate increases further when an unfamiliar stimulus is presented (Schmidt et al., 2007). Also, their stress hormone (cortisol) is higher and rises even more in response to an unfamiliar stimulus (Zimmerman & Stransbury, 2004). In addition, these children show greater pupil dilation and a rise in blood pressure when faced with a novel stimulus (Kagan et al., 1999). All these increased physiological processes point to a heightened activity of their amygdala as well as their sympathetic system (part of the nervous system activated when we are under stress). Heightened activity of these biological aspects further reduce the functioning of the prefrontal cortex (which helps us control our urges and fears) (Kagan & Fox, 2006). Since temperament is observable in the first few months of life (and therefore indicating its genetic foundation), it seems that genetic mechanisms influence the emergence of these physiological processes. Fortunately, the mentioned environmental influence (parental interventions) can reduce the impact of these biological influences.

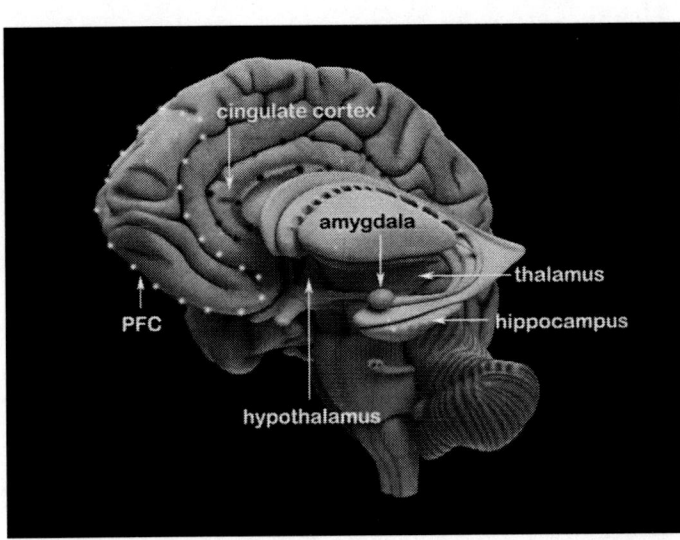

Figure 26. Amygdala and prefrontal cortex (PFC).

LIFE-SPAN PSYCHOLOGICAL DEVELOPMENT: ERIKSONIAN PERSPECTIVE

Erik Erikson (1902-1994) did not have a degree, yet he was trained by Anna Freud (Freud's daughter) to become a psychoanalyst with a focus on child development. Although Erikson utilized many aspects of psychoanalysis, he introduced numerous innovations into a view on personality. According to Erikson, the most important aspect of development is a *sense of trusting* others, which can result from proper parenting. A sense of trust is a foundation for the development of one's sense of predictability (the world is an ordered place), a sense of reliance on others (not being alone), a sense of having hope (a belief that a goal can be reached) and a sense of self-importance (self-respect). When a child experiences these mental processes, the child can develop independence to explore the world.

Erikson believed that there are certain stages of development that unfold throughout the entire life span. Obviously, he placed an emphasis on the importance of development through life, not on a specific time frame in childhood or midlife. Each one of these stages contains a certain crisis or a

275

problem that a person needs to overcome to move to the next stage of development. In order to move to the next stage, a person needs to adapt to a challenge/crisis of the previous stage. Once the person moves to the next stage, the person develops a strength (a virtue). Each movement to the next stage produces a different strength.

Stage 1: **Trust vs. Mistrust** (ages birth-1 year old). A child faces a crisis whether to trust others or not to trust them. If parents consistently provide the satisfaction of the child's needs, then the child will start to trust them and the world. If parents do not (like in cases of abuse and neglect), then the child will develop mistrust of them and the world. The virtue of this stage is hope (a belief that satisfaction can be attained).

Stage 2: **Autonomy vs. Doubt and Shame** (ages 1-3 years old). The crisis is whether to depend on others of to be independent. Motor skills (movements) develop during this age as well as the attachment with parents, and the child can start to explore the world independently (autonomously) knowing that parents are around (the child uses them as a security base). Through this independence, the child exercises free will. However, a high amount of parental criticism of the child's attempts to become independent and criticism of wrong behaviors can lead to the child's self-doubt and shame. The virtue that develops at this stage (after resolving the crisis) is will (a determination to exercise one's freedom of choice).

Stage 3: **Initiative vs. Guilt** (ages 3-5 years old). A child attempts to be even more independent in this phase, he or she expresses even more initiative to execute autonomous (independent) behaviors. Often times, the child will say "let me do it." The child approaches other children and takes an initiative to form friendships with those children. If the child is ridiculed for its attempts or punished for mistakes, it may develop guilt. The virtue that results from the successful resolution of the crisis is purpose (envisioning a goal and moving towards it). The challenge is whether the child will develop initiative or guilt.

Stage 4: **Industriousness** (or productivity) **vs. Inferiority** (ages 6-11 years old). During this phase, a child faces a crisis of whether to excel (be productive, industrious) in something or to stagnate. The main activity in this stage is learning, and the child wants to master everything that interests him/her. At this stage, children become knowledgeable about sports, math, dinosaurs, etc. Children compare themselves with other children and want to excel. Not being able to be at least equal to others may lead to a sense of being inferior to others. The virtue that develops is competence (pursuit and completion of a task).

Stage 5: **Identity Cohesion vs. Role Confusion** (ages 12-18 years old). At this stage, a person faces a crisis of whether to become a unique individual or not. The formation of ego identity (self-concept) is shaped mostly during this stage. At this time, a person goes through many changes such as bodily changes during puberty, sexual desire increases, and an increased interest in the opposite sex. There is a transition from elementary to high school; the end of high school is nearing so a person starts to think of a certain occupation (and in some countries individuals go to a mandatory army service). All these changes demand new behaviors and mental processes, influencing that person to experience role confusion (being confused about where one belongs,

276

who someone is, and where one wants to go with his or her life). At this time, it is easy to become impressed by others and to start following and imitating them at the expense of losing one's individuality. Loyalty to cult leaders is an example. However, a person experiences identity cohesion if her or she is able to understand what makes that person unique from others, is able to cherish that individuality, can realize where that person belongs, chooses a particular life goal or mission, and follows a path leading to goal attainment or mission accomplishment. The virtue that develops from this stage is fidelity (loyalty to oneself)

Stage 6: **Intimacy vs. Isolation** (ages 18-35 years old). During this stage, a person faces the crisis of deciding to be alone or to be intimate with someone? A person moves away from their parents as well as from the protective bubble of a college or University, and establishes his or her independence by holding a job. Romantic relationships (intimacy) and deep friendships (also intimacy) are formed. A person's identity starts to expand, so that he/she starts to perceive that person's self-concept as including others. Inability to form relationships will create a feeling of isolation associated with an avoidance of social communication, rejection of others, and even aggression towards others. Intimacy with someone becomes a threat to this person's identity. If intimacy can be formed, the strength of this stage is love (shared identity and mutual devotion)

Stage 7: **Generativity vs. Stagnation** (ages 35-55 years old). Should knowledge be passed onto others or not? That's the crisis of this stage. During this stage, a person experiences a need to teach a younger generation (this does not include only offspring, but people who are not family-related too). That need is called generativity. If an outlet for generativity is not found, however, then the person experiences stagnation: boredom and inner impoverishment. The strength that develops from this stage is care (concern for the progress of others).

Figure 27. Teaching the younger generation.

Stage 8: **Ego Integrity vs. Despair** (ages 55--end of life). To die fulfilled and at peace, or with a restless, troubled mind? A person faces this crisis during Stage 8. This is the period of examining one's life. Ego integrity refers to being able to reflect on one's life and one's choices with acceptance and satisfaction. Ego integrity also refers to the continuation of active participation in life, advising others, facing challenges and seeking stimulation. Therefore, a mere reflection on one's past life is not enough for serenity and fulfillment. Despair, however, refers to a sense of frustration, anger, regret, and disappointment due to missed opportunities and mistakes one has made. The virtue of this stage is wisdom (being knowledgeable about life and giving advice to others) (Schultz, 2005).

Research suggests that there is a support for Erikson's view and that a sense of trust early on is associated with well-being later in life. Infants 12 to 18 month old were evaluated on how well they are attached to their mother. Infants who had a strong (or secure) attachment (high level of trust) were more popular, more curious, more cooperative, and more willing to help other children 3 years later, than the children who did not have as strong emotional bond (insecure attachment) with their mothers (low level of trust) (Schultz, 2013). In another study, children (4, 8 and 11 years old) were asked to come up with their own stories about certain pictures that were presented to them. Researchers analyzed these stories to see whether they were able to tell what developmental stage these stories reflect, and it became clear that the stories entailed themes (trust, autonomy, initiative, industriousness) from the stages just completed. For example, a child who was 11 demonstrated a theme related to industriousness (Ciaccio, 1971). In yet another study, adult participants were asked to remember earlier events from their lives. When they recalled the first 10 years, the events related to trust, autonomy, initiative and industriousness were emphasized. When they recalled their life from 10 to 20, then the themes of intimacy became most frequent (Conway & Holmes, 2004). So, it does seem that some studies support Erikson's view that there are stages of the development in the way he conceptualized them.

Erikson stated that the identity forms between ages 12-18. A study showed that about 30% of research participants were in the process of searching for their identity until age 24 (Archer, 1982). Another study suggests that the process of identity formation is continuous throughout the entire lifespan (McAdams, 2001). It seems that Erikson's view is not supported regarding the cut off point for our identity formation. In terms of the generativity stage, a study showed that generativity was higher in research participants when they were in their 40s than when they were in their 20s, a finding that supports Erikson's view. The same study showed that the level of participants' generativity remained the same when they were in their 60s, which also supports Erikson's view that the final stage (Stage 8) is characterized with wisdom which is--like generativity--aimed at helping others navigate through the maze of life (Zucker, Ostvore and Stewart, 2002). Other studies support the notion that generativity encompasses Stages 7 and 8 (Warburton, McLaughlin and Pinsker, 2006; Sheldon and Kasser, 2001).

In terms of the final stage (ego integrity vs. despair), there are at least a couple of studies supporting the notion that individuals who are 55 and above engage in an examination of their past life, specifically to try to identify, comprehend, and resolve problematic experiences in their lives. Studies show that the individuals who engage more in these reflections also feel more satisfied with their life than those who engage less in these reflections (Taft and Nehrke, 1990; Torges, Stewar and Duncan, 2008). In some instances, Erikson is criticized for vague terms and conclusions without supporting evidence.

REFERENCES

Adolph, K. E., & Berger, S. E. (2012). Physical and motor development. In M. H. Bornstein & M. E. Lambs (Eds.), *Cognitive development: an advanced textbook* (pp. 257-318). New York: Psychology Press.

Archer, S. L. (1982). The lower age boundaries of identity development. *Child Development, 53,* 1551-1556.

Baird, A. A. (2010). The terrible twelves. In P. D. Zelazo, M. Chandler, & E. Crone (Eds.), *Developmental social cognitive neuroscience. The Jean Piaget symposium series* (pp. 191-207). New York: Psychological Association.

Barr, R. (2006). Developing social understanding in a social context. In K. McCartney & D. Phillips (Eds.), *Blackwell handbook of early childhood development* (pp. 188-207). Malden, MA: Blackwell.

Bates, E., Marchman, V., Thal, D., Fenson, L., Dale, P., Reznick, J. S., Reilly, J., & Hartung, J. (1994). Developmental and stylistic variation in the composition of early vocabulary. *Journal of Child Language, 21,* 85-123.

Baumrind, D. (2013). Authoritative parenting revisited: History and current status. In: Larzelere, R. E., Morris, A. S., Harrist, A.W., editors. *Authoritative parenting: Synthesizing nurturance and discipline for optimal child development.* Washington DC: American Psychological Association; 2013. pp. 11–34.

Bergman, A., Blom, I., & Polyak, D. (2012). Attachment and separation-individuation: Two ways of looking at the mother/infant relationship. In S. Akhtar (Ed.), *The mother and her child: Clinical aspects of attachment, separation, and loss.* Lanham, MD: Jason Aronson.

Belsky, J. K. (1990). *The psychology of aging* (2nd ed.). Pacific Grove, CA: Brooks/Cole.

Berk, Laura E. (2014). Development Through the Lifespan. Pearson Education, Inc.

Bernier, A., & Meins, E. (2008). A threshold approach to understanding the origins of attachment disorganization. *Developmental Psychology, 55,* 969-982.

Blake, J., & de Boysson-Bardies, B. (1992). Patterns in babbling: A cross-linguistic study. *Journal of Child Language, 19,* 51-74.

Blewitt, P., Rump, K., Shealy, S., & Cook, S. (2009). Shared book reading: WHen and how questions affect young children's word learning. *Journal of Educational Psychology, 101.*

Bornstein, M. H., Arterberry, M. E., & Lamb, M. E. (2014). *Development in infancy: A contemporary introduction* (5th ed.). New York: Psychology Press.

Brandone, A. C., Cimpian, A., Leslie, S., & Gelman, S. A. (2012). Do lions have manes? For children, generics are about kinds rather than quantities. *Child Development, 83,* 423-433.

Broer, L., Codd, V., Nyholt, D., Deelen, J., Mangino, M., Willemsen, G., ... Boomsma, D. I. (2013). Meta-analysis of telomere length in 19,713 subjects reveals high heritability, stronger maternal inheritance and a paternal age effect. *European Journal of Human Genetics, 21,* 1163-1168.

Bunge, S. A., & Toga, A. W. (2013). Introduction to frontal lobe development. In D. Stuss & R. Knight (Eds.), *Oxford handbook of frontal lobe functions*. New York: Oxford University Press.

Butterworth, G. (1994). Infant intelligence. In J. Khalfa (ed.), *What is Intelligence? The Darwin College lecture series* (pp. 49-71). Cambridge, England: Cambridge University Press.

Byers-Heinlein, K., Burns, T. C., & Werker, J. F. (2010). The roots of bilingualism in newborns. *Psychological Science, 21,* 343-348.

Carey, B. (2014a, January 27). The older mind may just be a fuller mind. *The New York Times.* Retrieved from http://newoldage.blogs.nytimes.com/2014/01/27/the-older-mind-may-just-be-a-fuller-mind/?action=click&contentCollection=U.S.&module=MostEmailed&version=Full&region=Marginalia&src=me&pgtype=article

Carstensen, L. L., Turan, B., Scheibe, S., Ram, N., Ersner-Hershfield, H., Samanez-Larkin, G. R., et al. (2011). Emotional experience improves with age: Evidence based on over 10 years of experience sampling. *Psychology and Aging, 26,* 21-33.

Cassidy, J., & Berlin, L. J. (1994). The insecure/ambivalent pattern of attachment: Theory and research. *Child Development, 65,* 971-991.

Celada, T. C. (2011). Parenting styles as related to parental self-efficacy and years living in the United States among Latino immigrant mothers. *Dissertation Abstracts International:*

Section B: The Sciences and Engineering, 71, 5783.

Ciaccio, N. (1971). A test of Erikson's theory of ego epigenesis. *Developmental Psychology, 4,* 306-311.

Cipriano, E. A., & Stifter, C. A. (2010). Predicting preschool effortful control from toddler temperament and parenting behavior. *Journal of Applied Developmental Psychology, 31,* 221-230.

Clifton, R. (1992). The development of spatial hearing in human infants. In L. A. Werner & E. W. Rubel (Eds.), *Developmental psychoacoustics* (pp. 135-157). Washington, DC: American Psychological Association.

Colapinto, J. (2000). *As nature made him: The boy who was raised as a girl.* New York, NY: HarperCollins.

Conway, M., & Holmes, A. (2004). Psychosocial stages and the accessibility of autobiographical memories across the life cycle. *Journal of Personality, 72,* 461-480.

Cooper, C., Sayer, A. A., & Dennison, E. M. (2006). The developmental environment: Clinical perspectives on effects on the musculoskeletal system. In P. Gluckman & M. Hanson (Eds.), *Developmental origins of health and disease* (pp. 392-405). Cambridge, UK: Cambridge University Press.

Corrow, S., Granrud, C. E., Mathison, J., & Yonas, A. (2011). Six-month-old infants perceive the hollow-face illusion. *Perception, 40*(11), 1376–1383.

Cratty, B. (1986). *Perceptual and motor development in infants and children* (2nd ed.). Englewood Cliffs, NJ: Prentice Hall.

Curtiss, S. (1977). *Genie: A psycholinguistic study of a modern-day "wild child."* New York: Academic Press.

Dasen, P., Ngini, L., & Lavalle, M. (1979). Cross-cultural training studies of concrete operations. In L. H. Eckenberger, W. J. Lonner, & Y. H. Poortinga (Eds.), *Cross-cultural contributions to psychology.* Amsterdam: Swets & Zeilinger.

David, K. M., & Murphy, B. C. (2007). Interparental conflict and preschoolers' peer relations: The moderating roles of temperament and gender. *Social Development, 16,* 1-23.

Eisenberg, N. (2010). Empathy-related responding: Links with self-regulation, moral judgment, and moral behavior. In M. Mikulincer & P. R. Shaver (Eds.), *Prosocial motives, emotions, and behavior: The better angels of our nature* (pp. 129-148). Washington, DC: American Psychological Association.

Feldman, R., Greenbaum, C. W., & Yirmiya, N. (1999). Mother-infant affect synchrony as an antecedent of the emergence of self-control. *Developmental Psychology, 35,* 223-231.

Feldman, Robert S. (2014). Development Across the Life Span. Upper Saddle River, NJ: Pearson Education, Inc.

Fenwick, K. D., & Morrongiello, B. A. (1998). Spatial colocation and infants' learning of auditory-visual associations. *Behavior & Development, 21,* 745-759.

Field, T. Diego, M., & Hernandez-Reif, M. (2009). Infants of depressed mothers are less responsive to faces and voices: A review. *Infant Behav Dev.* 32 (3): 239-244.

Fraley, R. C., & Spieker, S. J. (2003). Are infant attachment patterns continuously or categorically distributed? A taxometric analysis of Strange Situation behavior. *Developmental Psychology,* 39, 387-404.

Friedman, D. D., Ertegun, L., Lupi, T., Beebe, B., & Deutsch, S. (2013). Securing attachment: Mother-infant research informs. In J. E. Bettmann & D. D. Friedman (Eds.), *Attachment-based clinical work with children and adolescents* (pp. 45-60). New York: Springer.

Fu, G., Xu, F., Cameron, C., Heyman, G., & Less, K. (2007, March). Cross-cultural differences in children's choices, categorizations, and evaluations of truths and lies. *Developmental Psychology, 43(2),* 278-293.

Fujisawa, T., & Shinohara, K. (2011). Sex differences in the recognition of emotional prosody in late childhood and adolescence. *Journal of Physiological Science, 61,* 429-435.

Gliga, T., Elsabbagh, M., Andravizou, A., & Johnson, M. (2009). Faces attract infants' attention in complex displays. *Infancy, 14,* 550-562.

Grossman, L. (2005, January 24). Grow up? Not so fast. *Time, 165,* 42-53.

Guttuso, T., Jr. (2012). Effective and clinically meaningful non-hormonal hot flash therapies. *Maturitas,* 72: 6-12.

Haith, M. H. (1986). Sensory and perceptual processes in early infancy. *Journal of Pediatrics, 109(1),* 158-171.

Haith, M. H. (1991, April). Setting a path for the 90s: Some goals and challenges in infant sensory and perceptual development. Paper presented at the biennial meeting of the Society for Research in Child Development, Seattle, WA.

Harlow, H. F., & Harlow, M. K. (1966). Learning to love. *American Scientist, 54,* 244-272.

Hespos, S. J., & Baillargeon, R. (2008). Young infants' actions reveal their developing knowledge of support variables: Converging evidence for violation-of-expectation findings. *Cognition, 107,* 304-316.

Hewlett, B. S., and M. E. Lamb. 2002. Integrating evolution, culture and developmental psychology: Explaining caregiver-infant proximity and responsiveness in central Africa and the USA. In H. Keller, Y. Portinga, and A. Scholmerich (eds.), *Between Culture and Biology: Perspectives on Ontogenetic Development.* Cambridge, UK: Cambridge University Press.

Higley, E. R. (2008). Nighttime interactions and mother-infant attachment at one year. *Dissertation Abstracts International: Section B: The Sciences and Engineering, 68, 5575.*

Huffman, K., Dowdell, K. (2015). Psychology in Action. Hoboken, NJ: John Wiley & Sons.

Izard, V., Sann, C., Spelke, E., & Streri, A. (2009). Newborn infants perceive abstract numbers. *PNAS Proceedings of the National Academy of Sciences of the United States of America, 106,* 10382-10385.

Kagan, J., & Fox, N. A. (2006). Biology, culture, and temperamental biases. In N. Eisenberg (Ed.), *Handbook of child psychology: Vol. 3. Social, emotional, and personality development* (6th ed., pp. 167-225). Hoboken, NJ: Wiley.

Kagan, J., Snidman, N., Zentner, M., & Peterson, E. (1999). Infant temperament and anxious symptoms in school-age children. *Development and Psychopathology, 11,* 209-224.

Kalat, J. W. (2013). *Biological Psychology* (11th ed.). Belmont, CA: Wadsworth, Cengage Learning.

Kieffer, C. C. (2012). Secure connections, the extended family system, and the socio-cultural construction of attachment theory. In S. Akhtar (Ed.), *The mother and her child: Clinical aspects of attachment, separation, and loss.* Lanham, MD: Jason Aronson.

Kisilevsky, B., Hains, S., Brown, C., Lee, C., Cowperthwaite, B., Stutzman, S., et al. (2009). Fetal sensitivity to properties of maternal speech and language. *Infant Behavior & Development, 32,* 59-71.

Kochanska, G., Philibert, R. A., & Barry, R. A. (2009). Interplay of genes and early other-child relationship in the development of self-regulation from toddler to preschool age. *Journal of Child Psychology and Psychiatry, 50,* 1331-1338.

Kohlberg, L. (1966). A cognitive-developmental analysis of children's sex-role concepts and attitudes. In E. E. Maccoby (Ed.), *The development of sex differences.* Stanford, CA: Stanford University Press.

Kuhl, P. (2006). A new view of language acquisition. *Language and linguistics in context: Readings and applications for teachers.* Mahwah, NJ: Lawrence Erlbaum.

Labouvie-Vief, G. (2009). Cognition and equilibrium regulation in development and aging. *Restorative Neurology and Neuroscience, 27,* 551-565.

Larzelere, A. A. Morris, & A. W. Harrist (Eds.), *Authoritative parenting: Synthesizing nurturance and discipline for optimal child development* (pp. 11-34). Washington, DC: American Psychological Association.

Lemonick, M. D. (2000, October 30). Teens before their time. *Time,* pp. 68-74.
Lewis, M., Feiring, C., & Rosenthal, S. (2000). Attachment over time. *Child Development, 71, 707-720.*

Lindau, S. T., Schumm, L. P., Laumann, E. O., Levinson, W., O'Muircheartaigh, C. A., & Waite, L. J. (2007). A Study of sexuality and health among older adults in the United States. *New England Journal of Medicine, 357,* 762-774.

MacDonald, H., Beeghly, M., Grant-Knight, W., Augustyn, M., Woods, R., Cabral, H., et al. (2008). Longitudinal association between infant disorganized attachment and childhood post-traumatic stress symptoms. *Development and Psychopathology, 20,* 493-508.

Mahady, G. B., Locklear, T. D., Doyle, B. J., Huang, Y., Perez, A. L., & Caceres, A. (2008). Menopause, a universal female experience: Lessons from Mexico and Central America. *Current Women's Health Reviews, 4,* 3-8.

Marcus, G. F. (1995). Children's overregularization of English plurals: A quantitative analysis. *Journal of Child Language,* 22, 447-459.

Marcus, G. F. (1996) Why do children say "breaked"? *Current Directions in Psychological Science*, 5, 81-85.

Marieb, E., & Hoehn, K. (2013). *Human anatomy and physiology* (9th ed.). Glenview, IL: Pearson Education.

Marjoribanks, J., Farquahr, C., Roberts, H., & Lethaby, A. (2012). Long term hormone therapy for perimenopausal and postmenopausal women. *Cochrane Database of Systematic Reviews,* issue 7.

Martin, A., Onishi, K. H., & Vouloumanos, A. (2012). Understanding the abstract role of speech in communication at 12 months. *Cognition*, 123, 50-60.

Martin, J. A., & Buckwalter, J. J. (2001). Telomere erosion and senescence in human articular cartilage chondrocytes. *Journal of Gerontology and Biological Science, 56,* 171-179.

Martini H. G., Nath, L. J., Bartholomew, F. E., & Ober, C. W. (2012). *Fundamentals of anatomy and physiology.* (9th ed.). San Francisco, CA: Pearson Benjamin Cummings.

Maynard, A. (2008). What we thought we knew and how we came to know it: Four decades of cross-cultural research from a Piagetian point of view. *Human Development, 51,* 56-65.

McAdams, D. P. (2001). The psychology of life stories. *Review of General Psychology, 5,* 100-122.

McGrath, J. J., Petersen, L., Agerbo, E., Mors, O., Mortensen, P. B., & Pedersen, C. B. (2014). A comprehensive assessment of parental age and psychiatric disorders. *Jama Psychiatry, 71,* 301-309.

McMurray, B., Aslin, R. N., & Toscano, J. C. (2009). Statistical learning of phonetic categories: Insights from a computational approach. *Developmental Science, 12,* 369-378.

Melby, M. K., Lock, M., & Kaufert, P. (2005). Culture and symptom reporting at menopause. *Human Reproduction Update, 11,* 495-512.

Mennella, J. A. and Garcia, P. L. (2000), Children's Hedonic Response to the Smell of Alcohol: Effects of Parental Drinking Habits. Alcoholism: Clinical and Experimental Research, 24: 1167–1171. doi:10.1111/j.1530-0277.2000.tb02079.x

Meyer-Bahlburg, H. F. L., Dolexal, C., Baker, S. W., & New, M. I. (2008). Sexual orientation in women with classical or non-classical congenital adrenal hyperplasia as a function of degree of prenatal androgen excess. *Archives of Sexual Behavior,* 2008, 37, 85-99.

Miller, J. L., & Eimas, P. D. (1995). Speech perception: From signal to word, *Annual Review of Psychology, 46,* 467-492.

Mitchell, P., & Ziegler, F. (2013). *Fundamentals of developmental psychology* (2nd ed.). New York: Psychology Press.

Nelson, H. D. (2008). Menopause. *Lancet, 371,* 760-770.

Norton, A., & D'Ambrosio, B. (2008). ZPC and ZPD: Zones of teaching and learning. *Journal for Research in Mathematics Education, 39,* 220-246.

Paquette, D., Carbonneau, R., & Dubeau, D. (2003). Prevalence of father-child rough-and-tumble play and physical aggression in preschool children. *European Journal of Psychology of Education,* 18, 171-189.

Perry, W. G. (1981). Cognitive and Ethical Growth: The Making of Meaning. In A. W. Chickering and Associates, *The Modern American College.* San Francisco: Jossey-Bass.

Phillips-Silver, J., & Trainor, L. J. (2005, June 3). Feeling the beat: Movement influences infant rhythm perception. *Science, 308,* 1430.

Ping, R., & Goldin-Meadow, S. (2008). Hands in the air: using ungrounded iconic gestures to teach children conservation of quality. *Developmental Psychology, 44*(5), 1277-1287.

Pokhrel, P., Herzog, T. A., Black, D. S., Zaman, A., Riggs, N. R., & Sussman, S. (2013). Adolescent neurocognitive development, self-regulation, and school-based drug use prevention. *Prevention Science,* 14, 218-228.

Pomares, C. G, Schirrer J., & Abadie, V. (2002). Analysis of the olfactory capacity of healthy children before language acquisition. *Journal of Developmental Behavior and Pediatrics. 23,* 203-207

Popova, S., Lange, S., Burd, L., & Rehm, J. (2014). Canadian children and youth in care: The cost of fetal alcohol spectrum disorder. *Child & Youth Care Forum, 43,* 83-96.

Posner, M. I., & Rothbart, M. K. (2007). Temperament and learning. In M. I. Posner & M. K. Rothbart (Eds.), *Educating the human brain* (pp. 121-146). Washington, DC: American

Psychological Association.

Puchalski, M., & Hummel, P. (2002). The reality of neonatal pain. *Advances in Neonatal Care, 2,* 245-247.

Pundir, A., Hameed, L., Dikshit, P. C., Kumar, P., Mohan, S., Radotra, B., & Iyengar, S. (2012). Expression of medium and heavy chain neurofilaments in the developing human auditory cortex. *Brain Structure & Function, 217,* 303-321.

Putnam, S. P., Samson, A. V., & Rothbart, M. K. (2000). Child temperament and parenting. In V. J. Molfese & D. L. Molfese (Eds.), *Temperament and personality across the life span* (pp. 255-277). Mahwah, NJ: Erlbaum.

Raaska, H., Elovainio, M., Sinkkonen, J., Stolt, S., Jalonen, I., Matomaki, J., Lapinleimu, H. (2013). Adopted children's language difficulties and their relation to symptoms of reactive attachment disorder: FinAdo study. *Journal of Applied Developmental Psychology, 34,* 152-160.

Ramos, M. C., Guerin, D. W., Gottfried, A. W., Bathurst, K., & Oliver, P. H. (2005). Family conflict and children's behavior problems: The moderating role of child temperament. *Structural Equation Modeling, 12, 278-298.*

Reiner, W. G. (2005). Gender identity and sex-of-rearing in children with disorders of sexual differentiation. *Journal of Pediatric Endocrinology and Metabolism,* 18, 549-553.

Rossi, A. S. (2005). The menopausal transition and aging processes. In O. G. Brim, C. D. Ryff, & R. C. Kessler (Eds.), *How healthy are we? A national study of well-being at midlife* (pp. 153-201). Chicago: University of Chicago Press.

Rothbart, M. K., & Bates, J. E. (2006). Temperament. In N. Eisenberg (Ed.), *Handbook of child psychology: Vol. 3. Social, emotional, and personality development* (6th ed., pp. 99-166). Hoboken, NJ: Wiley.

Rothbaum, F., Rosen, K., & Ujiie, T. (2002). Family systems theory, attachment theory and culture. *Family Process, 41,* 328-350.

Rothbaum, F., Weisz, J., Pott, M., Miyake, K., & Morelli, G. (2000). Attachment and culture: Security in the United States and Japan. *American Psychologist, 55,* 1093-1104.

Schmidt, K.-H., Neubach, B., & Heuer, H. (2007). Self-control demands, cognitive control deficits, and burnout. *Work and Stress, 21,* 142-154.

Schmitz, S., Fulker, D. W., Plomin, R., Zahn-Waxler, C., Emde, R. N., & DeFries, J. C. (1999). Temperament and problems behaviour during early childhood. *International Journal of Behavioural Development, 23*, 333-355.

Schoppe-Sullivan, S., Diener, M., Mangelsdorf, S., Brown, G., McHale, J., & Frosch, C. (2006, July). Attachment and sensitivity in family context: The roles of parent and infant gender. *Infant and Child Development*, 15, 367-385.

Schultz, Duane P., & Schultz, Sydney Ellen. (2013). Theories of Personality. Belmont, CA. Wadsworth.

Shaeer, O. and Shaeer, K. (2012), The Global Online Sexuality Survey (GOSS): The United States of America in 2011. Chapter I: Erectile Dysfunction Among English-Speakers. *The Journal of Sexual Medicine, 9:* 3018–3027. doi:10.1111/j.1743-6109.2012.02976.x

Sheldon, K., & Kasser, T. (2001). Getting older, getting better? Personal strivings and psychological maturity across the life span. *Developmental Psychology, 37,* 491-501.

Sickmann, H. A., Patten, A. R., Morch, K., Sawchuk, S., Zhang, C., Parton, R., Christie, B. R. (2014). Prenatal ethanol exposure has sex-specific effects on hippocampal long-term potentiation. *Hippocampus, 24*, 54-64.

Siegler, R. S. (2012). From theory to application and back: Following in the giant footsteps of David Klahr. In J. Shrager, S. Craver (Eds.), *The journey from child to scientist: Integrating cognitive development and the education sciences.* Washington, DC: American Psychological Association.

Steinberg, Laurence., Bornstein, Marc H., Vandell, Deborah Lowe., Rook, Karen S. (2011). Lifespan Development: Infancy Through Adulthood. Belmont, CA. Wadsworth.

Styne, D. M. (2003). The regulation of pubertal growth. *Hormone Research, 60*(suppl. 1), 22-26.

Taddio, A., Shah, V., & Gilbert-MacLeod, C. (2002). Conditioning and hyperalgesia in newborns exposed to repeated heel lances. *JAMA: The Journal of the American Medical Association 288,* 857-861.

Taft, L. B., & Nehrke, M. F. (1990). Reminiscences, life review, and ego integrity in nursing home residents. *International Journal of Aging and Human Development, 30,* 189-196.

Tamis-LeMonda, C. S., Song, L., Leavell, A., Kahana-Kalman, R., & Yoshikawa, H. (2012).

Ethnic differences in mother-infant language and gestural communications are associated with specific skills in infants. *Developmental Science*, 15, 384-397.

Teller, D. Y., Morse, R., Borton, R., & Regal, C. (1974). Visual acuity for vertical and diagonal grating in human infants. *Vision Research, 14,* 1433-1439.

Thacker, H. L. (2011). Assessing risks and benefits of nonhormonal treatments for vasomotor symptoms in perimenopausal and postmenopausal women. *Journal of Women's Health, 20,* 1007-1016.

The Endocrine Society. (2001, March 1). *The Endocrine Society and Lawson Wilkins Pediatric Endocrine Society call for further research to define precocious puberty,* Bethesda, MD: The Endocrine Society.

Thompson, R. A. (2013). Attachment theory and research: Precis and prospect. In P. D. Zelazo (Ed.), *The Oxford handbook of developmental psychology: Vol. 3* (pp. 191-216). New York: Oxford University Press.

Tiffany Field, Miguel Diego, Maria Hernandez-Reif (2009). Depressed mothers' infants are less *responsive to faces and voices. Infant Behavior and Development, Volume 32, Issue 3.* Pages 239-244

Topham, G. L., Hubbs-Tait, L., Rutledge, J. M., Page, M. C., Kennedy, T. S., Shriver, L. H., & Harrist, A. W. (2011). Parenting styles, parental response to child emotion, and family emotional responsiveness are related to child emotional eating. *Appetite, 56, 261-264.*

Torges, C., Stewart, A., & Duncan, L. (2008). Achieving ego integrity: Personality development in late midlife. *Journal of Research in Personality, 42(4),* 1004-1019.

Trehub, S. E. (2003). The developmental origins of musicality. *Nature Neuroscience, 6,* 669-673.

Valiente, C., Lemery-Chalfant, K., Swanson, J., & Reiser, M. (2010). Prediction of kindergartners' academic achievement from their effortful control and emotionality: Evidence for direct and moderated relations. *Journal of Educational Psychology*, 102, 550-560.

Volker, S. (2007). Infants' vocal engagement oriented towards mother versus stranger at 3 months and avoidant attachment behavior at 12 months. *International Journal of Behavioral Development, 31,* 88-95.

Waite, L. J. (1995). Does marriage matter? *Demography, 32,* 483-507.

Walsh, K. E., & Berman, J. R. (2004). Sexual dysfunction in the older woman: An overview of the current understanding and management. *Therapy in Practice, 21,* 655-675.

Warburton, J., McLaughlin, D. & Pinsker, D. (2006). Generative acts: Family and community involvement of older Australians. *International Journal of Aging and Human Development, 63,* 115-137.

Warren, K. R., & Murray, M. M. (2013). Alcohol and pregnancy: Fetal alcohol spectrum disorders and fetal alcohol syndrome. In P. Boyle, P. Boffetta, A. B. Lowenfels, H. B. Burns, O. Brawley, W. Zatonski, & J. Rehm. (Eds.), *Alcohol: Science, policy and public health* (pp. 307-347). New York: Oxford University Press.

Whitbourne, S. K., & Whitbourne, S. B. (2012). *Adult Development and Aging: Biopsychosocial Perspectives, 5th Edition.* John Wiley & Sons, Inc. Hoboken, New Jersey

Yu, C., Hung, C., Chan, T., Yeh, C., & Lai, C. (2012). Prenatal predictors for father-infant attachment after childbirth. *Journal Of Clinical Nursing, 21,* 1577-1583.

Zimmerman, L. K., & Stansbury, K. (2004). The influence of emotion regulation, level of shyness, and habituation on the neuroendocrine response of three-year-old children. *Psychoneuroendocrinology, 29,* 973-982.

Zucker, A., Ostrove, J., & Stewart, A. (2002). College educated women's personality development in adulthood: Perceptions and age differences. *Psychology and Aging, 17,* 236-244.

Abnormal Psychology

Chapter Ten

Abnormal psychology explores *unhealthy* (pathological) mental processes and behaviors. Specifically, this field explores how they manifest, what causes them and how to treat them. But, when is a mental process/behavior unhealthy? How do we know? What are the criteria? It is unhealthy when one's mental process/behavior *interferes* with their daily functioning, so that the person cannot go to work or school, or cannot function adequately in those environments or various other daily environments (with adults, friends, children, in a grocery store). A person suffering from panic disorder, for example, cannot function in these environments due to frequent attacks of panic. An extreme example of an abnormality would be endangering one's own life (a suicide attempt, for example) or the life of others (due to a belief that one should commit murder to save humanity from earthquakes). Another component of abnormality is psychological suffering. If a person *suffers* due to his/her mental processes and behaviors, that suffering suggests a lack of health. Yet, in some conditions the person is mentally ill but does not really suffer (like when person is manic feeling euphoric and invincible, attempting to fly off from a roof). If one is unable to function within the normal situations of life, or if psychological suffering is present, one may be diagnosed as abnormal.

If we behave *differently* from the 95% of the population (meaning if we are in the category of 5% of people who behave unusually), this *may* indicate our abnormality (Coon & Mitlerer, 2012). However, being different (unusual) does not necessarily mean being abnormal. Albert Einstein, for example, saw space as something like a material made of rubber, and planets and stars as making an imprint in that material, so that other heavenly bodies are pulled towards those masses that warp the space. This enabled him to completely revolutionize the way physicists conceive of gravity. Einstein's way of thinking was very *unusual*, but it was not abnormal in the sense of an unhealthy set of mental processes and behaviors. When Nikola Tesla (an engineer and inventor) said in the 19th century that in the future we will have a device to communicate with people thousands of miles

Figure 1. Nikola Tesla.

away from us, that we will even be able to see each other on the device's screen, and that it will fit into the pocket, people thought that he was delusional (that he maintained false beliefs about reality). Forty years after his death in 1947, the cell phone was invented. We will see in the years to come if Tesla's next prediction will be realized – communication with the dead! Individuals (such as Tesla and Einstein), are rare and unusual in their beliefs, but not abnormal. If being different allows us to function and not suffer, difference is not abnormality, it is just the sign of a creative mind.

Behavior considered normal in one culture may be considered abnormal in another. Someone, for example, who is seen on the street of New York City wearing gloves infested with stinging ants that cause excruciating pain, will likely be perceived as "not playing with a full deck of cards." Yet this is a common practice in the Satere-Mawe tribe in Brazil to mark a teenage boy's transformation into an adult (Botelho & Weigel, 2011). The point is that the behavior should be evaluated in terms of the *context* in which it occurs. If the behavior of a member of a particular society is different from how the majority of its members behave, that behavior *may* be an indication of an abnormality. But, considering that in some other society that "strange behavior" is the *norm* (the acceptable behavior), the mentioned behavior is not necessarily abnormal. In fact, artists, philosophers, writers and scientists often do not conform to a norm and move the civilization forward with their novel directions.

Figure 2. Bullet ants were used in Satere-Mawe's practice. Their bite is exponentially more painful than a bee sting.

Being divorced from reality, is a sign of abnormality, right? A person who suffers from hallucinations (unreal sensory experience such as hearing voices or seeing demons) and/or delusions, lost touch with reality and is clearly showing symptoms of an abnormality. Yet people who are clinically depressed often have a more realistic understanding of the world than healthy people. For instance, most of us have unrealistically rosy views about how well liked we are, and about our positive character traits, while depressed people see themselves and their relationships more accurately. Thus, being "in touch with reality" does not necessarily lead to mental health— and it may even work against it (Alexander, 2014).

What is *insanity*? Insanity is a legal term referring to a situation in which a person is mentally ill to such extent that he or she is not in touch with reality, and therefore not responsible for his/her actions. Instead of belonging to a prison, in case of murdering someone, these individual should be in a hospital.

As far as most people are concerned, DSM-V can be R2D2's wife. But, in the world of psychology DSM-V is an abbreviation for a *diagnostic and statistical manual* of mental disorders, fifth edition. This is a book frequently used by psychiatrists and psychologists to diagnose mental illness. Diagnosis is a process of *labeling* a set of symptoms and signs. *Symptoms* are the subjective experiences of a condition (like hearing voices), and *signs* are observable manifestations (like a person looking depressed as judged by facial grimacing and posture) of a condition. A condition, say phobia, has a minimal number of symptoms that must be present in order to diagnose it as a phobia. This number of symptoms is called a *diagnostic threshold* (Aragona, 2009). It is a statistical manual since the book states how prevalent a condition is in the population. For example, one percent of people suffer from schizophrenia. The manual allows communication among mental health professionals so that they can all refer to the same condition regarding a diagnosed condition. However, the manual does not include causes or treatments for a condition. In the conditions that follow, we will use DSM-V to describe them, and we will mention some causes and treatments pertaining to each condition. Let's turn now to the more interesting stuff.

In this chapter, due to a large number of mental disorders in DSM-V, we will concentrate only on the most interesting and well-researched ones. We will examine their presentation, causes and treatments. In some cases, we will see only the presenting features, while I encourage you to discover their causes and treatments by taking an abnormal psychology course.

Figure 3. Psychologists refer to the DSM- V as the psychiatric Bible.

PERSONALITY DISORDERS

There are several personality disorders, so let's examine each one of them. Individuals with **antisocial personality disorder**:

- cause problems for others
- are deceitful, lying, lack empathy, exploit others
- engage (65 percent of them) in robbery, vandalism and rape

- are impulsive and irritable
- engage in repeated physical fights, assaults and recklessness
- are irresponsible (cannot hold a job, do not honor financial obligations)
- lack remorse for harming another person
- lack fear for engaging in a risky or illegal behavior
- show pattern of vandalism, stealing and physical cruelty towards people and animals before the person is 15 years old (APA, 2013).

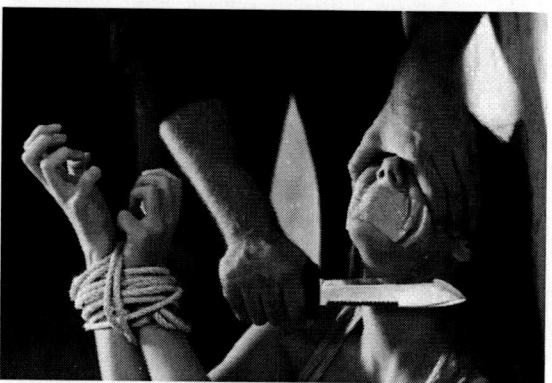

Figure 4. Another name for antisocial personality disorder is psychopathy or sociopathy.

Genetics moderately influences the emergence of this condition. This condition is also influenced by environmental factors such as marital conflict or divorce, legal problems and parents' psychopathology. In addition, these individuals usually have a history of negative upbringing such as parental physical abuse and neglect, having convicted parents, inconsistent parental discipline and lack of parental supervision. When children with genetic predisposition are *adopted* and raised in the mentioned negative environments, they are more likely to develop this condition than genetically predisposed children who experience more normal adoptive environment (Riggins & Caspers et al., 2003). Also, if a person is a victim of early maltreatment and has low levels of MAOa enzyme (that reduces the level of dopamine, serotonin and norepinephrine), that person is more likely to develop the condition, than a person living within the same environment but has high levels of MAOa enzyme. This research demonstrates an *interaction* between the level of the enzyme and the environment (Caspi et al., 2002). The disorder is usually preceded in childhood (around the age of 9) with a diagnosis of *conduct disorder* which consists of theft, avoiding school, running away from home and associating with delinquent peers. Children who have a healthy family environment, however, usually do not develop antisocial personality disorder and their conduct disorder is limited to adolescence (Butcher et al., 2014).

Within people who exhibit antisocial personality disorder, there seems to be a deficiency in the limbic system, specifically the amygdala, a structure important for the recognizing fear and sadness in others. This is an important component of empathizing towards those who suffer. Deficits in the amygdala are also associated with a reduction of fear, which is a well-known tendency in people with this disorder (who often do not fear the consequences of their behavior). Further, these individuals have reduced physiological manifestations of anxiety (sweating, increased breathing, and increased heart rate) when anticipating an unpleasant event which indicates lower activation of a sympathetic system. This can possibly explain their lack of or reduced anxiety when they anticipate the consequences of their actions (Marsh & Blair, 2008).

In terms of the treatments for this disorder, psychotherapies (talking to patients to change their mental processes and behaviors) do not work, and there is evidence that this form of treatment can make the condition worse (Harris & Rice, 2006). Some pharmacological treatments have shown a minimal benefit. For example, SSRI antidepressants have been shown to reduce aggression and impulsiveness, and increase social skills (Losel, 1998; Minzenbert & Siever, 2006).

A person with **borderline personality disorder**:

- has long lasting feeling of emptiness
- is highly aggressive (towards others and/or self)
- displays inappropriate, intense anger
- engages in recurring fights making relationship unstable
- has difficulty being alone and displays desperate efforts to avoid abandonment
- is moody, unpredictable, impulsive and easily frustrated
- engages in excessive eating, spending and promiscuity (APA, 2013).

Figure 5. Stay away from flowers with thorns if your partner has a borderline disorder.

Genetic factors play a considerable role in the development of this condition (Hooley et al, 2012; Distel et al., 2002). There is a lowered functioning of serotonin, a transmitter implicated in control of impulses, which may explain why these individuals have difficulties blocking their aggressive and self-mutilating behaviors (Schmahl & Bremmner, 2006). Decreased activation of certain brain areas (in prefrontal cortex) has been observed, and these brain areas are known to be the targets for serotonin (Lieb et al., 2004). Reductions of the volumes of hippocampus and amygdala have been observed, which correlates with aggression and being impulsive (Hooley et al., 2012). Most of these individuals recall a significant amount of childhood abuse, neglect, separation and loss, which may be factors contributing to this disorder (Bandelow et al., 2005; Battle et al., 2004). These individuals also have a history of being raised in families of marital discord and family violence (Paris, 2007).

In terms of the treatment of the borderline personality disorder, several therapies are available. *Dialectical behavioral therapy* (DBT) is a combination of cognitive and cognitive-behavioral therapy, and its focus is to encourage patients to acknowledge and accept their negative emotions without engaging in destructive and/or self-destructive behavior. The therapy consists of individual (working with a person), group (working with several people, such as family members) and phone (couching the patient over telephone) aspects. In a group setting, the patient learns to control negative emotions, and the individual and phone aspect teach patient to identify and alter dysfunctional behaviors and replace them with healthy social skills. This therapy seems to have a considerable effectiveness in reducing the symptoms of the condition (Lynch et al., 2007; Zanarini et al., 2005). Psychoanalythic psychotherapy seems to be as effective as DBT, and its goal is to strengthen the rational aspect (ego) of these individuals (Clarkin et al., 2007).

Narcissistic personality disorder refers to:
- an exaggerated sense of self-importance
- receiving attention from others, and a need to be admired and loved
- a disregard for the rights of others
- preoccupation with fantasies of success
- exploit others while pursuing own goals
- lacking empathy for others
- superficially charming and friendly
- see people as pawns
- a tendency to surround oneself with those who unconditionally praise them
- extreme vulnerability to being wounded by criticism from others

Figure 6. Admiring oneself.

There are two forms of this condition, grandiose and vulnerable. Its *grandiose form* is characterized by aggression, dominance and grandiosity (a belief in one's extraordinary worth), while the *vulnerable form* manifests as a fragile and unstable sense of self-esteem, shame and hypersensitivity to rejection and criticism. These aspects are the core and the narcissism is a façade. Grandiose narcissism is not linked with childhood abuse, neglect and poor parenting; instead, it seems that parental overvaluation is a contributing factor to the development of the condition. Its vulnerable form has been linked with physical and sexual abuse, and controlling, cold and intrusive parents (Horton et al., 2006; Miller, 2011; Otway & Vignoles, 2006). There is no meaningful data on the treatments and their effectiveness, since these patients do not believe that they need therapy, and thus do not participate in therapeutic settings (Crits-Cristoph & Barber, 2007).

Individuals who have **paranoid personality disorder**:
- are suspicious meaning that they have a tendency to interpret other people's actions as threatening or demeaning
- blame others for their own mistakes and failures

296

- are overly sensitive to criticism and hold grudges against others
- question sincerity and trustworthiness of friends and coworkers, and seldom confide in others
- defensive
- are perceived as cold, detached, scheming and humorless.

Schizoid personality disorder manifests as the following:
- being a loner, withdrawn, in pursuit of solitary interests
- focus on abstract ideas rather than thinking about people
- aloof without warmth or tender feelings for others
- indifferent to praise and criticism
- lack of emotions, rarely show nods and social smiles.

People with **schizotypal personality disorder**:
- think, dress and behave in strange ways
- experience unusual perceptions such as feeling the presence of a deceased person
- engage in magical thinking (such as believe they can affect the world with their own thoughts)
- believe that they can forsee the future
- are anxious in social situations, especially when around strangers
- engage in paranoid thinking that others are conspiring against them
- are socially withdrawn

Figure 7. Blowing air into a crystal ball could be the cure all for global warming.

Histrionic personality disorder refers to:
- displays of excessive emotionality
- being theatrical and/or sexually seductive to attract attention
- constantly seeking reassurance, approval or praise
- the excessive need to satisfy urges immediately).

Avoidant personality disorder consists of the following:
- withdrawal from society to escape rejection, shame or humiliation
- hypersensitivity to being negatively evaluated by others
- desiring affection yet too fearful of criticism to seek out others
- avoiding school or work to protect themselves against negative evaluation by others.

Obsessive-compulsive personality disorder (OCPD) consists of the following:
- being overly conscientious, rigid and excessively concerned with following rules, order, schedules, efficiency and work
- having difficulties relaxing and expressing feelings of warmth
- preoccupation with trivial details

- preoccupation with perfectionism to the point of not finishing projects
- <u>not</u> engaging in obsessive-compulsive rituals (washing hands 100 times per day, for example). These rituals are typical for another disorder -- obsessive-compulsive disorder (OCD).

Dependent personality disorder is characterized by:
- delegating one's responsibility about making decisions to other people (what job to take, where to live, and so on)
- lacking confidence
- believing themselves to be incompetent. As a result do not take initiative in various situations
- unwillingness to mature or take responsibility for themselves
- volunteering to do things that are unpleasant to make people like them
- fear of being abandoned
- seeking a new relationship immediately after one ends (APA, 2013).

ANXIETY DISORDERS

Let's continue with **anxiety disorders** that are characterized by a high level and long duration of anxiety that impair one's daily functioning. We will start with **generalized anxiety disorder** characterized by:

- constant state of worry, tension, and diffuse uneasiness
- restlessness, being easily tired, irritability
- disturbed sleep and/or concentration
- overreacting to sudden stimuli
- free-floating anxiety without a particular object, person or situation as a source
- a feeling of a lack of control over one's life

Figure 8. An expression of Generalized Anxiety Disorder (GAD).

What are the causal factors for this condition? These individuals are more likely to have a history of childhood trauma (Borkovec et al., 2004). Also, they have a low tolerance for uncertainty, coming from not being able to predict future events (Roemer et al., 2002). This is most likely due to recurring childhood situations in which unpredictable stressful events happened randomly (for example, father was sometimes nice and sweet towards the mother, and at other, seemingly random times, he was abusive). Thus, the child could not develop a concept for when to feel safe, and this constant feeling that something bad might happen at any given moment leads to anxiety (Mineka & Zinbarg, 1996). The feeling that one lacks control gives rise to anxiety, and can be traced back to over controlling, intrusive parenting style (Craske & Waters, 2005). When many patients are asked why they worry, they claim that they find some benefits from it, such as that worrying about a bad event makes it less

298

likely that the event will happen (superstitious thinking); or that worrying about this distracts them from some issues that the patient does not want to think about; or that worrying prepares one to deal with a bad event. Thus, a factor contributing to this condition is assigning a positive value to worrying, which just reinforces their worry (Dugas et al., 2007). Further, there is a tendency in these individuals to focus their attention to a threatening signal. For example, when patients are asked to remember this sentence: "They discussed the priest's conviction," the patients interpret it to mean that the priest was convicted of some horrible crime, rather than interpreting the word "conviction" as pertaining to the priest's firm faith (Wilson et al., 2006). Genetics influences the development of this condition to a modest extent (Hetterma et al. 2001). In terms of the neurotransmitters, it appears that the GABA system has a reduced level of functioning in this condition, especially in the limbic system, and that the stress hormone cortisol (released from an adrenal gland) is overactive (Butcher, 2016).

Pharmacological treatment consists of administering benzodiazepines to these patients that produce relaxation, but these medications can cause dependence and withdrawal symptoms. A more effective medication is buspirone which does not lead to these side effects. (Roy-Byrne & Cowley, 2007). Antidepressants are also safer and more effective than the benzodiazepines (Goodman, 2004). Cognitive-behavioral therapy, which seems to be as effective as benzodiazepines, consists of teaching a patient how to relax muscles (this is the behavioral component) and reduce negative perception of events (this is the cognitive component) (Barlow et al., 2007).

ANXIETY DISORDERS: PHOBIA

Let's turn to the next type of anxiety disorder – **phobias**. These refer to unrealistic, intense fears of specific objects, activities or situations that are actively avoided by the person. *Specific phobias* are associated with any situation or an object. Some examples are phobias of heights, snakes, spiders, the dark, tiny rooms (like elevators), germs and blood. *Social phobia* (currently termed *social anxiety disorder*) refers to the fear of situations such as speaking in public, dating, talking with authority figures or meeting new people. These individuals have fear of being evaluated negatively by others and humiliated. Another type of phobia is *agoraphobia* – fear of leaving one's home. An individual with agoraphobia does not want to feel trapped outside (in a bus, shopping mall, museum, store, museum, etc.) from which the escape would be difficult. These patients also fear having a panic attack when away from the safety of their home.

Figure 9. Feathers are typically seen as non-threatening but to people with a feather phobia, they may be terrifying.

What causes phobia? Learning is one factor. Research shows that people who experience fear associated with something non-threatening, start to fear that non-threatening thing. A person who has claustrophobia (fear of small spaces) recalls being locked in a tiny closet by her siblings in which she was terrified to be alone. These classically conditioned phobias are well known to researchers who ask the clients to remember sources of their phobia; 58 percent of clients are able to recall these situations (Acheson et al., 2007). However, a person does not have to be the one who experiences fear directly, since fear can be observed in others (called *vicarious conditioning*). For example, children who were asked to view photographs of animals paired with pictures of human faces displaying fear, later developed fear of those animals (a conditioned response that only lasted for about a week) (Askew & Field, 2008). Another example is a person who watched his grandfather vomit shortly before his death, thus later developing a phobia of vomiting (Mineka & Zinbarg, 2006). An additional factor is a cognitive one–patients overestimate the likelihood of something negative happening after a phobic stimulus is presented (Muhlberger et al., 2006).

Figure 10. Have you ever been stuck in an elevator? An experience such as this could cause a person to develop claustrophobia.

Another factor is evolutionary preparedness. It is an observation that people have a greater fear of snakes, water, heights and enclosed spaces, even though guns, motorcycles and cars are statistically more dangerous. How can this be explained? Throughout history and prehistory, humans have had negative experiences with snakes, water, heights, enclosed spaces (and other natural factors), and have only spent a relatively short time with the dangers of vehicles and guns. We have not had ample time, in the larger human development, to become conditioned to fear these things. This preparedness is demonstrated in a study that attempted to classically condition one group of people to fear pictures of snakes and spiders, and another group to fear flowers and mushrooms. It was more difficult to develop fear towards flowers and mushrooms, since humans are more accustomed to being attacked by spiders and snakes than flowers and mushrooms (Ohman & Milneka, 2001), so we developed susceptibility to fears of those stimuli. There is a modest genetic contribution to the development of phobias which is evident in studies that observed identical twins being more likely to suffer from phobias than dizygotic (non identical) twins (Kendler et al., 1999).

The most effective cognitive-behavioral therapy is called *gradual exposure therapy*. The patient is exposed to a small amount of the phobic stimulus, a photo of a spider presented at a distance, for example. While experiencing fear, the client is taught relaxation techniques (breathing, muscular relaxation) so that fear goes away in a few minutes (relaxation and fear cannot coexist). The client is also educated that the fear will go away as a consequence of relaxation. Next, the picture is brought closer to the client, and the process is repeated. The client eventually holds the picture, and the process is repeated until the client holds a real, small spider. Eventually, the client holds a large spider. This entire procedure is also called *systematic desensitization*, since in a controlled way (systematically), sensitization (being sensitive to the spider) is neutralized (desensitization). This therapy has another variation – *participant modeling* where a therapist models a behavior of touching the spider, so that the patient can engage in observational learning (observation and imitation). In this way the client learns (cognitive part) that touching the spider may not be harmful at all (Craske & Mystkowski, 2006). Some changes must occur at the level of amygdala since it is the part of the brain that it is involved in fear- formation and fear-recognition.

In terms of developing a social phobia, learning plays a considerable role. A large number of people with this condition report witnessing or experiencing a social situation where they (or someone else they observed) were a target of ridicule, humiliation, or severe teasing (Harvery et al., 2005). Thus, they developed fear of that situation and their fear generalized to various other social situations. Often, individuals with social phobia have parents that are cold, socially isolated and avoidant, thus the parents deemphasized the importance of harmonious social relationships

and did not stimulate their children to participate in social events (Harvery et al., 2005). These individuals usually have a cognitive bias, an expectation that others will reject and negatively evaluate them. Because of this anxiety, they cannot properly interact well with others. Due to their social awkwardness, others may indeed avoid and perceive them negatively (this is known as *self-fulfilling prophecy effect*) (Clark & McManus, 2002). Genes modestly influence this condition (Smoller et al., 2008).

Figure 11. Bullying can trigger a social phobia in a victim as well as in a witness.

Aside from the effectiveness of gradual exposure therapy, a *cognitive restructuring* method has also proved very effective. This approach consists of patients learning to *identify* cognitive bias such as: "I am nervous and I look stupid, nobody wants to be around me." A therapist perceives these thoughts as cognitive *distortions* and encourages the patient to change them through *logical reanalysis*: "Does being nervous always lead to looking stupid?" (Barlow et al. 2007). The treatment also consists of the administration of antidepressant medications. Although effective, they are still not as effective as cognitive-behavioral approach which does not last as long, and whose effects are longer lasting. Pure pharmacological treatments have a higher relapse rate once the patient ends medication use, and medication use is needed for excessively long periods of time to lower the chance of a relapse (Stein & Stein, 2008). However, gradual exposure and cognitive restructuring have comparable effectiveness (Clark et al. 2006).

ANXIETY DISORDERS: PANIC DISORDER

Panic disorder is characterized by the following:
Recurrent and unexpected *panic attacks*. A panic attack refers to a surge of intense fear or discomfort that reaches a peak within minutes, and during which time four or more of the following symptoms occur:

- Pounding heart
- Accelerated heart rate
- Sweating
- Trembling or shaking
- Shortness of breath
- Feelings of choking
- Chest pain or discomfort
- Nausea or abdominal distress
- Dizziness, lightheadedness or fainting
- Chills or heat sensations
- Numbness or tingling sensations
- Derealization (feeling of living in a world that is not real) or depersonalization (feeling detached from oneself)
- Fear of dying

Figure 12. Panic disorder sufferers may misperceive a simple chest pain as a heart attack.

Another aspect of panic disorder is a persistent worry about experiencing additional panic attacks. A factor that influences the emergence of this disorder is an increased activity of amygdala which further stimulates the locus coreuleus (in the brainstem) and the prefrontal cortex. These structures are termed the "fear network." The network is too sensitive and triggered easier than in healthy people. Reasons for this sensitivity are likely genetics and stressful life experiences (Ladd et al., 2000). Further, an increased activity of noradrenaline in brain areas can stimulate heart-related symptoms of panic. Serotonin levels, on the other hand, seem to be reduced, since serotonin reduces noradrenaline levels (Gorman et al., 2000). Gaba, a neurotransmitter that influences us to be calm, has an abnormally low presence in the individuals suffering from this condition (Mason et al., 2004). Cognitive factors influence this condition too, such as *catastrophic thinking* about bodily sensations. For example, when a person experiences a racing heart, he/she interprets this as an impending heart attack, which can, in turn, trigger a panic attack. Another cognitive factor that may play a role is the *perception of unpredictability.* When people are given a detailed account of what bodily sensations they will experience when given a medication, 30 percent experienced a panic attack in comparison to 90 percent of people who suffer from a panic attack who were not given an explanation (Schmidt et al., 2006).

Yet another cognitive factor plays a role: *perceived control* over a situation. When the sufferers were given a panic attack-inducing gas and were under the impression they could control the gas administration, they experienced less panic attacks than those sufferers who did not believe they could control the gas administration (Zvolensky et al., 1999). In addition, these individuals interpret ambiguous situation as threatening, when it can also be interpreted in a non-threatening way, so they focus too much on the threatening information (Mathews & MacLeod, 2005). Other cognitive factors play a role. For example, panic disorder is characterized by a fear of dying of a heart attack due to chest pain, which is common in panic attacks. However, this reasoning is difficult to understand since sufferers had many attacks without dying or ever even having a heart attack. Their rationale is that the only reason for their survival are the techniques they learned to relax themselves and their medications. This is why an effective therapeutic approach was designed, to which we now turn.

Figure 13. Therapy for panic disorders focuses on facing one's fear without safety behaviors.

This therapy consists of encouraging the patient to not rely on *safety behaviors* (medications, relaxation techniques) and rationally experience the attack, so that they can be convinced that the heart attack does not occur even though the safety behaviors are not used (Rachman et al., 2008). A similar cognitive-behavioral technique (*interoceptive exposure*) is used where a person is encouraged to induce bodily sensations that sufferers fear (hart racing, dizziness, etc.) through hyperventilation, running or spinning in a chair. The patient is asked to focus on those sensations until he/she gets used to them without experiencing fear. Another cognitive-behavioral approach (*panic control treatment*) is also used. A patient is educated about the condition, learns breathing techniques to relax, and confronts the inner sensations and external situations in order to become accustomed to them. These. The vast majority of patients were symptom free after several weeks of these two treatments (Arch & Craske, 2008). An additional cognitive intervention has also been used: changing one's thinking about bodily sensations (understanding that a racing heart can mean excitement, not necessarily a heart attack) can further reduce symptoms (Clark et al., 1997).

Medications usually prescribed for this condition are benzodiazepines. Although these medications reduce anxiety in 30-60 minutes, they often come with a number of side effects (drowsiness, slow movements and impaired thinking) and long-term use of these medications sometimes result in withdrawal symptoms such as nervousness, sleep disturbance, dizziness and panic attacks when these medications are discontinued (Polack & Simon, 2009). Antidepressants, specifically SSRIs and tricyclic, are another type of medications administered for this condition. While SSRIs are associated with impaired sexual function, tricyclics create dry mouth, constipation and blurred vision. It takes about 4 weeks for these substances to become effective. Physicians prefer to prescribe antidepressants over benzodiazepines since antidepressants do not produce withdrawal symptoms (Roy-Byrne & Cowley, 2007).

OBSESSIVE-COMPULSIVE AND RELATED DISORDERS

Obsessive-Compulsive Disorder consists of the following:

Figure 14. A cleaning compulsion is related to an obsession with germs.

- *Obsessions* (recurring, intrusive, anxiety-provoking thoughts and images) such as worrying about germs or whether one has locked all locks in the house

- *Compulsions* are irrational behaviors that one feels compelled to repeat many times, such as washing hands 100 times per day or checking whether the locks are locked 100 times per day. Compulsions are performed to get rid of obsessions, however obsessions come back.

Compulsions resemble rituals since they are so central in the life of a person, almost like a sacred activity. God forbid that a step of a compulsion is skipped (such as washing hands only 74 times instead of 76). To a compulsive person this would be a catastrophe. Compulsions are performed in a particular order, just like a ritual. Similarly they are repetitive like rituals.

What causes this condition? An effort to suppress thoughts usually produces even more of these thoughts in healthy people (Abramowitz et al., 2001). This is a cognitive pattern observed in people with OCD who often and intensely try to suppress obsessions (Purdon et al., 2007), only making them worse. Another cognitive pattern typical for the patients with OCD is *though-action fusion,* meaning they feel that an intrusive thought must lead into the corresponding behavior. Compulsions are performed to ensure that the materialization of a thought does not happen. What is evident here is a sense of inflated responsibility where a mere thought is perceived by a patient as something so bad that it needs to be eliminated (Rachman et al., 2006).

Genetics research indicates a moderate influence of genes in the development of this condition (if a parent has OCD, the offspring has 3-12 times higher chance of developing the condition than someone without a direct genetic link to OCD (such as having no first degree relative with OCD) (Hettema et al., 2001). An abnormally high level of activity has been detected in the frontal cortex of sufferers from OCD (the orbital cortex and the cingulate cortex) as well as in the subcortical caudate nucleus. In a healthy brain, the frontal cortex regions are usually associated with an urge to do something (clean every room in the house, for example), and caudate can block that impulse, but the mentioned deficits in these structures can lead to repetitive behavioral expression (compulsion) of an urge (Baxter et al., 2001).

Also, the white matter (axons) shows abnormalities in the already mentioned brain areas, and this matter facilitates communication among cells, resulting in miscommunication among the brain regions (Yoo et al., 2007). It seems that serotonin neurotransmitter overstimulates cells, possibly by serotonin receptors being too sensitive to serotonin's influence, or by this transmitter being too active (Baxter et al., 2000).

There are several treatment approaches to improve this condition. Antidepressant medications such as clomipramine and SSRIs increase the impact of serotonin on cells, which initially worsens OCD symptoms. However, after 6-12 weeks these medications reduce symptoms. How is this possible? When a neurotransmitter overstimulates cells, cells retract receptors and the transmitter's effect is reduced. It takes 6-12 weeks for the retraction to take place (Baxter et al., 2000). Forty to sixty percent of the patients show 25 to 35 percent reduction in symptoms, but if medications are discontinued the symptoms come back. The solution would require the patient to take medications indefinitely (Doughert et al., 2007). In people who fail to respond to these medications, antipsychotic medications (decreasing dopamine activity) are used for a reduction in symptoms (Bloch et al., 2006).

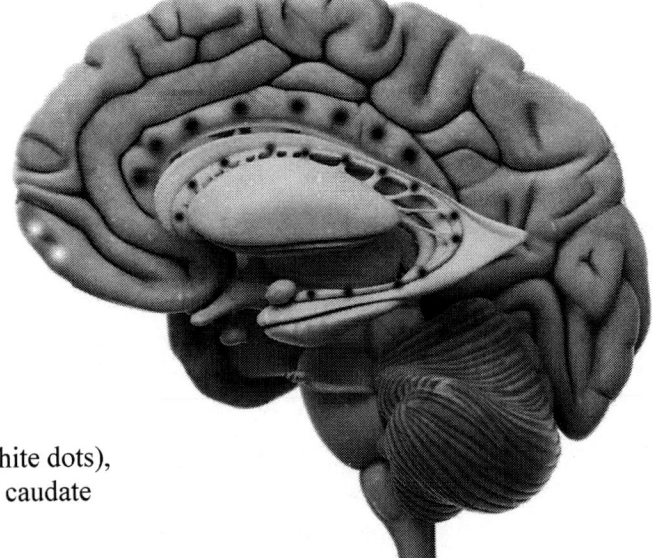

Figure 15. Orbitofrontal cortex (white dots), cingulate cortex (large black dots), caudate (small black dots).

The motivation behind behavioral treatment of OCD is to expose a person to a stimulus that bothers them – a person who fears germs may be asked to go through a trash can filed with garbage. When the person wants to engage in the ritual (say washing), he or she is not allowed to do so. For these reasons the therapy is termed *exposure and response prevention* therapy. After some time (it can be several hours), their anxiety subsides and they learn that the compulsion to wash hands (or another compulsion) is controllable. This therapy is very effective, accomplishing 50-70 percent reduction in symptoms, proving to be more effective than the medication therapy (Abramowitz et al., 2009). Combining medications and behavior therapy has been shown to be more effective in children and adolescents than in adults (March & Franklin, 2006). When all these therapies fail, brain surgery may be implemented. It is aimed at destroying brain tissue in one of the aforementioned brain areas. Thirty-five to forty-five percent of these cases respond with at least 30 precent reduction in symptoms (Ruck et al., 2008).

Figure 16. Sifting through trash is a standard treatment for germ obsession.

Let's consider the symptoms and signs of related disorders to OCD. **Body dysmorphic disorder** is marked by a preoccupation with a real or imagined defect in appearance. When a person has a minor physical defect, the person becomes extremely worried about it. **Hoarding disorder** refers to a person having an ongoing difficulty discarding or parting with possessions, regardless of their actual value. The person accumulates unnecessary possessions which clutter the living space and make otherwise healthy living difficult. **Trichotillomania** refers to a recurrent pulling out of one's hair, resulting in hair loss. Hair is most often pulled from scalp, eyebrows and eyelids. **Excoriation** is persistent picking at one's skin, most likely the face, arms and hands. Most pick with fingernails, but some use pins, tweezers and other devices. There may be skin rubbing, squeezing, lancing and biting too.

TRAUMA AND STRESSOR-RELATED DISORDERS

Post-traumatic stress disorder (PTSD), which can last months, years or decades, is characterized by an exposure to a traumatic event (combat, car accident, violent physical assault, etc.). This exposure can be direct (happening to the sufferer), or indirect, such as witnessing the event happen to others or learning that the event happened to a family member or a close friend. The following symptoms are typical of PTSD:

306

- Recurrent disturbing memories and/or dreams of the traumatic event
- Flashbacks in which the person feels or acts as if the traumatic events were occurring for the first time
- Distress to cues that symbolize or resemble the traumatic event
- Avoidance of stimuli (people, places, conversations, objects, etc.) associated with the traumatic event
- Inability to remember an aspect of the traumatic experience

- Negative beliefs and expectations about oneself
- Persistent negative emotional state (fear, horror, anger, guilt or shame)
- Inability to experience positive emotions (happiness, pleasure)
- Reckless or self-destructive behaviors
- Hypervigilance (constantly scanning the environment for threats)
- Exaggerated startle response
- Problems with concentration
- Sleep disturbance

Risk factors that influence the development of this condition are: lower level of social support, neuroticism (having a tendency to experience negative emotion), having preexisting anxiety or depression, family history of depression and substance abuse (McNally, 2013). Cognitive factors play a role too: a person has a higher chance of developing PTSD if he/she believes that PTSD is a sign of weakness and/or that others will be ashamed of them for developing the condition (Dunmore et al., 2001). People with higher intelligence scores are less likely to develop PTSD (Breslau et al., 2006). Why? Perhaps people with higher intelligence scores can make more sense of their traumatic experience and find something useful in it. Females tend to develop PTSD more than males. This may be due to an observation that females with PTSD have higher levels of the hormone cortisol secretions at times of stress in comparison to healthy women (Meewisse et al., 2007). People with PTSD have a tendency to have a smaller hippocampus (even before experiencing a traumatic event) (Gilbertson et al., 2002). It is not clear how this can influence the development of PTSD, though. Also, people who possess a certain gene (5HTTLPR) have a higher risk for developing PTSD (Kilpatrick et al., 2007).

Figure 17. Why do some people develop PTSD after a car accident and others do not?

Antidepressants and antipsychotic medications are sometimes helpful in reducing the symptoms (Reinceke et al., 2007; Bartzokis et al., 2005). Cognitive-behavioral therapy consists of *prolonged exposure*. The patient is encouraged to remember vividly the traumatic event over and over until there is a decrease in emotional response. This therapy includes relaxation training (Powers et al., 2010). The relationship between the therapist and the patient is very important for this condition due to the sensitive nature of the memories being revisited. The therapy, thus, also consists of being supportive, with therapists actively listening to the patient but not demanding more information than the patient is willing to provide. Care, warmth and kindness on the part of the therapist are significant (Charuvastra & Cloiter, 2008).

Other conditions belong in this category. For example, **acute stress disorder** is very similar to PTSD except that it lasts no longer than one month. It, too, results from a traumatic event. **Reactive attachment disorder** affects children who, due to an exposure to a traumatic event, become withdrawn, minimally seeking comfort when distressed. They show minimal social and emotional responsiveness to others, diminished expression of positive emotions and episodes of fear, sadness and irritability. **Disinhibited social engagement disorder** manifests in a child who is actively approaching and interacting with strangers, and in their willingness to go away with the stranger.

MOOD DISORDERS

A well-researched mood disorder is **bipolar disorder**, also called manic-depression. It comes in two types: bipolar I and bipolar II. The bipolar I disorder is characterized with a period of *depression* and a period of *mania*. Depression refers to the following experiences (at least five) for at least two weeks:

- Feeling sad, empty or hopeless
- Markedly diminished interest or pleasure in all or almost all activities most of the day, nearly every day
- Significant weight loss or gain (change of more than 5 percent of body weight in one month).
- Insomnia or hypersomnia (too much sleep)

- Restlessness or slowing down of movement
- Fatigue (loss of energy)
- Feelings of worthlessness or excessive/inappropriate guilt
- Reduced ability to concentrate, indecisiveness
- Recurrent thoughts of suicide without planning suicide

Figure 18. Contemplating suicide.

Depression can also occur with *psychotic* features (hallucinations and delusions) and *catatonic* features (inability to move or talk). Mania, on the other hand, refers to the following:

- Inflated self-esteem
- Euphoria (feeling on the top of the world)
- Grandiosity (a belief that one can fly, for example)
- Decreased need for sleep (feeling well-rested after 3 hours of sleep, for example)
- Flight of ideas (racing thoughts)
- Distractibility
- Increase in goal-directed activity (work, school, hobbies, sexual life)
- Purposeless non-goal-directed activity

- Excessive involvement in activities that have a high potential for painful consequences (foolish business investments, buying sprees, sexual promiscuity)

Figure 19. A healthy person may buy a couple guitars. A person with bipolar disorder will buy 30 of them in one day.

The bipolar II form consists of a period of a serious depression alternating with a period of hypomania (not full-blown mania).

Genetics plays a very prominent role in this condition. This is obvious in the finding that out of 50 pairs of identical twins (twins with the exact same genetic material), where one twin has the condition, 60 of these twin pairs are *concordant* (both twins have the disorder) for the condition. In dizygotic twins whose genetic material is much less similar than in the identical twins, the concordance rate is only 19 twin pairs out of 50 twin pairs. In terms of the neurotransmitter unbalance, noradrenaline activity is increased during a manic episode, and decreased during a depressive episode (Goodwin & Jamison, 2007). Manic symptoms of hyperactivity, grandiosity and euphoria are associated with an increased activity of dopamine in the brain (Cousins et al. 2009). High doses of cocaine and amphetamine, drugs that increase dopamine activity, usually lead to mania (Cousins et al., 2009). In depression there is a reduction in the activity of dopamine (Goodwin & Jamison, 2007). Cortisol (stress hormone) levels are increased in the depression aspect of the condition, but not in the manic aspect (Goodwin & Jamison, 2007). Blood flow to the prefrontal cortex is reduced in depression, but is increased in the prefrontal cortex in mania. These biological influences contribute to deficits in problem solving, planning, working memory, attention shifting and sustained attention, all functions of the prefrontal cortex (Chen et al., 2011).

Further, the thalamus and amygdala (both aspects of the limbic system/emotional center) are enlarged in individuals with bipolar disorder, which indicates a disturbed relationship between the prefrontal cortex and the limbic system (Chen et al., 2011). Stressful life events precede manic and depressive episodes (Goodwin & Jamison, 2007).

Pharmacological treatments utilize drug *lithium*, a mood stabilizer. Mania is a high mood and depression is a low mood. Lithium stabilizes the moods to a middle level. It is not advisiable to treat bipolar disorder with antidepressants since they can trigger a manic episode, unless they are administered with lithium (Thase & Denko, 2008). Lithium is effective for 75 percent of patients, but only one third remained free of an episode over a five year follow-up period (Keck & McElroy, 2007). Long term lithium use can lead to kidney malfunction, but this happens only occasionally (Goodwin & Jamison, 2007). *Anticonvulsant medications* are also used in patients who do not respond well to lithium or who experience lithium side effects (gastrointestinal problems, weight gain, slowing of thinking, reduced motor coordination). Studies show, however, that incidence of suicides is higher in people who use anticonvulsants than in those who are prescribed lithium (Thase & Densko, 2008). Sometimes bipolar disorder includes psychotic symptoms (hallucinations and delusions), in which case antipsychotic medications are prescribed (Rotschild et al., 2004).

Electroconvulsive therapy (ECT) is used for the treatment of manic episodes, and it significantly reduces symptoms in about 80 percent of patients (Goodwin & Jamison, 2007). ECT therapy consists of passing electrical current through the brain, by positioning electrodes on the temples. This therapy induces seizures in a controlled environment. For this procedure the patient is put under general anesthesia and given muscle relaxants (to prevent muscle injury when a person experiences a seizure). There are a total of 6-12 treatment sessions, 2-3 per week. The electrical current is applied to temples very briefly, only a couple of seconds. Side effects of ECT include confusion, slowed response time and memory loss. This is usually temporary, but long term side effects are also known to occur, though rarely (Sackeim et al., 2007). Lithium is given after ECT to maintain the effects of the ECT.

Figure 20. Mindfulness meditation.

There are various cognitive-behavioral therapies used for bipolar disorder. *Mindfulness-based cognitive* therapy is frequently used. The therapy consists of teaching a patient to mediate. The goal of the meditation is to identify negative thoughts and sensations, become aware of them, and accept them without avoiding them. The patient is encouraged to discover that these negative thoughts and sensations are simply momentary, temporary mental processes, not a reflection of an unchangeable reality, not something set in stone (Piet & Hougaard, 2011).

310

Major depressive disorder is another mood condition. Its features are listed above, but occurs without mania (that's why it is also called also a *unipolar depressive disorder*). When it occurs as

a component of the bipolar disorder, depression is more severe than when it occurs by itself. An additional mood disorder is **dysthymia** or persistent depressive disorder. This is a less intense yet relatively constant experience of

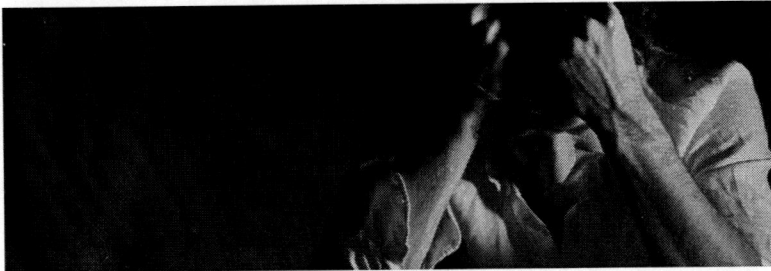

Figure 21. Major depression.

depression for at least two years. During this period, the person may not be experiencing symptoms for more than 2 months. Further, there is **cyclothymic disorder** which is a less intense version of bipolar disorder. These patients exhibit hypomanic and depressive symptoms for two years. However, these symptoms amount to neither a full-blown hypomanic nor a full-blown depressive episode. Symptoms may be exhibited for half of this two year period but not for more than 2 months at a time (Butcher, 2014). **Premenstrual dysphoric disorder** manifests itself as irritability, mood swings, depression and anxiety that all occur repeatedly during the premenstrual phase of the cycle and begin to go away around the onset of menses or shortly after (APA, 2013).

PSYCHOTIC DISORDERS

Psychosis refers to a state of mind in which a person has lost touch with reality. **Schizophrenia**, a psychotic disorder, is characterized by positive and negative symptoms. Positive symptoms are not considered valuable or good; instead, the term "positive" describes mental processes and behaviors that are usually not present in a healthy person. For example, *loosening of associations* (also called *thought derailment*) refers to jumping from topic to topic (which makes sentences difficult to follow by a listener). *Word salad*, another positive symptom, refers to putting random words in a sentence that make sense only grammatically, not semantically (meaning-wise). For example: "I am elected by princess ocean, who blings, sings, dings and rings until death do us part forever never after". "Blings, sings, dings" (and so on) is called *clang association* – repetitious use of words that sound similar. *Neologism* refers to making up new words like "…they met with a bunch of *triloglited* children." All these aspects are examples of a *thought disorder* – deficits in thinking clearly and expressing a coherent train of thought (Bucher, 2014).

Delusions and *hallucinations* are positive symptoms too. Delusions are false beliefs about reality that persist in spite of evidence that proves them wrong or inaccurate. *Delusions of influence* are false beliefs that: one's thoughts are controlled by some external forces; an enigmatic agency has stolen one's thoughts; thoughts of the patients are being broadcasted through radio waves to many people; thoughts have been imported into one's mind by aliens. These individuals may often wear helmets in an attempt to prevent these "interventions" by external entities and organizations.

Delusions of grandeur (grandiosity) are such that a person believes that he/she possesses supernatural abilities, for example to summon rain, move mountains, fly, resurrect the dead, etc. *Delusions of persecution* (paranoia) are such that a person falsely assumes that he/she has been followed and/or that others plot to harm him/her. *Delusions of reference* are those in which a person believes that he/she has stumbled across a tv show, movie, song, or picture specifically

designed to send a very important message directly to the patient. *Somatic delusions* are false beliefs pertaining to one's body, such as a conviction that one's blood is evaporating and that the only way to replace the blood is to obtain it from others like a vampire – by biting them for the neck. *Religious delusions* are false beliefs that one has an important religious function, like being the second coming of Jesus Christ.

Figure 22. Paranoid delusion.

Hallucinations are unreal sensory experiences such as seeing things that are not there, hearing voices, tasting something not produced by a real stimulus, smelling scents that do not exist (especially vomit, rotting eggs, urine, feces or smoke), or sensing objects that do not exist (like bugs crawling on one's skin) (Alexander & Yakel, 2014). The most common are hearing (or auditory) hallucinations, voices that are bossy, criticizing ("You are so stupid.") and abusive ("Ugly bitch!"), but some voices are pleasant ("My darling"). Especially dangerous are *commanding voices* that demand some action, which can sometimes lead to self-harm, and injury or murder of others (Nayani & David, 1996). Research shows that the brain area for speech production is active when auditory hallucinations occur, which indicates that these hallucinations are produced by the patients' brain, not by some non-existent entities (Hoffman et al., 2005). An additional positive symptom is *disorganized behavior*, such as catatonia, waxy flexibility, echopraxia and echolalia. *Catatonia* refers to remaining in a bizarre posture for hours. *Waxy flexibility* refers to an observation that a person can be moved and reshaped by another person as if the patient is made of wax; *echopraxia* (mimicking the actions of others); *echolalia* (mimicking what another person is saying).

Negative symptoms include *flattening of affect* or lack of emotional expression, *alogia* or very little speech, *social withdrawal* (reclusive life), and *avolition* or an inability to initiate behaviors (staring at one dot for hours, with no interest in outside work or social activities) (Butcher, 2014). Some subtypes of schizophrenia are *paranoid schizophrenia* which is dominated by paranoid delusions, *disorganized schizophrenia* characterized by disorganized thinking, disorganized behavior and flat affect, and *catatonic schizophrenia* which is dominated by catatonia (Butcher, 2014).

What factors influence the development of schizophrenia? Genetics plays a significant role in influencing schizophrenia since the concordance rate in identical twins is 28 percent, and the concordance rate in dizygotic twins is much less – only 6 percent. When a child with a genetic risk is adopted by a family with dysfunctional patterns, he/she is more likely to develop schizophrenia than a child who is raised in a healthy family environment. Obviously, genetics creates vulnerability for schizophrenia and the negative environment transforms the vulnerability into an actual disorder, thus we can say that genes and environment interact (Tienari et al., 2004). Some studies show that rates of schizophrenia are elevated in individuals whose mothers contracted the a virus (influenza or rubella) during their fourth to seventh months of pregnancy. It is likely that mothers develop *antibodies* (chemicals produced by the immune system to fight the virus), which enter the baby through the placenta (a structure in the uterus allowing communication between the mother's bloodstream and the baby's) (Wadington et al., 1999; Brown, 2011).

Further, individuals conceived during the height of a famine, are more likely to develop schizophrenia than people who were not exposed to the same levels of famine (Brown, 2011). Obviously, some aspect of nutrition influences the emergence of schizophrenia, although it is not known what that specific aspect may be. Also, if a mother goes through a heightened level of stress (death of a relative), her child has a 67 percent increased risk for developing schizophrenia (Khashan et al., 2008). It is likely that stress hormones are transferred from mother to child in uterus, negatively impacting the child's brain which can contribute to schizophrenia. The onset of schizophrenia is often associated with the patient experiencing stress. Stress is known to trigger a release of stress hormones

Figure 23. Famine.

(cortisol from adrenal glands) that stimulate dopamine activity (McMurray et al., 1991) which can encourage the emergence of schizophrenia. Families in which the patient is criticized/disliked, and subjected to hostility and excessive concern about the patient's illness, create stress for the patient, and often induce the *relapse* (experience a new episode of schizophrenia) (Butzlaff & Hooley, 1998).

Brain volume is usually lower in patients with schizophrenia even before the onset of the illness, suggesting that these brain abnormalities also influence the emergence of the illness (Karlsgodt et al., 2010). Brain areas that show the most reduction are the frontal lobes (important for rational thinking, being in touch with reality), the amygdala (emotions), the hippocampus (memory) and the thalamus (receives sensory input from the environment) (Ettinger et al., 2001; Keshavan et al., 2008). Abnormalities are also visible in the myelin sheath. This deficit is associated with impairments in cognitive functioning. White matter (myelin) abnormalities are evident even in individuals who show initial genetic susceptibility to this illness, thus it may also influence the emergence of the disorder (Francis et al., 2017). Frontal lobe functioning is in some patients hyperactive and in others is hypoactive. This frontal lobe dysfunction is believed to influence some negative symptoms and to stimulate attention deficits (Goldman-Rakic & Selemon, 1997).

ION CHANNEL

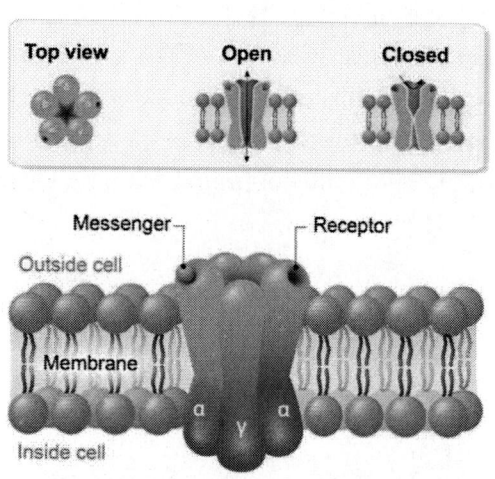

Figure 24. When receptors are blocked, the messenger (neurotransmitter) does not bind to it.

In the 1960s Chlorpromazine (a drug) was successfully used to treat schizophrenia. Chlorpromazine blocks dopamine receptors from receiving dopamine transmitter. Amphetamine (a stimulant drug) produces an excess of dopamine, and sometimes the abuse of this drug leads to hallucinations and delusions. Also, L-DOPA medication, used to treat Parkinson's Disease, increases the amount of dopamine in the brain, but this sometimes leads to psychosis (hallucinations and delusions). These observations point to the dopamine system for influencing schizophrenia. Thus, schizophrenia is characterized with an excess of dopamine. However, dopamine can overstimulate the cells not only by being overabundant, but also by its receptors being too dense or too sensitive to dopamine. The density of dopamine receptors (D2 subtype) has been found in several studies (Seeman, 2011; Wong et al., 1986). It has also been observed that patients with schizophrenia have a greater number of a dopamine receptors (D2) which are supersensitive to dopamine transmitters (Seeman, 2011).

Glutamate neurotransmitters play a role in this disorder too. PCP, a drug also called "angel's dust," blocks glutamate receptors from binding with glutamate transmitters, and produces both positive and negative symptoms. Ketamine, an anesthetic, also blocks glutamate receptors producing positive and negative symptoms (Krystal et al., 2005). These observations suggest that glutamate are lower than normal in a person with schizophrenia, something that has been supported by research findings

Figure 25. Angel dust blocks glutamate receptors, preventing glutamate from binding to it.

(Marsman et al., 2011, Goff & Coyle, 2001). Is there a relationship between dopamine and glutamate? Dopamine is known to inhibit glutamate activity, so it seems that overactive dopamine suppresses the activity of glutamate (Butcher 2014). Interestingly, the THC chemical in marijuana increases the synthesis of dopamine. Does smoking weed increase the risk of developing schizophrenia? Studies show that people who engage in heavy marijuana smoking and who have a particular form of a gene are at a higher risk to develop this condition. People who do not possess this form of the gene are much less likely to develop this illness even they smoke marijuana (Caspi et al., 2005).

PSYCHOTIC DISORDERS: TREATMENT OF SCHIZOPHRENIA

Pharmacological treatments are central for this condition through the administration of *typical* and *atypical* antipsychotic medications. Typical antipsychotics (the *first generation*) were invented in the 1950s and, while effective in significantly reducing the positive symptoms, produce side effects such as drowsiness, dry mouth, weight gain and movement abnormalities (muscle spasms, rigidity, shaking) (Butcher, 2014). In the 1980s atypical antipsychotic medications were invented, and while equally effective as the typical, the atypical medications produce less movement abnormalities (Lieberman & Stroup, 2011). These medications come with side effects such as drowsiness, weight gain, diabetes and (rarely) a drop in white blood cells (Sernyak et al., 2002). How do typical and atypical medications work? They block dopamine receptors (D2 subtype), and by doing so they prevent the binding of dopamine transmitters to their receptors, reducing dopamine's impact on the brain cells (Tandon et al., 2010).

Family therapy is effective in treating schizophrenia after medications are administered. Family members are educated about the illness and about the importance of improving the clarity of family communication. This therapy lowers the chance of relapse (Pfammatter et al., 2006). A combination of these therapies results in about 38 percent of patients recovering from the illness (but indefinite medication use is still necessary) they still need to take the medications for the rest of their lives). This treatment does not ensure a definite cure but enables the patient to function relatively well (Harrison et al., 2001).

OTHER PSYCHOTIC DISORDERS

Schizoaffective disorder is characterized by features of schizophrenia mixed with periods of major depression or bipolar disorder. **Schizophreniform** disorder is schizophrenia that lasts no longer than 6 months. A **brief psychotic disorder** is schizophrenia that lasts for only a few days and never returns (Butcher, 2014). **Delusional disorder** refers to holding a delusion. A well-known subtype is *erotomania* – a delusion that one is loved by another person when that other person is not even aware of the delusional patient's existence (Purcell et al., 2001).

REFERENCES

Abramowitz, J. S., Braddock, A. E., & Moore, E. L. (2009). Psychological treatment of obsessive-compulsive disorder. In M. M. Antony & M. B. Stein (Eds.), *Oxford handbook of anxiety and related disorders* (pp. 391-404). New York: Oxford University Press.

Abramowitz, J. S., Tolin, D. F., & Street, G. P. (2001). Paradoxical effects of thought suppression: A meta-analysis of controlled studies. *Clin. Psychol. Rev., 21*(5), 683-703.

Acheson, D. T., Forsyth, J. P., Prenoveau, J. M., & Bouton, M. E. (2007). Interoceptive fear conditioning as a learning model of panic disorder: An experimental evaluation using 20% CO-sub-2-enriched air in a non-clinical sample. *Behav. Res. Ther., 45*(10), 2280-2294.

Alexander, P., Flint, W. R., Flome, R., Hakala, C., Hayashi, C., Jones, J., July, W., Nguyen, B., Patry, M., Shobe, E., Sweetman, A., Thomas, B., Vukov, B., Wark, V., & Yakel, A.D. (2014). *Psychology: exploring our universe within* (4th edition). Boston, MA: Pearson Custom Publishing.

American Psychiatric Association. (2013). *Diagnostic and statistical manual of mental disorders* (DSM-5). (5th ed.) Washington, DC: American Psychiatric Association.

Arch, J., & Craske, M. G. (2008). Panic disorder. In W. E. Craighead, D. J. Miklowitz, & L. W. Craighead (Eds.), *Psychopathology: History, diagnosis, and empirical foundations* (pp. 115-158). Hoboken NJ: John Wiley & Sons.

Askew, C., & Field, A. P. (2008). The vicarious learning pathway to fear 40 years on. *Clin. Psychol. Rev., 28*(7), 1249-1265.

Bandelow, B., Krause, J., Wedekind, D., Broocks, A., Hajak, G. R., & Ruther, E. (2005). Early traumatic life events, parental attitudes, family history, and birth risk factors in patients with borderline personality disorder and healthy controls. *Psychiat. Res., 134*(2), 169-179.

Barlow, D. H., Allen, L. B., & Basden, S. L. (2007). Psychological treatments for panic disorder, phobias, and generalized anxiety disorder. In P. E. Nathan and J. M. Gorman (Eds.), *A guide to treatments that work.* New York: Oxford University Press, pp. 351-394.

316

Bartzokis, G., Lu, P. H., Turner, J., Mintz, J., & Saunders, C. S. (2005). Adjunctive risperidone in the treatment of chronic combat-related posttraumatic stress disorder. *Biol. Psychiat.*, 57(5), 474-479.

Battle, C. L., Shea, M. T., Johnson, D. M., Yen, S., Zlot-nick, C., Zanarini, M. C., et al. (2004). Childhood maltreatment associated with adult personality disorders: Findings from the collaborative longitudinal personality disorders study. *J. Pers. Disord.*, 18(2), 193-211.

Baxter, L. R., Jr., Ackermann, R. F., Swerdlow, N. R., Brody, A., Saxena, S., Schwartz, J. M., et al (2000). Specific brain system mediation of obsessive-compulsive disorder responsive to either medication or behavior therapy.l In W. K. Goodman & M. V.

Rudorfer et al. (Eds.). *Obsessive-compulsive disorder: Contemporary issues in treatment. Personality and clinical psychology series* (pp. 573-609). Mahwah, NJ: Erlbaum.

Bloch, M. H., Landeros-Weisenberger, A., Kelmendi, B., Coric, V., Bracken, M. B., & Leckman, J. F. (2006). A systematic review: Antipsychotic augmentation with treatment refractory obsessive-compulsive disorder. *Molecular Psychiatry*, 11, 622-632.

Borkovec, T. D., Alcaine, O. M., & Behar, E. (2004). Avoidance theory of worry and generalized anxiety disorder. In R. G. Heimberg, C. L. Turk & D. S. Mennin (Eds.), *Generalized anxiety disorder: Advances in research and practice. (pp. 77-108).* New York: Guilford Press.

Botelho, JB. & Weigel VA. (2011). The Sateré-Mawé community of Y'Apyrehyt: ritual and health on the urban outskirts of Manaus. *Hist Cienc Saude Manguinhos.*

Breslau, J., Aguilar-Gaxiola, S., Kendler, K. S., Su, M., Williams, D., & Kessler, R. C. (2006). Specifying race-ethnic differences in risk for psychiatric disorder in a USA national sample. *Psychol. Med.*, 36(1), 57-68.

Brown, A. S. (2011). The environment and susceptibility to schizophrenia. *Progress in Neurobiology, 11,* 23-58.

Butcher, James N., Hooley, Jill M., Mineka, Susan. (2016). Abnormal Psychology. Sixteenth Edition.

Butzlaff, R. L., & Hooley, J. M. (1998). Expressed emotion and psychiatric relapse: A meta-analysis. *Arch. Gen. Psychiat.*, 55(6), 547-552.

Caspi, A., Moffitt, T. E., Cannon, M., McClay, J., Murray, R., Harrington, H., et al. (2005). Moderation of the effect of adolescent-onset cannabis use on adult psychosis by a functional polymorphism in the Catechol-O-Methyltransferase gene: Longitudinal evidence of a gene x environment interaction. *Biol. Psychiat.*, 57, 1117-1127.

Caspi, A., Sugden, K., Moffitt, T. E., Taylor, A., Craig, I. W., Harrington, H., et al. (2003). Influence of life stress on depression: Moderation by a polymorphism in the 5HTT gene. *Science*, 301, 386-389.

Charuvastra, A., & Cloitre, M. (2008). Social bonds and posttraumatic stress disorder. *Annu. Rev. Psychol.*, 59, 301-328.

Chen, C. H., Suckling, J., Lennox, B. R., Ooi, C., & Bullmore, E. T. (2011). A quantitative meta-analysis of fMRI studies in bipolar disorder. *Bipolar Dis.*, 13(1), 1-15.

Clark, D. M., & McManus, F. (2002). Information processing in social phobia. *Biol. Psychiat.*, 51, 92-100.

Clark, D. M., Ehlers, A., Hackmann, A., McManus, F., Fennel, M., Grey, N., et al. (2006). Cognitive therapy versus exposure and applied relaxation in social phobia: A randomized controlled trial. *J. Consult, Clin. Psychol.*, 74(3), 568-578.

Clark, D. M. (1997). Panic disorder and social phobia, In C. G. Fairburn (Ed.), *Science and practice of cognitive behaviour therapy* (pp. 119-153). New York: Oxford University Press.

Clarkin, J. F., Levy, K. N., Lenzenweger, M. F., & Kernberg, O. F. (2007). Evaluating three treatments for borderline personality disorder: A multiwave study. *Am. J. Psychiatry*, 164, 922-928.

Coon, D., & Mitterer, J. O. (2010). *Introduction to psychology* (12th ed.). Gloucester, MA: Thomson Learning, Inc.

Couzin, J. (2004). Volatile chemistry: Children and antidepressants. *Science*, 305(5683), 468-470.

Craske, M., & Mystkowski, J. (2006). Exposure therapy and extinction: Clinical studies. In M. Craske & D. Hermans (Eds.), *Fear and learning: Contemporary perspectives.* Washington, DC: APA Books.

Craske, M. G., & Waters, A. M. (2005). Panic disorders, phobias, and generalized anxiety disorder. *Annu. Rev. Clin. Psychol.*, 1, 197-225.

Crits-Christoph, P., & Barber, J. P. (2007). Psychological treatments for personality disorders. In P. E. Nathan & J. M. Gorman (Eds.), *A guide to treatments that work* (pp.641-658). New York: Oxford University Press.

Distel, M. A., Rebollo-Mesa, I., Willemsen, G., Derom, C. A., Trull, T. J., Martin, N. G., et al. (2009). Familial resemblance of borderline personality disorder features: Genetic or cultural transmission? *PLoS ONE*, 4, 4.

Dougherty, D. D., Rausch, S. L., & M. A., J. (2007). Pharmacological treatments for obsessive-compulsive disorder. In P. E. Nathan & J. M. Gorman (Eds.), *A guide to treatments that work* (pp. 447-474). New York: Oxford University Press.

Dugas, M. J., Savard, P., Gaudet, A., Turcotte, J., Laugesen, N., Robichaud, M., et al. (2007). Can the components of a cognitive model predict the severity of generalized anxiety disorder? *Behav. Ther., 38*(2), 169-178.

Dunmore, E., Clark, D. M., & Ethlers, A. (2001). A prospective investigation of the role of persistent Posttraumatic Stress Disorder (PTSD) after physical and sexual assault. *Behav. Res. Ther., 39,* 1063-1084.

Ettinger, U., et al. (2001). Magnetic-resonance imaging of the thalamus in first-episode psychosis. *Am. J. Psychiatry*, 158, 116-118.

Gilbertson, M. W., Shenton, M. E., Ciszewski, A., Kasai, K., Lasko, N. B., Orr, S. P., et al. (2002). Smaller hippocampal volume predicts pathologic vulnerability to psychological trauma. *Nature Neuroscience*, 5, 1242-1247.

Goff, D. C., & Coyle, J. T. (2001). The emerging role of gltamate in the pathophysiology and treatment of schizophrenia. *Am. J. Psychiatry, 158*, 1367-1377.

Goldman-Rakic, P. S., & Selemon, L. D. (1997). Functional and anatomical aspects of prefrontal pathology in schizophrenia. *Schizo. Bull., 23,* 437-458.

Goodman, W. K. (2004). Selecting pharmacotherapy for generalized anxiety disorder. *J. Clin. Psychiatry,* 65(113), 8-13.

Goodwin, F. K., & Jamison, K. R. (2007). *Manic-depressive illness: Bipolar disorders and recurrent depression* (2nd ed.). New York: Oxford University Press.

Gorman, J. M., Kent, J. M., Sullivan, G. M., & Coplan, J. D. (2000). Neuroanatomical hypothesis of panic disorder, revised. *Am. J. Psychiatry*, 157, 493-505.

Harris, G. T., & Rice, M. E. (2006). Treatment of psychopathy: A review of empirical findings. In C. J. Patrick (Ed.), *Handbook of the psychopathy* (pp. 555-572). New York: Guilford Press.

Harrison, G., Hopper, K., Craig, T., Laska, E., Siegel, C., Wanderling, J., et al. (2001). Recovery from psychotic illness: A 15- and 25-year international follow-up study. *Brit. J. Psychiatry*, 178, 506-517.

Harvey, A. G., Schmidt, D. A., Scarna, A., Semler, C. N., & Goodwin, G. M. (2005). Sleep-related functioning in euthymic patients with bipolar disorder, patients with insomnia, and subjects without sleep problems. *Am. J. Psychiatry*, 162, 50-57.

Hettema, J. M., Neale, M. C., & Kendler, K. S. (2001). A review and meta-analysis of the genetic epidemiology of anxiety disorders. *Am. J. Psych.*, 158(10), 1568-1578.

Hoffman, R. E., Gueorguieva, R., Hawkins, K. A., Varanko, M., Boutros, N. N. Wu, Y.-T., et al. (2005). Temporoparietal transcranial magnetic stimulation for auditory hallucinations: Safety, efficacy and moderators in a fifty patient sample. *Biol. Psychiatry*, 58, 97-104.

Hooley, J., Cole, S., & Gironde, S. (2012). Borderline personality disorder. In T. Widiger (Ed.), *The Oxford Handbook of Personality Disorders* (pp. 409-436). Oxford: Oxford University Press.

Horton. R. S., Bleau, G., & Drwecki, B. (2006). Parenting narcissus: What are the links between parenting and narcissism? *J. Pers.*, 74, 345-376.

Karlsgodt, K. H., Sun, D., & Cannon, T. D. (2010). Structural and functional brain abnormalities in schizophrenia. *Curr. Dir. Psych. Sci.*, 19, 226-231.

Keck, P. E., & McElroy, S. L. (2007). Pharmacological treatments for bipolar disorder. In P. E. Nathan & J. M. Gorman (Eds.), *A guide to treatments that work* (3rd ed., pp. 323-350). New York: Oxford University Press.

Kendler, K. S., Karkowski, L. M., & Prescott, C. A. (1999). Fears and phobias: Reliability and heritability. *Psychol. Med., 29*, 539-553.

Keshavan, M. S., Tandon, R., Boutros, N. N., & Nasrallah, H. A. (2008). Schizophrenia, "just the facts": What we know in 2008 part 3: Neurobiology. *Schiz. Res., 106*, 89-107.

Khashan, A. S., Abel, K. M., Mc Namee, R., Pedersen, M. G., Webb, R. T., Baker, P. N., et al. (2008). Higher risk of offspring schizophrenia following antenatal maternal exposure to severe adverse life events. *Arch. Gen. Psychiat, 65*, 146-152.

Kilpatrick, D. G., Koenan, K. C., Ruggiero, K. J., Acierno, R., Galea, S., Resnick, H. S., et al. (2007). The serotonin transporter genotype and social support and moderation of posttraumatic stress disorder and depression in hurricane-exposed adults. *Am. J. Psychiatry, 164*, 1693-1699.

Krystal, J. H., Perry, E. B., Gueorguieva, R., Belger, A., Madonick, S. H., Abi-Dargham, A., et al. (2005). Comparative and interactive psychopharmacologic effects of ketamine and amphetamine. *Arch. Gen. Psychiatry, 62*, 985-995.

Ladd, C. O., Huot, R. L., Thrivikraman, K. V., Nermeroff, C. B., Meaney, M. J., & Plotsky, P. M. (2000). Longterm behavioral and neuroendocrine adaptations to adverse early experience. In E. A. Meyer & C. B. Saper (Eds.), *Progress in brain research: Vol 122. The biological basis for mind-body interactions.* Amsterdam: Elsevier.

Lieb, K,. Zanarini, M., Schmahl, C., Linehan, M., & Bohus, M. (2004). Borderline personality disorder. *Lancet, 364*, 453-461.

Lieberman, J. A., & Stroup, T. S. (2011). The NIMH-CATIE schizophrenia study: What did we learn? *Am. J. Psychiatry, 168*, 770-775.

Losel, F. (1998). Treatment and management of psychopaths. In D. J. Cooke, A. E. Fourth, & R. D. Hare (Eds.), *Psychopathy: Theory, research, and implications for society* (pp. 303-354). Dordrecht, Netherland: Kluwer Academic Publishers.

Lynch, T. R., Trost, W. T., Salsman, N., & Linehan, M. M. (2007). Dialectical behavior therapy for borderline personality disorder. *Ann. Rev. Clin. Psych., 3*, 181-205.

March, J. S., & Franklin, M. E. (2006). Cognitive-behavioral therapy for pediatric obsessive-compulsive disorder. In B. O. Rothbaum (Ed.), *Pathological anxiety: Emotional processing in etiology and treatment* (pp. 147-165). New York: Guilford Press.

Marsh, A. A., & Blair, R. J. R. (2008). Deficits in facial affect recognition among antisocial populations: A meta-analysis. *Neuroscience and Biobehavioral Reviews*, 32, 454-456.

Marsman, A., van den Heuvel, M. P., Klopm, D. W. J., Kahn, R. S., Luitjen, P. R., & Hulsoff Pol, H. E. (2011). Glutamate in schizophrenia: A focused review and meta-analysis of 1H-MRS studies. *Schizo. Bull.*

Mason, W. A., Kosterman, R., Hawkins, J. D., Herrenkohl, T. I., Lengua, L. J., & McCauley, E. (2004). Predicting depression, social phobia, and violence in early adulthood from childhood behavior problems. *J. Am. Acad. Child Adoles. Psychiatry 43*(3), 307-315.

Mathews, A., & MacLeod, C. (2005). Cognitive vulnerability to emotional disorders. *Annu. Rev. Clin. Psychol.,* 1(1), 167-195.

McMurray, R. G., Newbould, E., Bouloux, G. M., Besser, G. M., & Grossman, A. (1991). High-dose nalolone modifies cardiovascular and neuroendocrine function in ambulant subjects. *Psychoneuroendocrinology, 16,* 447-455.

McNally, R. J. (2013). Posttraumatic stress disorder and dissociative disorders. In P. H. Blaney, T. Millon, & S. Grossman (Eds.). *Oxford textbook of Psychopathology* (3rd ed.). Oxford, UK: Oxford University Press.

Meewisse, M.-L., Reitsma, J. B., de Vries, G.-J., Gerson, B. P. R., & Olff, M. (2007). Cortisol and post-traumatic stress disorder in adults. *British Journal of Psychiatry,* 191, 387-392.

Miller, G. (2011). Healing the brain, healing the mind. *Science,* 333, 514-517.

Mineka, S., & Zinbarg, R. (1996). Conditioning and ethological models of anxiety disorders: Stress-in-Dynamic context anxiety models. In D. Hope (Ed.), *Perspectives on anxiety, panic, and fear: Nebraska symposium on motivation.* Lincoln: University of Nebraska Press.

Mineka, S., & Zinbarg, R. (2006). A contemporary learning theory perspective on the etiology of anxiety disorders: It's not what you thought it was. *Am. Psychol.*, 61, 10-26.

Minzenberg, M. J., & Siever, L. J. (2006). Neurochemistry and pharmacology of psychopathy and related disorders. In C. J. Patrick (Ed.), *Handbook of the psychopathy* (pp. 251-277). New York: Guilford Press.

Muhlberger, A., Wiedemann, G., Herrmann, M. J., & Pauli, P. (2006). Phylo- and ontogenetic fears and the expectation of danger: Differences between spider- and flight- phobic subjects in cognitive and physiological responses to disorder-specific stimuli. *J. Ab. Psych.,* 115(3), 580-589.

Nayani, T. H., & David, A. S. (1996). The auditory hallucination: A phenomenological survey. *Psychol. Med.,* 26(1), 177-189.

Ohman, A. & Mineka, S. (2001). Fears, phobias, and preparedness: Toward an evolved module of fear and fear learning. *Psychol. Rev.,* 108, 483-22.

Otway, L. J., & Vignoles, V. L. (2006). Narcissism and childhood recollections: A quantitative test of psychoanalytic predictions. *Pers. Social Psychol. Bull., 32,* 104-116.

Paris, J. (2007). The nature of borderline personality disorder: Multiple dimensions, multiple symptoms, but one category. J. *Pers. Disord., 21(*5), 457-473.

Pfammatter, M., Junghan, U. M., & Brenner, H. D. (2006). Efficacy of psychological therapy in schizophrenia: Conclusions from meta-analyses. *Schizo. Bull., 32*(S1), S64-S80.

Piet, J., & Hougaard, E. (2011). The effect of mindfulness-based cognitive therapy for prevention of relapse in recurrent major depressive disorder: A systematic review and meta-analysis. *Clin, Psychol. Rev.,* 31(6), 1032-1040.

Pollack, M. H., & Simon, N. M. (2009). Pharmacotherapy for panic disorder and agoraphobia. In M. M. Antony & M. B. Stein (Eds.), *Oxford handbook of anxiety and related disorders* (pp. 295-307). New York: Oxford University Press.

Powers, M. B., Halpern, J. M., Ferenschak, M. P., Gillihan, S. J., & Foa, E. B. (2010). A meta-analytic review of prolonged exposure for posttraumatic stress disorder. *Clin. Psychol. Rev.,* n.p.

Purcell, R., Pathe, M., & Mullen, P. E. (2001). A study of women who stalk. *Am. J. Psychiatry,* 35(2), 121-136.

Rachman, S., Radomsky, A. S., & Shafran, R. (2008). Safety behaviour: A reconsideration. *Behav. Res. Ther.,* 46(2), 163-173.

Rachman, S. J., Shafran, R., & Riskind, J. (2006). Cognitive vulnerability to obsessive-compulsive disorder. In L. B. Alloy & J. H. Riskind (Eds.), *Cognitive vulnerability to emotional disorders* (pp. 235-249). Hillsdale, NJ: Lawrence Erlbaum.

Reinecke, M. A., Washburn, J. J., & Becker-Weidman, E. (2007). Depression and suicide. In F. M. Dattilio & A. Freeman (Eds.), *Cognitive behavioral strategies in crisis intervention* (pp. 68-92). New York: Guilford Press.

Riggins-Casper, K. M., Cadoret, R. J., Knutson, J. F., & Langbehn, D. (2003). Biology-environment interaction and evocative biology-environment correlation: Contributions of harsh discipline and parental psychopathology to problem adolescent behaviors. *Behav. Gen.,* 33, 205-220.

Roemer, L., Orsillo, S. M. & Barlow, D. H. (2002). Generalized anxiety disorder. In D. H. Barlow (Ed.), *Anxiety and its disorders* (2nd ed, pp. 477-515). New York: Guilford.

Rothschild, A. J., Williamson, D. J., Tohen, M. F., Schatzberg, A., Andersen, S. W., Van Campen, L. E., et al. (2004). A double-blind, randomized study of olanzapine and olanzapine/fluoxetine combination for major depression with psychotic features. J. *Clin. Psychopharm.,* 24(4), 365-373).

Roy-Byrne, P. P., & Cowley, D. S. (2007). Pharmacological treatments for panic disorder, generalized anxiety disorder, specific phobia, and social anxiety disorder. In P. E. Nathan & J. M. Gorman (Eds.), *A guide to treatments that work* (pp. 395-430). New York: Oxford University Press.

Ruck, C., Karlsson, A., Steele, D., Edman, G., Meyerson, B. A., Ericson, K., et al. (2008). Capsulotomy for obsessive compulsive disorder. Long terms follow up of 25 patients. *Arch. Gen. Psychiatry,* 65, 914-921.

Schmahl, C., & Bremner, J. D. (2006). Neuroimaging in borderline personality disorder. *J. Psychiatr. Res.,* 40(5), 419-427.

Schmidt, N. B., Richey, J. A., Maner, J. K., & Woolaway-Bickel, K. (2006). Differential effects of safety in extinction of anxious responding to a CO-sub-2 challenge in patients with panic disorder. *J. Abn. Psych.,* 115(2), 341-350.

Seeman, P. (2011). All roads to schizophrenia lead to dopamine supersensitivity and elevated dopamine D2high receptors. *CNS Neuroscience and Therapeutics, 17,* 118-132.

Sernyak, D. L., Leslei, D. L., Alarcon, R. D., Losonczy, M. F., & Rosenheck, R. (2002). Association of diabetes mellitus with use of atypical neuroleptics in the treatment of schizophrenia. *Am. J. Psychiatry, 159,* 561-566.

Smoller, J. W., Gardner-Schuster, E., & Misiaszek, M. (2008). Genetics of anxiety: Would the genome recognize the DSM? *Depression and Anxiety,* 25(4), 368-377.

Stein, M. B., & Stein, D. J. (2008). Social anxiety disorder. *Lancet,* 371(9618), 1115-1125. Tandon, R., Nasrallah, H. A., & Keshavan, M. S. (2010). Schizophrenia, "just the facts" 5. Treatment and prevention past, present, and future. *Schizophrenia Research,* 122, 1-21.

Thase, M. E., & Denko, T. (2008). Pharmacotherapy of mood disorders. *Ann. Rev. Clin. Psych., 4,* 53-91.

Tienari, P., Wynne, L. C., Sorri, A., Lahti, I., Laksy, K., Moring, J., et al. (2004). Genotype-environment interaction in schizophrenia-spectrum disorder. *Brit. J. Psychiatry,* 184, 216-222.

Waddington, J. L., O'Callaghan, E., Youssef, H. A., Buckley, P., Lane, A., Cotter, D., et al. (1999). Schizophrenia: Evidence for a "cascade" process with neurodevelopmental origins. In E. Z. Susser, A. S. Brown, & J. M. Gorman (Eds.), *Prenatal exposures in schizophrenia* (pp. 3-34). Washington, DC: American Psychiatric Press.

Wilson, E. J., MacLeod, C., Mathews, A., & Rutherford, E. M. (2006). The causal role of interpretive bias in anxiety reactivity. *J. Abn. Psych., 115*(1), 103-111.

Wong, D. F., Wagner, H. N., Jr., Tune, L. E., Dannals, R. F., Pearlson, G. D., Links, J. M., et al. (1986). Positron emission tomography reveals elevated D2 dopamine receptors in drug-naive schizophrenics. *Science, 234,* 1558-1563.

Yoo, S. Y., Jang, J. H., Shin, Y. W., Kim, D. J., Park, H. J., Moon, W. J., et al. (2007). White matter abnormalities in drug-naive patients with obsessive-compulsive disorder: A diffusion tensor study before and after citalopram treatment. *Acta Psychiatrica Scandinavica,* 116(3), 211-219.

Zanarini, M. C., Frankenburg, F. R., Hennen, J., Reich, D. B., & Silk, K. R. (2005). The McLean Study of Adult Development (MSAD): Overview and implications of the first six years of prospective follow-up. *J. Personal. Discord., 19,* 505-523.

Zvolensky, M. J., Eiffert, G. H., Lejeuz, C. W., & McNeil, D. W. (1999). The effects of offset control over 20% carbon-dioxide-enriched air on anxious response. *J. Abn. Psychol.*, 108, 624-632.

Social Psychology

Chapter Eleven

WHAT IS SOCIAL PSYCHOLOGY?

Social Psychology explores how group situations influence an individual's behavior and, vice versa, how a person influences a group dynamic. Social psychology similarly examines how individuals influence one another. This section examines some major processes within this psychological subfield, such as: social cognition, social influence, and social relations.

SOCIAL COGNITION

Social cognition, or how we perceive other people and ourselves, incorporates the following concepts: attribution, attitude and prejudice. *Attribution* refers to our perception of what causes another person's behavior. However, our process of discovering what causes other peoples' behavior is prone to errors. *Fundamental attribution error* (FAE) refers to our tendency to perceive the *personality* of another person as the singularly direct cause for that person's behavior, without taking into consideration any possible *situational* factors (Hooper et al., 2015). For example, when someone cuts us off on the highway, we are very quick to exclaim "what in idiot!" But what if that person is rushing his pregnant wife, who is going into labor, to the hospital? We also engage in attribution thinking whenever we explain *our own* behavior. *Self-serving bias*, for example, is our tendency to perceive our success as resulting from our own personality and personal initiatives, while blaming our failures on external, situational factors. This is typically done so that the individual is able to maintain positive self-esteem and a positive public image (Wiggin & Yalch, 2015). Here is an example: When I was a college student, I went to a bank to deposit a check. The bank teller was a very attractive woman. I was embarrassed to ask her out since she did not give me any cues signifying her interest. A few days later a card with the bank's logo arrived in the mail. It read: "Thank you so much for coming, and I hope to see you again." Signed by the attractive bank teller. That note gave me an incredible confidence boost. I was convinced

Figure 1. We are often very quick to judge others, even when we do not know the other person's situation.

that she liked me. I attributed my success to my personality and looks, and I was ready to act upon her signal. During my next visit to the bank I very confidently asked her out. As I expected, she gave me her phone number without hesitation. On our date, I thanked her for the card with which she revealed that she liked me. Then, she asked "What card? Oh, you mean the one that my coworker Edward sent to all of the customers?" I was convinced that my success was due to her liking my personality, when in reality the bank has a practice of sending those cards to every member. Without the card, I would not have asked her out, considering how many men were probably already pursuing her. But, sometimes, ignorance is bliss.

Another example of FAE exhibition is during gameplay, say soccer, baseball, tennis or basketball. When we lose, we blame it on the situational factors such as an unfair referee, a non-regulated court or field, insurmountably difficult or cheating opponents, unbearable weather, or a lack of luck. We do not say that we lacked motivation, creativity, stamina, precision, determination, or skill, but instead focus on external circumstances (situational) that prevented us from winning. How do we explain this tendency to attribute success to ourselves, and our failures to outside forces? The answer is known as the *actor-observer effect*. This effect states that when we analyze our own behavior we are like an actor who is aware of his/her mental processes as well as the

situation he/she is in. Since we are aware of our situation, we take into consideration the outside world, but when we are just observers of others we are unable to grasp their position of the situation (Blanchard-Fields et al., 2007). FAE seems to happen more in individualistic societies (in the USA, for example) where people are perceived as responsible for their own successes (Peng et al., 2000), and less in collectivistic societies where people are seen as members of a larger social network whose behavior is largely influenced by cultural expectations and codependence (Blanchard-Fields et al., 2007).

Figure 2. When a player loses a tennis match, we rarely attribute the failure to an annoying crowd, a slippery court, or an injury. Instead we place the blame on some personality aspect (like being disturbed by a recent breakup).

SOCIAL COGNITION: ATTITUDES

An attitude is a *learned* tendency to respond positively or negatively to a particular person, event, or object. An attitude consists of a feeling (or feelings), behavior (action or actions) and cognitions (thoughts or beliefs). What is your attitude about a technology that would allow us to read someone's mind? Someone may have a bad feeling about this. He or she may think that this would be an invasion of privacy. Their bad feeling would dictate how the person then acts. This person may participate in some public gathering that protests against this hypothetical technology. All this, the negative feelings and the corresponding actions, are what make up the attitude towards that technology. Attitudes are formed via learning, specifically through *direct contact* (a child eats peanuts, has an allergic reaction, and forms a negative attitude towards peanuts), *direct instruction* (a teacher delivers information about the dangers of drugs and the student adopts the same attitude) and *observational learning* (a child witnesses their parents enjoying a certain band, and starts liking the same band too). But attitudes are not set in stone; they are prone to alteration. *Attitude change* can occur through persuasion and cognitive dissonance. *Persuasion* is a process of altering a person's belief or a course of action by relying on an argument or emotional/logical pleading. It has been proven that a persuasion is most successful if the person doing the convincing is: attractive, seen as trustworthy or similar to the audience, and perceived as an expert. An exceptionally successful persuasion requires a clear and well-organized message. Other practices used to ensure persuasion include: logically acknowledging both sides of the argument, employing a *moderate* amount of fear ("you must elect me president since only I will be able to save us from unavoidable disaster), and providing information on what the person can do to avoid the problem. Audiences most susceptible to persuasion are individuals between the ages of 16 and 25 (Ciccarelli et al., 2017).

Figure 3. What are the ingredients of successful persuasion?

An attitude can also change due to a mental process called *cognitive dissonance*. This discrepancy occurs when our thoughts do not match our actions, which creates discomfort. For example, consider a priest who preaches about the importance of forgiveness, yet does not truly forgive others. He is aware of this contradiction, which starts to bother him producing an inner frustration and tension. How he can deal with this cognitive dissonance? He can change his attitude about forgiveness, not believe in that notion any longer, perhaps never preaching about that subject again. This way there is no inconsistency between his beliefs and actions. On the other hand he could adopt a more forgiving nature so that his actions are synchronized with his attitude (Huffman & Sanders, 2017)

PREJUDICE

Prejudice refers to an unsupported and negative attitude towards members of a particular group. Since prejudice is an attitude, it contains a negative action of discrimination against specific individuals. The cognitive component of prejudice is a *stereotype*, an overgeneralized negative belief encompassing all members of a group (Fiske, 1998). Different types of prejudice include:

prejudice towards teenagers, the elderly, ethnic groups or races, those from different economic level, of different sexual orientation, etc. One of the most prevalent types of prejudice is a perception of an *in-group* and *out-group*, commonly manifested as an "us" versus "them" mentality. When a person identifies with all members of a group, that group becomes their in-group, and consequently everyone outside of the group is seen as a detached, out-group (Hawstorne, et al., 2002). *In-group favoritism* is an observation that in-group members perceive themselves as being more attractive, having better personalities and deserving more resources compared to the out-group members (Effron & Knowles, 2015, Hoogland et al., 2015; Sierksma et al., 2015). The out-group is usually looked down upon, increasing the self-esteem of the members of the in-group (Festinger, 1954). The out-group homogeneity effect is a tendency to perceive the out-group members as more alike and less diverse than the members of an in-group. This effect can easily lead to stereotypes (Brewer, 2015; Kang & Lau, 2013). Discrimination of an out-group usually is a form of *scapegoating*, a process where an out-group serves as a target for the frustration of the in-group. For example, the in-group of Nazi members exterminated the out-groups of Jews, Gypsies and Homosexuals (to name a few out-groups), as they believed this to be the final solution to the worlds problems. The AIDS epidemic of the 80s was initially blamed on homosexuals, yet the HIV virus was actually most likely contracted by chimpanzee hunters in West Africa whose blood was infected with the virus. When the housing market crashed in 2008, the working class was blamed for buying houses they could not afford yet the true irresponsibility lies with the lenders and bankers who allowed the haphazard purchases (Huffman & Sanders, 2017).

Figure 4. A popular, fun-loving in-group.

But what causes prejudice? In line with classical conditioning, repeated displays of negative images associated or paired with a group of people (or members of a particular group) can influence prejudice (Gatino & Tartaglia, 2015). I witnessed this first-hand in the 1990s prior to a war between different ethnic groups in my home country of Yugoslavia. I am Serbian and went to visit a Croatian friend. We watched TV with her parents and I was shocked to see a Serbian death camp built to imprison Croatians during World War II (in the 1940s). When I returned back to Serbia I saw on TV the same death camp, but this time the Serbian news stated that the Croatians had built it to imprison Serbs! It became obvious that the media was being manipulated in order to create a stereotype of an ethnic out-group, in this case the Croatians. Why? To stimulate prejudice, and create a fuel for the war (the war broke Yugoslavia into Croatia, Serbia, and other countries). The formation of prejudice can also be influenced by a lack of critical thinking. One of critical thinking's major aspects is to verify the credibility of information that presented to us; when we absorb new information critical thinking allows us to consider the source of the information. Is it something that we heard from a friend of a friend? Did it come from a reputable research study? Even if the information came from a trustworthy study, typically one research study is not enough. The most credible study is that which is replicated in completely different labs.

Personal expectations and treatment can influence prejudice as well. For example, a teacher named Jane Elliot informed the blue-eyed children that they are special, destined to succeed. She gave them extra time at recess and lunch. She also kept them separated from the brown-eyed children in the class. Elliot was critical of brown-eyed children, and found out that the blue-eyed children criticized them too, belittled them and even attacked them. Soon it became apparent that the brown-eyed students were underperforming on their tests compared to the blue-eyed students. However, when Elliot reversed the situation, she started treating the brown-eyed children as being superior and the blue-eyed children as inferior. Soon, the blue-eyed children underperformed on their tests too. This was an amazing demonstration of how it is easy to induce prejudice and discrimination as well as to influence mental processes and behaviors on others via our expectations (Peters, 1971). Another study demonstrated the power of self-fulfilling prophecy, or expectations that embody themselves in reality. In the 1960s two researchers, Rosenthal and Jacobsen, administered an intelligence test to students. Then, they randomly selected a group of the students, and informed their teachers that those particular students had the best chance to perform well at school. The teachers were not aware of the random nature of this identification. In reality, some of those students did not perform exceptionally well on the test, so the researchers intentionally misrepresented the facts to teachers. However, at the end of the school year these students (the "bloomers"), who were identified as most likely to succeed, really did have the best scores in the class. Most likely their success was due to their teachers' high expectations of them. The teachers acted upon their expectations and provided more attention and encouragement to the "bloomers" than other students. The positive treatment led to a better performance on the part of the students. (Grisson et al., 2017).

Figure 5. Who is smarter, blue-eyed or brown-eyed children? What did Elliot's study show? Does eye-color make a difference?

PREJUDICE: HOW TO REDUCE IT?

Prejudice can be reduced when people are encouraged to *cooperate* instead of compete. A famous study from the 1960s by Muzafer Sherif proves this point. He divided teenage boys into two groups, kept them in separate cabins and assigned certain tasks to be performed by each group. Boys from each group started to perceive the other group as an out-group. Then groups were encouraged to participate in competitive tasks. This in-group versus out-group perception and competition led to aggressive interactions between the groups (boys raiding each other's camps, for example). Then, Sherif created situations that required cooperation from boys of different groups to reach *superordinate goals*—goals that could not be reached by one group alone, but required the groups to join efforts to overcome common problem. Once the groups worked together, they reached their goals, and all members of both groups were equally rewarded. Prejudice in both groups towards the other group was successfully reduced (Sherif, 1966). Modern research also supports the idea that cooperation leads to a reduction in prejudice (Zhang, 2015).

Other studies have shown that prejudice can be reduced if groups or individuals are encouraged to contact each other, given that the contact has aspects of cooperation and recognition of *equal status* (meaning that some members are not assuming more power or higher status over others) (Pettigrew & Tropp, 2000). My personal experience supports these findings very well. Before war broke out in Yugoslavia (among different ethnic groups), members of different ethnic groups were encouraged by the president to maintain a close contact with each other as well as to cooperate in overcoming a superordinate goal. For example, a performance (a superordinate goal) was sponsored that included approximately a thousand high-school students. The performance very closely resembled the opening and closing ceremonies of the Olympic games. This performance took place in the capital of Yugoslavia. Students from all ethnic groups travelled from their states to the capital to live together in dormitories for about one month, spending entire days with each other. Time together included practicing

Figure 6. If ballerinas fail to work together, their *Swan Lake* performance will become desynchronized and difficult to follow

dance routines, a major part of the performance. In order to attain a high level of synchronous choreography, students needed to work together for many hours a day. After a hard day's work they would unwind and enjoy their time together in the dormitories and the city. By spending extensive amounts of quality time together, students gained a better understanding of people from other backgrounds. They came to understand that everyone, regardless of their ethnic group, was a unique individual. They discovered they all had many things in common (music, hobbies, dreams, sport activities, etc.). Students were equal in status, especially during the performance and as well as during practice. The realizations the students reached through their cooperation significantly reduced any possible prejudice. In 1980 the president who organized this annual performance died, and these performances (and other organized contacts) ceased about 5-6 years later. Why? Politicians from different ethnic groups wanted to become presidents of their own independent states, so that they could have a metaphorical piece of the pie as opposed to having a unified country with only one president who supervises them all.

Cognitive retraining is another method used to reduce prejudice. Individuals tend to see people as belonging to certain groups, categorized by race, ethnicity, and so on. By doing this we perceive people as very similar if not identical to the other people associated with the same group. This is typical thinking, but cognitive retraining is when we oppose this pattern of thought. We should focus on people for their unique personalities instead of as a generalized whole (Sanders & Huffman, 2017). *Cognitive dissonance* can also reduce prejudice. For example, take the claim "all gay men are effeminate." That's the attitude of many people, but when we encounter a masculine gay man, we experience dissonance since the observation does not match our attitude. What do we do? We rationalize the observation by considering the masculine gay man an exception. By saying this we correct the dissonance and go back to the old attitude that all gay men are effeminate. Until we meet many other masculine gay man. At that point we a forced to correct the dissonance by simply modifying our attitude ("not all gay men are effeminate").

Figure 7. You may be familiar with an image of a masculine cowboy riding ino the sunset. However, regardless of how masculine he appears, he can be attracted to men.

Another method of reducing prejudice is *empathy induction,* which refers to our ability to assume the perspective of another person. Consider the following study: research participants took a survey about their attitudes towards transgendered people. Then, participants were exposed to one of two conditions: either they were visited in their home by a transgendered individual or by a non-transgendered person. The transgendered person talked to the participant about what it is like to be transgendered, and the other individual talked about recycling. Then, the visitors asked the participants to recall the time when he/she was the subject of prejudice or judgment, and to recall how they felt. After that, the participant was asked to reflect on how his/her experience is related to someone who is a transgendered individual. Then, the participant took the same survey again. The point of this was to stimulate people to engage in empathetic thinking, taking the perspective of the transgendered person who is often treated with prejudice. The study found that the prejudice of the participants towards transgendered individuals was significantly reduced, regardless of whether or not they were visited by a transgendered individual (Broockman & Kalla, 2016).

Social influence is a field within social psychology that explores how others influence an individual's mental processes and behaviors, and how a person influences others. Aspects of social influence are conformity, obedience, and group processes. Let's examine conformity first. *Conformity* refers to changing one's behavior to match the behavior of others due to real or imagined group pressure. Asch (1951, 1956) demonstrated this concept very well. He formed a group of research participants in a room. Seven of them were *confederate* participants (meaning they were predetermined to behave the way Asch instructed them) and one was a *naïve* participant (meaning they did not know that the others were confederates). Asch showed two cards to the group, on one card there was a single line (A). On the other card there were three lines (B, C, and D). Only B was identical in length to A, and C and D were clearly shorter. However, when confederates all stated that C equaled A, the naïve participant was confused but concurred with what the others said. This tendency expressed itself in 1/3rd of the naïve participants (in conditions where no confederates chose the same conclusion, conformity did not occur). It was an amazing demonstration. Some later studies performed in the United States showed less conformity (Lalancette & Standing, 1990; Nicholson et al., 1985), while studies in other societies found levels of conformity similar to Asch's study (Neto, 1995). Studies in collectivistic cultures (such as Hong Kong and Japan) found more conformity (Kim & Markus, 1999). Gender does not appear to play a role when it comes to conformity (females and males conform at the same level), but when the behavior of interest is displayed in public, females tend to be more likely to conform to the majority consensus (Eagly & Carly, 2007).

But why do people conform in the first place? What motivates them to do so? One reason is that individuals tend to go

Figure 8. Non-conformity.

along with group norms, or expected behaviors displayed by members of a group. Sticking to accepted norms satisfies our need for approval and acceptance by a group. It also allows us to believe that we are not appearing foolish or strange. This type of conformity is called *normative conformity* (Oarga et al., 2015). *Informational conformity*, conversely, is when one assumes that other people have more information than us. In Asch's study, people who conformed to the majority consensus reported that they thought that the others must have seen something they did not. This clearly indicates one's lack of confidence in his/her own perception. *Referential conformity* is yet another source of conformity – going along with the behaviors of others whom we perceive as important in our lives, people we admire, respect, and want to resemble (such as parents, friends, teachers, movie stars) (Schultz et al., 2015).

Figure 9. A non-conformist in the midst of Nazi Germany. His defiance deserves the entire page and our admiration.

SOCIAL INFLUENCE: OBEDIENCE

Obedience is adhering to and following someone's orders/commands. In the 1960s researcher Stanley Milgram was very curious about why Nazi soldiers obeyed their officers who ordered them to kill millions. Milgram thought there was something wrong about the Nazi mind. He thought that a simple study would demonstrate the difference between the mind of a normal, healthy person and Nazi psychopaths. For his study, Milgram recruited research participants who were psychiatrically evaluated and confirmed as healthy subjects. Research participants were divided into "teachers" and "learners." The teachers' role was to read a list of words to the learners, and the learners were responsible for remembering the words and reciting them back to the teacher in a particular order. When a learner made a mistake, the teacher administered an electric shock. With every mistake the learner made, the voltage of the shock was increased by increments of 15 volts. The last switch (450 volts) was labeled "severe shock." Prior to the experiment, the teachers experienced a sample of a 45-volt shock, which is not pleasant at all, so the teacher is somewhat aware of the pain they are inflicting. A wall separated the teacher from the learner while an authority figure (presumably one of the researchers) remained in the room with the teacher, verbally persuading them to stay continue administering shocks if the teachers showed signs of hesitancy upon hearing the learner screaming and begging for the shocks to stop. Milgram hypothesized that only 1 percent of teachers would administer the final 450-volt shock. He was proved wrong as the results showed 65 percent of teachers eventually flipped the last switch! The authority figure was crucial in persuading the teachers to continue. They used verbal persuasions such as: "the experiment requires you to continue," "once we started, we cannot stop," "it is absolutely essential to continue." When the teachers asked, "are you going to take the responsibility (for the state of the individual receiving near fatal shock)?" the authority figure affirmed they would. This removal of responsibility allowed the teachers to administer shocks without attached guilt. Milgram's results were shocking since this behavior of the teachers was reminiscent of Nazi soldiers who were similarly obeying their superiors. Fortunately, the learners were not really shocked at all. They were *confederates*, actors who lead teachers to believe that they were shocking real people, which was not the case as they were merely acting like they were receiving shocks. This was a deceptive study, aimed at seeing how the teachers would react to believing that everything was real. This study has been replicated several times since with very similar results, where obedience in teachers varies from 61-66 percent (Slater et al., 2006; Corti & Gillespie, 2015).

Milgram varied the conditions in his study. One condition was having the orders come from an ordinary person, not an authority figure in a lab coat believed to be a researcher (as in the original study). Under that condition, only 20 percent of teachers administered the 450 volts level of electricity. When the authority figure left the room and issued orders by phone, again 20 percent of teachers administered the 450 volt shock. When the learner was not in a separate room from the teacher, but was instead only a matter of feet away from the teacher, 40 percent of teachers administered the final shock. When the teacher had to hold the learner's hand on the shock plate, 30 percent of people used the last switch. When the teacher watched two other teachers refuse to shock the learner, 10 percent of teachers used the last switch. When teachers watched two other teachers administer the final switch, 70 percent of the teachers used the last switch. When the teacher could chose the level of shock, only 3 percent of teachers used the last switch. These percentages varying over different circumstances, illustrate that varying the conditions can increase or decrease obedience (Sanders & Huffman, 2017). Other factors that contribute to

Figure 10. Full obedience to authority allows those in charge to be in total control. But obedience can be reduced.

obedience are *socialization* (when we are raised on the idea of listening and respecting authority figures) and *lowering of the moral guard* (the authority figure in Milgram's study did not appear to have evil intent; he was a researcher at Yale, and people lowered their moral guard not noticing that excessively electrocuting others is evil).

SOCIAL INFLUENCE: COMPLIANCE

Compliance refers to going along with a request of a group or another person. (In this case the person/group would not be a figure of authority, if they were then it would be considered obedience.) There are several techniques used to facilitate compliance. The first one we will talk about is the *foot-in-the door* technique, which consists of the following: a smaller, inconsequential request is made, and when the person complies, then a larger one follows. The person will most likely comply with the larger request, since people strive towards consistency in their behavior (Meineri & Gueguen, 2008). For example, a family member asks you to bring him/her a bottle of water from the refrigerator. After that another family member asks you to bring the entire box of bottles from the garage or basement and you will likely do so, as to remain consistent in your actions. Another technique to ensure compliance is *door-in-the face*. This consists of making an unreasonable request first which is presumably going to be rejected. After the initial rejection, a much more reasonable request is made and is usually complied with. I trick my daughter all the time using this technique. I tell her that mommy will come to do homework with her. Our daughter knows that her mother finds it necessary to spend about an hour on homework. My daughter starts hiding in the house rejecting the idea of spending such an unbelievable amount of time on homework. Then I offer that she can do the homework with me for 30 minutes, and she immediately agrees without question. Sometimes, however, when I try to do the homework with her for 30 minutes without invoking the "mother" trick, she hides in the house and does not want to do it. But why is this technique dubbed the door-in-the face technique? It recalls the practices

of door-to-door salespeople. If they ask for a high price for an item, we "slam the door in their face," in other words we say, in effect, "thanks, but no thanks." Then, they ask for a lower price, and we agree to it, without realizing that the reduced price is still a great deal for them.

The *low-ball technique* accomplishes compliance too. It is another trick and it proceeds as follows: once a commitment has been made, then the person who struck the deal with us increases their request. For example, a few years ago I found a professional-

Figure 11. I wish our homework experience were as idealistic as this one pictured here.

looking company to install laminate floors in my home. We agreed on a price. I was surprised that professionals could afford the work at such a reasonable price. Then, in the midst of the installment, I was confronted with several additional items that I needed to buy for the job to be done, even though those additional costs were never mentioned when we made the deal originally. If I did not agree to the additional costs, though, half of my home would go unfinished. Of course, I never recommended this company to other people, and from then on have only purchased services and items from reputable and well-known companies, even if they sometimes cost much more (Weyant, 1996; Bator & Cialdini, 2006).

SOCIAL INFLUENCE: GROUP PROCESSES

A *role* we play within a group can have a considerable influence on our behavior. A study conducted by Philip Zimbardo in the 1970s demonstrated the powerful impact certain roles can exert on us. In the basement of Stanford psychology department, Zimbardo created a setting that resembled prison with cells for inmates. He recruited research participants, young college men without any mental problems, and randomly assigned some of them to a group of "prisoners" and some to a group of "guards." The prisoners and guards received corresponding uniforms (the guards even received nightsticks, though physical abuse was never suggested or condoned) and were tasked with acting like their assigned roles. The participants were scheduled to live like this in the "Stanford Prison" for two weeks, while Zimbardo assumed the role was of prison warden. But the situation proved to get out of hand very rapidly. The study got out of control, guards started to behave in an abusive manner (preventing prisoners from eating, sleeping, and showering). The prisoners initially defied the guards until prisoners were psychologically crushed, and sunk into depression and passivity. Zimbardo even started to act like a real warden so much so that his girlfriend could not recognize him any longer. It is clear that prisoners, guards, and Zimbardo, got carried away with their respective roles. After 6 days the study had to be aborted. Still, the main reason why the experiment ended was Zimbardo's girlfriend's threat of leaving him if he didn't call it off (Zimbardo et al., 1977; Zimbardo, 1993) The study could have played out smoothly; Guards and prisoners could have mutually agreed on acceptable rules, reminding each other that it was just a study, not a real prison. They could have agreed to live in peace for the duration of the experiment, receive their paychecks, and call it a day. But the roles they were playing consumed them. In addition to the power of a role, this study demonstrated the power a particularly instigative *situation* (being a guard versus a prisoner) can have on the participants.

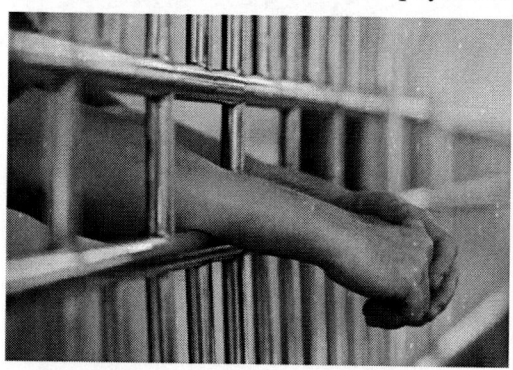

Figure 12. The Stanford Prison study showed that a role we are assigned can have a powerful impact on human behavior.

Another group-related process that has a powerful influence on individuals is *group decision-making*. When members of a group make decisions, these decisions are typically more in the middle of the road, meaning less prone to extremes. Since a group consists of different people and a decision is meant to satisfy as many as possible, there would be some compromise. This is, however, not the case. Groups actually tend to make more extreme decisions. For example, if the initial position of the group was risky, the final round of the decision-making process will give rise to an even riskier position. If the initial position was conservative, the final decision will be even more conservative. This tendency towards extremes in the group-decision making process is called *group polarization* (Davis & Mason, 2016; Keating et al., 2016).

Groupthink is another process that has a powerful influence on people. In groupthink it is more important that a group's members make a decision together, and less important that the decision be the best one possible. A regularly cited example is when Bush's administration launched a war on Iraq in 2003. What motivated the war was the belief that Saddam Hussein's regime had acquired weapons of mass destruction. Bush's administration, later on, said that the informant who provided this decisive information was simply wrong, and that it was a mistake to go after weapons that didn't exist. The questions became, "why was the claim not checked…why didn't anybody ask for more supporting facts from different informants about the weapons?" The answer seems to be: groupthink (Mackenzie, 2006; Rodrigues, Assmar & Jablonski, 2005). Another example comes to mind: a rock musician Sixto Rodriguez. Sixto was perceived by a record company in the 1970s to be a major rock star in the U.S. with the potential for a huge following. This record company saw his music as revolutionary. However, when his album was released, only a few copies were sold and it quickly sunk into obscurity. Sixto was unknown until 2012 when a documentary about him became an Oscar winner. In that documentary it was revealed that he had been famous in South Africa, Australia, and New Zealand before he attempted fame in the U.S., and that Sixto did not even know about his status of a rock hero until late 1990s! How is this related to groupthink? Well, the members of the American record label who published Sixto's album in the 1970s should have performed some type of a survey of the general public, calculating his true popularity in the U.S., before recording and releasing his record. Had they done this, they would have known that the American public was not interested in Sixto's type music at the time. However, the record company was absolutely convinced that Sixto was the next big thing. This perception that one cannot possibly fail, is called an *illusion of invulnerability*. In addition to illusion of invulnerability, why does groupthink occur? An *illusion of unanimous consensus* is often times an important factor. This illusion refers to an observation that even though there *appears* to be a unanimous consensus,

individual members still have doubts and disagreements that they do not vocalize. For groupthink to occur there is usually *pressure to conform* (whether spoken or unspoken) among members or by the group's leader. There is also a *bias towards out-group disagreeing members,* individuals who are perceived as not only less useful and insightful, but as enemies, weak, and inferior. Similarly, group members are sometimes convinced that their decision is moral or better, and thus the other group members display *no examination of the morality* of their decision (Janis, 1972, 1982).

Figure 13. What do you think about Sixto's songs? Do you enjoy music?

What can be done to reduce or even eliminate groupthink? Group members should be held responsible for their contributions. This will counteract the illusion of invulnerability as well as the lack of moral examination of decisions. Opinions of the people outside of the group should not only be considered but sought, which can also counteract the bias towards perceived out-group members. Members of groups should be encouraged to anonymously state their opposing views, free from direct criticism. This would counteract the illusion of unanimous consensus. Group leaders should not take a dominatingly strong stance on a given issue, which would counteract the pressure by an authority figure. A group member or members should have the role of "devil's advocate," or those who will challenge the group's decision and propose a counterargument leaving room for discussion on given topics (Hart, 1998; Moorhead et al., 1998).

Figure 14. How can we reduce groupthink?

FACILITATION, INHIBITION, LOAFING AND DE-INDIVIDUATION

Facilitation, inhibition, loafing and de-individuation are some additional group processes that effect individuals' actions. If a member of a group perceives a task as easy and benefits from the presence of others, then their performance will increase. This is called *social facilitation*. If a member of a group perceives a task as difficult, however, that person's performance will suffer as a result of the presence of a group. This is called *social impairment* (Aiello & Douthitt, 2001).

Figure 15. Presence of others makes it difficult to perform on some complex task (like chess).

What explains the influence of others? Their presence increases *arousal* in individuals, and the arousal and associated excitement aids the person's performance of a simple task. However, an increased arousal (induced by the presence of others) often works against one's performance when the task is too complicated (Rosenbloom et al., 2007). The presence of others has proved to have an impact on certain personality characteristics. Lazy individuals tend to perform better when they are not under the influence of a group. This is known as *social loafing*. A lazy person (a social loafer) hides their laziness in a group of people, by avoiding being evaluated alone and shifting the workload to other people in the group. When the same person works alone, however, they suddenly become the focus of their own evaluation and the work can no longer be shifted to other individuals (Suleiman & Watson, 2008). In collectivistic societies (China, for example) where people are more interdependent and feel more inherent responsibility to contribute to a group's effort, there is more social loafing than in individualistic societies such as the US (Menon et al., 1999).

When a group member experiences a reduction in his/her responsibility and a sense of personal identity, this is called *deindividuation (*Diener et al., 1980). People in a group feel a higher sense of anonymity than when they are alone. Due to this unknown and un-identified, de-individuated

340

feeling, people act more on their impulse (have less logical control of their behavior) (Cicarelli & White, 2017). De-individuated people exhibit a higher tendency for cheating and engaging in various other deviant behaviors (Chen & Wu, 2013). The Stanford prison study reflected de-individuation in the guards who "departed" from their usual, every day selves, assuming a role of vicious guards, completely separated from ties to the outside world. This de-individuation facilitated their devious behavior. Prisoners were given identical uniforms stripping them of their individuality, and they were addressed by their respective serial numbers instead of their names. Thus, they too were de-individuated. It is likely that their ordeal in the simulated prison was influenced by their loss of individuality. Zimbardo was also de-individuated, as is evident in the fact that his girlfriend threatened to leave him for becoming detached from his old self. Cults have a habit of de-individuating their members. Members often wear the same uniforms, have the same haircuts and are given new names by the cult leaders. De-individuation stimulates cult members to identify themselves with the group and blindly follow its rules, discouraging individuals from evaluating and challenging the leader's opinions and commands.

SOCIAL INTERACTION: AGGRESSION

Aggression is a mental process/behavior of intentionally harming another person. This harm can be physical or psychological (humiliation, for example). Aggression can be violent (physical harm) or non-violent (verbal criticism, gossip, insults, etc.) (Moore & Pepler, 2006). Further, aggression can be *instrumental* (when an assassin is paid to eliminate or wound a target) and *hostile* (an angry woman finds her husband cheating and runs him over with her car). Instrumental aggression has

for its ultimate goal something other than causing harm, such as earning money (as in assassin example). But hostile aggression is aimed at causing harm directly (physical and/or psychological damage to a victim) (Berkowitz, 1993; Anderson & Bushman, 2002). Research has proposed that any unpleasant event can be a cause of aggression. For example: heat, crowding, loud noises, provocation from another person, cigarette smoke, bad smells, and unsatisfactory life situations can cause aggression (Anderson, 1987).

Figure 16. Is this an instance of instrumental aggression or does she want to get rid of her ex-husband?

But, as we saw aggression can similarly result simply from doing a job with no true malice towards the victim (the assassin example). Biology acts as a factor influencing aggression. Specifically, identical twins (individuals with identical or nearly identical genetic makeup), raised separately from birth will both exhibit aggressive tendencies, given that at least one proves to have aggressive character. The degree of this similarity is higher in identical twins than in fraternal twins (those who do not have identical genetic material) (Miles & Carey, in 1997). Aside from genetic makeup, there are numerous examples of individuals who suffered brain damage and, as a result, became much more aggressive than before (Lavergne, 1997). Does testosterone trigger aggression? Men secrete more testosterone then women and men are much more often the aggressors in situations than women. However, concluding that testosterone leads to aggression does not logically follow, since studies show that when volunteers are injected with testosterone their aggression does not always increase (O'Connor et al., 2004). Similarly, boys during puberty are not more aggressive even though they are experiencing a surge of testosterone in their bodies (Bokhoven et al., 2006). Violent male criminals usually have higher levels of testosterone and lower levels of serotonin (Dabbs et al., 2001; Robbins, 1996), but do these chemicals stimulate aggression? On the basis of the previously mentioned study, this is most likely not the case. Perhaps these chemical imbalances in the violent criminals are a result, and not a cause of their inclination towards aggression. The influence of alcohol has been experimentally tested: volunteers who participated in a Milgram-like study administered more shocks to the learners if the teachers were under the influence of alcohol than those who were not (Bushman, 1997). But that begs the question: were the inebriated teachers more aggressive or were they simply more inclined to follow orders?

Zimbardo (1971) showed that enactment of a *role* can lead to aggression. Another study showed that one third of children who are abused, grow up to abuse others (Glaser et al., 2001; Oliver, 1993). What explains this observation of some abused individuals becoming abusers themselves, instead of recalling what happened to them and sheltering others from harm? Perhaps observational learning can provide an answer. Bandura (1980) showed in a study that when children observe aggressive adults harm a doll, children imitate those adult behaviors. So *learning* may influence emergence of aggression (including in those who were once abused). This is similarly indicated in studies on violence in *media* where even

Figure 17. Do females display more indirect aggression than men? Keep reading to find out.

a short-term exposure to violent media significantly increases the likelihood of children engaging in both physical and verbal aggression. In terms of aggression in men versus women, it is clear that proportionately many more men violently aggress than women (Archer, 2004). But when it comes to *indirect* aggression (speaking maliciously about another person, ostracizing others from a group) females and males do not differ significantly (Anderson et al., 2003). Why are men more physically aggressive than women? The true answer is that we really do not know. An educated guess would be that the media portrays men in such a light (there are rarely movies about armies of women fighting, yet so many movies about a lot of men fighting), and those males who view this become influenced to act on it. They may be trying to fulfill the masculine images with which they are presented. It is an educated guess, but it would fit into previous research findings.

How does one reduce aggression? The best method is often thought to be venting (called *catharsis*: punching a pillow, a punching bag, or vigorously exercising). However, research does not support the idea that catharsis reduces aggression (Kuperstok, 2008; Sebauer, 2014). A much better approach would be to engage in mental processes and behaviors that are *opposite* from our aggression or aggression of another person, meaning we should aim to relax ourselves or that other person, to engage in humor (but our humor should not be interpreted by the other person as ridicule). One could similarly attempt to show understanding of the other person's point of view (Maldonado et al., 2014). Additional approaches can reduce aggression, such as developing better communication skills (misunderstanding can stimulate aggression), locating conflict-mediation services, locating counseling services that work with individuals at risk for aggression, and locating anger management programs (American Psychological Association, 2013).

PROSOCIAL (HELPING BEHAVIOR)

Why do we help others? One view, called *evolutionary perspective* of helping, claims that we do so to ensure that our own genes' survive, since when we help our child or a relative, we are prolonging that person's (and our genes') survival (Richardson, 2015). Other studies indicate that we help others because we would also expect help from that person. Helping others makes us feel virtuous, which boosts our self-respect; it also helps us avoid feelings of distress and guilt. These are *egoistic* (self-centered) *motivations* for helping, meaning that we help others so that we can

ultimately benefit ourselves (Dickert et al., 2015; Schroeder & Graziano, 2015). However, some theories embrace *an empathy-altruism view* that states that we help others since encountering a suffering person awakens our empathy (perception of what it is like to be in that person's situation) which triggers our natural altruism, helping behavior for the sake of that other person alone (without our own benefit at all) (Batson, 2014). But why do we sometimes not help a person suffering? The more vague a situation becomes, the less likely we are to help. If it is not clear whether an

Figure 18. Would this person be helped quickly (or at all) if more people were present?

argument is typical behavior of a couple, for example, or if the argument appears to be escalating to violence, we are more likely to intervene. Many other factors determine the likelihood of a person helping. If a person is in a good mood, that person is more likely to help. If a bystander is a male, he is more likely to help a victim who is female. But, if the bystander is a female she is

343

less likely to help a female. Physically attractive people are more likely to be helped. Further, if a victim appears to be "deserving to be in a victim situation" (like a homeless individual who is perceived as lazy and careless, or drunk), that person is less likely to be helped (Richards & Lowe, 2003; Tukuitonga & Bindman, 2002).

An especially interesting phenomenon is the *bystander effect*, an observation that a person will be less likely to help if there are more people present at the scene. If there is only one person present during an individual's suffering, it is more likely that the bystander will help the victim (Darley & Latane, 1968). The bystander effect occurs due to a *diffusion of responsibility*; if more people are present, we tend to think that someone else will call the police, that the responsibility is spread (or diffused) to everyone involved. Diffusion of responsibility also occurs since we tend to think that others (anyone else) are more qualified to decide what to do (Glasman & Hadad, 2008; Leary & Forsyth, 1987).

ATTRACTION

What factors influence our attraction to another person? The answer is multi-factored: physical attractiveness, proximity, similarity and reciprocity of liking are some influences. In comparison to less attractive people, we *perceive* attractive people as more cooperative, poised, achieving, sociable, healthy, warm, and intelligent (Sofer et al., 2015; Mattes & Milazzo, 2014). Although we sometimes see couples where one of the partners is very good looking and the other one is not at all, it is still likely that people end up in relationships with someone who resembles their own level of attractiveness (McClintock, 2014). A way to increase attractiveness is by *flirting*. In terms of the nonverbal flirting, *smiling* and *eye-contact* do the trick, both behaviors indicate that the person is available and interested (Hall & Xing, 2015; Sprecher et al., 2015).

Proximity or geographical (spatial) closeness also increases attractiveness. People who are physically near each other tend to be more attracted to each other than people who don't live or work close together (Finkel et al., 2015). Of course, proximity can be a reason for frustration if you dislike somebody who is geographically close to you, but in most cases proximity does increase attractiveness. This is evident in online dating where this pattern is clear: more physical distance between people, less attraction and thus no action (Nguyen & Szymanski, 2012). Why is proximity so effective? The phrase "it grew on me" explains it. The more people experience something, the more they tend to like it. This

Figure 19. What are the factors that stimulate attraction in humans?

is known as the *repeated exposure effect*. Similar to this is our disposition to be less threatened by people with whom we are familiar (Konghtong et al., 2014; Yoshimoto et al., 2014).

It turns out the old saying "opposites attract" is misleading. People tend to stay together with others who are similar in terms of ethnic background, social class, interests, and attitudes (Watson et al., 2014; Brown & Brown, 2015; Neimayer & Mitchell, 1998). Romantic partners can enjoy a few differences they have, but more *similarity* is the key to a quality romantic relationship (Berscheid & Reis, 1998; Mc Pherson et al., 2011). *Reciprocity of liking* means that we have a tendency to like people who like us rather than people who don't like us. In a study by Curtis and Miller (1986) students were placed in groups of two. One member of each pair was chosen randomly, and some of these members were informed that the other member of their group really liked them, and other members were informed that the other member did not like them. When given a chance to meet and spend some time with the other member of their pair, those who were told they were liked acted in a warmer, more open, and friendlier way than those who were told that they were not liked. However, if a person has low self-worth, reciprocity of liking usually does not apply, since the person who does not like him/herself will always question why another person likes them. And mistrusting others can lead to a true dislike (self-fulfilling prophecy effect) (Murray et al., 1998).

LOVE IS ALL WE NEED

It is famously said that all we need is love. But what is love? Many psychologists have embraced Sternberg's view of love (1997). Sternberg views love as being composed of several aspects: intimacy, passion, and commitment. *Intimacy*, in his view, refers to emotional closeness, self-disclosure and high levels of familiarity/comfortableness with each other. This type of love is often seen in friends. *Passion*, on the other hand, is attraction, desirability, the physical aspect of love (feeling a sexual and emotional arousal towards another person), and a process of intense longing for another person. Sex, holding hands, and hugs are all manifestations of passion. *Commitment* is a decision to be with another person in a relationship. Commitment also includes a feeling of security, permanence and stability. When intimacy and passion dominate in a relationship, it is considered a *romantic love*, a basis for a more lasting relationship (Diamond, 2003). Romantic love has been identified in 147 out of 166 societies studied (Jankowiak & Fischer, 1992). Intimacy and

Figure 20. The frequent impact of the L (love) and C (commitment) words.

commitment dominating in a relationship is known as *companionate love*, which is seen in marriages where people lead intertwined lives involving children, paying bills, and passion that is less prominent than in romantic types of love (Gottman & Krokoff, 1989). Companionate love has been identified in the online dating world, and research shows that there is a higher marital satisfaction and a significantly lower divorce rate in companionate love that started online in comparison to non-online version of this type of love (Cacioppo et al., 2013). When intimacy, passion and commitment equally dominate in a relationship a couple has achieved a *consummate love*, the ideal form of love, an ultimate and fulfilling goal.

REFERENCES

Aiello, J. R., & Douthitt, E. A. (2001). Social facilitation from Triplett to electronic performance monitoring. *Group Dynamics: Theory, Research, and Practice,* 5(3), 163-180.

American Psychological Association (2013). Gun violence: Prediction, prevention, and policy. Public and Member Communications, Public Affairs Office. Washington, DC: American Psychological Association.

Anderson, C. A., & Bushman, B. J. (2002). Human aggression. *Annual Review of Psychology,* 53, 27-51.

Anderson, C. A. (1987). Temperature and aggression: Effects on quarterly, yearly, and city rates of violent and nonviolent crime. *Journal of Personality and Social Psychology,* 52(6), 1161-1173.

Anderson, C. A. (2003). Video games and aggressive behavior. In D. Ravitch & J. P. Viteritti (Eds.), *Kid stuff: Marketing sex and violence to America's children* (p. 157). Baltimore/London: The Johns Hopkins University Press.

Archer, J. (2004). Sex differences in aggression in real-world settings. A meta analytic review. *Review of General Psychology,* 8, 291-232.

Bandura, A. (1980). The social learning theory of aggression. In R. A. Falk & S.S. Kim (Eds.), The war system: *An interdisciplinary approach* (p.146). Boulder, CO: Westview Press.

Bator, R. J., & Cialdini, R. B. (2006). The nature of consistency motivation: Consistency, consistency, and inconsistency in a dissonance paradigm. *Social Influence,* 1, 208-233.

Batson, C. D. (2014). *The altruism question: Toward a social-psychological answer.* New York, NY: Psychology Press.

Berkowitz, L. (1993). Pain and aggression. Some findings and implications. *Motivation and*

Emotion, 17, 277-293.

Blanchard-Fields, F., Chen, Y., Horhota, M., & Wang, M. (2007). Cultural differences in the relationship between aging and the correspondence bias. *Journals of Gerontology Series B: Psychological Sciences and Social Sciences, 62*(6), 362-365.

Brewer, M. B. (2015). Motivated entitativity: When we'd rather see the forest than the trees. In S. J. Stroessner & J. W. Sherman (Eds.), Social perception from individuals to groups (pp.161-176). New York, NY: Psychology Press.

Broockman, D., & Kalla, J. (2016). Durably reducing transphobia: A field experiment on door-to-door canvassing. Science, 353, 220-224

Bushman, B.J. (1997). Effects of alcohol on human aggression: Validity of proposed explanations. In M. Galanter (Ed.), Recent developments in alcoholism. Vol. 1: *Alcohol and violence- Epidemiology, neurobiology, psychology, family issues* (pp.223-243). New York: Plenum Press.

Chen, V. H. H., & Wu, Y. (2013). Group identification as a mediator of the effect of players' anonymity on cheating in online games. *Behaviour & Information Technology, 34*(7), 658-667.

Ciccarelli, S. & Noland White, J., (2017). Psychology (5th ed.). Boston, MA: Pearson.

Corti, K., & Gillespie, A. (2015). Revisiting Milgram's cyranoid method: Experimenting with hybrid human agents. *The Journal of Social Psychology,* 155, 30-56.

Dabbs, J. M., Jr., Bernieri, F. J., Strong, R. K., Campo, R., & Milun, R. (2001). Going on stage: Testosterone in greeting and meeting. *Journal of Research in Personality,* 35, 27-40.

Davis, N. T., & Mason, L. (2016). Sorting and the split-ticket: Evidence from presidential and subpresidential elections. *Political Behavior.*

Dickert, S., Västfjäll, D., & Slovic, P. (2015). Neuroeconomics and dual information processes underlying charitable giving. In E. A. Wilhelms & V. F. Reyna (Eds.), *Neuroeconomics, judgement, and decision making* (pp.181-199).

Diener, E., Lusk, R., Defour, D., & Flax, R. (1980). Deindividuation: Effects of group size, density, number of observers, and group member similarity on self-consciousness and disinhibited behavior. *Journal of Personality and Social Psychology,* 39, 449-459.

Eagly, A. H., & Carli, L. L. (2007). *Through the labyrinth: The truth about how women become leaders.* Boston: Harvard Business School Press.

Effron, D. A., & Knowles, E. D. (2015). Entitativity and intergroup bias: How belonging to a cohesive group allows people to express their prejudices. *Journal of Personality and Social Psychology*, 108, 234-253.

Festinger, L. (1954). A theory of social comparison processes. *Human Relations*, 7, 117-140.

Fiske, S. T. (1998). Stereotyping, prejudice, and discrimination. In D. T. Gilbert & S. T. Fiske (Eds.), *The handbook of social psychology* (4th ed., Vol. 2, pp. 357-411). New York: McGraw-Hill.

Gattino, S., & Tartaglia, S. (2015). The effect of television viewing on ethnic prejudice against immigrants: A study in the Italian context. *International Journal of Intercultural Relations*, 44, 46-52.

Glaser, M., Kolvin, I., Campbell, D., Glasser, A., Leitch, I., & Farrelly, S. (2001). Cycle of child sexual abuse: links between being a victim and becoming a perpetrator. *British Journal of Psychiatry*, 189, 482-494.

Glassman, W.E., & Hadad, M. (2008). Chapter eight: Perspectives on social behaviour, altruism and bystander behavior. In William E. Glassman & Marilyn Hadad (Eds.), *Approaches to Psychology* (pp. 399-401). London: Open University Press.

Hart, P. (1998). Preventing groupthink revisited: Evaluation and reforming groups in government. *Organizational Behavior & Human Decision Processes*, 73(2-3), 306-326. Hoogland, C. E., Ryan Schurtz, D., Cooper, C. M., Combs, D. J. Y., Brown, E. G., & Smith, R.

Hoogland, H. (2015). The joy of pain and the pain of joy: In-group identification predicts schadenfreude and gluckschmerz following rival groups' fortunes. *Motivation and Emotion*, 39, 260-281.

Hooper, N., Erdogan, A., Keen, G., Lawton, K., & McHugh, L. (2015). Perspective taking reduces the fundamental attribution error. *Journal of Contextual Behavioral Science*, 4, 69-72.

Janis, I. (1972). *Victims of groupthink.* Boston: Houghton-Mifflin.

Kang, S.-M., & Lau, A.S. (2013) Revisiting the out-group advantage in emotion recognition in a multicultural society: Further evidence for the in-group advantage. *Emotion*, 13, 203-215.

Keating, J., Van Boven, L., & Judd, C. M. (2016). Partisan underestimation of the polarizing influence of group discussion. *Journal of Experimental Social Psychology*, 65, 52-58.

Kim, H., & Markus, H. R. (1999). Deviance or uniqueness, harmony or conformity? A cultural analysis. *Journal of Personality and Social Psychology*, 77, 785-800.

Kuperstock, N. (2008). Effects of exposure to differentiated aggressive films, equated for levels of interest and excitation, and the vicarious hostility catharsis hypothesis. Dissertation Abstracts International: Section B: The Sciences and Engineering, 68, 4806.

Lalancette, M.-F., & Standing, L. G. (1990). Asch fails again. *Social Behavior and Personality,* 18(1), 7-12.

Lavergne, G. M. (1997). *A sniper in the tower: The true story of the Texas Tower massacre.* New York: Bantam.

Leary, M. R., & Forsyth, D. R. (1987). Attributions of responsibility for collective endeavors. *Review of Personality and Social Psychology,* 8, 167-188.

Mackenzie, D. L. (2006) (Abstract only). Group hope. An antecedent of groupthink? Dissertation Abstracts International. Section B. The Sciences and Engineering Vol. 66 (10-B). Maldonado, R. C., DiLillo, D., & Hoffman, L. (2014). Can college students use emotion regulation strategies to alter intimate partner aggression-risk behaviors? An examination using I3 Theory. *Psychology of Violence*, 5, 46-55.

Meineri, S., & Gueguen N. (2008). An application of the foot-in-the-door strategy in the environment field. *European Journal of Social Sciences,* 7, 71-74.

Menon, T., Morris, M., Chiu, C. Y., & Hong, Y. I. (1999). Culture and the construal of agency: Attribution to individual versus group dispositions. *Journal of Personality and Social Psychology,* 76, 701-727.

Miles, D. R., & Carey, G. (1997). Genetic and environmental architecture of human aggression. *Journal of Personality and Social Psychology*, 72, 207-217.

Moore, T. E., & Pepler, D. J. (2006). Wounding words. Maternal verbal aggression and children's adjustment. *Journal of Family Violence*, 21, 89-93.

Moorhead, G., Neck, C. P., & West, M. S. (1998). The tendency toward defective decision making within self-managing teams: The relevance of groupthink for the 21st century. *Organizational Behavior & Human Decision Processes*, 73(2-3), 327-351.

Nero, F. (1995). Conformity and independence revisited. *Social Behavior and Personality,* 23(3), 217-222.

Nicholson, N., Cole, S., & Rocklin, T. (1985). Conformity in the Asch situation: A comparison between contemporary British and U.S. students. *British Journal of Social Psychology,* 24, 59-63.

Oarga, C., Stavrova, O., & Fetchenhauer, D. (2015). When and why is helping others good for well-being? The role of belief in reciprocity and conformity to society's expectations. European *Journal of Social Psychology,* 45, 242-254.

Oliver, J. E. (1993). Intergenerational transmission of child abuse: Rates, research, and clinical interpretations. *American Journal of Psychiatry*, 150, 1315-1324.

O'Connor, D. B., Archer, J., & Wu, F. C. W. (2004). Effects of testosterone on mood, aggression and sexual behavior in young men. A double-blind, placebo-controlled, cross-over study. *Journal of Clinical Endocrinology and Metabolism*, 89, 2837-2845.

Peng, L., Verkhratsky, A., Gu, L., & Li, B. (2015). Targeting astrocytes in major depression. *Expert Review of Neurotherapeutics*, 1-8.

Peters, W. A. (1971). *A class divided.* Garden City, NY: Doubleday.

Pettigrew, T. F., & Tropp, L. R. (2000). Does intergroup contact reduce prejudice? Recent meta-analytic findings. In S. Oskamp (Ed.), *Reducing prejudice and discrimination: Social psychological perspectives* (p. 93-114). Mahwah, NJ: Erlbaum.

Richards, C. F., & Lowe, R. A. (2003). Researching racial and ethnic disparities in emergency medicine. *Academic Emergency Medicine,* 10(11), 1169-1175.

Richardson, R. C. (2015). Evolutionary psychology, altruism, and kin selection. In T. Breyer (ed.), *Epistemological dimensions of evolutionary psychology* (pp. 103-115). New York, NY: Springer.

Robins, L. N. (1996). *Deviant children grown up*. Baltimore: Williams & Wilkins.

Rodrigues, A., Assmar, E. M. L., & Jablonski, B. (2006). (English abstract only). La psicología y la invasión de Irak (Psychology and the invasion of Iraq). *Revista de Psicologia Social,* 20, 387-398.

Rosenbloom, T., Shahar, A., Perlman, A., Estreich, D., & Kirzner, E. (2007). Success on a practical driver's license test with and without the presence of another testee. *Accident Analysis & Prevention*, 39(6), p. 1296-1301.

Sanderson, C., & Huffman, K., (2017) Real World Psychology (2nd ed.) USA: John Wiley & Sons.

Schroeder, D. A., & Graziano, W. G. (Eds.). (2015). *The Oxford handbook of prosocial behavior.* Oxford, UK: Oxford University Press.

Schulz, H. M. (2015). Reference group influence in consumer role rehearsal narratives. *Qualitative Market Research: An International Journal*, 18, 210-229.

Seebauer, L., Froß, S., Dubaschny, L., Schönberger, M., & Jacob, G. A. (2014). Is it dangerous to fantasize revenge in imagery exercises? An Experimental study. *Journal of Behavior Therapy and Experimental Psychiatry,* 45, 20-25.

Sherif, M.(1966). In common predicament: Social psychology of intergroup conflict and cooperation. Boston, MA: Houghton Mifflin.

Sierksma, J., Thijs, J., & Verkuyten, M. (2015). In-group bias in children's intention to help can be overpowered by inducing empathy. *British Journal of Developmental Psychology*, 33, 25-56.

Slater M., Antley, A., Davison, A., Swapp, D., Guger, C., Barker, C.,... Sanchez-Vives, M. V. (2006). A virtual reprise of the Stanley Milgram obedience experiments. PLoS ONE 1(1), e39.

Suleiman, J., & Watson, R. T. (2008). Social loafing in technology-supported teams. *Computer Supported Cooperative Work*, 17, 291-309.

Tukuitonga, C. F., & Bindman, A. B. (2002). Ethnic and gender differences in the use of coronary artery revascularization procedures in New Zealand. *New Zealand Medical Journal*, 115, 179-182.

Weyant, J. M. (1996). Application of compliance techniques to direct -mail requests for charitable donations. *Psychology and Marketing,* 13, 157-170.

Wiggin, K. L., & Yalch, R. F. (2015). Whose fault is it? Effects of relational self-views and outcome counterfactuals on self-serving attribution biases following brand policy changes. *Journal of Consumer Psychology*, 25, 259-472.

Zimbardo, P. G., Ebbeson, E. B., & Maslach, C. (1997). Influencing attitudes and changing behavior. Reading, MA: Addison-Wesley.

Zimbardo, P. G. (1993). Stanford prison experiment: A 20-year retrospective. Invited presentation at the meeting of the Western Psychological Association, Phoenix, AZ.

INDEX

A

Abraham Maslow · 18, 63
absolute refractory period · 143
accommodation · 103, 111, 204, 260
acetylcholine · 192, 238
action potential · 141, 142, 143, 144, 145, 147, 148, 171
actor-observer effect · 328
acute stress disorder · 308
addiction · 240
adolescence · 89, 222, 269
adulthood · 48, 232, 271, 272, 290, 322
aggression · 24, 341
Albert Bandura · 70
Alfred Adler · 55
all or none law · 144
alpha activity · 227
altruism · 343, 346, 348, 350
Alzheimer's disease · 191, 195, 196, 198
AMPA · 170, 171, 172, 174
amphetamines · 238
amygdala · 18, 169, 171, 187, 188, 192, 197, 208, 223, 275, 294, 295, 301, 302, 310, 313
anal stage · 45
anal-expulsive personality · 45
anal-retentive personality · 45
anaxonic synapse · 128
androgen hormones · 270
antagonistic (opposing) muscles · 109
anterograde amnesia · 187, 188, 189, 190
antisocial personality disorder · 293, 294
anxiety disorders · 298, 320, 322
archetype · 15, 51, 52
assimilation · 260
association · 41, 111, 154, 156, 169, 184, 229, 284, 311
astrocytes · 130, 131, 132, 148, 150, 350
attachment · 262, 279, 282, 284, 287, 288, 289
attention · 10, 225
attraction · 344
auto-immune condition · 95
automatic processing · 225
avoidant personality disorder · 297
axon collateral · 127
axon hillock · 139, 140, 141, 143, 144, 145
axon terminal · 124, 125, 127, 128, 130, 141, 143, 144, 147, 148, 237
axoplasm · 124, 125

B

B.F. Skinner · 16, 161
barbiturates · 237
basal nuclei · 94, 98, 167, 169, 189, 239, 240

basic anxiety · 60
basic needs · 64
behavioral definition · 24
behavioral genetics · 74
behaviorism · 17
belongingness and love needs. · 64
benzodiazepines · 237, 299, 304
beta activity · 227
binocular effects · 203
biological makeup · 253, 255, 256
bipolar disorder · 269, 308, 310, 311, 315, 318, 320
Blade Runner · 2
body dysmorphic disorder · 306
borderline personality disorder · 295, 316, 318, 319, 321, 323, 324
bottom-up processing · 206
brain death · 227
brain stem · 98, 105, 108, 116, 149, 238
brief psychotic disorder · 315
Broca's area · 164
bystander effect · 344

C

Carl Jung · 50
Carl Rogers · 18, 67
case study · 30, 31, 48, 186
castration anxiety · 46
cataplexy · 230
caudate nucleus · 94, 189, 305
causation · 26, 184, 217
central nervous system · 97, 98, 102, 104, 108, 130, 131, 132, 133
centration · 257, 258
chemically-sensitive channels · 137, 138, 139, 140
circadian rhythm · 226, 250
circadian rhythm · 226
classical conditioning · 17, 153, 154, 155, 156, 157, 160, 169, 172, 243, 330
cocktail party phenomenon · 201, 203
cognitive dissonance · 329
cognitive perspective · 17
cognitive retraining · 333
cognitive-behavioral approach · 302, 303
cognitive-behavioral technique · 303
collective unconscious · 15, 50, 51
colliculi · 98
coma · 113, 227
comorbidity · 94
companionate love · 345
compensate · 55, 127, 242
complexes · 50, 51, 228
compliance · 336
compulsions · 93, 94
concentration gradient · 136, 137, 142

concentration pressure · 135, 147
concrete operational stage · 258
conditioned response · 154, 155, 169, 243, 300
confabulation · 184
confirmation bias · 218
conformity · 334, 349, 350
connexins · 148
consciousness · 225, 245, 249
context-dependent memory · 180
controlled processing · 225
conventional morality · 267
convergence · 203
convergent ways of thinking · 218
correlation · 2, 6, 26, 184, 217, 324
cortex · 98, 105, 164, 165, 166, 167, 174, 187, 188, 189,
    190, 191, 195, 197, 201, 207, 229, 232, 240, 244,
    245, 248, 274, 275, 287, 295, 302, 305, 309
cranial nerves · 100, 103, 104, 108, 110, 111, 116, 118
creativity · 73, 218, 219
creative power of self · 56, 58
critical period · 254
cross-cultural perspective · 16
curcumin · 192
cyclothymic disorder · 311
cytoplasm · 124

D

Dark Ages · 6, 7
declarative memories · 181
defense mechanism · 39, 40, 42, 46, 85
delta activity · 228
delusional disorder · 315
delusions · 192, 311
dendrites · 124, 171
dendritic spines · 124, 192
dependent personality disorder · 298
dependent variable · 25, 27, 29
depolarization · 139, 141, 143, 144, 145, 148, 170, 171
depressants · 237
depressive disorder · 311, 323
disinhibited social engagement disorder · 308
divergent thinking, · 218
door-in-the face · 337
dopamine · 94, 138, 167, 173, 175, 237, 238, 239, 240,
    242, 245, 294, 305, 309, 313, 314, 315, 324, 325
dorsal root · 106, 107
dream analysis · 41, 42, 56
drugs · 27, 28, 30, 215, 217, 237, 238, 239, 240, 242,
    243, 244, 309, 329
DSM-V · 293
dyad · 64
dysthymia · 311

E

echoic sensory memory · 179
Edward Thorndike · 16, 161

Edward Tolman · 162
ego · 14, 36, 37, 38, 39, 40, 41, 42, 43, 44, 45, 46, 77,
    276, 278, 281, 288, 289, 296
egocentrism · 257, 258
Electra complex · 47
electrical synapse · 148
electroconvulsive therapy · 310
electroencephalography · 227
electromyogram · 229, 249
electrostatic gradient · 135, 142
electrotonic signal · 138
empathy induction · 333
empiricism · 9
encoding · 177, 199
end button · 127
environmental influence · 205, 253, 254, 255, 275
enzymatic degradation · 148
episodic · 177, 181, 186, 188, 190, 195, 199, 222
Erik Erikson · 62, 275
estrogen · 270, 271
evolution · 19, 283
evolutionary perspective · 18, 343
excitatory neurotransmitters · 137, 141
excitatory post-synaptic potential (EPSP). · 139
excoriation · 306
explicit memories · 181, 189
extracellular fluid · 124, 130, 134, 135, 136, 137, 142
extraverted · 52, 53, 54, 73

F

false memories · 184, 185
fetal alcohol syndrome · 244, 269, 290
fictional finalism · 56
fight or flight response · 112
first-born child · 57
flashbulb memory · 177, 186
focal point · 235
follicle-stimulating hormones · 270
foot-in-the door technique · 336
formal operational stage · 259, 260
free association · 41
functional fixedness · 218
functionalism · 12
fundamental attribution error · 327

G

GABA · 230, 237, 238, 239, 299
ganglion · 107, 108, 226
gap junction · 148
gender role · 215
generalized anxiety disorder · 298, 316, 317, 319, 324
Gestalt · 11, 12, 174, 202
G-factor · 209
glial cells · 124, 126, 130, 131, 132, 133, 149
globus pallidus · 94
glutamate · 131, 167, 170, 171, 237, 239, 244, 314

gonadotropins · 270
Gordon Allport · 72
gratification · 37, 44
gray matter · 106, 107
group polarization · 338
groupthink · 338

H

hallucinations · 4, 23, 77, 192, 207, 229, 230, 239, 241, 292, 309, 310, 311, 312, 314, 320
Hans Eysenck · 73
Henry Molaisson · 186, 189
hippocampus · 99, 149, 167, 171, 177, 178, 181, 187, 188, 191, 192, 195, 197, 239, 244, 248, 295, 307, 313
histrionic personality disorder · 297
hoarding disorder · 306
Humanism · 7
humanistic perspective · 18, 63
hyperpolarization · 140, 142, 143
hypnosis · 185, 234, 235, 245, 247, 248
hypothalamus · 96, 191, 226, 231, 238, 239, 240
hypothesis · 24, 27, 28, 163, 262, 320, 349

I

iconic memory, · 178
id · 14, 36, 37, 38, 39, 40, 41, 42, 43, 44, 45, 46, 47, 48, 174
ideal-self · 68, 69
illusion · 12, 41, 68, 207, 220, 221, 229, 281, 339
illusion of unanimous consensus · 339
immunity · 93
Implicit memories · 181, 189
impulses · 14, 15, 36, 37, 38, 42, 44, 48, 50, 78, 99, 145, 150, 237, 240, 261, 273, 295
incongruence · 68
independent variable · 25, 27
individuation · 52
inferiority complex · 55
inferiority feeling · 55, 56
influx · 140, 143
in-group favoritism · 330
inhibitory neurotransmitter · 138, 140
inhibitory post-synaptic potential (IPSP · 140
innervation · 104, 105, 106, 107, 110, 111, 112, 115, 116, 145
insomnia · 231, 308
intelligence · 86, 201, 209, 212, 213, 214, 219, 220, 221, 222, 280
intelligence quotient (IQ) · 212
interference view · 182
internal conflict · 39
interoceptive exposure · 303
interview · 19, 30, 75, 183
introspection · 10, 11
introverted · 52, 53, 54, 73, 81
inventories · 76

ions · 123, 124, 126, 134, 135, 136, 137, 138, 139, 140, 141, 142, 143, 144, 145, 147, 148, 168, 170, 171, 244

J

Jean Piaget · 255, 279
Jonah Complex · 66
jump-like conduction · 145

K

Karen Horney · 59
K-complex · 228, 246
Korsakoff's syndrome · 195, 196, 244, 190

L

language development · 265
latent learning · 162
learned helplessness · 163
leutenizing hormones · 270
Lev Vygotsky · 261
local signal · 138
long-term depression · 172, 173
long-term memory · 149, 167, 180, 194
love · 345

M

maintenance rehearsal, · 179
Malleus Malleficarum · 6
mania · 77, 308, 309, 311
MBTI test · 54
medial temporal lobe · 187, 194
meditation · 236, 247
melatonin · 226, 246
membrane · 125, 128, 134, 135, 136, 137, 138, 139, 140, 141, 142, 143, 144, 147, 148, 170, 241
membrane potential · 134, 139
memory consolidation · 188, 228, 234, 248
menopause · 271, 285
meta-needs · 64
methamphetamines · 238
microglia · 131, 132
midbrain · 98, 167, 173, 237, 238, 239
minimally conscious state · 227
mirror neurons · 165
misinformation effect · 183, 184
MMPI · 77, 83
monocular effects · 204
moral development · 267
motion parallax · 204
motivated forgetting · 182
motor cranial nerves · 103
myelinated axons · 107, 126, 127, 144, 145

N

narcissism · 46, 77, 296, 320
narcissistic personality disorder · 296
narcolepsy · 230, 231, 247, 250
nature · 5, 7, 18, 71, 79, 87, 135, 142, 210, 220, 253, 281, 282, 307, 323, 329, 331, 346
negative punishment · 158
NEO PI test · 74, 77
neocortex · 187
nerves · 97, 98, 100, 101, 102, 103, 104, 105, 106, 108, 110, 111, 112, 113, 115, 116, 117, 118, 119, 231, 266
neuro-muscular junction · 110
neuron · 106, 123, 124, 125, 126, 127, 128, 130, 132, 135, 136, 137, 138, 139, 140, 142, 143, 144, 146, 147, 148, 168, 170, 171, 172, 174, 175, 230, 239, 244
neurotic competitiveness · 61, 62
neurotic personality · 61
neurotransmitters · 6, 97, 123, 124, 125, 127, 128, 130, 135, 137, 139, 140, 144, 147, 148, 168, 170, 171, 231, 237, 238, 299, 314
neutral stimulus · 154, 156, 158, 172
nicotine · 238
night terrors · 232
NMDA receptor · 170, 244
nodes of Ranvier · 126, 127, 144
non-working memory · 179, 190
nurture · 220, 222, 253, 264

O

obedience · 335
object permanence · 256, 257
obsessive-compulsive disorder · 94, 95, 298, 304, 305, 306
obsessive-compulsive personality disorder · 297
OCEAN · 74, 181
Oedipus complex · 45, 47, 49
oligodendrocytes · 126
operant conditioning · 16, 160, 161
operational definition · 24
opiates · 238
oral personality · 44, 49
orexin · 231, 240, 246, 249

P

panic disorder · 302, 316, 318
paradigm shift · 8
paranoia · 77, 312
paranoid personality disorder · 296
parasympathetic system · 112, 115, 116, 117, 149
parenting styles · 263
participant observation · 25, 30
penis envy · 47, 49
perceptual constancies · 205

peripheral nervous system · 97, 102, 104, 108, 110, 132, 133
permeability · 135, 142
personality · 35, 48, 74, 76, 77, 84, 85, 86, 87, 88, 89, 90, 91, 185, 190, 220, 221, 281, 288, 289, 317, 320, 346, 347, 348, 349, 350
personality disorders · 293
person-centered therapy · 68, 69
phagocytosis · 131
Philip Zimbardo · 337
phobias · 299, 300, 316, 319, 321, 323
photographic memory · 178
phrenology · 218
physical development · 268
physiological reactions · 2
placebo effect · 29
plasticity · 240
pleasure principle · 37
positive punishment · 158
positive regard · 67, 68, 69, 88
postconventional morality · 267
post-traumatic stress disorder · 306
prefrontal cortex · 164, 190, 201, 309
prejudice · 329, 331
premenstrual dysphoric disorder · 311
premotor cortex · 167
prenatal development · 132, 269
preoperational stage · 257
primary sex characteristics · 270
proactive interference · 182
procedural memory · 182, 189, 234, 250
pruning · 260
psyche · 1, 43
psychoanalysis · 15, 36, 41, 51, 59, 62, 275
psychodynamic perspective · 14
psychosexual development · 43
puberty · 47, 48, 255, 269, 270, 276, 289, 342
punishment · 158, 159, 166, 167, 168, 173, 267
putamen nucleus · 94, 189

R

random assignment · 29
random selection · 28, 29
Raymond Catell · 72
reactive attachment disorder · 308
receptor · 129, 137, 140, 141, 147, 148, 167, 170, 171, 174 192, 230, 237, 239, 242, 244
reciprocal determinism · 70
reflex arc · 110
reflexes · 1, 8, 70, 110, 253, 255, 256, 269
relative refractory period · 143
reliable · 67, 76, 81, 83
REM sleep disorder · 230
REM stage · 229
Renaissance · 7, 8, 9
repeated exposure effect · 345
repolarization · 142, 143
repressed memory · 185, 196

repression · 40, 46, 50
resting potential · 135, 136, 137, 139, 142, 168
retinal disparity · 203
retroactive interference · 182
reuptake · 130, 148, 237, 238, 245
Rorschach Inkblot Test · 82

S

safety need · 60, 64
safety needs · 64, 67
saltatory conduction · 145
savants · 217
scaffolding · 261
scapegoating · 330
schemas · 260
schizoaffective disorder · 315
schizoid personality disorder · 297
schizophreniform · 315
Schwann cells · 126, 133
scientific method · 24, 67, 176
secondary sex characteristics · 270
seizures · 186, 187, 237, 244, 310
self-actualization · 63, 66
self-concept · 68, 69, 86, 276, 277
self-fulfilling prophecy effect · 215, 301, 345
self-propagation · 142
semantic memories · 181
sensitization · 168, 241, 301
sensorimotor stage · 255, 256, 257
sensory development · 265
S-factor · 209
shadow · 15, 51, 204
short-term memory · 32, 179, 190, 191, 211
Sigmund Freud · 14, 15, 28, 35, 36, 39, 40, 41, 42, 43, 44,
    45, 46, 47, 48, 49, 50, 54, 56, 60, 62, 89, 275
sleep deprivation · 195, 233
sleep paralysis. · 230
sleep spindles · 228, 232
sleepwalking · 232
slips of the tongue · 41, 42
slow-wave sleep · 228, 233, 234
social cognition · 327
social facilitation · 340
social impairment · 340
social influence · 334
social loafing · 340
sodium-potassium pump · 136, 143
somatic system · 108, 109, 110, 119
spinal cord · 96, 97, 98, 102, 104, 105, 106, 107, 108,
    110, 111, 116, 124, 129, 132, 230, 239, 266
spinal nerves · 102, 103, 108, 110, 111, 117
SSRI · 94, 95, 295, 304, 305, 295
stages of sleep · 227, 233
Stanford prison experiment · 338
Stanley Milgram · 335, 351
state-dependent memory · 181
stereotype threat · 214
Sternberg's view of love · 345

stimulants · 237
strange situation · 262
structuralism · 11
subconscious · 49
subcortical · 98, 166, 167, 229, 305
subject variables · 29
sublimated · 47
subliminal · 49, 153, 208, 209, 223
superego · 14, 36, 38, 40, 41, 42, 44, 45, 46
superiority complex · 55
suprachiasmatic nucleus · 226
survey · 30, 31, 198, 323, 333, 339
sympathetic system · 112, 114, 115, 116, 117, 275, 294
synapse · 124, 125, 128, 129, 130, 146, 147, 148, 169,
    172, 230, 237

T

telodendria · 127
temperament · 273, 286, 287, 288
temporal cortex · 164, 166, 189, 201
teratogens · 269
testosterone · 18, 270, 272, 342, 350
thalamus · 99, 191, 232, 238, 310, 313, 319
Thematic Apperception Test · 82, 83
theta activity · 228
threshold of excitation · 139, 143, 144, 171
tolerance · 240, 241, 298
top-down processing · 205
tract · 108, 115
trait view · 72
triadic reciprocity · 70
trichotillomania · 306
tyranny of the should · 61

U

unconditioned response · 154, 158
unconditioned stimulus · 154, 158, 172
uconscious · 41
United States · 2, 12, 13
unmyelinated axons · 107, 126, 144

V

validity · 24, 54, 76, 77, 81, 82, 83, 86
variable · 25, 26, 27, 172
vegetative state · 227
ventral root · 106, 108
vesicles · 112, 125, 127, 128, 147, 148
vicarious experience · 71
voltage-sensitive channels · 139, 141, 142, 143, 144,
    145
voluntarism · 10
voluntary behavior · 1

W

walking · 1, 37, 55, 56, 123, 178, 208, 217, 218, 230, 237, 255, 256, 269
Wechsler Intelligence Scale · 212, 214
Wernicke's area · 164
white matter · 106, 305
withdrawal · 44, 168, 231, 240, 241, 242, 243, 274, 297, 299, 304, 312

within-subject design · 31
working memory · 179, 190, 194, 195, 197, 198, 309

Z

zone of proximal development · 261

Credits

CHAPTER 1: EXPLORING PSYCHOLOGY

All images are obtained from www.shutterstock.com. Figure 1 by Cameron Whithman; Figure 2 by Lightspring; Figure 3 by Hispan; Figure 4 by Bruce Rolf; Figure 5 by Master 1305; Figure 6 by Laroslav Neliubov; Figure 7 by Malei; Figure 8 by Johan Swanepoel; Figure 9 by Yuganov Konstantin; Figure 10 by Arid Ocean; Figure 11 by Elena Ray; Figure 12 by Public Domain; Figure 13 by Lightspring; Figure 14 by Wiliyam Bradberry; Figure 15 by Vadim Sadovski; Figure 16 by Se Media; Figure 17 by Tomasz Bidermann; Figure 18 by Cranach; Figure 19 by Propositive; Figure 20 by Coffeemill; Figure 21 by Kiselev Andrew Valerevich; Figure 22 by Andrey-Popov; Figure 23 by Anastasiia Kazakova; Figure 24 by B Calkins; Figure 25 by Monkey Business Images; Figure 26 by Neo Edmund; Figure 27 by Cresta Johnson; Figure 28 by Photographee.eu; Figure 29 by Esteban de Armas; Figure 30 by Kutlerveserova Stuchelova; Figure 31 by Quorthon 1; Figure 32 by Sashkin; Figure 33 by ESB Professional. All images are obtained from www.shutterstock.com.

CHAPTER 2: PERSONALITY

All images are obtained from www.shutterstock.com. Figure 1 by Photoagent; Figure 2 by Lightspring; Figure 3 by Lovely Color Photo; Figure 4 by Sean Nel; Figure 5 by Cranach; Figure 6 by Vkilikov; Figure 7 by Conrado; Figure 8 by Gigava; Figure 9 by Niyazz: Figure 10 by ArTDi101; Figure 11 by Solarseven: Figure 12 by Djinn; Figure 13 by Kamira; Figure 14 by ESB Professional; Figure 15 by Getmilitaryphotos; Figure 16 by Wallenrock; Figure 17 by XiXinXing;Figure 18 by realpeople; Figure 19 by Andril Muzyka; Figure 20 by Studio M; Figure 21 by Mansiliya Yury; Figure 22 by Sayanny; Figure 23 by Alexander Sviridov; Figure 24 by Kiselev Andrey Valerevich; Figure 25 by Jarhe Photography; Figure 26 by Ollyy; Figure 27 by Gercen; Figure 28 by Frankie's; Figure 29 by Elina Leonova; Figure 30 by Karen Struthers; Figure 31 by Pathdoc; Figure 32 by rangizz; Figure 33 by arbit; Figure 34 by Ruksutakarn studio; Figure 35 by Evgenii Bobrov; Figure 36 by Andrei_R; Figure 37 by Razoomanet and Andrey-Popov; Figure 38 by Pixelheadphotodigitalskillet; Figure 39 by Sergey Nivens; Figure 40 by Aloha Flamingo; Figure 41 by Brocreative; Figure 42 by Elena Shashkina; Figure 43 by Pahtdoc; Figure 44 by Gaudilab; Figure 45 by Jason Stitt; Figure 46 by Fcscafeine; Figure 47 by Antonio Guillem; Figure 48 by Kzenon; Figure 49 by Gamenacom; Figure 50 by Marilyn Volan; Figure 51 by Iakov Filimonov.

CHAPTER 3: BIOLOGICAL PSYCHOLOGY I

All images are obtained from www.shutterstock.com. Figure 1 by Sebastian Kaulitzki; Figue 2 by Alila Medical Media and Nerhuz; Figure 3 by Sebastian Kaulitzki; Figure 4 by Alila Medical Media; Figure 5 by Sebastian Kaulitzki; Figure 6 by Sebastian Kaulitzki; Figure 7 by decade3d-anatomy online; Figure 8 by Vasabii; Figure 9 by Stihii; Figure 10 by Vasabii; Figure 11 by Sebastian Kaulitzki; Figure 12 by ellepigrafica; Figure 13 by Alila Medical Media; Figure 14 by Marina_Ua; Figure 15 by Nerthuz; Figure 16 by Biomedical; Figure 17 by Alila Medical Media;

Figure 18 by Sebastian Kaulitzki: Figure 19 by Blamb; Figure 20 by Designua; Figure 21 by Jubal Harshaw; Figure 22-25 by Alila Medical Media; Figure 26 by Stihii; Figure 27 by Designua; Figure 28 by ducu59us: Figure 29 by Stihii; Figure 30 by Designua; Figures 31-34 by Alila Medical Media; Figure 35 by Blamb.

CHAPTER 4: BIOLOGICAL PSYCHOLOGY II

All images are obtained from www.shutterstock.com. Figure 1-7 by Designua; Figure 8 by Blamb; Figures 9-13 by Designua; Figures 14-15 by Evgeniy Mahnyov; Figure 16 by Alila Medical Media; Figures 17-18 by Alexilusmedical; Figure 19 by Figure 20 by Designua; Figure 21-24 by Anya Ku; Figure 25-26 by Designua; Figure 27-28 by Joshya; Figures 29-30 by Designua.

CHAPTER 5: LEARNING

All images are obtained from www.shutterstock.com. Figure 1 by KK Tan; Figure 2 by Sergo 1972; Figure 3 by Loannis Pantzi; Figure 4 by Minerva Studio; Figure 5 by Halay Alex; Figure 6 by Bildagentur Zooner Gmbh; Figure 7 by Diana Indiana; Figure 8 by Elena Shashkina; Figure 9 by Creative Images; Figure 10 by TinnaPong; Figure 11 by Sue McDonald; Figure 12 by Neil Lockhart; Figure 13 by Grigorita Ko; Figure 14 by Vasabii; Figure 15 by Designua; Figures 16-17 by Vasabii; Figure 18 by Alexilusmedical ; Figure 19 by Naart; Figure 20 by Vasabii; Figure 21 by Ellepigrafica; Figure 22 by Designua.

CHAPTER 6: MEMORY

All images are obtained from www.shutterstock.com. Figure 1 by Sebastian Kaulitzki; Figure 2 by Sarah Holmlund; Figure 3 by Sergey Lavrentev; Figure 4 by Elnur; Figure 5 by Gino Santa Maria; Figure 6 by Seyomedo; Figure 7 by Ollyy; Figure 8 by Yiucheung; Figure 9 by ra2studio; Figure 10 by Everett Historical; Figure 11 by Vasabii; Figure 12 by Sebastian Kaulitzki; Figure 13 by Vasabii; Figures 14-19 by Sebastian Kaulitzki; Figures 20-21 by Alila Medical Media.

CHAPTER 7: COGNITION

All images are obtained from www.shutterstock.com. Figure 1 by Rawpixel.com; Figure 2 by Sebastian Kaulitzki; Figures 3-4 by Imagewriter; Figure 5 by Miloje; Figure 6 by Big Bigbb1; Figure 7 by Lcoks; Figures 8-9 by lassedesignen; Figure 9 by lassedesignen ; Figure 10 by Igor Maltsev; Figure 11 by Peter Hermes Furian; Figure 12 by Barsukov Vladimir; Figure 13 by Luis Louro; Figure 14 by Mikael Damkier; Figure 15 by NikoNomad ; Figure 16 by Aleksandris Bondars; Figure 17 by Rangizz; Figure 18 by Anatomy Insider; Figure 19 by Chameleonskye; Figure 20 by t legend; Figure 21 by Poprotskiy Alexey; Figure 22 by g-stokstudio; Figure 23 by Pressmaster.

CHAPTER 8: CONSCIOUSNESS

All images are obtained from www.shutterstock.com. Figure 1 by Stanisic Vladimir; Figure 2 by Alila Medical Media; Figure 3 by Daniela Sachsenheimer; Figure 4 by pathdoc; Figure 5 by Alila Medical Media; Figure 6 by ellepigrafica; Figure 7 by Ljupco Smokovski; Figure 8 by Milkovasa;

Figure 9 by Sebastian Kaulitzki; Figure 10 by Boris Vukov; Figure 11 by BlueRingMedia; Figure 12 by Milles Studio; Figure 13 by Monika Wisniewska; Figure 14 by Sunti; Figure 15 by Blamb; Figure 16 by ChameleonsEye; Figure 17 by Alexilusmedical; Figure 18 by Voyagerix; Figure 19 by Igor Stevanovic; Figure 20 by Raj Creationzs; Figure 21 by artpixelgraphy Studio; Figure 22 by Africa Studio; Figure 24 by Oleg Golovnev.

CHAPTER 9: DEVELOPMENTAL PSYCHOLOGY

All images are obtained from www.shutterstock.com. Figure 1 by arbit; Figure 2 by Sashkin; Figure 3 by Komolo Tavani; Figure 4 by Krystyna Taran; Figure 5 by leungChopan; Figure 6 by Eugenio Marangiu; Figure 7 by Ollyy; Figure 8 by TopPhotoEngineer; Figure 9 by Meilun; Figure 10 by hxdbzxy; Figure 11 by StockLite; Figure 12 Karl Rosecrants; Figure 13 by Julza; Figure 14 by Postolit; Figure 15 by Pedalist; Figure 16 by Alila Medical Media; Figure 17 by Vitstudio; Figure 18 by Sebastian Kaulitzki; Figure 19 by Flashon Studio; Figure 20 by Designua; Figure 21 by Sabphoto; Figure 22 by Sene Gal; Figure 23 by Designua; Figure 24 by diez artwork; Figure 25 by Nomad-Soul; Figure 26 by Sebastian Kaulitzki; Figure 27 by debasige.

CHAPTER 10: ABNORMAL PSYCHOLOGY

All images are obtained from www.shutterstock.com. Figure 1 by miroslav110; Figure 2 by Ryan M. Bolton; Figure 3 by Boris Vukov; Figure 4 by Antonio Guillem; Figure 5 by Art Family; Figure 6 by Tinxi; Figure 7 by Teodor Lazarev; Figure 8 by ESB Professional; Figure 9 by musicman; Figure 10 by SG Shot; Figure 11 by Syda Productions; Figure 12 by Pop Paul-Catalin; Figure 13 by Sergey Nivens; Figure 14 by KarenFoley photography; Figure 15 by Sebastan Kaulitzki; Figure 16 by Monning; Figure 17 by Sir Travelalot; Figure 18 by lassedesignen; Figure 19 by Africa Studio; Figure 20 by Picoso.kz; Figure 21 Photographee.eu; Figure 22 by Fresnel; Figure 23 by Suzanne Tucker; Figure 24 by Designua; Figure 25 by Conrado.

CHAPTER 11: SOCIAL PSYCHOLOGY

All images are obtained from www.shutterstock.com. Figure 1 by tostphoto; Figure 2 by Nicholas Picciollo; Figure 3 by Matej Kastelic; Figure 4 by Juri Pozzi; Figure 5 by Masiko 553; Figure 6 by melnikof; Figure 7 by Seita; Figure 8 by Pop Paul-Catalin; Figure 9 by Public Domain; Figure 10 by Sergey Nivens; Figure 11 by Creative Images; Figure 12 by Sakhorn; Figure 13 by Elena EFimova; Figure 14 by Denis Production.com; Figure 15 by 3445128471; Figure 16 by Katalinks; Figure 17 by SkyPics Studio; Figure 18 by Frankie's; Figure 19 by hagit berkovich; Figure 20 by Anetlanda.